Remaking the City Street Grid

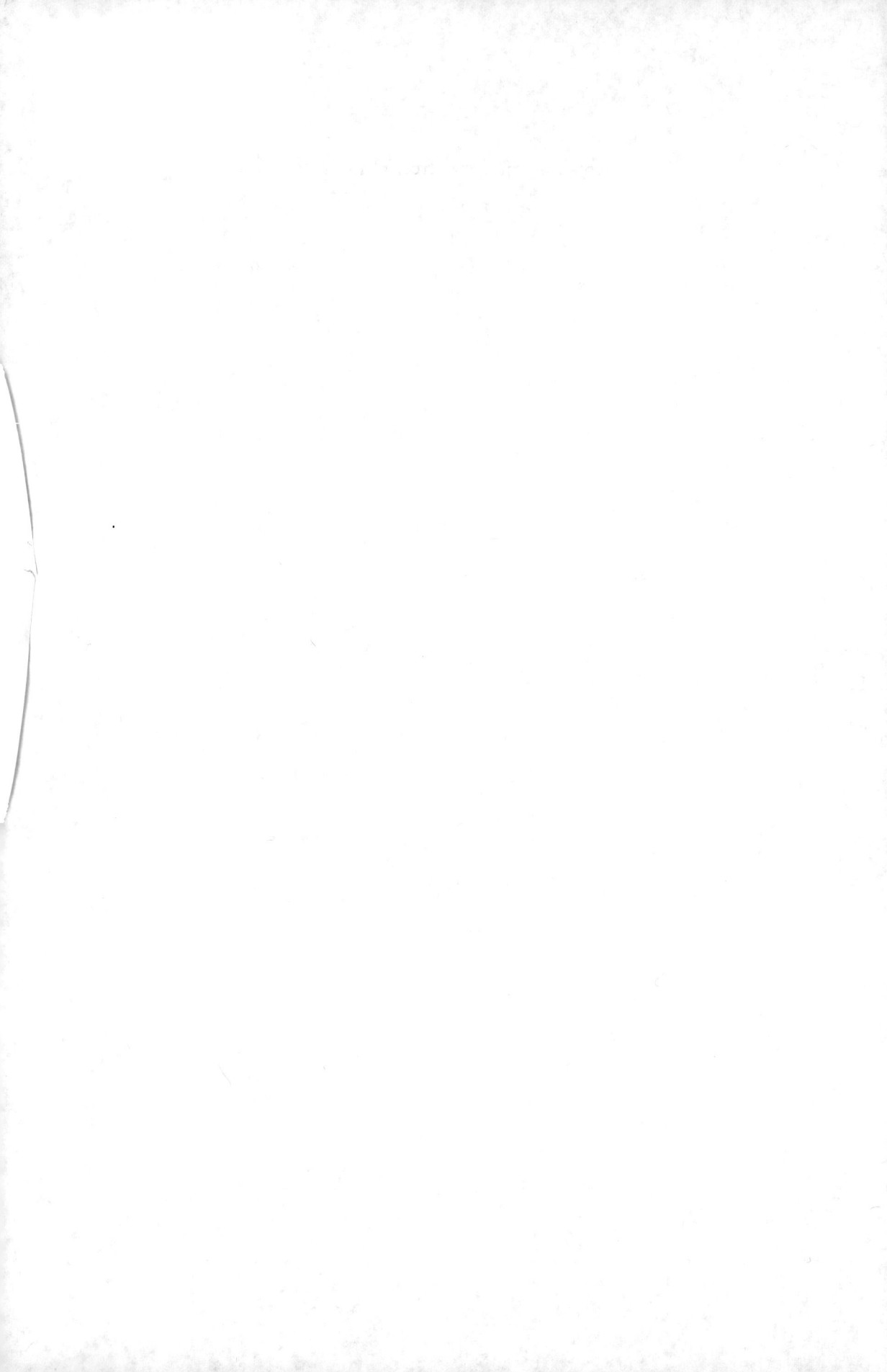

Remaking the City Street Grid

A Model for Urban and Suburban Development

FANIS GRAMMENOS and
G.R. LOVEGROVE

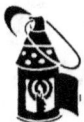

McFarland & Company, Inc., Publishers
Jefferson, North Carolina

All photographs, drawings, and charts are works by the authors unless otherwise noted.

LIBRARY OF CONGRESS CATALOGUING-IN-PUBLICATION DATA

Grammenos, Fanis, 1941–
Remaking the city street grid : a model for urban and suburban development /
Fanis Grammenos and G.R. Lovegrove.
p.   cm.
Includes bibliographical references and index.

ISBN 978-0-7864-9604-4 (softcover : acid free paper) ∞
ISBN 978-1-4766-1768-8 (ebook)

1. City planning.   2. Streets—Design and construction.
I. Lovegrove, G. R.   II. Title.

HT166.G6825 2015   307.1'216—dc23   2015000099

BRITISH LIBRARY CATALOGUING DATA ARE AVAILABLE

On the cover: A contemporary thoroughfare: similar to incidental
one-way couplets in central-city districts, this is a planned
arrangement for major boulevards that connect districts

Printed in the United States of America

*McFarland & Company, Inc., Publishers
Box 611, Jefferson, North Carolina 28640
www.mcfarlandpub.com*

Table of Contents

Preface

This book was born in part after observing knowledge gaps in our respective land-use planning and transportation engineering professions. Those gaps (identified further below) are wide, due in large part to professional or institutional inertia, which hinders the application of innovations that increase community sustainability.

Compounding this problem, everyone has a different "vision" of the ideal form; hence, we are reluctant to boast that this book is "the" panacea to all issues facing communities. Nonetheless, we are excited about it. As often happens, a happy coincidence took place in 2007 that allowed us to meet and realize a breakthrough in knowledge. Like beggars in the desert stumbling upon an oasis, we offer what we found for use, for practitioners to solve at least part of these knowledge gaps.

While the coauthors had never met before, and lived on opposite ends of Canada, both had been working on community planning and design principles, like the rest of those in our respective professions. Grammenos was looking for a user-responsive neighborhood development pattern as part of his work at the Canada Housing & Mortgage Corporation (CMHC), while Lovegrove was looking for more sustainably safe and energy-efficient neighborhood transport systems as part of his PhD research at UBC. Neither knew the other until Grammenos came across a paper published by Lovegrove on a neighborhood street pattern that reduced collisions by over 60 percent. Numerous e-mail and phone conversations ensued, and the rest, as they say, is history. This book is the culmination of our journey of discovery. We hope you will find it both enlightening and helpful in your pursuit of sustainable community layouts, whatever your definition and context.

Many current planning books on the topic of shaping communities have been written from the pulpit by aspiring evangelists; ours has been written from the nave by perspiring serfs. We decided to write this book, as opposed to simply continuing disparate discussions and knowledge transfers at conferences and in journal papers, because of the complex, system-based concepts involved. We see ourselves as doers rather than talkers, as tinkerers rather than promoters, hoping to help fix a complex problem that defies clear definition, but that is critical to our journey's success. We are only fixing a car that's already on the road toward an unknown destination—simply making the trip smoother. For that reason, neither of us could have written this book alone; it was a team effort, an integrated, multi-disciplinary collaboration necessitated by the scope of discussion that spans land-use planning through transportation engineering. To that end, we welcome, even wish for, any suggestions you have to improve it in future editions.

The knowledge gaps that this book can address for people attempting to sustain a reasonable quality of life in cities are explained next. While we see no villains or victims, we do see six troubling inconsistencies in neighborhood design practices.

First, we observe a contradiction between reverence for renowned urban thinkers such

1

as Raymond Unwin, Christopher Alexander, Kevin Lynch, Lewis Mumford and Jane Jacobs and the selective, outright dismissal of certain of their ideas. Some planners wholeheartedly use parts of these thinkers' ideas while rejecting or sidestepping others, without justification. This selective use is troubling, and it negates the system-based approach that great urban thinkers must use.

Second, we see a misattribution of effects to unrelated, or at least unproven, causes.[1] For example, a street type—the cul-de-sac—has been identified as a cause of low-density development on the pretense that low-density neighborhoods exhibit that type of street form. Certain observers extrapolate that if low-density development is undesirable, the cul-de-sacs that cause it must be banned. Yet, historically and culturally, there are good examples of cul-de-sac neighborhood patterns with high population and home density (e.g., False Creek in Vancouver, BC). However, this opinion persists in North America and, until challenged by research presented in this book, will continue to reinforce the unfounded perception of a causal relationship. Other misattributions likewise abound.

Third, we are concerned about the pervasive tendency to espouse and mimic past forms in planning advocacy and practice. Just as in other contemporary artifacts, it is presumed that a modern neighborhood will be satisfactory only if it takes the shape of an old one. "Back to the Future" is a constant slogan in contemporary writing and neighborhood design reflecting this intellectual tendency. Yet we know it to be a case of idealizing past forms and of acute disassociation of form and function. Ultimately, past forms that survive into the present and beyond should do so on the grounds of their persistent utility, regardless of our affinity for them.

Fourth, we are troubled by the intellectual trend of blaming the transportation engineering discipline as a scapegoat for many of the proclaimed ills in contemporary cities. (Wait a minute, transportation is a derived demand of land use, isn't it?!) Rather than identifying the forces at work and the tensions between them that need resolution, some critics prefer to assign low value or intelligence to the work of a specific profession (engineers, architects, developers, etc.). This cross-discipline "racism"—let's be blunt about these disrespectful and unprofessional attitudes—contributes little to understanding, and even less to solving, complex problems that require system-based, integrated solutions. We see no differences in the degree of collective diligence or ingenuity among professions involved in shaping the city, and we are delighted that many of our younger colleagues are starting to coin the phrase "plangineer," reflecting the fact that a team-based, community-focused approach is needed.

Fifth, we are concerned that planning practices divergent from the current view of "correct" doctrine are presumed to have detrimental, even apocalyptic, consequences, and thus are promptly dismissed. Yet we learn from history that a city's destiny is shaped by a myriad of factors, only one of which relates to physical planning, of which the relevant importance can be shown to be proportional to the viewer's professional perspective. We also learn that "correctness" is just as transient for planning ideas as for all other disciplines.

Sixth, an old and persistent issue, is the use of statistical analysis to substantiate a view or proposed solutions. Always placed in a context favored by a proponent, with the metrics also predetermined, conclusions so arrived at often do little more than reinforce the investigator's bias. Revisited, revised and discarded studies have revealed the stark truth of the all too common "experimenter's error"—the wishful expectation of a result overriding the data analysis.[2] And as cross-references multiply, the noise of conviction overwhelms attempts to deconstruct the false method or logic. Science-based theory, tested and validated by sound experimental design, and adopted by practitioners in several successful case studies, represents the goals and content of this book.

Overall, the inconsistent use of theory, incorrect conclusions regarding causes and effects, overreliance on tradition in thought and practice, lack of professional respect, and arrogant positioning of physical planning as a dominant means of influencing the fate of cities have all led us to a new perspective that underpins this book. An evolutionary view of cities, which absorb and incorporate many ideas (sometimes contradictory) into their fabric—physical, political, economic, social, and technological—to varying degrees, at different times, shape a city's destiny.

If you are an innovator, this book is for you. We think you and your community will profit greatly. If your community is somewhat conservative, you may find these ideas more challenging to implement, because anything new requires a coalition of supportive planners and engineers, not to mention visionary leaders at the decision-making level. Regardless, we hope you will be encouraged to try something new that others are doing across Canada (e.g., British Columbia, Alberta, and Saskatchewan to date) and in our global village (China and India to date). We offer this book as a systems approach to promote integrated, resilient community land-use and transportation planning and design decisions. The systems approach—theory, practice, and case studies—contained in this book has been peer-reviewed and tested, including numerous conferences and print/online publications. In the interest of expediting knowledge transfer to you in your pursuit of successful communities, we felt justified in consolidating and presenting in one book what has spanned these past several years of dialogue, analysis, and results.

This book intends to contribute a new systematic neighborhood design, derived from a synthesis of previous ones. We hope it will become an evolutionary adaptation that will allow people to maximize the benefits they (and future generations of city dwellers) can reap from living in new and existing neighborhoods. The book flows such that the chapters take you on a journey from theory to practice and, finally, case studies. We provide examples of in-situ applications of the fused grid design principles, including retrofits to existing neighborhoods as well as designs of new ones. In each case, we focus on context, design challenges, results, and lessons learned. As the design process is not an exact science, there will be many more permutations and case studies to consider going forward, which we will welcome and illustrate in future editions; meanwhile, these are early days.

Acknowledgments

This book would not have been possible without our colleagues, our families, our publisher and our collective life experiences. Each of you has shaped, fed, mentored, and critiqued our work, to refine our craft and open our minds so as to help us discover knowledge, and to facilitate its transfer, throughout our accumulated 80 years of work.

Starting from the closest and moving outward, we would like to thank Jason Grammenos for the convincing graphics/animations that allowed us to expose and discuss the concept clearly; our employers, UBC and CMHC, for giving us an opportunity to explore and solidify the concept; colleagues such as Sevag Pogharian, Douglas Pollard, Ian Melzer and Barry Craig for the early encouragement, always welcome and vital during a concept's formative stages; Larry Frank, Chris Hawkins, James Sun, and Xiongbing Jin for devoting academic time to investigating aspects of the concept; and numerous others who expressed their support at workshops and conferences, too many to name individually. On the implementation quest, thanks go to Barbara Dembek, planning director, who ushered the first municipal secondary plan to approval. And a big thank-you is due to Jeff Blair, who embraced the concept early and built the first-ever example of it in Calgary—a tribute to his foresight and forward thinking. Indirectly, we also owe a debt to those who critiqued the concept in its early stages, forcing us to develop more cogent arguments and supportive examples.

Thank you all.

Introduction

Building a neighborhood, whether it happens gradually on the ground or abstractly on a desk, always reflects a set of intentions, whether codified, subconscious or newly conceived. These intentions influence the built outcome and its fitness for human activities. Thus a spiral is formed between intentions and outcomes, whereby intentions are modified and refined to improve outcomes. These modifications normally become incorporated within vernacular tradition, in civic norms or manuals of practice. This evolutionary perspective permeates these pages; it sees cities as organic, but not as organisms.[1]

There would be little need for modification of either intentions or outcomes were it not for the constant changes in the activities of production, provision, protection, transportation, communication and governance—the patterns of survival—the sum total of which constitutes the evolving human culture. In the animal world, shelter modes have remained constant throughout the existence of a species; in the human world, change is constant.

Every new planning idea can be judged in the context of the changes in the *patterns* of living that it is designed to respond to and from the perspective of its potential to accommodate them.

Recent work in fractal geometry has revealed the intuitive understanding that patterns of living are bound up with patterns of form in which or through which living is accommodated. A cursory look at surviving towns and villages that have remained unchanged may well surprise the observer with the dramatic difference in layout and building shapes from the average contemporary city experience that they display. But when comparing these towns to one another, an obvious similarity emerges. The reason for the similarities and the differences can be found in the patterns of use and in the rules that codified them. As in the genesis of living organisms, codes, written or vernacular, shape the physical form of a settlement and inevitably reflect the culture (the patterns of living) of its inhabitants. Similar cultures will produce analogous forms.[2]

This book is about street patterns. It fits in the spiral of the feedback loop at the junction where forcibly modified or malfunctioning patterns beg for change. The focus on street patterns rests on many grounds:

- First, out of all the physical elements of a neighborhood, the street infrastructure is the most enduring; some cities still retain the layouts of districts that have been in place for over a thousand years. Buildings and functions changed regularly around them, but not the layouts. Finding an appropriate layout is critical because modifications to malfunctioning networks may be impossible or, if feasible, disruptive and costly. Yet, recognizing their tenacity as well as society's large capacity for adaptation, this focus is pursued with humility. Any new street pattern will do given sufficient later modifications, as have all surviving old patterns.[3]

- Second, by taking up land, streets remove it from other potential uses that make up a neighborhood's living tissue. A balance of space allocation must be struck between their essential role as connectors and the presence of functions that they connect.
- Third, streets can enable or constrain movement and, consequently, enhance or degrade mobility and access by their overall geometry and their specific characteristics, such as width, pavement, grade, and so on. Decreased mobility means reduction of productive or leisure time.
- Fourth, from the physical street perspective, that is the channel which provides space for the transportation that connects all parts of a settlement. There have been three typical periods in the history of cities and their networks: (a) the foot and hoof, (b) the wheel and hoof, and the current (c) wheel and motor period. Each period influenced the shape, size and use of streets.
- Fifth, each transportation period introduced new advantages for enhancing daily life but also, albeit inadvertently, new risks in degrading it. Inventing adaptations to preempt degradation reinforces the positive effects of transportation evolution. Developing new patterns is part of that constant effort.
- Sixth, rarely in the history of cities do new comprehensive patterns displace the old; adaptation is the normal mode of response. Given the twentieth century's numerous additions to the range of transportation means, which includes trains, trams, subways, buses, trucks, bicycles, motorbikes and private cars, all of which compete for movement space, a fresh look at street patterns is warranted.

Permanence, land uptake and circulation deserve close attention in any proposal for a new street pattern because all three determine its viability and fitness for living. Careful scrutiny and justification based on evidence is equally crucial, regardless of whether a pattern is chosen from the historical repertoire or created based on a set of performance parameters.

A closer look at street networks also rests on the observation that transport functions, and the means and networks that support them, are fundamental to all systems that support life. Not only are they present and directly observable at a meso-scale level—plants and animals—but they also have been found to occur at even the micro sub-cellular scale.[4] Transportation in its widest sense includes the moving of items ranging from matter to messages (e.g., nutrients to electric impulses) by means varying from bronchial tubes to ganglia plexus. Each transport network evolved to serve a specific function by specialized means. A street network of a settlement would be no different from this perspective. Co-temporal networks can coexist in complementary roles but also (at times) with conflicting physical demands.

This book will lay out a proposal for a new, *contemporary* street network pattern based on observation and research. Observation will focus on the "squeaking wheel" where malfunctioning comes to light and where spontaneous adaptations have occurred. It will also look at the gradual, imperceptible adaptations that are now taken for granted and, therefore, unlikely to trigger new solutions. However, research will ground the rationale for, and fitness of, the proposed new patterns. Living in an era of transition between technologies in transportation and communication, and the resulting stress of adjustment, begets research on these aspects and, even though at times inconclusive, can provide at least some grounds for action. Action often must rely on intuition based on available evidence.

As might be expected, when the old models show signs of stress, numerous proposals surface as people try to identify the causes of malfunction and propose cures; these vary widely and at times are contradictory. Both the diagnosis, which is usually proportional to the depth of understanding of the complex systems that cities are, and the prescriptions are frequently off the mark. Comprehension usually rests on metaphors, whether practical or abstract, and given that metaphors are projected rather than derived from the working system, they sustain a set of logical assumptions that often misrepresent the actual system, which, in essence, remains indescribable.[5]

On the side of the diagnosis, for example, some observers find cause for despair in the "ugliness" of certain areas of cities, and others, upon realizing that cities are growing in a way different from in the past, pit the old parts of the "city" against the new as if they were built by distinct, strange species. Yet "ugliness" can be quickly shown to be both subjective and ever present, and it can likewise be demonstrated that evolution of technology and economy are the common forces that built both the past and the present, and each built segment of the city is a reflection of the sum total of the prevalent "culture." Culture is never ugly; like every other organic growth, it just is.[6]

On the side of the prescription, some have suggested that designing new districts at the periphery to look like early small towns will not only improve life in the suburbs themselves but also solve a myriad of other problems, including climate change (a preposterous claim, sustained only by its idealism). A second thread of prescriptions dwells in the imaginary world of another era as yet to emerge either through changes in technology or in people's habits. These "if only" radical solutions also foresee a wholesome cure to all of the city's intractable problems—clearly an unrealistic expectation.

We believe that cities, as the complex "ecosystems" that they are, transcend any individual idea both in scope and in time, and that to grant such an enormous potential to a conceptual system is entirely unrealistic, if not naive. In this vein, expectations for the outcomes resulting from applying a new street network pattern are moderated by the fact that the numerous patterns that have survived from the past, though they may be judged unsuitable on functional grounds, have been made to work through ingenious and laborious, if imperfect, adaptations.

Consequently, the intentions of this book are modest. It will look at past and current street patterns critically and draw lessons from historic and current developments; it will also survey ideas from a range of thinkers and propose a new pattern for developments that, hopefully, will be more fitting for the current culture and the daily activities it has brought about.

In the continuing line of adaptations, this proposal will simply add one that, ideally, will be adopted sporadically in different places, modified where necessary, and applied to create fitting environments for today's culture.

The introductory chapter on patterns discusses the pervasive presence of patterns in the natural world, inanimate, biotic, and animate, as well as in human artifacts, including the largest—cities. It reiterates with examples from literature and practice the old truth that it is inefficient, and possibly risky, to reinvent the wheel each time that it could be the answer to a given problem. A pattern preempts this wastefulness and directs creativity to refinements or new tasks, embedding and transmitting previously gained intelligence.

The second chapter presents and elaborates two aspects of adaptations: the stress that networks experience under the dual impacts of population growth and change in transport means, and the stress that residents experience when using the networks during their daily cycle of activities. It puts forward the case that built systems are slow to change, which inevitably triggers a set of personal adaptations that occur faster. It lists and discusses the major stressors of distance, effort, topography, and speed, and how each of these generates the friction that ultimately leads to adaptive solutions, some of which emerge unexpectedly from innovations unrelated to settlement building.

The third chapter mirrors the flow of the second and surveys the sequence of adaptations that have occurred in response to the stressors surveyed previously. It shows the constant interplay between stressors and solutions, which in turn can themselves become stressors. Through this survey, the chapter extracts a few general principles that are necessary for shaping a contemporary network. Principles such as hierarchy, filtered permeability, and differentiation of modes and paths, among others, are shown to be essential for contemporary mobility and accessibility.

Chapter 4 articulates the elements of the proposed network model. Following a discussion and explanation of general principles, it presents the logic for structuring a network that reflects them. Such logic, in addition to being extracted from naturally occurring evolutionary adaptations, is also grounded in explicit or implicit rules found in contemporary writings on street networks.

Chapter 5 is a hands-on description of how the proposed network can be laid out at the neighborhood and district scale. It lays out the network as a diagram that incorporates the principles and performance criteria discussed in previous chapters. It also explores the degree of freedom and flexibility to modify the diagram to suit specific site constraints while maintaining full adherence to the organizing principles espoused by the model.

Chapter 6 presents available research that provides inferential evidence of the potential fitness of the proposed network for contemporary living patterns and culture (both social and technological). It covers all current issues of priority, such as walkability, mobility, health, safety, security, infrastructure cost, and greenhouse gas emissions.

Chapter 7 presents case studies of neighborhoods and districts that followed the emergence of the new network model or that preceded it but incorporate its essential principles. They also cover national and international communities.

A relevant and persistent question about the origins of network patterns and, in particular, what has become mistakenly known as the Greco-Roman rectilinear, orthogonal grid is treated in a speculative manner in the Appendix.

1

The Idea of Pattern and Its Use

This book is about a contemporary street network pattern. Introducing a new pattern inevitably raises questions, such as what we mean by "pattern," whether there is evidence of patterns in existing networks and whether patterns are necessary in the first place. This chapter will try to address these and related questions. A reader interested only in the proposed network may skip this chapter without loss.

It has been repeatedly shown that the human brain has an innate propensity to see patterns; even where there is no pattern, the brain often projects one.[1] Patterns appear everywhere in nature—whether inorganic or biotic—and several observers speculate that they are the fundamental building *method* of the living world. The discovery of the genetic code, which underlies the morphogenesis of individuals belonging to a given species, sealed the case that patterns shape the entire biological world as we see it. But patterns extend beyond the biological world: language, for example, consists of structural patterns for which the human brain appears to have a genetic predisposition.[2] The pervasive presence of patterns speaks to their inevitability, at least where they occur naturally, as, for example, in botanical or animal circulatory systems. In consciously conceived human artifacts, where the adoption of a pattern is optional, their emergence follows the recognition of their effectiveness in achieving desirable ends.

This aspect of patterns—their capacity to deliver optimal results—leads us to the distinction between visually identifiable patterns and the logic, function or forces that produce it. A snowflake has a recognizable pattern that results from molecular structural properties, which are not readily available for visual inspection. Generally, there is a generative pattern behind the visual pattern.

All patterns have three essential characteristics:

- They have intelligible structure.
- They are repeatable and adaptable.
- They have a whole-part indivisibility.

Ideal whole-city patterns, for example, were created with specific aims in mind, but natural or emergent patterns also embody intent, although it is often not immediately revealed. Created patterns, which concern us here, exhibit all the above characteristics.

We find a clear expression of created pattern characteristics in the archetypal spoked wheel:

Intelligible structure: A circular, continuous rim and radiating spokes emanating from a hole (the hub) have an easily graspable and memorable configuration.
Repeatable and adaptable: While the geometry and structure stay the same, the dimen-

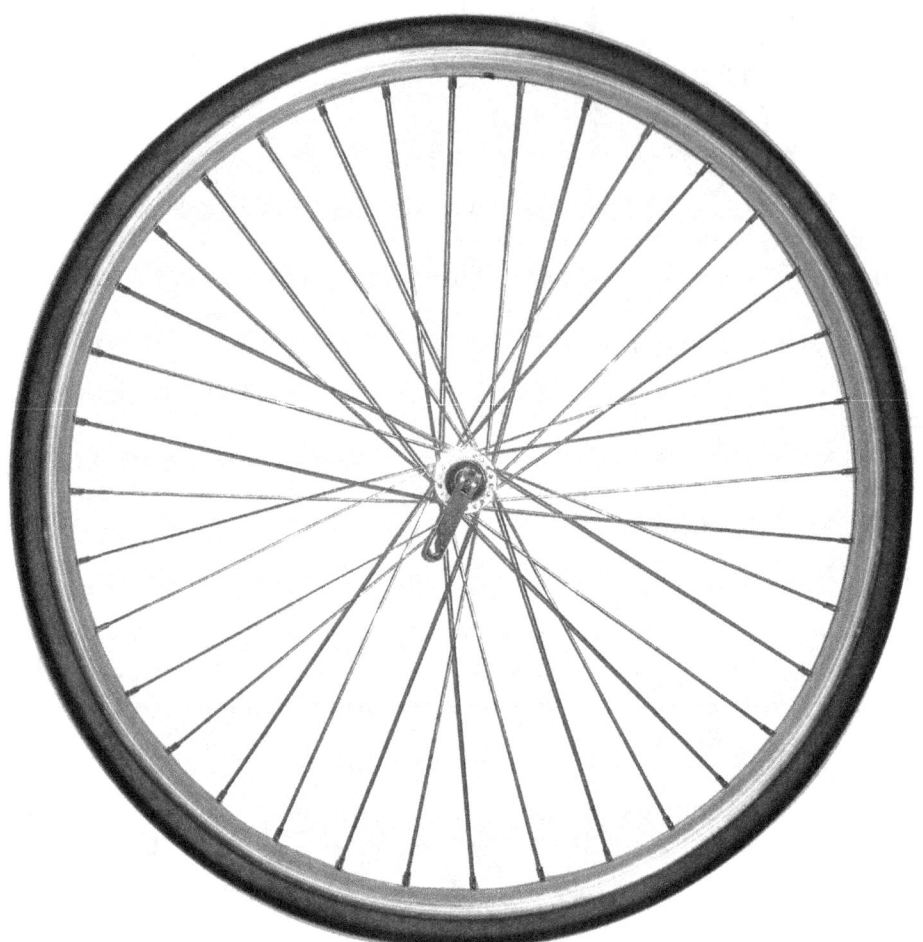

The Wheel: A supreme example of the prime characteristics of a pattern—intelligibility, repeatability and whole-part indivisibility. Its adaptations encompass an entire universe of mechanical devices.

sions of, materials for, and connections between components can vary, while always yielding the same effect.

Whole-part indivisibility: Each part depends on another to function, and the concept fails when one single part fails. The integrity (or wholeness) of the concept depends on its parts, and the parts can only be understood in the context of the whole.

From a cognitive perspective, a pattern has a characteristic common to all patterns: embedded intelligence, a solution to a problem; it is imbued with intent.

Intent expresses the organizing logic when it relates to human artifacts, but *laws* or *functions* describe the shaping forces better when a pattern emerges in nature. A spiral sunflower or galaxy is the outcome of generative processes that obey specific laws, which we may or may not understand. (They both appear too orderly to be accidental, or, from a perceptual perspective, we recognize order even when we cannot describe it.) We recognize a geometric visual pattern promptly, and we can often reproduce its image on paper, but we cannot readily articulate the underlying laws that formed it—an ellipse or a spiral, for example.

This distinction between the visible pattern, which is the outcome, and the processes that create it, which are driven by physical laws or (in the case of humans) cultural and technological norms, is a critical one for this discussion. Its importance rests on the frequently presumed, and mistaken, reversal of causality: that the outcome could itself engender the forces that created it.

While a visual pattern itself is easily perceived, its intent is not revealed to us spontaneously; to be understood, it must be placed in the context that generated it, including the forces that shaped it. Thus, it is meaningless to invoke perceptual patterns without knowing the processes that shape them. Jane Jacobs has warned planners and architects about the distinction between functioning and visual order: "The look of things and the way they work are inextricably bound together, and in no place more so than in cities.... It is futile to plan a city's appearance, or speculate on how to endow it with a pleasing appearance of order, without knowing what sort of innate functioning order it has."[3]

Understanding a pattern's intent intuitively without conceiving its mechanisms happens regularly. Small-scale implements that incorporate patterns, for example, produce their desired effect by us acting *on them* (breaking a walnut with a nutcracker, for example). The action and the immediate outcome register the utility (or intent) of the pattern indelibly, even when it is not understood in abstract terms. The pattern-effect relationship is thus fully assimilated. Replicating the same pattern—a lever—for another use (e.g., cutting cloth), however, will run into problems unless the pattern is understood as a force diagram.

The intuitive assimilation of pattern-effect relationship is not as readily attainable with large-scale patterns, such as neighborhoods, villages and cities, for two reasons:

a) Their perception differs in that we act *in them*, and we ourselves are the recipients of their effect. That effect may be intermittent or long term, and its association with the pattern not directly discernible. For example, low levels of sunlight due to the narrowness of streets or height of buildings (or both) could, over the long term and in association with other factors (e.g., humidity), lead, in some cases, to health or building problems. This connection or "pattern" may escape observation.

b) Because of their scale, we are rarely able to conceive them in their entirety and, consequently, unable to project a pattern (much like ants that build pattern-based ant-hills for millions of inhabitants without a blueprint). In addition, the assimilation is made harder by our innate capacity to adapt to prevailing conditions, thereby obscuring the pattern-effect relationship and its perception.

Visible vs. Opaque, Veiled Patterns

For these reasons of scale, longer-term effect and human adaptability, patterns of settlements can become opaque to direct observation, their intent veiled and their effects unattributable.

Opaqueness of the relationship between visible, observed patterns and the causative mechanisms is common in many other natural and man-made things. The genetic code, which was unveiled less than a century ago, is clearly an elaborate pattern that causes the creation of a recognizable entity, itself a pattern of components in defined functional relationships. Not only do the visible components have characteristic attributes and relationships in animate individuals, but there are also totally undetectable *patterns of behavior* that become overt and observable only after they are triggered by a predetermined stimulus (e.g., aggressive/passive, fight or flight). And though the code has been laid bare and, in certain cases, specific parts of it have been linked with certain specific attributes, the process from code to morphogenesis still remains unknown.

How to Make a Fabric

A simple example of the unintelligibility of the relationship between a code pattern and the visible outcome closer to daily observation lies in the weaving of fabrics. Single or multicolored fabrics display a wide range of textures and recognizable shapes (e.g., Tartan patterns). We know that this variety is achieved with two interacting thread sets intertwined in perpendicular directions. The textures and geometric pattern outcomes, however, remain opaque upon seeing the fabric on display. The code that determines the outcome may involve many warp heddles, warp colors and a prescribed sequence for their up-down positions at each passing of the weft, which can also be multicolored. None of this coded sequence of movements or materials matters in our appreciation and use of the fabric. Yet without the

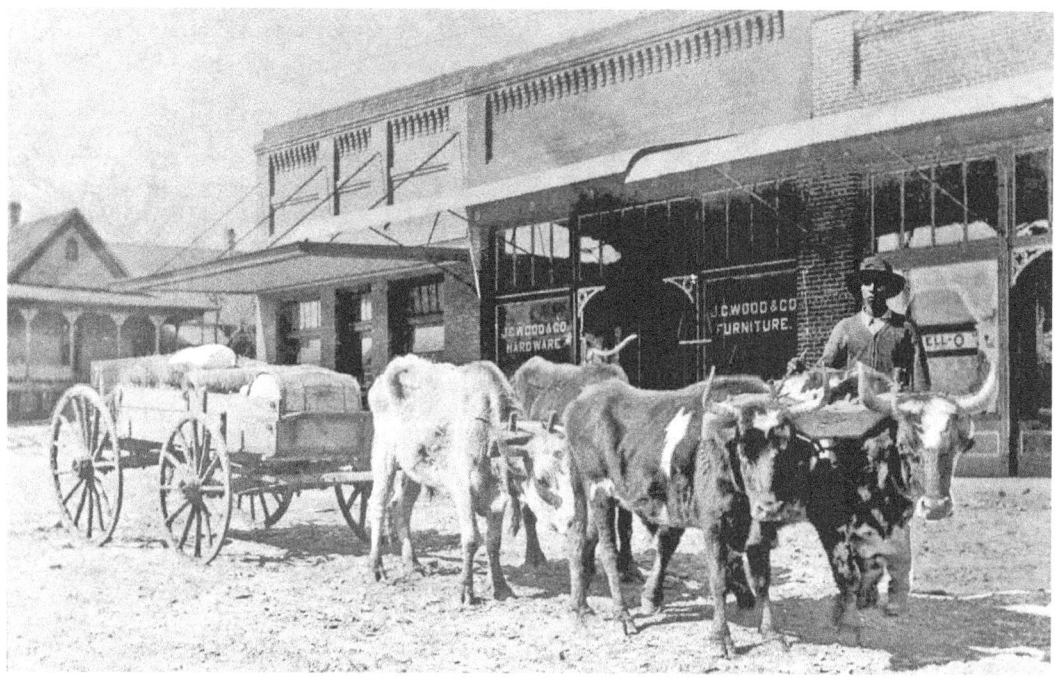

Settlement Network Designer: The hybrid device of four-oxen-plus-cart required specific street dimensions for moving and turning that become a repeatable pattern, a code (Southern Methodist University, Central University Libraries, DeGolyer Library).

generative code that produces a specific fabric texture (e.g., a towel or a bed sheet), the fabric could not serve its intended purpose. This up-down sequence could require the movement of as many as 16 heddles—too many for an operator to control or remember. Inevitably, these were patterned as a code on a circulating chain of on-off triggers (analogous to 0–1 in computing). The relationship between the chain pattern and the fabric outcome is impossible to fathom through mere observation. The missing link to understanding is the mediating mechanism and materials that produce the specific fabric. Just as a change in the "code" would alter the weaving pattern, so would a change in materials affect the outcome.

Extending the fabric analogy to a settlement's street network configuration, which is often an implied component in the metaphorical expression "city fabric," we can promptly see that the use of a network may satisfy known requirements regardless of whether its users understand the code of its formation. From the simplest, most repetitive and uniform pattern to the most labyrinthine, the "heddles" that determined its weaving remain obscure, undetected. (This analogy could also be extended to the land-use "patterns," albeit with some caution.)

The examples that follow show that street patterns conceived and applied in the past may be either concealed or misinterpreted and always need a translation of their codes.

Veiled Patterns

Street Width

Salt Lake City: Laid out in 1847, it has some of the widest roads (132 feet–40 m) among U.S. cities—double the width of most, and up to 10 times that of historic European city streets. One might wonder: Why such an excessive width?

If a street design code were to be classified as a "pattern" (a resolution of design requirements with a functional intent), then this excessively large width cannot be explained by the familiar transportation context of the 1800s in America: travel mostly on foot, with a few horses for war or transport and oxen for heavy loads and field work. Such a context is normally expressed in narrow streets and compact buildings, such as those appearing in European towns and Arab Medinas. This unusual "pattern" becomes clear only when we understand its designer's stated intent: that carts drawn by a team of four oxen should be able to turn around in the street without having to backtrack.[4] This pattern makes even greater sense when it is revealed that certain central-city streets were used for trade. Loaded carts would bring in goods and usually become the display benches too—a store in the street that took up street space.

For today's smaller, flexible, mechanical replacement for bovine power, the turning requirement is not only obviated but also a *prohibited* maneuver, a fact that makes Salt Lake City's wide roads even less intelligible. The bovine-age pattern misaligns with the motor-age functions and makes it incomprehensible, particularly in residential districts.

Ancient Chinese Cities: The width of streets of ancient Chinese cities, a second example, is revealed only in sacred texts: the *Book of Rites* (150 BCE) specifies that the nine major north-south straight roads in a new (ideal) city be 9 times the carriage gauge of a chariot in width, about 30 meters (98 feet, similar to the Salt Lake City dimensions). Using a chariot as a unit of measurement underscores its importance in city life, whether for defense, ceremony or transportation. However, as with Salt Lake City's streets, the width cannot be understood in the predominant pedestrian mode of transportation in BCE China. Chariots were used only by few and mostly on special occasions. A road so wide would be sparsely used most of the time. The same road today is readily accepted as an arterial that accommodates the ubiquitous, motorized replacement of the chariot and, coincidentally, raises no questions, as it matches the new requirements (arterial roads range from 85 to 110 feet, or 26 to 33 meters). However, the intent of the original pattern in this case remains obscure even though its width evidently is pegged to a means of transport.

Arab Medinas: A third example comes from the other extreme of the street scale: the narrowest possible, constrained by overhead bridges or buildings and free of geometric rules. Such streets can be found in hillside villages and towns, and they are prevalent in most old Arab cities (Medinas).

The street width, which is exceptionally small, has been interpreted as an indication of scarcity of land or an adaptation to a hot climate, both of which could be contributing causes for this pattern. There are, however, examples of it in places where either one or both of these conditions do not apply (i.e., island villages or Arab cities in milder Mediterranean climates that are built on level, unconstrained ground). These exceptions call for another cultural explanation.

A plausible one lies in the available means of transport, which also links indirectly to the terrain. As long as the predominant means of transport are humans or loaded animals, the width of a street need not be larger than that required for one or two loaded animals to travel. This is connected to the terrain by way of the limitation it imposes on the means of transport: a hill side location, usually chosen for defense purposes, may not be accessible by any other means of transport except animals and humans.

The next condition that perpetuates this conventional street width is codification. From 600 CE on, most Arab cities followed a street code that was implicit in the Koran or explicated by the interpreters of it.[5] Other codes in the Mediterranean region were influenced either directly by the conquering nations or by cultural diffusion.[6] The influence of these codes eroded and ceased with the emergence of automotive transport. Twentieth-century expansions of all Arab Medinas use wider street dimensions adapted to the new transport modes.

Truncated City Blocks: A fourth, and unique, example of revealed intent is Barcelona's expansion plan. Residents of or visitors to Barcelona may wonder why the city's blocks have their corners cut off. Explanations and reactions vary with the perspective of the viewer: Architects and planners find them meaningful because they create an "urban room"; in the unrelenting, rigid linearity of the grid, a break provides a welcome relief of space. Walkers find them inconvenient because they have to march longer to cross a street, while drivers appreciate the convenience of easy turning and being able to look further into the intersecting street for oncoming traffic.

The truncation's rationale has drifted from view in the 100-plus years since its application and explanations for this pattern of block geometry remain personal, based on experience and training. Only drivers have an intuitive appreciation of its original intent, but they would likely be unable to articulate it as a "pattern."

However, the intent of this truncation can be retrieved from the writings of its designer, an engineer with strong social reform convictions and no architectural ambitions. The trun-

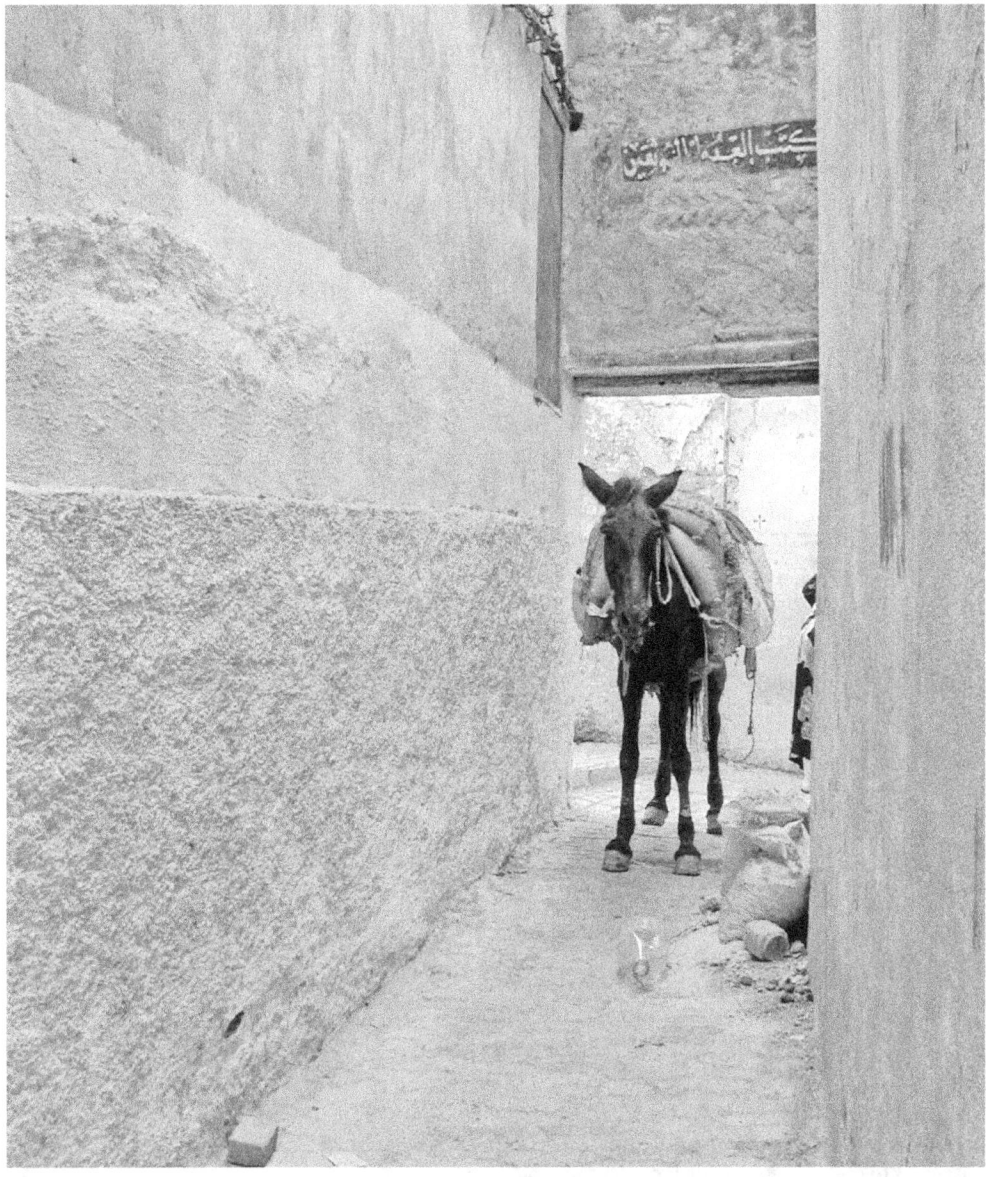

Settlement Network Designer: Pack animals dictate a specific street width—just enough for them to pass through.

cation is set in the transportation context of 1859, its inception time: mostly people traveled on foot, with a few horses and coaches, carts drawn by oxen and the "news" from elsewhere of horse-drawn omnibuses and trams on tracks. Idelfons Cerda consciously drew a "plan for the future" that would make it easy for these emerging large means of public transport to negotiate turns anywhere in the expanded city. Tram lines could be laid on any street and turn onto any other. Truncating the corners was the pattern that met this turning requirement well.[7] The large block size, 370 by 370 feet (113 by 113 meters), which he chose for additional reasons, accommodated the truncation easily. Such a design proved prophetic, as current spe-

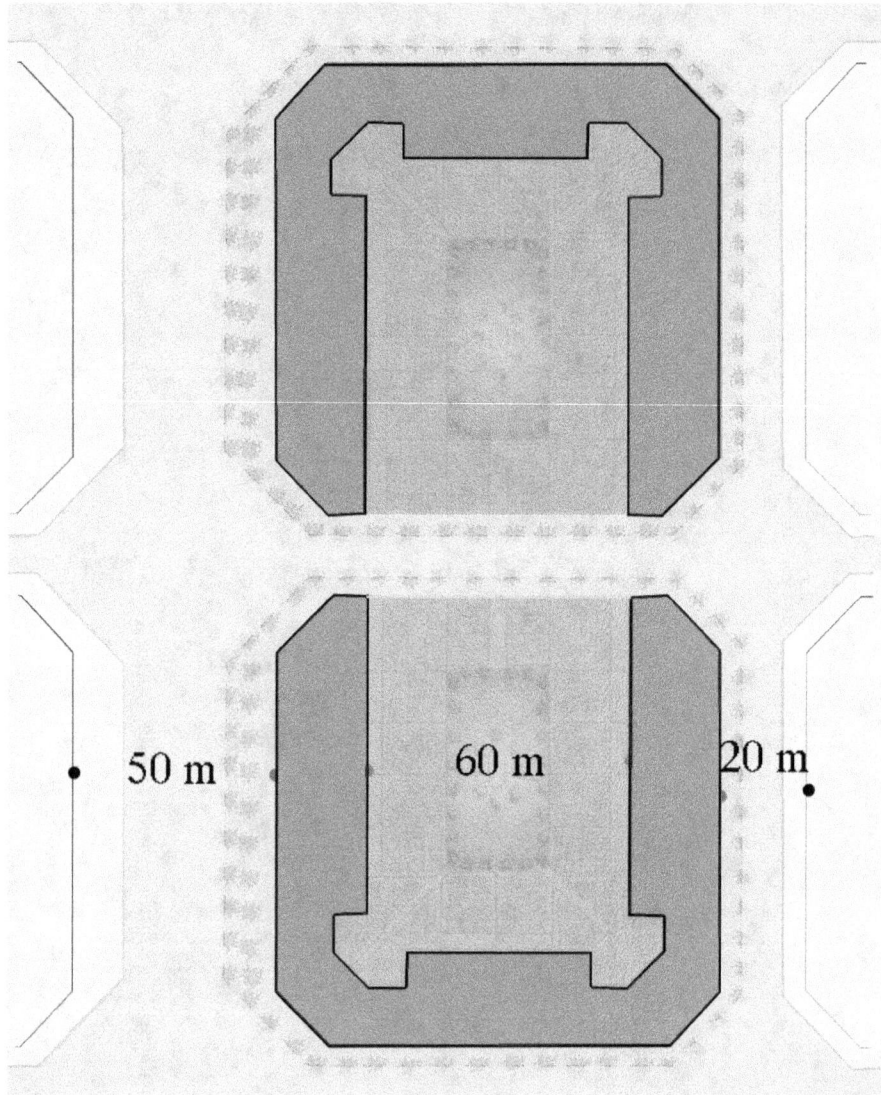

City Blocks Designed for Mobility: Barcelona displays a "pattern" of identical chamfered blocks intended to ease the turning of large wagons and carts.

cial means of heavy transport have grown to sizes unimaginable at his time (e.g., 70 feet, or 21 meters), for a transport truck and a city bus) and they now negotiate these turns easily.

    The Salt Lake City prescription, the Chinese *Book of Rites* rules, Cerda's book on the Barcelona expansion and the Koran all reveal and make intelligible patterns that today bewilder the visitor, the regular user and the student of cities. These four examples unveil a relationship with transportation means that explains the patterns of street width and block configuration. They open a window to research and speculation on network patterns in towns and cities in general. All four belong to the category of conceived and prescribed patterns with a declared functional intent. Other patterns of accretion and emergence that may not have analogous explanations in contemporary texts will be discussed in a later section.

From Single Street to Network

While street width can be traced in specific cases to the means of transport, explanations for street network configurations remain largely a matter of speculation. Characteristics of the network, such as rectilinearity, intersection type, angles and frequency, as well as the shape and size of blocks that are generated by the network, constitute topics of continuing curiosity and debate.

Irregular and non-geometric layouts can often be attributed to sloping, uneven terrain, but not always. Some cities built on level ground (e.g., Marrakech) exhibit irregularity similar to hill towns, thus prolonging the question of intent and the "pattern" that translated it into practice.

Straight, Crooked or Curved

Straight streets appeared in early cities in Mesopotamia, Egypt, the Hindu Valey and elsewhere.[8] Crooked streets also have a long history and are associated with "organic," unplanned cities such as ancient Athens and Rome, as we shall see. Several well-known, more recent layouts display curvilinear streets, often of irregular, random direction and curvature (e.g., Riverside, Illinois, 1868). Their existence and continuing use raises the question of the rationale for the straightness of streets found in Indian, Greek, Roman, Chinese and other cities of certain periods. Regarding contemporary curvilinear streets, we know from written sources that the rationale, in general, stands on aesthetic grounds—the picturesque effect.[9] But the grounds for long, straight streets remain largely indecipherable. References to aesthetic effect and military purpose seem to apply only to specific streets. In this case, aesthetics is the justification for a straight street according to Leon Battista Alberti: "When they [victorious armies] come to town, if the city is noble and powerful, the streets should be straight and broad, which carries an air of greatness and majesty." Palladio notes a functional purpose: "The ways will be more convenient if ... there be no place in them where armies may not easily march." Similar processional and celebratory reasons appear to have been the case in the layout of some streets of Babylon. Streets conceived to play such a role were dubbed "military streets."

A more general, but insufficient, explanation for rectilinear streets rests on "common sense"—the natural tendency of people to walk in a straight line, barring obstacles.[10] Yet many early unplanned settlements, and others that coincided with or followed the Roman period of rectilinear layouts, disregarded straightness and, in certain cases, repudiated it by transforming a preexisting straight-line pattern (e.g., Damascus) into a quasi-maze. This disparity and contradiction of the presumed natural tendency begs for additional explanations. A tentative explanation is proposed in the Appendix rather than here, since it treads on uncertain ground and is tangential to the topic of this chapter. The same explanation includes the probable byproduct of rectilinearity—orthogonal layouts and rectangular city blocks (but not in every case, as we shall see).

A Patterns Theory

The necessity for and inevitability of patterns was articulated by Christopher Alexander in his 1967 book. He selected many context-based solutions that seem to spontaneously, and repeatedly, emerge and, after illuminating their rationale, tabulated them in text and drawing as "patterns" in a comprehensive "pattern language." Though listed separately, the individual patterns are linked in ways analogous to the words of a language—each pattern has necessary antecedent patterns on which it rests, and it in turn becomes a precondition for other patterns that follow. They form a language nexus, each "word" (or pattern) depending on context to be fully functional ("understood").[11]

Since its publication, the book's influence grew steadily, but mostly outside the architectural and planning professions. However, shortly afterward, the entry of the mathematics of fractals—in the 1980s—as an explanatory tool in many research fields reinvigorated the idea of patterns in city building and city evolution. Fractals unveiled the pervasive presence of geometric order that covers much of the observable world, including what might seem to be random configurations. Computing embraced patterns in hardware and software architecture as a means of improving computational efficiency and speed.

The recent mapping of the human genetic code revealed that specific patterns determine what beneficial features continue to survive. Just like all other patterns, genetic code patterns absorb and bequeath advantageous, adaptive characteristics. Speculating on these grounds, it is conceivable that, just as any genome (human or other) produces a characteristic outcome, the entire pattern language "genome" sequence proposed by Alexander can in fact produce a characteristic city or region. Such a synthesis has not been attempted, however. Distinct "patterns" continue to be referenced and applied sporadically. Some of them re-emerge in this book, which attempts a synthesis at the neighborhood and district level.

This convergence of several disciplines around the idea of patterns confirmed their value as tools for mapping observable phenomena and, in turn, as means of solving practical problems.

Application and Reaction

The veiled quality of intent creates two classes of pattern replication or application: copying or adapting. Copying presumes a pattern's utility, while adaptation interprets its utility as understood. Both are valid, each in a specific context.

The same veiled quality also generates two distinct reactions by professionals to using patterns: disdain or affection. The first reaction is based on the common (and true) perception that copying and repetition repudiates a person's intelligence and capacity for invention; therefore, it is demeaning. The second, affection, springs from appreciation of the intelligence in the pattern and the freedom it bestows in adapting it to specific conditions—in other words, starting the creative process with the power of an essential idea in hand, fully understood.[12]

The disdain for using patterns overlooks the fact that, in daily life, we use patterns embedded in implements with an expectation of their effect and no awareness of their presence. A classic example of this idea is the use of the ubiquitous "lever" pattern, as we saw earlier. From an abstract concept of a principle and relation of parts, it has spawned myriad implements for daily use. All of them are applications of the same pattern; yet each is directed to a different purpose. The lever pattern morphs each time to suit a specific goal while its principle remains intact.[13]

Conclusion

This chapter attempted to show the pervasive presence of patterns in human settlements, whether implicit or explicit, concealed or revealed. The main ideas that it presented are as follows:

1. Patterns are pervasive and necessary.
2. Patterns underpin physical, observable constructs but are distinct from them.
3. It is counterproductive to copy the observable outcome without instituting the processes that created it.

The following chapters will trace the changes in city network patterns, unveil some of the forces behind them and ultimately provide the rationale for a new network pattern.

2

Networks and Their Users Under Stress

In the preceding pages, we set the context of this search with a distinction between the patterns of survival—the activities of production, provision, protection, transportation, communication and governance—that can be summed up as human culture and the traceable network configurations ("patterns" in the most general sense) of settlements. It is in these settlements, as they have been formed over time, that culture manifests itself, and, in a way, they embody it in stone and space. Conversely, as culture evolves, it strives for new settlement patterns that enable its better manifestation. In this dynamic interaction between culture and settlement patterns, friction is constant and adjustments are a work in progress.

In the first chapter we saw the pervasive presence of patterns in natural and man-made things. In human artifacts, patterns may have been conceived to express an idea (e.g., the order of the cosmos as represented in Indian canonical city patterns) or solve a specific problem (e.g., elaborate, geometric city fortifications to repel attacks). In this chapter we will look at how such man-made patterns are eventually superseded and need revision, adaptation or, in some cases, a complete overhaul.[1]

The Networks

From villages to metropolises, and from favelas to exclusive gated communities, settlements consist of two basic, tangible, visible elements: single buildings (or clusters of them) and access networks. Network evolution and layout is this book's central theme, and network pressures are the focus of this chapter. We will look at network stressors, ancient as well as contemporary, to set the context for a change that could respond to contemporary culture. What, then, stresses a network and its users?

Take, for example, the simplest network: a set of corridors in an apartment or office building. They have a 5-foot (1.5 m) width, slightly wider than an average street from an old Arab city (Medina) or a hilltop village. The corridors and these streets are found at the outermost branches of a network tree and are intended exclusively for residents on foot. Neither the frequency nor the type of movement creates any friction in apartment corridors or village streets; both are fixed, known quantities. Hauling bulky goods or belongings is far too infrequent an event to generate conflicts among residents crossing paths.

However, in a similarly large building, a hospital, corridor size may become an issue, even though traffic still consists typically of people. The friction stems from the increase in the frequency (volume) of traffic and the occasional movement of patients in wheelchairs, stretchers or wheeled beds. The size of these mechanical objects and their turning radii cannot be accommodated within the width of a typical residential-building corridor—hence the regulation (pattern) for an 8-foot (2.4 m) width in hospitals. While an apartment corridor size may cause annoyance on a rare occasion, a malfunctioning hospital corridor could be a matter of life and death in episodic, critical cases. Conflicts with elevated risks generate serious discomfort and thus demand a new pattern that accommodates a new use. Put in general transportation terms, the network issues in this case are *congestion* and *travel-mode conflict*—familiar, contemporary themes. We will look at several themes, both old and new, in the subsequent sections.

But first, we will take a snapshot of the interaction between pattern stressors and residents, and the process of mutual adaptation by settlements and residents.

Evolution on Its Head

This instance of change in building use shows that problems arise when a system has been conceived with one set of conditions in mind and is subsequently put to a use in which different conditions prevail. It also shows that new technologies (in this case, wheelchairs and wheeled beds), when they enter an existing system, demand adjustments in the design standards (patterns). This is the reverse of the familiar story of the adaptation of living organisms to their changing environment: in this case, it is the built environment that requires adaptation to the changing functions that humans perform in it. But, as we shall see later, this reverse evolution of the environment to fit the demands of its human inhabitants is only part of the story. While "environment" is generally understood to mean the natural environment, the ecosphere in which all organisms live, cities may also fit this definition, since they are the de facto territory in which individuals live and, increasingly, fulfill most of their needs. Purposeful interactions with the "natural" environment in survival activities such as fishing and hunting have mutated to sport and pastime diversions—a recreation. Just like the natural environment, settlements predate each distinct individual and endure for countless generations. Individual adaptation to settlement patterns at the formative stages is a normal, regular process. But the adaptation of them to a new collective set of requirements occurs at longer time intervals. The two processes are in constant interplay.

The Big Difference

In the natural evolution story, organisms that fail to adapt perish. In the built settlement version, a maladaptation simply increases the intensity of friction between the settlement and its inhabitants. Such friction instigates a process of reconsideration but rarely leads to a settlement's demise. But there are exceptions. One obvious, notable exception, for example, would be inadequately developed city defenses up against an unexpected assault tactic. The discovery of their inadequacy could, at times, come too late for their redesign, as the settlement could already lie in ruins, with its population decimated and enslaved. (Other settlements will derive usable lessons from the demise of one.) In general, however, settlements rarely perish completely; they merely go through periods of severe decline only to revive after modest or extensive transformations. Rome, for example, went from the seat of an empire numbering nearly a million people to a provincial medieval town of about thirty thousand and on to a revival and repopulation in modern times.

TIME LAG AND ADAPTATION

Modifying fortifications, for example, would invariably be a massive, costly and lengthy undertaking. During this period of planned change, often generations long, another form of adaptation takes place. A city's rulers, staring into potential extinction, explore partial, intermediate solutions to shield the city from disaster. For example, when the first cannons damaged city walls, one intermediary, pragmatic response was to increase the width of the surrounding moat just beyond the cannon range (inevitably, this was useful only until the next, longer-range cannon materialized). Similarly, citizens acting at the personal level improvise temporary adaptations to alleviate the intensity of a dysfunctional condition. For example, bicycle and moped riders, and even pedestrians, in certain contemporary cities wear breathing masks to lessen the impact of air pollution, which is a new, unanticipated urban condition.[2] A proper solution seems unlikely in the short term. Until a long-term one is found, it is the citizens who develop adaptive strategies to a city's changing conditions brought about by a new culture (in this case, the manufacturing of goods and the provision of power).

THE INTERPLAY

This interplay between cities being adapted to suit their citizens' new culture and citizens adapting their daily patterns of living to match the city's physical conditions produces a curious effect: a temporary solution that alleviates the severity of a problem and endures for more than a generation can eventually hide the existence of a problem. For example, stop signs at four-way intersections hide the problem of the ambiguity in motorized movement priority inherent in that type of intersection. Drivers obey the sign reluctantly and, in some cases, with resentment. (Priority was not an issue in such a network where only pedestrians moved.) Occasionally drivers reveal the basic problem of the inherent unsuitability of such an intersection to motorized movement by simply ignoring the sign, with catastrophic consequences. The underlying problem is further obscured by focusing the criticism on the "antisocial" or abnormal behavior of the disobedient individual. Ironically, the same behavior is perfectly social and legal when on foot. The real problem becomes evident when the sixteen possible points of collision are drawn on paper. When the probabilities for collisions increase, as the diagram shows, so do the worrisome statistics; it is the intersection type that raises the probabilities, not the drivers. A five- or six-leg intersection would predictably produce more collisions as the conflict points increase geometrically.

Citizens who are born into a malfunctioning condition often cannot "see" the source of the friction, having never been without it—a de facto acceptance, an acculturation. For example, walking on the entire city street was for centuries a normal, casual activity. However, for a number of generations born into the automobile era, it is neither casual nor normal. Instead, it is highly regimented, controlled and tense, due to perceived and actual risk. Citizens simply accept walking in the city as a stressful activity, one of the many stressors of city life, and they search for antidotes at the personal level, as solutions to this problem are understood to be beyond their reach as individuals.

Similarly, people who grew up on a street that became heavily trafficked in the preceding generation may find the condition annoying, but they tolerate it as inevitable, a given. Others, who earlier experienced the transition from quiet and peaceful to noisy and risky, were unsettled by the change and chose to move. The incompatibility remains, but for some it is an accepted fact (hidden) and for others an insoluble problem to be evaded.

The preceding discussion and examples allude to a four-step process that takes place in discovering and resolving conflicts between the citizens and their city environment:

1. Emerging Problems—subconscious nuisance becomes conscious thought
2. The System Reacts—conscious thought initially is led by instinctive reaction
3. Initial Organizing Principles—instinctive reaction gives way to strategic responses
4. Institutionalized Change—strategic response leads to system retrofit and planning

These four steps occur spontaneously over prolonged periods and become complicated and protracted by the involvement of many actors with diverse perspectives and interests. There is neither an expected time frame nor a guiding hand, much less a predetermined outcome.

The remainder of this chapter will focus on a set of emerging network problems and the factors that triggered their emergence. It will leave the discussion of adaptations for the next chapter. It is worth noting here parenthetically, however, that solutions to emergent problems may come from quarters totally unrelated to the parameters of the problem at hand, as the following example demonstrates.

Solutions Out of Nowhere

Technology that is in full use and appreciated by its users can create side effects of unforeseen dimensions. For example, at the turn of twentieth century, planners could not find a way to deal with the filth, contamination, congestion and accidents caused by the growing number of horses serving bustling metropolises. The solution came, unforeseen and unplanned, virtually overnight through the displacement of horse power by mechanical power and, along with it, the Industrial Revolution. By the 1900s, horse power had been in use for over 4,000 years, serving practically for every labor-demanding task; it was not a new, unexpected intrusion into the life of the city. Yet, suddenly, when horses proliferated significantly within a few decades, it came to be seen as an intractable planning issue, particularly with respect to transportation within the city. In the case of the engine that replaced the horse in the "horseless carriage," the idea came from outside the planning discipline and had little to do with solving city planning issues, such as the horses' unhealthy and unpleasant side effects; it simply obviated the source of the problem.[3]

Network Issues

Any discussion of transport network issues inevitably involves the transport means; they are manifestations of the same activity—mobility: one is the act of locomotion and the other its imprint on the ground.

There have been essentially three overlapping eras in the history of transportation on land: *foot and hoof* (walking and riding), the longest[4]; *hoof and wheel* (chariot, cart, coach),

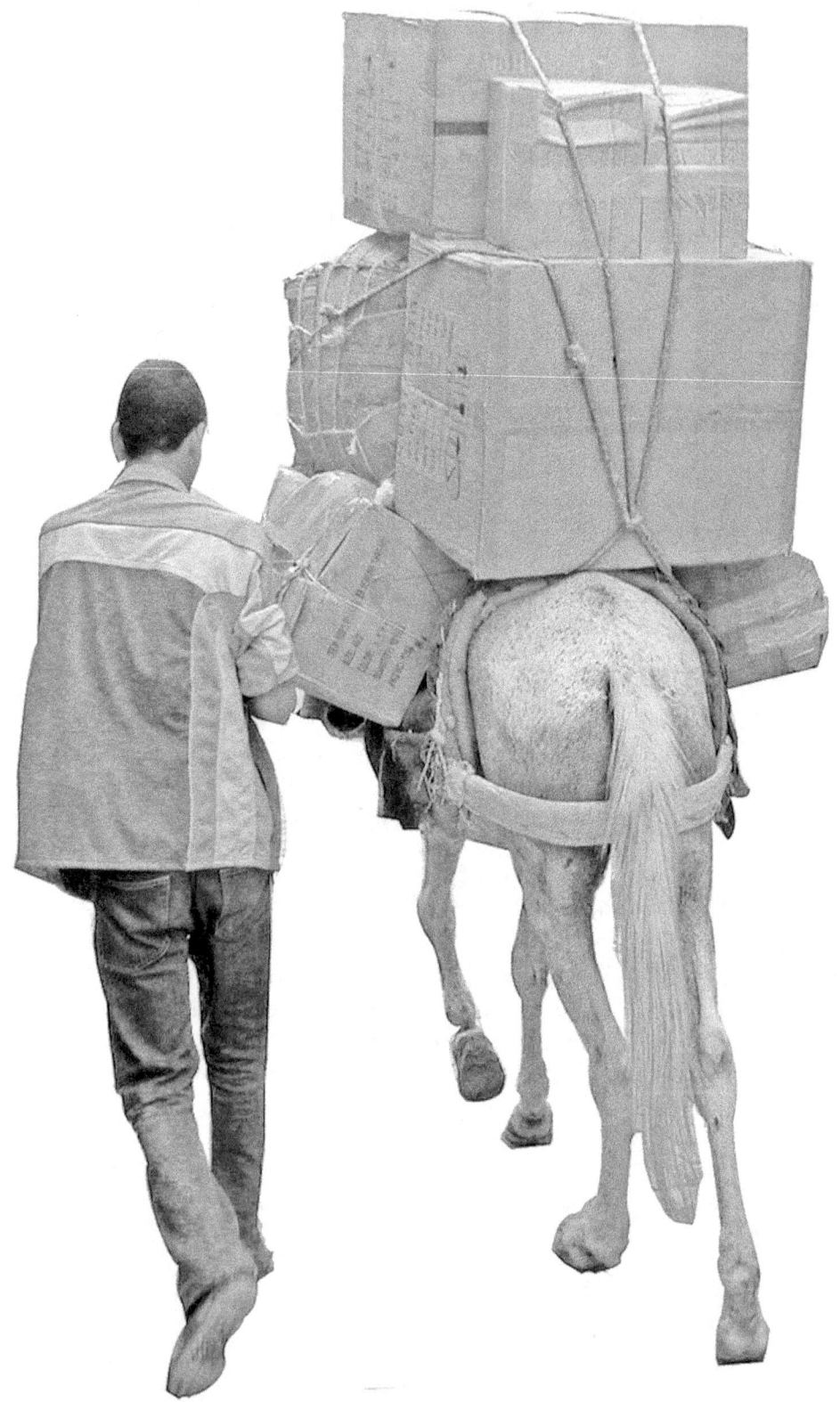

beginning about 4,000 years[5]; *wheel and engine* (mechanized), beginning about 150 years ago.[6] As we saw earlier, it is generally the new culture (in this case, transport technology) that creates friction and conflicts between an existing network and the need for mobility. We shall frequently refer to these three eras in the subsequent discussion.

DISTANCE AND EFFORT

A primal and critical stressor of a network user is travel distance, which affects effort (i.e., energy) and time expenditure.

In early settlements, food production and daily procurement of essential goods (e.g., water, firewood and foodstuff) were demanding, arduous tasks; the distance to the destination of their fulfillment could set up a friction between required effort and achieved benefit. For the first 5,000 years of settlement building, when foot-based transportation was the only option, network distance (and settlement size) was limited to a range of 2,600 to 3,600 feet (800 to 1100 meters) from edge to edge,[7] and resulting areas ranging from 160 to 300 acres. This network circumscription, within a roughly circular area, balanced the demands for transportation, food distribution, provision, housekeeping, governance and defense into a self-contained settlement unit with a walk-scaled diameter.[8] The network layout within these defined perimeters varied among settlements depending on the growth process and local topography, but the rule of total distance remained inviolable mostly because another primary factor was at play—preventing uncontrolled or hostile access to the city.[9] This pattern was repeated continually in Greek and Roman colonies during their respective hegemonies, and also in other new settlements until the 1800s Industrial Revolution, when the steam locomotive broke through the perimeter confines by making travel practically effortless. Not only persons but also heavy goods could find their way from and to distant locations far beyond the 3,300-foot (1,000-meter) diameter of a settlement.

The distance constraints of networks had another outcome that could not have been predicted at the outset of a settlement's founding—population density. Most early cities were largely self-sufficient, though they frequently traded with nearby and distant colonies and other cities, mostly via seafaring and (less often) caravans of hoofed animals. A few of them, particularly the centers of empires, amassed considerable wealth, traded vigorously and offered many opportunities for a good life.[10]

ATTRACTION AND COMPROMISE

Inevitably, these prosperous cities became magnets for people seeking new prospects and advancement. In addition, for every new "citizen" there would be a number of "noncitizens," or slaves, as households and the city as a whole typically depended on manpower for their daily operations.[11] The outcome of this attraction was that more people needed accommodation within walking distance and found it in fully built-up city blocks and crowded,

Opposite: **Foot and Hoof Transport: These extremely arduous, limited-capacity and time-consuming modes circumscribed a settlement's area and the reach of its networks.**

substandard buildings.[12] The crowding, absence of sanitation and poor hygiene practices cultivated and helped spread infections.

Rome had a peak population density of 322 people per acre (800 p/ha), and a surviving example of this condition, Fez, Marrakech, has a density of 200 p/acre (500 p/ha).[13] The same constraint and impact would also emerge in the early industrial city, where factories and businesses were concentrated in a small walk-distance diameter, as were the living quarters of the work force. New York, London, Paris and other major industrial cities such as Liverpool reached unprecedented population densities at the end of the nineteenth century. The resulting stress on the residents was enormous, as crowding precluded any sense of privacy, autonomy and personal pursuit without distractions or intrusions. Quality of life for many became a victim of the city's success. In addition, the high densities, substandard housing and rudimentary sanitation infrastructure, if any, proved a fertile ground for infectious diseases; not only quality of life but also life itself was at risk.[14]

The same distance-related friction resurfaced, however, in the automotive twentieth century, and in this case it was centered mostly on the time aspect of travel. Distance is now measured in time units, given that the personal calorific expenditure has been obviated by mechanized transport means. Citizens try to optimize their time expenditure for the movements that constitute their daily cycle. And as cities continue to absorb ever larger numbers of people, their expansion becomes inevitable, as does the range of travel distances.[15] Residents seek to reduce the time spent on daily travel in order to optimize opportunities for other activities.[16] Consequently, speed emerges as a dominant design requirement for network configuration and transportation infrastructure. But speed, as we shall see later, creates its own tensions and conflicts.

The distance limit of networks was removed, but the friction that their sheer size created thus mutated into a new conflict between time for travel and time for personal and social activities. Apart from distance, other factors can limit accessibility, one of which is topography (e.g., hills, rivers, mountains, forests, etc.).

THE HILL, THE VALLEY, THE RIVER AND THE PLAINS

For a defense advantage, and likely also for sanitary reasons, a majority of early settlements were built on hill slopes and hilltops: Athens (3000 BCE) hugged the Acropolis hill and Rome (700 BCE) perched on an assemblage of seven hills within its walls, to cite only two well-known examples.

The network of a hillside settlement inevitably has parts in it that resemble a zigzag, donkey-path configuration for ergonomic reasons. Workers and pack animals can ascend a modest slope, although with difficulty and exertion; the descending part of the journey is the riskier of the two. In this configuration, distances increase as routes become indirect, unless one chooses a shortcut, usually a steep stair, which is not accessible to loaded animals. But as long as defense dominates the scale of survival priorities and the main carriers are humans and pack animals, the stress of travel is taken as a given.

A conflict arises when the dominant, and more efficient, mode of goods transport becomes the cart. Loaded carts cannot easily negotiate uphill gradients and even less so the occasional step. And, surprisingly, downhill hauling is even harder with primitive carts. This

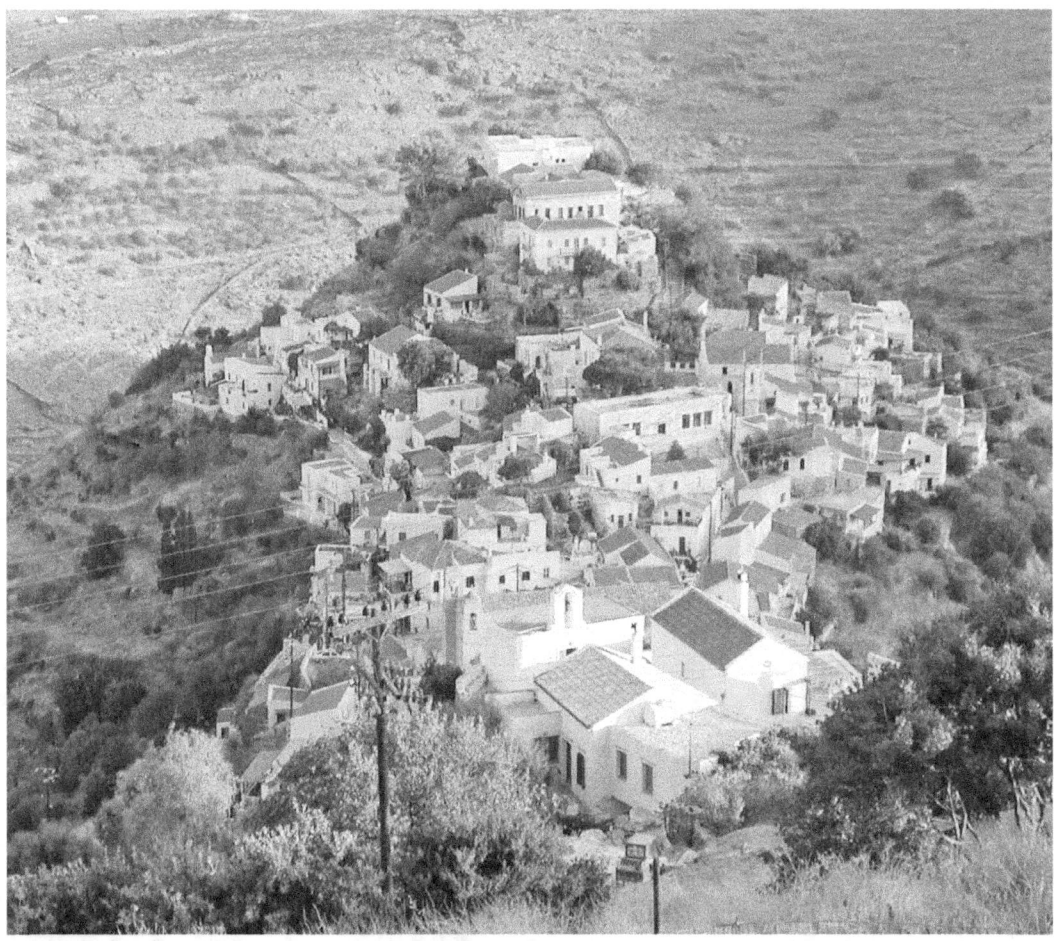

Hilltop Settlement: A network of steep climbs and stairs excludes all wheeled transport. Foot (mainly) and hoof (partially) are the only transport means of serving this community.

condition of low transport efficiency may have been recognized as an economic disadvantage. Some settlements chose a twin solution that addressed this issue: a productive place in the flat valley and a defensible place up on the hill for the times of assault. The wheeled cart, when it proliferated, propelled the economic life of cities and may have also influenced the selection of new city sites based on its requirement for low or no-gradient locations. Some cities in the Euphrates area and the Nile Delta started off with an advantageous topography for all early modes of transport—an almost level plain (Babylon is a supreme example of this case and a prime instance of a successful metropolis).

Many Roman outposts (castra) at the height of the empire's power (30 CE to 300 CE) were laid out on nearly flat sites (e.g., Timgad). When city-states eventually merged into nations, new cities, particularly in the colonial Americas, were sited on flat or rolling hill terrain that avoided the conflict between topography and transport means. By then (in the 1600s and 1700s), inter-city wars were far less frequent, being displaced by colonial warfare, and, consequently, transportation efficiency may have assumed a higher priority for site selection over city defense. Battles were fought on open plains as frequently as around cities. Cannons, which became a winning component of warfare, even more so than carts, could not easily negotiate steep, rough terrain.

With the onset of early canal and railway networks, which supplemented the street networks, the inaccessibility disadvantage of hilly sites placed them off the new network lines and on the path to economic isolation; trains cannot negotiate slopes.[17] This network-related isolation would persist until the next, more versatile means of transport emerged—the motorized vehicle. It eased the tension of network inaccessibility and linked such settlements to the surrounding land and cities, but its use brought about a new conflict: the size of transport means versus the size of network elements that we discuss under the element of size.

Many settlements that were founded at the navigable end of the river, such as Rome and London, for example, grew initially only on one shore. Their street network stopped at the water ("River Road" or "Front Street"). During the human carriage and pack animal era, commuting and transporting goods to other side of the river by boat was a slow, arduous process. Another network stressor became all too present: inability to expand to or trade with places beyond the dividing water body.

The entrance of motorized vehicles in the urban network may have made most sites accessible irrespective of topography, but it also introduced new stressors, one of which—noise—we discuss next.

NOISE

Produced by vehicles when using the network, noise results from the method of propulsion and from their interaction with the street surface. From the iron hoofs of horses to the iron rims of cartwheels, to the roaring engines of buses and trucks and the whistles and rhythmic track sounds of trains, noise emanates and disturbs residents irrespective of the network configuration. In the foot and hoof transport era, noise was produced by the hoofs and wheels hitting a stone pavement.[18] This wheel-induced noise, combined with loud voices, continued on for many centuries; the noise on main streets was proportional to the wealth of the settlement and its resulting density. With the emergence of trains, more noise was added to the central settlement districts as rail networks brought passengers and goods to the city core.[19]

With motorized vehicles, the major noise source shifted to the engine and its exhaust, although the wheels still remain an emitter of sound in spite of the rubber-based design. Combustion engines had no effective noise-abating devices for the first fifty years of their existence. Their noise, particularly when they malfunctioned, could be above the pain threshold. Not only powerful engines of large hauling trucks but also numerous mechanical devices designed for the construction, repair and maintenance of roads, whether mobile or stationary, operate at the higher-decibel sound level, often exceeding ear safety levels (e.g., jack-hammers, street excavators, etc.). Though improvements continue to be made to the internal combustion engine's silencing devices, traffic noise remains a source of stress for city residents.[20]

This friction becomes more apparent under certain conditions related to network configuration: (a) frequency of stops, (b) steep gradients, (c) speed and (d) distance to sources of loud noise.

Stops involve engine deceleration, brake application and subsequent acceleration. Each of these actions increases the noise levels produced by a vehicle, and it becomes louder in proportion to the size of the vehicle. Exceptions to this size rule are the two-wheeled vehicles that produce higher-decibel noise compared to automobiles. Networks, either by design or through management, can limit the number of stops and types of vehicles that travel on specific streets.

Steep gradients, which depend on site choice, require higher engine torque on the ascend portion of the trip and deceleration engagement when descending; both of these are noise-producing operations.

High speeds, which involve increased revving of the engine, also result in increased noise. A network element may anticipate, invite or inhibit high speeds by its configuration. Highways with no at-grade intersections and local streets with multiple at-grade crossings stand at the ends of the spectrum of potential for speed but, as we have seen, not necessarily at the respective ends of noise-level inducement.

Distance from loud sources can influence the number of people affected by the generated noise. Distance is determined by network configuration and placement of land uses.

Transportation on rails since its introduction has been an emitter of irritating noise that has compromised the quality of life of citizens and affected the values of property adjacent to the railway line.[21]

As we shall see in the next section—element size—street width has intentionally or inadvertently limited the size of vehicles entering residential streets since antiquity. However, it has also exacerbated circulation jams, and consequently noise, where drivers attempt to find the shortest route, disregarding its inadequate width and the traffic on it. This stressor from an inherited network is instructive: limiting street width can be used as means to prevent large vehicles from traveling on it, but it will not work if a given street is a shortcut to a desired destination.

ELEMENT SIZE

Regulated streets in ancient Rome were to be 12.2 meters (40 feet) wide; a main road, 6 meters (20 feet) wide; and 4.5 meters (15 feet wall-to-wall) for most neighborhood streets. The actual pavement was about half of that, or 2.25 meters (7.5 feet). Some preexisting streets, dating before the wheel's use, were even narrower. Arab cities as well as Mediterranean town streets were mostly about 1.3 meters (4.3 feet) wide or, occasionally, its double, 2.6 meters (8.6 feet). In these instances, the given width meant a wall-to-wall dimension, as there was no distinction between pavement and total space; the entire space between buildings *was* the street. At intersections, turning radii were practically nonexistent, and a building's corners defined the limits of the movement space.

These elements and their dimensions are still present in many old town centers, medinas, historic towns and old villages. Strolling villagers or visitors move through these streets and turn at corners today as easily as they have done for centuries; it is a well-functioning transportation network based on and used by people on foot and animals on hoof. In fact, visitors to these districts delight in the *absence* of motor traffic.

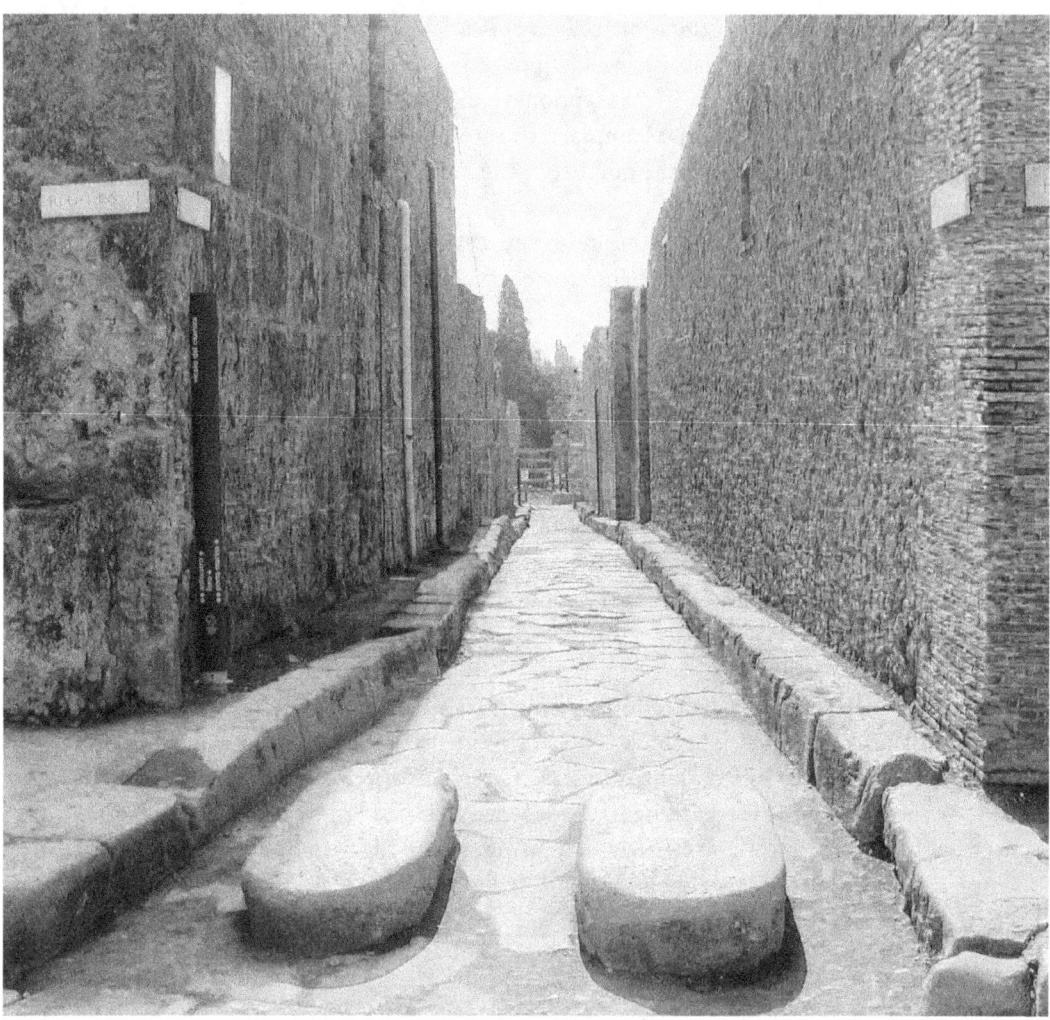

A Narrow Street in Ancient Pompeii: Serving as a walk path and a drain channel, this roadway can barely accommodate a cart. It is flanked by barren walls with an occasional entrance—an inhospitable and, at times, treacherous space.

The conflicts between network element sizes and its users arose when the first animal-drawn wheeled vehicles, a new technology, entered the network. The width and length of the cart and oxen (or horse) combination put many of these streets virtually out of service. The 4.3 feet (1.3 meters) wall-to-wall street effectively barred any vehicles such as chariots, wagons and carriages that use the standard gauge of 4.7 feet (1.4 meters) between wheels. Consequently, the vast majority of streets were (and still are in historic centers) inaccessible to these modes.

The regulated Roman streets with a 7.5 feet (2.25 meters) (slightly bigger than a person's stretched arms) pavement allow only one cart to move on them and no passing. This size could prove satisfactory if one assumes the infrequent appearance of a cart on a neighborhood street. A prosperous and populous city with vibrant trade activity and frequent movements of goods, however, may encounter increasing conflicts in its narrow streets, as did Rome and Pompeii.

With the advance of the Industrial Revolution, the services and materials that could be obtained multiplied rapidly: daily milk, vegetables, bread, and ice could arrive at the citizens' doorsteps if the network allowed the wagon to reach it. Similarly, building materials, house furniture and appliances could be delivered. For most families living in the old town center, these services were denied.

In current times, sanitation and fire trucks, as well as ambulance vehicles, being even wider and longer that carts or wagons, would also be inadvertently excluded from these districts, to the detriment of the residents' safety. Cars that generally have the same wheel gauge and buses or trucks, which have an overall width of 8.5 feet (2.6 meters), are clearly unable to reach many street destinations.

With these restrictions imposed by its network's dimensions, a settlement by necessity retains the culture of a previous era and, inevitably, its social and economic expectations. Of those who become aware of the new mobility opportunities and find the imposition unacceptable, many escape, an act that leads to settlement depopulation and economic depression. Since the network cannot adapt to the new mobility culture, certain citizens evade its problems by moving elsewhere.

Street size restrictions affect more than circulation and provision of services. From a contemporary aesthetic and environmental perspective, they also eliminate the possibility of embellishing the street with trees and other greenery. A landscaped street is not only more attractive but also pleasant and, evidently, healthier, as we shall see in Chapter 6. The Roman, medieval, and Renaissance dimensions leave no room for tree planting. Surviving drawings of such cities show no street greenery, nor have excavations found any proof of street vegetation. After experiencing contemporary cities where the practice is common, the contrast becomes stark—another point of friction, a reason for dissatisfaction and a propellant to escape from streets that lack vegetation.

In addition to greenery, street size, including the entire right of way and the building set-back, also affects the adaptability of the street's use: the bigger the distance between facing buildings, the greater the potential for transformations.

With the influx of more people and increasing number of vehicles, there develops fierce competition for street space between walkers, vehicles and store owners.[22]

Restaurants and coffee houses usually extend their territories into the sidewalk to attract customers, the classic street-side café or restaurant. Network element size can limit this potential, which normally adds to the vibrancy of a city and its social life.

We may conclude here that the size of network elements both expresses a culture and conditions its evolution. We will examine the reverse side of this issue, size of transportation means, in the section on speed.

Shape and Configuration

We saw earlier that hillside village or town networks inevitably include irregularly shaped streets that conform to the topography and inherently obey ergonomic principles that lessen the effort of climbing. This necessary irregularity, combined with the customs of land parceling and development, creates a top view (plan) of a network that has little geometric order, regularity or identifiable shapes. But since there was no predetermined plan as a starting point of the settlement, which simply grew piecemeal over time, a "top view" is a

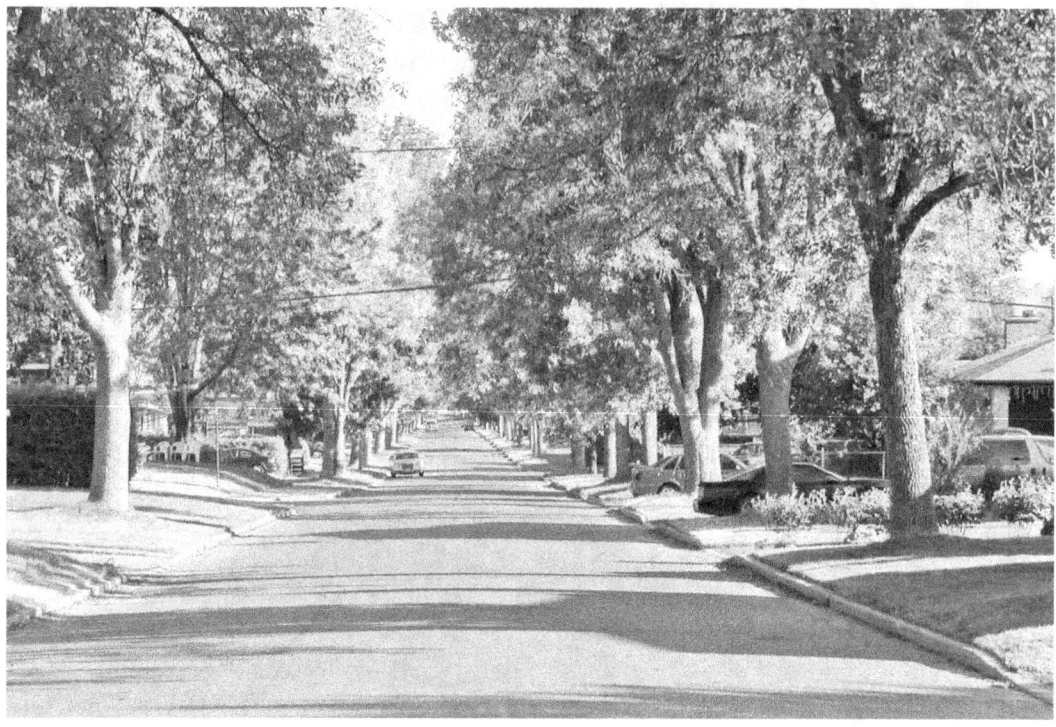

Contemporary Residential District Street: Four to ten times wider than its Roman and Arab equivalents, it provides space for plentiful greenery—a desired attribute.

meaningless abstraction that could not be expected to make geometric sense. For reasons that remain unclear, so far shrouded in historic obscurity, this irregularity seems to have emerged in sites that are plain (or almost so). References allude to the defensive value of a labyrinthine network,[23] but it is uncertain whether this was an intentional objective in the layout of settlements such as Athens or Rome, which grew by accretion. No plans have been discovered that are attributed to a city founder of previous eras and show a willfully constructed labyrinthine network. The opposite is generally true: most preserved plans show some geometric order. There is even some evidence of a tendency to move from geometric to haphazard through incremental, perhaps unregulated, incursion,[24] which intensifies the question of intent for such configurations.

Organic, labyrinthine networks display multiple street directions, a variety of intersection angles and generally narrow street widths that can vary along the length of the same path. As we saw above, width alone can be a decisive impediment to the movement of wheeled vehicles that emerged at some point during a town's long history. When small widths are combined with frequent acute angles in the system, they put carts and wagons effectively out of service for a good portion of the network, if not the entire network. When they do fit within the width of street, carts may be unable to negotiate a sharp turn on to another without repetitive back-ups. Some evidence exists that shows that the economics of owning and using a cart drawn by animals, as compared to simply animals, for the transportation of goods fluctuated substantially in time and by location, but the cost remained generally high, which might explain the long periods of coexistence of multiple modes of transport—pack animals and loaded carts, and, of course, not ignoring the ever present human labor, available and competitive in earlier periods. It also explains the endurance of towns with labyrinthine networks, which are mostly unsuitable for wheeled transport; men and beasts of burden accomplished all the hauling that was needed.

Such networks also coexisted with what evidently are planned networks, which exhibit geometric regularity. Though their origin remains a matter of speculation (see Appendix), there is a sufficient number of excavated ancient city sites and recorded samples, along with some evidence of rationale, to indicate that they represent an evolution and an adaptation to the new means of transport. These discovered plans (Hindu canonic, Chinese *Book of Rites*, Hippodamian, Roman, etc.) use straight lines and repetitive elements that give the plan a sense of regularity and order; a logic (or pattern) permeates them. While their exact logic may be inscrutable for the present, it will suffice to note that they constitute a clear departure from the previous informal, irregular layouts of towns that grew by accretion.

It is intuitive and also reasonable to see a connection between wheeled transportation and rectilinear networks as well as orthogonal intersections. Chariots, which were used for war (the equivalent of a contemporary armored vehicle) from the third millennium BCE onward, and for ceremonial or personal transport of those who could afford to own one, would roll far more easily in straight lines than through a sequence of twisting street segments requiring frequent turns. As early as 1600 BCE, charioteers were competing in races. Experiencing this advantage in mobility in preexisting straight streets would be sufficient inspiration

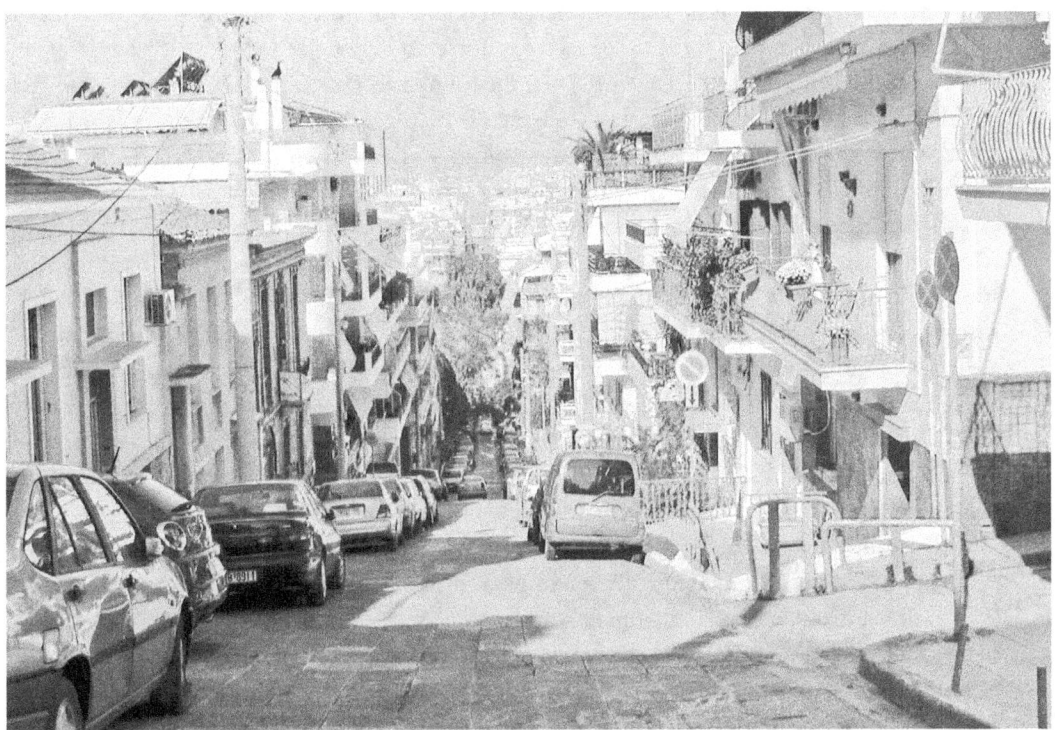

Geometry and Topography: The grid geometry applied inflexibly on steep topography reduces accessibility and makes access inconvenient, arduous and risky.

to introduce it in a plan for a new city or rebuilding a destroyed one. The same is true about intersection angles. If a land division system is to have intersections that are convenient for turning, the most logical solution is to avoid sharp angles and make all angles equal, which means 90 degrees, or "right" angles. This approach was taken by Hippodamus (498–408 BCE) in the plan for the reconstruction of Miletus (475 BCE). Independently, or through diffusion, the Romans followed this pattern, or "system," throughout their empire when they established new outposts or colonies (e.g., Timgad, Corinth, etc.). As long as the width of a street was sufficient for at least one cart, the network pattern made all of its parts accessible to all then-common modes of transport—foot, hoof and cart. Curiously, for all its rationality in resolving network conflicts, it was far less effective when applied to hill slopes, as was the case with Miletus, Piraeus, Priene and other cities in the city-state era; streets running against the grade were often a series of stairs unsuitable even for animal transport.[25]

Many new cities were based on this orthogonal pattern. It removed the tension between new transportation means and network design. Transportation culture, however, after a virtual stasis of four millennia that relied on human and animal power, evolved to include more and drastically different means, on account mostly of their speed and also, importantly, their size—motorized transport. Speed introduced new network stressors that we discuss in the next section. Speed also affected the configuration of network patterns, as we shall see in the chapter on adaptations.

Speed

Speed and its network layout ramifications could not have been missed by the Greek and Roman planners who built racetracks for horse and chariot racing, which has been a sport since 1600 BCE in Greece, before even the foundation of Rome. On the track, horses could easily attain 40–50 km/hr, up to ten times the regular city traffic speed. (This high speed is now the norm, although modest, for automobiles.) Its effects must have also been imprinted indelibly upon seeing the wreckages of chariots on the hippodrome grounds.

When motorized transport took hold of the network, it effectively transformed city streets into virtual racetracks overnight. "Race Street" was a name given, and retained, to streets in cities such as Philadelphia; Hartford, Indiana; and Cincinnati, Ohio, among many, where occasional horse races were held; now the race was on in every street. The differences are that the "track" used to be the traditional public space, where citizens normally strolled, walked and chatted, and that the race is no longer occasional—it is a daily event. An enormous tension arose between the competing occupants of the street—pedestrians and horseless carriages. This tension is still ongoing, and we will examine responses to it in the following chapters.

Speed influenced another aspect of networks: the limits of travel distance. As we saw earlier, once the calorific expenditure is removed from the travel equation, distance is measured in time units. Under variable speed, similar time units produce variable distances. Consequently, speed relieved some of the previous tension between mode of transport and place of residence. A city could now offer a greater range and variety of habitable land than was available during the horse, train and tram eras; plains, hills, ravines and mountains became equally accessible.

Speed was simply one expression of the transition to a new source of power: from animate to chemical (which, ironically, is still measured in animate equivalents—horses). And as the horses packed under the hood continued to increase, so did the range of places that were made accessible. Settlements reappeared on hillsides and hilltops as city extensions— this time not for defense but for escape, proximity to nature and the expansive, inspiring views.

Increasing horsepower brought another network stressor—large to very large vehicles. The automobile retained the average dimensions of its carriage predecessor in its varieties (about 13 feet [4–5 meters] long and 6 feet [2 meters] wide). New vehicles, however, such as city and inter-city buses (40–60 feet [12–18 meters] long, by 8.5 feet [2.6 meters wide), small and big transportation trucks (from 4.25 meters [14 feet] to 16 meters [53 feet]) long and 2.3 meters [7.6 feet] wide), articulated transport trucks (from 23 meters [75 feet] to 27.5 meters [90 feet] long) and sanitation and fire engine trucks (up to 8 meters long and 2.5 meters wide) exceeded the car length and weight many times over. Truck size becomes strikingly manifest when a truck carries eight average cars in two layers. This doubling or quadrupling of length and a widening of chassis require wider lanes, larger turning radii and more space for service functions without blocking traffic.

Existing networks of older cities were experiencing unprecedented stress. Speed required more travel space. Each car lane had to be increased from the inescapable Roman rut size of 1.43 meters (4 feet 8 inches) to around double, 3 meters (10–11 feet). Turning radii had to be increased from near zero to at least 3 meters (10 feet) and up to 7.6 meters (25 feet) for the proliferating larger vehicles. Even small vehicles such as motorbikes require a 25-foot radius at normal speeds of 20 km/hr.

Adding to the street width stress was the need for convenient stalls for vehicles (that is, on-street or off-street parking). This space pressure, resulting from speed and vehicle size, in many cases meant that most of the street space taken up by travel lanes. Where sidewalks existed, they gradually shrank to sizes that could no longer accommodate crossing pairs of pedestrians, much less street (sidewalk) life. Walking in such meager space became inconvenient, stressful and unpleasant.

Older parts of the city gradually became less serviceable and adaptations at the personal level were inescapable, as we shall see. The case for changing the traditional patterns of networks when building new city districts could not be made more vividly or convincingly.

Speed was also the cause of a yet another stress mediated by networks, as we shall discuss in the next section.

Safety

Injurious collisions are simply unimaginable between walkers, as speed and kinetic energy are by far the key elements in injuries and fatalities. At the horse and buggy speed, collisions can be injurious and also, albeit infrequently, fatal. As speed increases with motorized power, which amplifies the kinetic energy of the car's mass, so does the severity of injuries to people on the street or in cars. Network configuration plays a major role in the rate at which collisions occur by:

- enabling speed in general and where it may not be warranted (e.g., residential neighborhood streets)

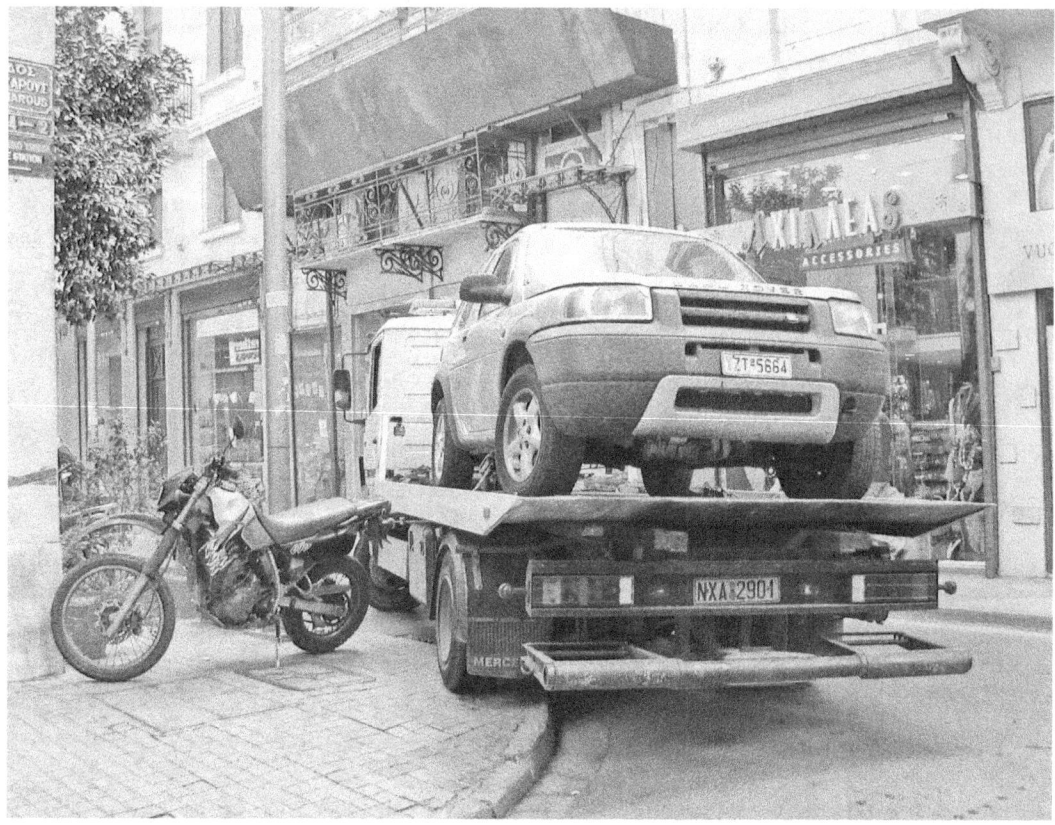

The Burden of Inheritance: A nineteenth-century street burdens all modes of movement with obstacles and constraints that generate chaotic, unpleasant and dangerous conditions.

- confusing or frustrating drivers through inadequate network clarity, as they must react in time measured in fractions of a second
- the de facto and often presumed priority it offers to vehicles over pedestrians when the two are both present
- mixing the various wheeled and motorized vehicles and pedestrians excessively at times

As we saw in the previous section, purely rectilinear networks gave the chariot and cart an advantage in speed and convenience. However, street widths in the cart era prevented both implements from traveling on a residential street in most instances. Even when present, due to size constraints, their speed was moderate, thus lessening the risk of collision. The same network configuration that served the cart has a speed *disadvantage* in the automobile era; it endangers the people it is presumed to serve. This is particularly true in otherwise tranquil neighborhoods.

Speed also brought into sharp relief the unsuitability of the cross intersection (four-way) for motorized transport. First, the repetitive stops at frequent corners, which degrade the speed advantage of motorized transport, frustrate drivers and prompt aggressive, risky behavior. Second, the ambiguity of movement priority often leads to wrong moves, particularly under emotional stress. Third, given the numerous ways in which a collision can occur at such intersections, the likelihood of one occurring rises considerably. Studies and statistics have confirmed this fact repeatedly.[26]

The conflict between network performance and citizens' well-being is currently more than an abstraction of city functionality and economic outcomes; it is a matter that affects citizens at the personal level. Deaths and injuries are simultaneously statistics and tragic events in citizens' lives. And as statistics become bleak, so do the lives of many citizens. They resent this condition and react; the "system" must also react and evolve. In the foot and hoof era, many citizens died in armed conflicts as soldiers; now just as many die as civilians in road conflicts.

The safety stress of the network on its users demands more than personal adaptations; it calls for a transformation. The chapter on adaptations will look at these potential network transformations.

DENSITY OF TRAFFIC AND GRIDLOCK

Since goods are produced within cities and are also consumed in them, most travel happens within the city boundaries. In addition, there has been a dramatic increase in available services, which, when combined with the procurement of goods, creates a picture of substantial change in travel density, proportionately far higher than in the period when most production occurred outside the city walls. This change implies increases in traffic volumes on the road network.

And given the multifold expansion of the city, made possible by motorized vehicles of all types, more traffic is generated, particularly around hubs of economic activity such as offices, institutions, large shops, and entertainment/sports complexes. In addition, periodic events, such as national celebrations or group gatherings or annual routines (e.g., Christmas shopping, Major League games), further intensify the traffic to be borne by a transportation network.

All of these factors, whether acting synchronously or separately, test the network's capacity and stress its users. Occasionally, the system breaks down; the presumed advantage of speed is neutralized by severe congestion, so that average speeds revert back to the horse and carriage era.

Many factors contribute to the breakdown. At least one reason is found in the network geometry: the grid. A grid, particularly one with frequent intersections, leaves little room for queuing. When the density of the traffic increases, the queue enters the intersection and inadvertently stops the traffic moving in the perpendicular direction; a *gridlock* ensues that brings traffic to a standstill in a series of surrounding streets—a new event and a new word in the dictionary of cities, whose meaning has now expanded to include any dysfunctional operation.

In such conditions, another stressor emerges—impure air. Transport emissions rise substantially at low speeds or while idling, and drivers as well as the neighboring residents find themselves engulfed in foul and often noxious air. The transportation network shows its inability to cope and demands attention.

When such devaluation of network performance occurs regularly, the stress on its users increases, and pressure for changes to the network or for other solutions intensifies. Given that a large percentage of the transportation network is already in place, relief may come through a combination of adaptations, personal and of the system, as we shall see in the adaptations chapter. It could also emerge out of an unforeseen source, as did the solution to the intractable horses-in-the-city problem.

The Era of Travel

Travel by the city residents can and does stress its network, as we saw, particularly in a large and dense metropolis. But street networks of small cities can also be under stress for a different reason—influx of visitors.

Since motorized travel removed calorific expenditure and reduced travel time by at least an order of magnitude while also improving comfort, no destination within 8 hours of driving is too far. (The same distance would have taken at least 15 days in Mozart's wunderkind years, which would necessarily include several stops at uncomfortable inns along the way.) Anything less than 8 hours is considered "a short day's trip." In addition to individual and family travel, people also travel in groups on trips offered by coach and ship lines.

Millions flock to Disneyland, national parks, ski resorts, Olympic sites, baseball tournaments, and other permanent or annual events hundreds of kilometers away because they can. Hundreds of people may land on a small island for just a day or two. Suddenly the transportation network of a small or medium-sized town experiences extreme stress. It is asked to handle multiple times the normal town population and its vehicles.

What is true for smaller towns also applies to metropolises. They offer multiple reasons for visiting: from business opportunities and learning and teaching events to unique entertainment and sports events and specialized shopping unavailable in smaller cities. These additional numbers of people and cars that invade the city daily can be a sizable addition to the numbers of citizens going about their usual activities.[27]

Motorized transport introduced an era of affordable and comfortable travel that made previously very distant places reachable only by very few accessible to practically everyone. Twenty kilometers (or a day's trip) was the travel horizon for most people during the foot and hoof era, and such a trip would be taken only very rarely (and for some never). It is now often the case that the visitors outnumber the residents during the peak travel season. As a result, networks of small and large cities either cyclically or permanently are subjected to extreme pressure due to the number of visitors attracted by the city's opportunities—a welcome boost to the city's wealth but also a stressor of its transportation network.

Visitors, particularly when arriving at places where an entirely inscrutable language is spoken, can easily get lost within a city's network, highlighting a new network stressor that we discuss next—legibility.

Legibility

Nothing raises anxiety to a fever pitch as much as the sensation of being lost in a foreign city. When on foot, a person can absorb a multitude of sensory clues, other than street names, that reinforce the ability to recognize a place, a street, a square, without knowing the local language.[28] When driving, however, that ability is diminished, as the rate of incoming sensory perceptions increases dramatically due to the speed of movement and, simultaneously, is restricted by the forced attention to the events on the road, resulting in too little time to process information and too little detail to form a memorable picture. This dual imposition leaves a driver heavily dependent on signs, which cannot be deciphered. The outcome is a high level of anxiety. Missing a turn in a town in which many streets have been adapted to one-direction traffic could lead to sense of total loss of direction and orientation. The same would be equally true when missing a highway exit and arriving at a different, entirely unfamiliar part of the town.

Local residents have no difficulty navigating their district within a kilometer's diameter no matter what the network configuration; no maps or street signs are necessary, and these, in any case, were unavailable for most of city history.[29] Visitors, however, cannot find their way without maps and printed guides (and, in many cases, even when using them).

A network configuration can thus become a source of stress for visitors in the era of large cities and of extensive, instant, universal travel.

Stress and Cure

In this chapter we saw how transportation networks are stressed by their users and how they, in turn, stress them. If the means of transport had not evolved, cities would have remained the small, walking-distance-radius places that they were when they began. While transport means evolved, their adoption occurred at different rates. Their impact was relatively small until very recently, when the change in their speed and size was dramatic and their use became nearly universal. It is in the last two hundred years, and more so in the twentieth automotive century, that the speed and variety of vehicles increased, as did their ownership by individuals and organizations.

City growth was driven by the means of transport, and they are now stressing city networks as well as the citizens. The pressure to find solutions that balance mobility, the main function of networks, and maintain a high quality of life, which cities are known for, is enormous.

The next chapter looks at the series of reactions, adaptations and proposed solutions.

3

Adaptations, Transformations
and Innovations

"Everything is the way it is because it got that way ... the form of an object is a 'diagram of forces,' in this sense, at least, that from it we can judge of or deduce the forces that are acting or have acted upon it." —D'Arcy Wentworth Thompson

In the previous chapter, we saw how networks can stress their users, and how in turn their users, equipped with new means of transport, can render networks dysfunctional. We have also discussed the interplay between evolving "culture," a collective name for all human activity patterns, and movement network patterns. We suggested that this interplay forces the network system to adapt to each new culture with a range of temporary or permanent measures (or both), but also compels city residents to make personal adjustments in their daily cycle patterns. Network adaptation happens slowly in existing areas and more readily in new districts. This chapter will look at both types of adaptations: network system and personal. It presumes that people are attracted to cities for their advantages, but not without reservations about their disadvantages; achieving a balance drives the mutual adaptations.

Network Systems

Network systems, particularly street networks, are slow to adapt (or never do) for good reasons: (a) they represent enormous public investments, and (b) they enshrine private property boundaries that represent residents' wealth—in many cases, all their wealth. For these reasons, it is still possible to walk on the very streets that Roman, Athenian and Marrakech citizens did millennia ago. Wholesale adaptations are rare: the transformation of the network of Paris by Baron Haussmann, for example, was precipitated by an autocratic government (that of Emperor Napoleon III), and it required vast public expenditures; it has not been repeated in any other city to the same extent. While the built environment resists physical changes, the rules of its use can be modified fairly easily. These can also be aided by management systems that guide user behavior as well as punishing misbehavior. For example, the traffic cop in the middle of an intersection, an early response, represents a management adaptation of a system that could no longer function if left unattended.

The most visible adaptations are those that are made to the street network, which we experience daily, and which has been synonymous with the *transportation* and *communication* network for most of history—but no longer. The nineteenth and twentieth centuries brought to the stage many new "ways" that complement, expand or supplant the role that streets once played exclusively—the railways, tramways, subways, freeways, expressways, airways—and a number of "lines," often with a dedicated right of way, such as telegraph, telephone,

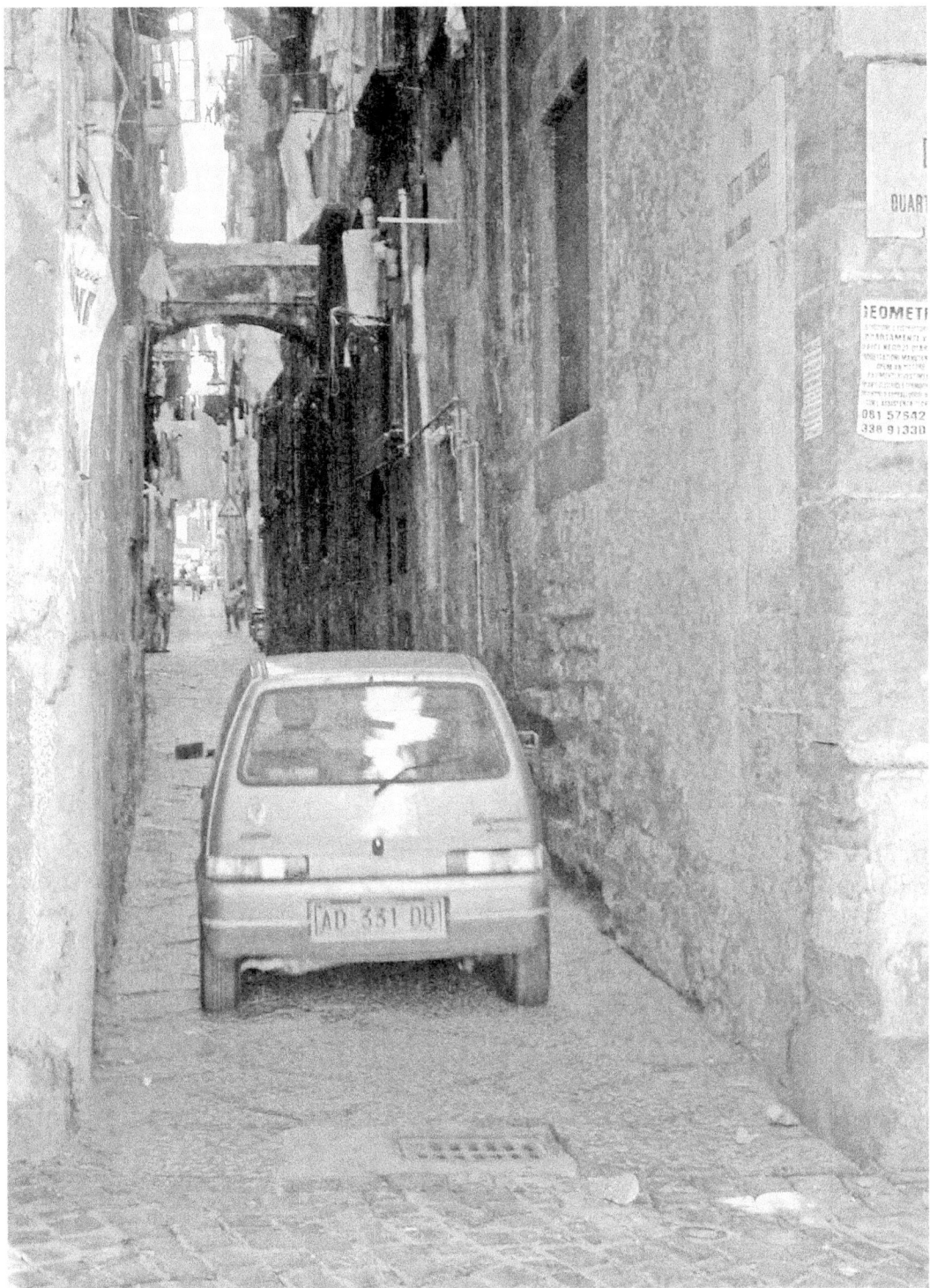

Greco-Roman Street in Naples: A transformation with negative outcomes. Too narrow for people crossing, too risky for mixing modes, too dark and damp for health and most unsettling at night—a remnant that persists in spite of the loss of its utility.

power and digital lines. To these "lines," more must be added that are also involved in transporting materials: water lines, gas lines and sewer lines. In addition to the "ways" and "lines," a new stream of (erroneously named) air-*waves* has been added to the expanding set of "networks." These also have a dedicated right of way—a specified bandwidth, now progressively in diminishing supply.[1]

While examining system adaptations, we will look at reactions and their outcomes with an eye to charting a balanced course to network configuration.

PERSONAL ADAPTATIONS

We mentioned earlier the masked riders of bicycles and mopeds in heavily polluted cities as an example of personal adaptation to an intractable network-wide stressor—air pollution. Personal adaptations respond to an issue with speed and flexibility and can be viewed as early and clear evidence of the existence of a stressor—symptoms of an underlying conflict.

This chapter will trace system and personal adaptations in response to each of the stressors elaborated in the previous chapter, highlighting the important differences between the two. It will also try to distinguish between transient adaptations and emergent permanent solutions that address the stress source, where such solutions exist. By reviewing the commonalities in the stressors and adaptations, it will attempt to set the context for the next chapter, which proposes a systematic approach for removing network stressors altogether in new districts or planned cities.

Elements of Friction and Adaptations

DISTANCE AND EFFORT

As we saw in the previous chapter, the combined effect of network size and the implied effort to reach destinations in the city was to limit the physical area of most cities and, at the same time, as they attracted more people, to increase their population density. Most walled cities were 2,600 feet (800 meters) by 3,300 feet (1,000 meters), or about 200 acres (80 hectare) in area. Greek and Roman cities of that size had population densities in the range of 80–140 people per acre (200–350 p/ha), as did Pompeii (180 p/ha) and Ostia (320 p/ha). Larger cities, usually capitals, such as Rome and Babylon, were contained in an area of 6 square miles (16 square kilometers), with a radius of about 1.25 miles (2 kilometers). Within this half-hour walking distance from the edge to the center, the most populous cities reached a population of 900,000, perhaps the maximum that could be compacted within such area. Population densities spiked to 250 people per acre (600 per hectare), and cities with such densities inevitably developed multiple centers to serve their people. London and Paris, still essentially walking cities in the mid–1700s, reached their critical size of 800,000 and their population densities reached 250 per acre (600 p/ha). By 1900, population density in these cities peaked at over 280 per acre (700 p/ha), while in New York it reached 520 per acre (1,300 p/ha). This extraordinary compaction of citizens, by contemporary standards, demonstrates the enormous attraction of the city and, at the same time, its limitations.[2]

While distance and effort played a decisive role in confining the city area, and thereby increasing its density, defense and communication also played an important role in the pre-cannon period. Defense necessitated the construction of protective walls, a very large public undertaking that consumed a disproportionate share of a city's resources; they had to be designed to an optimal size. It was far more economical to add people to the city than to expand the wall perimeter, though a few cities succumbed to the enormous pressure and constructed new walls further away—Constantinople, for example. Communication also acted as a constraint when it came to managing the city in general, and particularly in the eventuality of hostile attacks or great emergencies, both of which required oral transmission of messages that was limited by the reach of voice.

This need for vocal messaging found a practical expression in the size of Roman garrison towns, restricted to about 2,300 by 1,600 feet (700 by 500 meters), so that all parts of town were within hearing distance of the perimeter walls, where sentinels were stationed, and, similarly, of the central square, from which new civic proclamations were made by trained town criers (with voices in the range of 100 decibels).[3] The death of the first marathon runner, following his delivery of the victory message, underscores the critical role verbal communication played in foot-based cultures.

Both of these stressors on city networks (and size) were removed via intentional and unintentional technological adaptations. The cannon (in the 1600s), an offensive weapon, obviated the need for city walls for strategic defense, a purposeful deterrent against an attacking enemy. Three hundred years later (late 1900s), electricity—in the form of the telegraph—would replace foot and hoof in conveying messages, a task entirely unrelated to its main purpose of providing power.

The density effect of the distance and effort limitations is still evident in districts of cities that predate the industrial era, and also in newer cities that still rely predominantly on human-powered transport. Fez (within the walls of the old city), for example, has a population density of 180 per acre (450 p/ha). By comparison, contemporary cities that grew mostly after the Industrial Revolution show much lower density figures even in their densest central districts. For example, New York now registers 43 per acre (106 p/ha) and Los Angeles, 12.5 per acre (31 p/ha). These numbers put Fez, Ostia and Pompeii multiple times and, in certain cases, an order of magnitude above modern cities. Similarly, the Philadelphia and Toronto cores, the densest part of each city, count, respectively, 32 per acre (80 p/ha) and 30 per acre (75 p/ha), which are less than one fifth that of Fez.[4] Considering that contemporary cities make use of multi-story buildings unavailable in older cities, it can be reasonably inferred that crowding in early settlements must have been extreme. Records of personal stories and surveys of late nineteenth-century neighborhoods depict conditions in which several children of a single family shared one room.

Cities acted as people magnets but also as compressors. Larger populations often meant crowding, even overcrowding. The inevitable stress from overcrowding led to personal adaptations, at least for a small minority of the general population—the affluent. Well-to-do citizens moved to the fringes of the city or beyond to the adjacent land. A clay tablet from Babylon dated 539 BCE explains the attraction: "Our property seems to me to be the most beautiful in the world: it is so close to Babylon that we enjoy all the advantages of the city, and yet when we come home we are away from all the noise and the dust." The majority, however, would not exercise this option until two millennia later, when the friction of distance/effort was overcome by economical communal or personal means of transport, such as trains, omnibuses, trams, and bicycles.

Animate Power

The problem of exertion was first overcome around 2500 BCE by the domestication and use of animal power for transportation. Horse riding may have occurred as early as 3500 BCE, most likely for hunting and corralling. Bulls, horses and camels quickly assumed mythological standing (i.e., semi-religious) for their unquestionable benefits, and they conferred power and status on their owners. Distances could still be long, but the effort to cover them was diminished for the riders. Similarly, a load could be unmanageable and overwhelming for a man, but once transferred to an animal, the burden could be carried over longer distances.

With animate power, city networks would now grow to some extent, though still limited, due to the time expenditure, a second constraining factor, and, more importantly, the extent of horse ownership in cities. The cost of maintaining a horse was too high for the vast majority of citizens; horses remained a possession of a minority throughout city history. For this minority, the horse offered a double benefit: reduction of walking effort and choice of place of residence—a horse ride of half or three quarters of an hour could bring affluent citizens to the "country," a sufficient four kilometers away from the crowded, smelly, dusty, noisy central city. An even smaller minority of rulers developed another adaptation for the reduction of effort in reaching destinations, particularly in uneven, steep or stepped terrain: a personal enclosed coach (litter) carried by four men. This adaptation demonstrates the continuing prevalence of inexpensive labor and the extreme hierarchical structure of most preindustrial societies.

With later complementary technological advances, a few millennia after domestication, horses entered the public domain and, for several decades before the proliferation of the steam engine and the electric motor, they powered a limited public transportation system of buses on rails or on wheels. Overcoming the unwelcome effort of walking home after a long (usually 10–12 hours) and exhausting workday, these urban innovations eased the restriction on the distance from workplace to home. Horses and wheels provided that relief.

Two Wheels and a Pedal

The millennia-old invention that reduced effort when transporting goods, or eliminated altogether when a man was being carried by horses harnessed to a wheeled vehicle, found a new expression in the late 1800s—the bicycle. It was as flexible and as personal as a horse and far more economical to purchase, maintain and store: no food, no stable, no manure, no grooming or veterinarian care.

Exceeding the regular speed of horses and doubling the speed of walking, it also required half the effort for traveling to destinations. A 2-kilometer distance, when walked at a normal (4 km/hr) or brisk (7 km/hr) pace, burns 93 and 100 calories, respectively. The same distance at two different speeds (9 km/hr and 16 km/hr) by bicycle would use up 54 and 48.7 calories, respectively: that is, about half the calorific expenditure of walking and double the speed.

The boundary of distance and effort was pushed again and networks could stretch somewhat beyond the perimeter of a settlement into adjacent surrounding land.[5] When combined with a train ride, as was the case in certain instances, more distant places could be reached with little effort. Bicycles also revealed a new network conflict: ride discomfort on account of the street surface.[6] These two means of transport, trains and bicycles, which grew in use almost synchronously, allowed more citizens the personal adaptation of their Babylonian urban predecessors—a place to live that would be less crowded and perhaps in more pleasant surroundings.

Invisible Home Fuels

A seemingly unrelated transportation system that impinges on the street network lightly, but does not "use" it, is the transport of power—electricity. The thin lines of wire overhead, with the complement of mechanical devices at their terminal points, ultimately displaced the transport of millions of tons of wood, coal, oil, kerosene and ice used for heating and lighting buildings and for refrigerating perishable food articles. This displacement also resulted in fewer vehicles on the streets and reduced the effort for attaining desired comfort at home or at work.

Similarly invisible and non-intrusive is the natural gas delivered to streets and homes starting in the nineteenth century and proceeding from then until its current widespread use. Buried lines within the right of way of the street make the delivery unobtrusively, with the exception of the occasional disruption to install or repair them. They displaced innumerable hours of walking and hauling of wood and coal to homes and factories—in fact, an entire service industry.

Iron Roads

Steam power and electricity eased the distance restriction still more. A new type of road was to emerge and spread in the city and between cities—the railroad. Rails were laid out on major city streets and extended beyond existing city boundaries, creating new streets and, with them, new city districts.[7] These roads (or railways) had entirely new design requirements for street width, turning radii and safety rules, particularly within the settlement. They made travel convenient, comfortable and effortless. A fifteen-minute trip by tram or train could cover a distance of four to six miles (6–10 kilometers), allowing far more people to experience the advantages of city life and to live in compact, yet less crowded, quarters. Haussmann, who, as we shall see, transformed the street network of Paris, also introduced the first two suburban railways: a large one transporting goods and a small version for passengers to suburbs such as Auteuil and Passy, two of 11 earlier out-of-town villages that by 1860 had been annexed to the capital. These two early rail suburbs were, and still remain, the wealthiest districts of Paris.

With these developments that created a new culture of transportation, distance and effort lost most of their power as factors in shaping a settlement. The city finally broke the stranglehold of its walls and the tyranny of distance.

A Mechanized Street

A radical network adaptation occurred starting in 1863 in London that soon after was emulated by numerous other cities. Unlike all previous adaptations that used the streets,

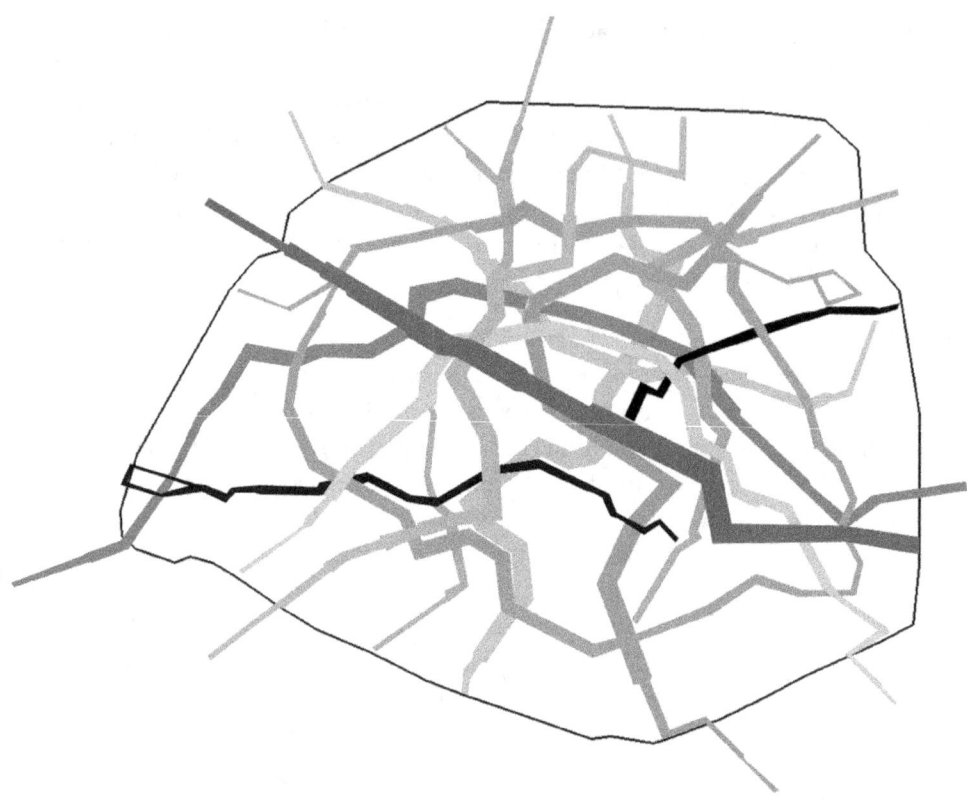

Paris Metro Lines by Passenger Traffic: Transcending the surface street network constraints, the Metro moves far greater numbers of people and much faster than any other transport method operating within a metropolis.

such as horse-drawn omnibuses and later electric trams, this one ignored the streets and their constraints and charted its own way below the surface—the subway. From the city dweller's perspective, it can be viewed as a moving street with imaginary, fixed buildings on either side above. This view rests on the fact that the subway moves people only, a function that streets have performed inherently since the birth of settlements. By avoiding the constraints of street dimensions and network configuration, it created a new network that in fact complements and extends the existing network while being far more efficient in reducing the distance/effort constraint and responding to the growing time constraint. An indication of how much more movement (virtual street) space was added to on-grade streets is given by the track kilometer length for major city systems: Moscow, 269 kilometer; Tokyo, 293; New York, 1,102; London, 408; Washington, 166. For comparison, consider that the entire street network length of imperial Rome was 89 kilometers.[8] Also indicative of their influence is the area that the tracks serve measured as a "ped-shed"—a 10-minute walk from each station.

Effortless Climb

While the subway extended the street below grade, another adaptation extended it vertically above the surface—the elevator. Starting in the coal mines, it eventually became a building apparatus by late nineteenth century. It eliminated the effort in climbing up to a habitable space and removed the five-to-six-story practical height limit of buildings that had dominated settlements up to the time of its invention (1852). The city could now accommodate more inhabitants in the same area; a single building could house the population of a village in a minuscule portion of its area. Building tall structures also helped intensify the workplace in multiple-story offices and add daytime population to central districts. When applied to residences, the result was ambivalent: in some cases, both unit and people count in an area increased, but in others, depending on family composition, the habitable unit count went up but the population count remained the same—the gain amounted to more space available per person. By this means, the average height of central districts increased and their population density decreased, by pre-industrial standards. The height innovation brought forward another stressor, however: dark streets and lack of sky-view, at least for pedestrians and dwellers of lower-level apartments.

Moving Drinkable Water

A second invisible and vital vertical transportation system—pressurized piped water— became more common around the last half of the nineteenth century. For example, up to 1852, only 6,000 houses in Paris, a city of one million people, had piped water, which reached the lower floors only. The remaining four floors were served manually using buckets, an arduous and messy (but inescapable) daily task. This new essential hygienic convenience, combined with the effortless elevator climb, increased the attractiveness of tall buildings and of living on upper floors, which up to that point were occupied by lower-income dwellers. By the end of the 1800s the number of dwellings supplied with piped water was increasing steadily, as were the populations of cities.

The Automobile

The trajectory of the influence of distance and effort on city size and shape took another sharp drop with the introduction of the internal combustion engine and the resulting culture of private mobility and mass movement enabled by cars, buses, trucks and diesel trains. Cars had all the advantages of a horse—personal, flexible door-to-door transportation and speed— but, at the same time, also some of its disadvantages—purchase and maintenance cost as well as space for storage. They also propagated much faster than horses and continue to do so globally. Within a hundred years they displaced horses entirely for personal travel, at least in the industrialized countries. With their use, costing hardly any effort and permitting travel in complete comfort, a territory of 100–200 square kilometers is accessible in one hour's return trip.

The Death of Distance

The final and ultimate assault on the distance/effort factor, the "tyranny of distance," came with the parallel development of electronic communications, wired or wireless, and high-speed trains and aviation: one provided instant exchange across vast distances, and the second reduced many days of travel to simply hours.[9] And though cities continue to have administrative, geographic boundaries and distinct civic governments, through these developments they are now interwoven into a network of mutual economic exchange and dependency and, in some cases, are physically abutting with indiscernible boundaries.

With the distance constraint removed, the imperative for very high densities also disappeared; average city densities entered a long period of gradual decline even as their populations mushroomed during the high-mobility century. This decline became most pronounced at their centers, which historically had been the densest.[10]

As we shall see under the *element size* and *speed* sections, cities adapted their networks to suit and serve these new transportation options. And as networks spread, time became the new point of friction. It has been found that, on average, people allocate one hour per day to travel, which has remained constant throughout the history of settlements (the Marchetti constant). To reach desirable destinations (e.g., work, shops, service, entertainment, civic functions, etc.) and leave sufficient time for personal and family activities, speed becomes a necessary and desirable objective.

At the personal level, citizens adopted these new methods of transport, which branched off in a multitude of types and hybrids that made it possible to choose where to live in the city, how much time to spend traveling, and how much effort to assign in accomplishing the daily cycle of activities that required transportation. Walking, bicycling, and using the tram, train, subway or bus were all available choices; none was imperative, though the range of choices *was* limited for some due to cost. The city magnet grew stronger with additional advantages, while the compression eased substantially.

Topography

In the previous chapter we saw that the introduction of wheeled transport of goods and people, in carts and coaches, demonstrated the disadvantages of networks on slopes that had been previously used only by pack animals and people. Anticipating only that type of circulation, such networks matched the dimensions of man and animal. The slope gradient was often hard, and for some impossible, to negotiate. Consequently, the combination of slope and tight spaces made such networks partially or wholly inaccessible to the new means of transport. Founders of new settlements may have responded to this obvious conflict by seeking sites on flat or rolling plains appropriate for such transport.

Hillsides

New sites on flatter land avoided both the restrictive gradient and the inevitable sharp turns of hill sites. The settlement network's elements could now be of sufficient width and in the straight lines that made transport convenient, comfortable and efficient.

But the topography constraint would reemerge in specific land-locked cities that grew enough to use all the land available that was framed by mountains, wide rivers or lakes. Since the networks could not grow, buildings did, using new construction technology that increased height and vertical transport that made climbing to higher floors effortless. Land-locked cities grew taller faster than those on large plains. Cities such as Vancouver and Hong Kong, for example, show this tendency vividly. This adaptation indirectly increased city population density (generally in the center), though not necessarily crowding, as personal space in such buildings could still be adequate, even generous. This network constraint

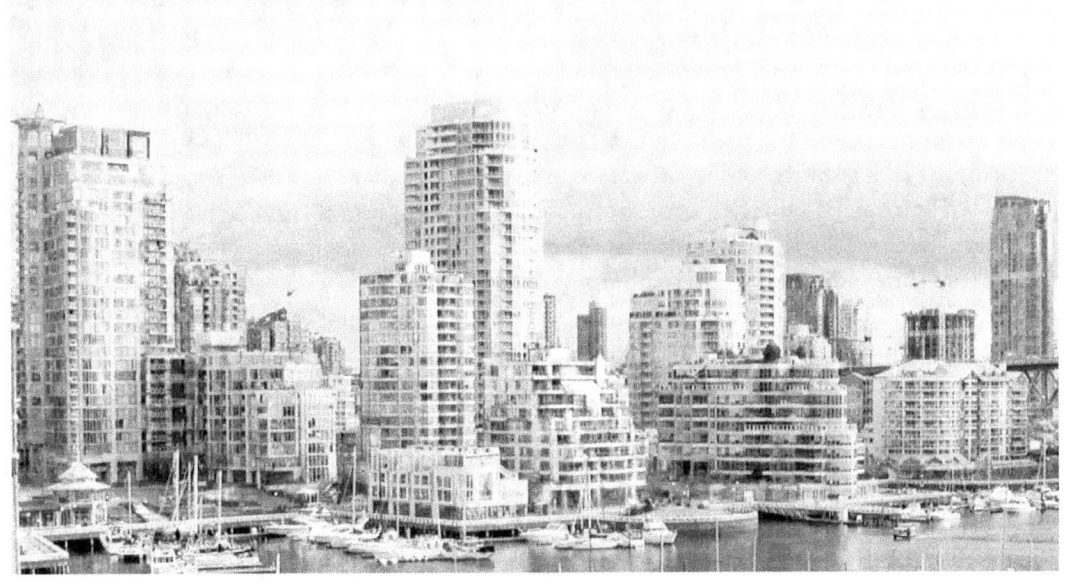

Landlocked Cities Grow Tall: Vancouver, British Columbia, shows the effects of land pressure in its skyline, with more towers than similar-sized cities built on unlimited flat land.

shaped settlements until 1920, the effective beginning of the automotive era, when car ownership reached about 8 million vehicles in the United States (87 vehicles/1000 people) and rivaled horse ownership a few years later (8 million horses in 1946). This density, however, combined with the concentration of work and services, did create a new stressor—traffic congestion (a later topic).

From the emergence of automobiles onward, however, hill slopes were once again available for settlement that could now be reached without excessive effort; the combustion engine provided all the necessary power. These new sites conferred desirable advantages on their inhabitants: expansive views, plentiful sunlight and natural, fresh air ventilation—all desirable attributes for a home, particularly in a city.

Inadvertently, these new desirable sites on hills practically eliminated the two most common and economical means of transport—foot and bicycle. They also made public transport means either inapplicable or barely so with special technical modifications (e.g., engaging gears or cables for trams). This new tension between networks and choice of travel means continues today: a slope approaching 10 percent is impossible to negotiate when riding a bike and daunting for many on foot. Sites accessible only via high-gradient streets are effectively out of range for bicycles and pedestrians.

Mountains and Water Bodies

Other topographic limitations related to water bodies such as rivers, lakes, sea channels and inlets constrained the growth of cities and the networks that serve them. Early in their history, cities chose sites on the shores of navigable rivers or sea inlets for their transportation and trade advantage; much later these water bodies became obstacles to their growth. And though vessels morphed into innumerable types that place no limit on what can be transported (including cars, buses and even trains), the logistics of such transport and its speed make it highly uncompetitive with the newest land-based vehicles. Speed and flexibility, as we saw, have emerged as overriding determinants of efficiency and productivity. With advanced engineering and seemingly unlimited power in the twentieth century, cities overcame such topographic limitations through a proliferation of bridges (of previously unimaginable lengths) and, recently, underwater roads and rails.

Topographic obstacles were also subdued in mountainous regions. Advanced tunnel boring technology allowed networks to continue through, not over, mountains, thus connecting cities and regions of neighboring countries.

Such large network improvements led to a wider range of personal adaptations of not only places to live but also places of work, shop and recreation. It is now possible to live in one country and work in a second that is separated by water from the first, and then go shopping in a third behind the mountains. Topography imposes little stress on network users with the exception of trams, bicycles and pedestrians. Apart from restricting bicycle and pedestrian mobility, steep gradients are now a factor in noise increase, the subject of a subsequent section.

Cross-Continent Connections

Topography was also subdued when it posed obstacles to inter-city and international trade that supplied each city with necessary, locally unavailable materials and products. Two historically unprecedented public works, both in magnitude and cost, were carried out to create new, shorter routes to continental destinations—the Suez (1869) and Panama canals (1914), the latter being named one of the seven wonders of the modern world. Traffic on the Panama Canal increased from 1,000 vessels in 1914, when it opened, to 14,000 in 2008. Similar increases in traffic and cargo occurred after the opening of the Eurotunnel (Chunnel): from 7 million passengers in 1995 to 17 million in 2007, and from about 6 million tons of freight to 19 million in the same period—about three-fold increases in 12 years in both cases. Whether by fast train, car or plane, inter-country or inter-continent travel may not seem so outlandish if seen from the perspective of time that networks and the means of transport permitted in the foot-and-hoof and hoof-and-carriage eras. Cities and their merchants traded with proximate villages or towns that were half a day or even a full day of travel away. The same time is now sufficient to cover continental distances and a sufficient reason to venture on such exchanges.

It would seem that both the distance and topography obstacles to the growth of networks and cities have long been overcome, and the city emerges even more attractive than it has been, offering a greater set of advantages and lifestyle choices than its earlier incarnations.

ELEMENT SIZE

Several sources confirm the codification of network element dimensions: (a) the earliest Roman regulations (450 BCE) specified 1 foot (0.3 meters) of width for footpaths, 3 feet (0.9 meters) for horse-riding paths, and 4 feet (1.2 meters) for carriageways for single vehicles;

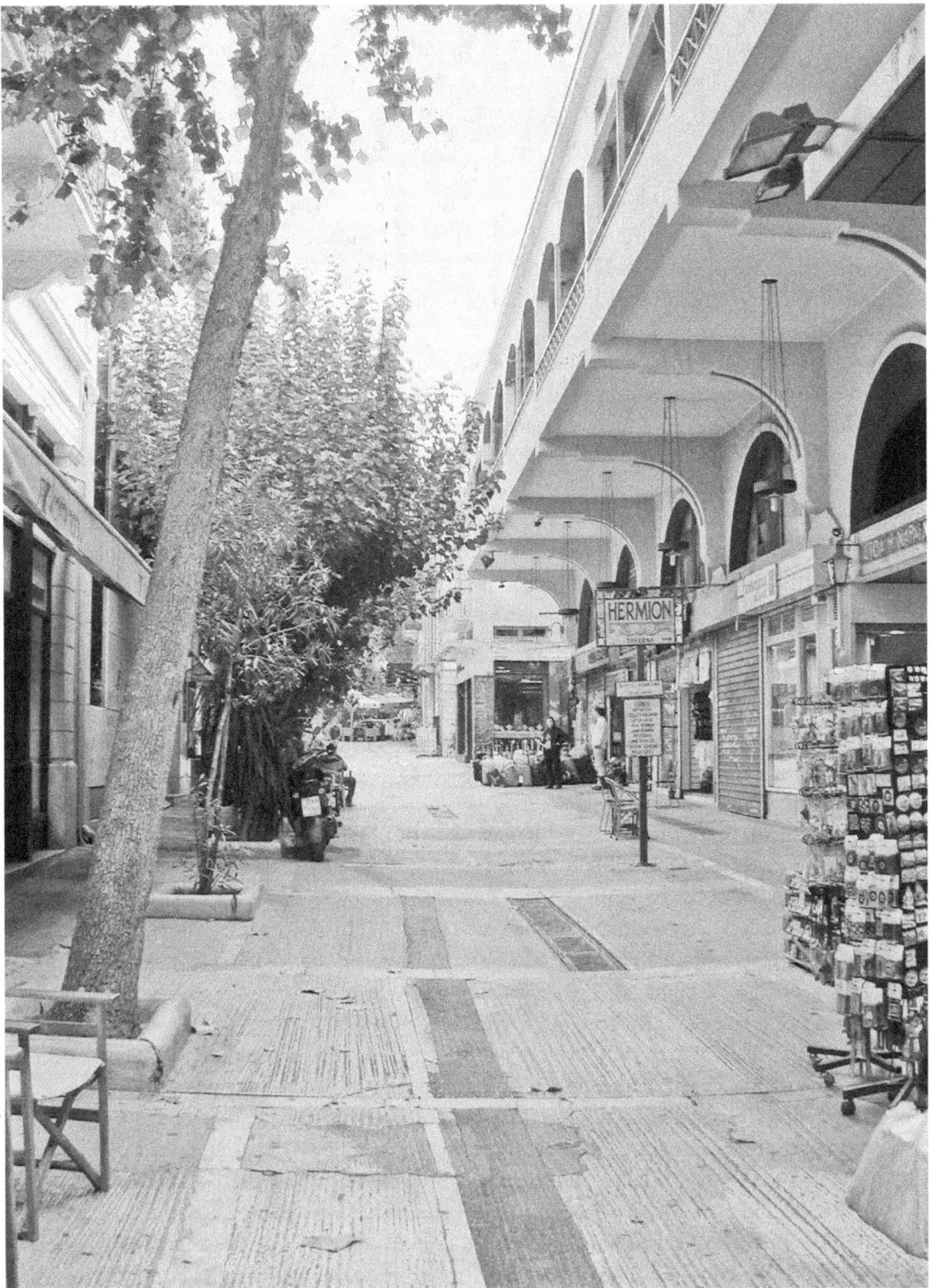

Street Adaptation and Retrofit: A millennia-old residential street becomes an open-air bazaar crowded with local and itinerant global shoppers. The pressure leads to recessing the ground floor to make room for the displays and the unforeseen crowds.

(b) later Roman law (100 BCE) regulated a minimum street right of way of 15 feet (4.5 meters), and at about 15 BCE new regulations specified three classes of streets: 40 feet, 20 feet and 15 feet (12.2 meters, 6 meters, and 4.5 meters); (c) a section of the Koran speaks of two types, 4.3 and 8.5 feet (1.3 and 2.6 meters); and (d) the Chinese *Book of Rites* (1500 BCE) specifies a major avenue dimension as nine carriage widths, or 98 feet (30 meters). A medieval decree by Henry I (1135 CE) called for all English roads to be two carriages wide, an event suggesting that, as in all European medieval towns, most existing roads could only accommodate one carriage at a time, if at all. The numbers from the successive Roman regulations show a clear trend toward wider streets and, in some cases, over a period of 5 centuries, an almost tripling of their width. This trend can only be interpreted as an adaptation to transportation pressures.

Excavations or standing remnants of older cities also provide evidence of street widths. From Egypt, dating about 1900 BCE, a new settlement for pyramid workers had a street width of 10–13 feet (3–4 meters). Early Greek cities had many 11.5-feet (3.5-meters) wide streets, but also occasionally a wider main street (platys), which became a shopping avenue.

These codifications appear to respond to common means of transport, and also to major city functions. The Koran encodes the almost exclusive use of pack animals. Roman regulations in turn discuss pack animals and wheeled vehicles with reference to their wheel gauge of about 1.4 meters (which has remained practically the same ever since). The larger dimensions that apply to very few streets catered to regular ceremonial civic and religious events that involved large crowds and multi-horse drawn chariots (*quadriga*) and carts.

A Tool's Hold

Another, later influence on the street width has been the use of a standardized measuring tool, the surveyor's chain (1620 CE), which resulted in many pre-industrial U.S. and Canadian cities having this exact measure as the right-of-way width for most of their streets, particularly the concession roads that were evenly spaced at 100 chains apart. In fact, the use of a one-chain (66 feet, or 20 meters) right of way was implicitly regulated in the division of agricultural lands (1862) in the United States by the requirement that each farmer leave a half-chain public access strip around the one-mile square of his land parcel. (In Canada, one or one-and-a-half chains were added to the parcel.) The resulting 66-foot right of way between cultivated fields was presumed to accommodate the turning radius of a horse-and-cart assembly. We also saw in the patterns chapter evidence of a similar rationale for the dimensions of the Salt Lake City streets (120 feet wide), which were to accommodate a team of four oxen and a four-wheel cart turning within the street without backing up.

Medieval cities exhibited dimensions ranging from 4 feet (1.2 meters) to a rare 33 feet (10 meters). Renaissance cities, particularly those that followed a preconceived plan, either replicated the Roman dimensions or increased them. The transportation backdrop for all these regulated or customary dimensions has been human power, animal power, and an array of wheeled vehicles. Such vehicles were pulled by oxen and horses. Animal power and vehicles were high-value commodities that few individuals owned throughout city history. The extent of their use would have depended on the economics of competing transport resources. For example, the massive stones that were used to build the Egyptian pyramids were transported to their final destination by hundreds of men. By comparison, an emperor or his dignitaries paraded in the city on chariots pulled by four horses. These transport means—man, animal and harnessed animal—coexisted for millennia, and still do in many contemporary settlements: existing or regulated streets may have not posed insurmountable friction, as appropriate means may have been used on each street type, though, inevitably, such accommodation to existing network conditions would have reduced the efficiency of transport functions.

These regulated systems and their adaptations reveal the rationale for the chosen element sizes and the friction that such sizes generated. Not only the size of individual elements but also their assembly into a system may likewise reveal preexisting frictions and their resolution. In theory, at least, no change is necessary unless there is a perceived or actual pressure for it.

Alleviating, Managing Stress

System stress first emerged in large and densely populated cities, such as Rome and later Constantinople, Paris and London. As the empire expanded and Rome blossomed as an administrative, military and trading center, its old, narrow streets became so congested as to render them entirely dysfunctional—movement became inefficient, no matter the means. In response, two administrative adaptations were introduced: first, the designation of a number of city streets as one-way, and then, as things continued to deteriorate, the declaration of the center of Rome off limits to all vehicles between 6 a.m. and 4 p.m. by Julius Caesar in 45 BCE. About 100 years later (in 50 CE), with the continuing expansion of the Roman Empire, Emperor Claudius extended the daytime ban to all towns in Italy. He also was to construct the world's first dual carriageway road that connected Rome to its port of Ostia, a very busy thoroughfare. (Its median strip was paved and intended for travelers on foot only—a unique innovation for its time.) Within another 130 years (around 180 CE) Marcus Aurelius extended the ban to all towns of the Roman Empire. As a result, within two centuries all major towns in the Roman world functioned without wheeled traffic during the day (exemptions were granted to town and visiting dignitaries and special construction crews). All these sequential administrative adaptations reveal the tension between preexisting street size and the amount of pedestrian and vehicle traffic.

Excavations in Pompeii, a Roman city, reveal evidence suggesting that certain streets, on which wheeled vehicles were once used, became one-way in the first century CE. Other streets in the city bear no marks of wheeled traffic, from which archeologists surmise that they were closed to (or inappropriate for) wheeled traffic.

Two millennia later, in a repeat of the Roman experience, cities have turned many city-center streets into one-way roads, and a trend of limiting entry into the central district is under way and apparently growing; several cities at the start of the twenty-first century have placed restrictions on private car traffic entering their centers. Some introduced a tax (congestion charges) for entering, and others have regulated entry via license plate numbers.[11] Notably, what took two centuries in the Roman Empire to assess and regulate happened within a quarter of that time in the twentieth automotive century.

These regulatory adaptations speak to two crucial, and surprisingly contemporary, issues: (a) the likely unsuitability of an existing network system for new, unforeseen transport means, and (b) the potential for a network system to be overwhelmed by an increasing number of users even if it is suitably designed for current means of transport. Invasive intervention may be the only remedy in such cases.

Baron Haussmann's Scalpel

A well-known and admired physical adaptation of a network is the massive surgery performed by Baron Haussmann on Paris during the 1850s and 1860s. The rationale for this transformation points to many motives, all of which converge on enabling movement, be it for cavalry, cannons, coaches, troops or citizens. It took 140 kilometers of new streets to adapt the inherited medieval network to these contemporary demands. Following this intervention, average street widths doubled in Paris. More importantly, the configuration of the network changed dramatically, as we shall see in a subsequent section.[12]

Since Haussmann's time, average street dimensions have been increasing in all cities, either by using more of the available right of way for traffic lanes in existing districts or by regulating more generous dimensions in new areas. A carriage (traffic) lane ranges from 9 feet (2.7 meters) to 13 feet (3.6 meters), even though the wheel base (or gauge) is practically identical to that of the Roman chariot. Most regulated streets today have at least two lanes, plus a parking lane, altogether producing a pavement width of about 28 feet (8.5 meters) and, with the set-backs, are larger than the largest regulated Roman street, of which there were very few.

Parking Stalls Pressure

Unfortunately, the increase in width and the addition of lanes provided only temporary relief, particularly in existing pre-automotive networks: first, because of the burgeoning number of vehicles entering the city, and, second, due to the need for parking stalls. The demand for parking space and the struggle to regulate it takes us back to the Assyrian King Sennacherib (705–681 BCE), who forbade illegal parking on the Royal Road of Nineveh on pain of death.[13] Julius Caesar later introduced requirements for off-street stalls for horses and wagons. Parking restrictions were also applied in Pompeii. Street parking management currently is a major city operation. Regulations disallow parking during certain hours of expected high-traffic volumes and exact steep fines from offenders. However, violations do occur and, when they happen, reduce the effective road width at peak time. Another network adaptation to enable the optimum use of road space on two-way streets is "switching," in which one of the available lanes switches direction at prescribed times to respectively accommodate incoming or outgoing traffic. Such management solutions make up partially for the lack of adequate room for traffic and parking.

Current municipal planning regulations prescribe ratios of parking stalls for all new buildings in central districts as well as in new developments. In spite of these adaptations, however, availability of parking in central districts during business hours remains a point of friction for citizens of many cities, particularly in cities that receive large numbers of visitors. Plans for new city districts have gradually adapted their street dimensions to include parking lanes on the street as an expected feature. Numerous new city districts can be found, however, that were designed in the 1950s and 1960s, the middle of the automotive century (particularly in cities where automobile ownership was low), where this adaptation does not show up in the layout, as evidenced by cars occupying sidewalk space. An inevitable and proliferating counter-adaptation to secure space for pedestrian movement is the installation of bollards along the sidewalk edge, a ubiquitous presence in old city centers.

MY TIME, TRAFFIC TIME

Unplanned relief for the pressure of the road system came from the change in the demographics of the work force. As more women entered the work force from mid-century onward, a strong need for more flexible work arrangements emerged, one of which has been widely adopted—flex time (i.e., flexible work hours). Such varying times of reporting to and leaving work reduced the number of people traveling simultaneously and distributed the traffic load over a longer period; whether traveling by car, tram, bus or subway, the pressure on the network system lessened somewhat. The network remained physically the same, but the demand for travel space was reduced, at least transiently.

The Underground Revolution

As we saw in the distance/effort section, a radical change in the network capacity for moving pedestrians occurred with the introduction of below-grade railways—the Underground (or Subway, or Tube). Ridership numbers speak to a dramatic effect on the mobility of citizens, the distance they could travel in a relatively short time and the equivalent street space that was freed up as a result. Subways, since they move pedestrians, can be viewed as an addition to the street network—increasing the existing street capacity by mechanical means. Seen from the perspective of a historic city such as Rome, the number of citizens that move within the city and the distances they cover are of astounding magnitude. The major subways in the world carry daily passengers as follows: Beijing, 7.5 million; Tokyo, 6.0 million; Moscow, 6.6 million; Paris, 4.5 million; Toronto, 1.0 million; and Montreal, 1.1 million. Though these daily figures represent a minority of the total trips in each city, from a historical perspective of network systems, they would be equivalent to moving the entire population of Rome many times around the city without treading on the city's streets.

Yet, just as in the Roman era the increased population and its mobility needs overwhelmed the streets, so did a similar trajectory of growth apply to the contemporary subway systems of certain major cities. On certain lines to key destinations, neither the frequency of trains nor their size can satisfy the demand; coach overcrowding, often extreme, occurs at peak hours. Certain lines have reached their absolute capacity, similar to an overcrowded street, an arterial or a stadium exit corridor.

INVISIBLE STREETS/PATHS

Two additional network system adaptations provide more circulation space for foot traffic: below-grade streets and above-grade (plus–15) pedestrian networks. The need for these paths emerged as less and less of the street space was available for pedestrian movement, which was confined to narrow sidewalks (in some cases, no more than two people abreast), and the environment became increasingly unpleasant and rife with risk. Street crossing at designated spots generated a large proportion of accidents. In addition to risk, extreme weather conditions in certain cities made a protected environment more desirable. Morphologically, these "street networks" exhibit the characteristics of incremental growth settlements, where the act of building defines the street space, not the other way around; the paths are not laid out in advance—they simply happen. Leftover space varies in width and winds its way from building to building as the circumstances permit. This adaptation was soon seen as an opportunity for commercial activity and exploited for that purpose.[14]

The need for more movement street space resolved (albeit unintentionally) the tension between height of buildings and daylight at street level. New streets twice the width (or wider) of early existing ones allowed more light and better circulation of air in new districts. This improvement, however, coincided with the rapid development of elevator technology, which allowed buildings reach unprecedented heights, reintroducing the same lack of sunlight at the street level. Air movement, on the other hand, became a converse problem. At least under certain specific weather and building configuration conditions, tall buildings caused air flow at the street level to rise to intolerable speeds. Such conditions render the below- and above-grade paths even more desirable.

Street size, whether for movement or parking or both, has been and remains an issue in existing pre-motor city districts, and it has become a contentious issue in the design process for new districts. The debate centers on the transformation of the streetscape and street use as flow and speed increase, the topic of the next section.

Speed

Speed rewards the predator or its prey, the hunter or the hunted, by outpacing the other. About three millennia ago, Olympic runners glorified human speed and horse riders pushed the limit to new thresholds. (In legends horses have wings, expressing the exhilarating difference between running and riding.) Speed also expands the reach for resources, be it prey, water, wood, ripe fruit or, more recently, jobs and goods. With a full list of daily and seasonal activities, limiting travel time becomes a priority. Evidence suggests that the pursuit of speed, though not exclusively, has shaped the networks of human settlements since their birth.

The first network adaptation for speed relates to the directness of the path. Meandering or detouring paths reduce average speed in reaching a destination. At low speeds (i.e., walking), even small detours matter. As speeds increase (horse, carriage, bicycle and car), small detours matter less to the overall trip; speed more than compensates for the slightly increased distance.

Speed can be seen as the duration of a trip or the pace at which a distance is covered; both aspects are interrelated. Directness reduces distance and pace reduces time: for equal pace, distance matters, and for equal distance, pace matters.

A settlement where all origins and destinations are connected by the most direct route possible—a straight line—is inconceivable; it would consist mostly of paths and little else. The larger the settlement, the more unrealistic such an ideal becomes as the cross-connections increase exponentially.

A Balancing Act

Two adaptations to resolve the tension between directness of route and habitable space have emerged in the layout of network systems: the Milesian (or Hippodamian) plan and the spider-web (radial) plan. Both provide direct routes to only a portion of the possible destinations, balancing the needs for buildable land area and for network space. (This balance will reemerge as a critical criterion in the twentieth-century city expansions as land prices dominate the value of buildings.) As a settlement grows and destinations diversify—and also disperse—it can be shown that the differences of average trip length become insignificant between these two geometrically distinct patterns. Speed emerges as the dominant factor in trip duration.

Straight lines that characterize both plans are not only needed for directness of route but also essential for vehicle speed. Only by maintaining a straight trajectory can a moving object maintain a constant speed, and the higher the speed, the straighter the trajectory must be. The importance of straight-line movement for speed was understood by Haussmann in his transformation of Paris, as we shall see. In addition to straightness of path, other factors affect speed, which we examine next.

Space to Move

One such factor is available street width. The faster a vehicle moves, the more space it needs to move through. Conversely, limiting its movement space will force a lower speed on the vehicle as the rider or driver exercises caution to avoid impinging on the adjacent travelers. To organize movement in restricted space, lane markings appeared regularly on paved roads from about 1920, when cars equaled the number of horses on urban streets. Prior to that, a street was simply movement space for any vehicle to occupy, in whatever spot was available and in whichever direction. The outcome of this free mix of horse-drawn vehicles of all types and pedestrians on any part of the pavement was a disturbingly high number of accidents on crowded streets.[15]

Since the demarcation of lanes began, lane widths increased steadily as street space allowed (or required) and as vehicle speeds increased. For new roads, design standards were adopted to conform to engineering calculations of space required at specified speeds. These design and regulatory adaptations quickly became universal and helped address the twin pressures of speed of movement and accident toll.[16] As we saw under the discussion of element size, starting in imperial Rome, where size was already fixed by existing buildings, streets were turned into one-way roads to accommodate both volume and speed.

Deciphering Priority

A serious impediment to speed in a network is the frequency of intersections. And since a network by definition is a set of intersecting paths, identifying and managing the priority of movement of vehicles on each path becomes a stress point.

In existing networks, where physical adaptations were either limited or impossible, controlling priority of passage at intersections was achieved via regulatory measures. Their first

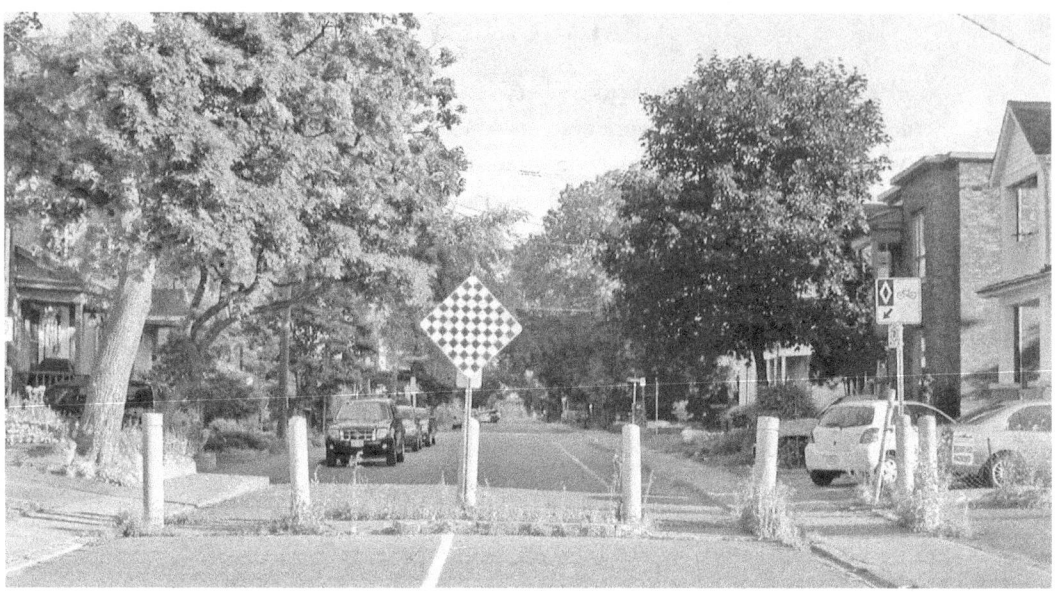

Beneficial, Modest Street Transformation: Preventing car access to a main artery using bollards returns three benefits: eases the traffic flow on the artery, calms the neighborhood street and retains full active-mode connectivity.

manifestation was the introduction of signs that codified priority through a new language of signals. This language, which had to be assimilated before permission to drive a vehicle was granted, was also accompanied by a code of vehicle behavior, which was taught in advance of being a licensed driver. Signs proliferated during the automotive twentieth century, and they now number in the dozens. Signs, however, do not remove the ambiguity of priority in all cases, nor are they strictly enforceable. Four-way stop signs, for example, leave room for subjective judgment and the frequent bias that goes with it—the cause of accidents and violent disputes.

As a progression beyond the signs, and in response to their observed malfunctions, particularly in heavy traffic conditions, a second major adaptation emerged: traffic lights at jammed intersections. They improved movement (flow) and thereby decreased the time for reaching destinations. Later in the twentieth century, automatic lights were synchronized (using computers) in the direction of the primary flow, thus assisting vehicles to achieve reasonable speeds in town. In the case of Los Angeles, for example, synchronization has reduced travel times by as much as 24–29 percent.[17]

However, traffic lights, even with priority given to major thoroughfares, still impose a delay on vehicle flow, raising the possibility of gridlock, due to inevitable slow turns and circumstantial street incidents (goods delivery or passenger drop-off, for example). With this realization, streets that previously connected to what eventually became a major road were selectively severed from it by closing their connections. This adaptation improved flow on the major road but also created an incidental, unintended residential cul-de-sac on the other side of the closure. Moreover, it confirmed the role of each street in a naturally emergent hierarchical system that had not been envisioned at the layout stage of the neighborhood, usually half a century or more earlier.

GRIDLOCK

In spite of these adaptations to accommodate speed, gridlock at intersections is a frequent source of speed degradation and driver frustration—a prime example of system breakdown. The inability to achieve speed, even modest horse-trotting speed, in inherited, traditional networks was obvious by the end of the nineteenth century and an inescapable conclusion as motorized transport entered the roads. The most populous of the industrial cities, Paris, London and New York, realized that speed in a densely inhabited region can only be achieved by ignoring the existing network and moving people underground. The subway (Underground, Metro, Tube) remains the fastest means of transport in urban settings (ever since its introduction in London in 1863), particularly at peak hours. At-grade alternatives such as buses and trams attain only a fraction of the users of underground systems. Riding the subway, at the cost of personal mobility at either end of the trip, is a personal adaptation chosen by many citizens in balancing time expenditure and convenience.

Historically unprecedented speeds resulted in a network modification unknown and unnecessary in previous eras—road pavement banking. First introduced in a race track, it became common on freeways that permitted speeds over 60 km/hr. Interestingly, it was resisted by coach owners because of the sliding effect it had on their vehicles, which traveled at lower speeds. The car design requirements ultimately won the pavement banking battle.

THE LITTLE TUBE THAT COULD

The pursuit of speed in a foot and hoof–dominated era, progressively being industrialized but not yet fully mobile (1800s), brought about another tube-like system that overcame street obstacles—the PTT, or Pneumatic Tube Transport—within buildings and between buildings. Now considered an anachronism, though still in limited use, the PTT once had 400 kilometers of routes in Berlin, 460 kilometers in Paris and an extensive network in New York City until 1953. These numbers correspond surprisingly well with subway track lengths, such as London's 408 kilometers, Moscow's 269 kilometers and Tokyo's 293 kilometers. PTT systems are capable of delivering mail and small objects inside a capsule at speeds reaching 36 km/hr, many times faster than an office clerk in a building or a taxi downtown. Hospitals, which have grown to become immense building complexes, still use this method for the delivery of medical supplies between departments.

Interestingly, the idea of moving people between cities using an improved version of this technology resurfaced recently. The intent is to compete with air travel for speed by avoiding the intermediary airport functions and their increasing distance from the city center, which often take as much time as the air trip itself.[18]

TWO-WHEELED FLEXIBILITY

A personal adaptation for achieving speed in congested urban environments is the two-wheeled motorized vehicle in all its varieties. Initially adopted for its low cost by city dwellers who could not afford cars, it soon became a convenient and fashionable way to gain end-to-end speed of travel. A motorbike (or scooter) can maneuver between car traffic and accelerate ahead of it at traffic stops, thus avoiding gridlock conditions. It can take shortcuts through narrow lanes and park close to its destination, since it requires little space. In total door-to-door trip time, it outperforms cars, taxis and buses. Given this speed advantage, it has emerged as an alternative taxi vehicle at a competitive price in certain cities. But only a minority accept its high risk.

An alternative adaptation for speed in central areas is the use of the bicycle. Though the risk deters many from using it, the bicycle does have a speed advantage for door-to-door travel. For this advantage, small package- and food-delivery companies use it.

The speed advantage of motorized vehicles brought a new friction and a major concern, both social and personal—injuries and deaths. A strong correlation has been established between travel speed and injury severity.

Speed Implications

Mechanical adaptations were quickly introduced and legislated to increase driver safety, such as seatbelts and airbags, along with modifications to a vehicle's structural frame. These devices protected the driver but left the pedestrian and the cyclist still exposed. Between the two, they count for one quarter of all fatalities due to collisions. Adaptations to resolve this conflict include a range of traffic-calming measures that, in the majority of cases, aim at reducing speed—a pragmatic solution but counterproductive with respect to reducing travel time. Dozens of measures and initiatives have been proposed and implemented with measurable positive results, but the number of collisions is never low enough from a societal or personal perspective. For many, the fact that the most natural form of transportation within a city—walking—entails higher risk of injury than driving seems anomalous.

Noise

When used in transport, human and animal power produce little noise, and generally that of low-decibel level—perhaps annoying but hardly ever harmful. This is particularly true when the majority of the network retains its natural compacted earth surface, as was the case with most early city streets.

But since many city street networks also functioned as drainage systems for rainwater (and frequently for sanitation as well, stone paving was introduced to fulfill these functions and, simultaneously, prevent detrimental erosion. Around 4,000 BCE, when the first urban places appeared in Mesopotamia, villages with paved streets also appeared on the record. With the street surface paved in stones, the noise level would have inevitably increased. The invention and growing use of wheeled vehicles, particularly when iron wheel rims came into common use, made that noise ever present and frequently extremely disturbing, as we saw previously.

In Roman cities, which grew in population and trade activity as the empire blossomed, the problem of noise was exacerbated by the prohibition of wheeled vehicles within the city walls during daylight hours (45 BCE). This adaptation to the issue of traffic density, as we shall see later, caused excessive disturbance at night to citizens who lived on and around the heavily trafficked roads. Records from Rome of that period allude, with some exaggeration, to citizens living in a permanent state of insomnia, as expressively exaggerated by Juvenal.

One instance of a regulatory adaptation to this stress surfaced in the city of Paris in 1487 with the banning of trotting and galloping. Such a prohibition would have reduced the noise intensity and may have also contributed to road safety.

The second source of noise, merchants selling wares and people settling disputes, was an inevitable part of a bustling city. Certain disputes arose on account of deciding the right-of-way priority; many streets were only wide enough for one cart but not limited to one-directional traffic. Incidentally, such a dispute caused the first recorded patricide in history—the murder of King Laius by his reportedly lost son Oedipus.[19] These problems were exacerbated by the enormous population density, caused, as we saw, by the distance limitation, itself the outcome of the available means of transport.

As we can surmise from the Babylon tablet quoted in Chapter 2, it was through a personal adaptation that a segment of citizens found relief from this source of stress: they moved away from busy streets, even though this might have meant an increase in the distance they had to travel to procure their daily necessities—a compromise and a conscious balance of priorities.

The noise stressor has been present throughout city history, and it remains the focus of attention today. In addition to its effect on people, it also impacts the value of property, compounding an owner's stress. Several network-related causes of noise have been eliminated while new ones appeared.

At around the end of the 1800s, roads gradually changed from earth or stone surface to a bitumen mix that produces a smooth finish. In parallel with this development, but much later, the wheels of carts, coaches, bicycles and cars were fitted with rubber and pneumatic tires. The combination of the network surface change and the tire innovation produced a dramatic drop in the noise intensity.

The noise-reduction effect of these innovations was entirely incidental. They were introduced for the comfort of bicycle, coach and car riders, who were said to suffer serious discomfort, and even muscle or back pain, after a long ride. Its incidental effect notwithstanding, the innovation was used for its silencing effect even in delivery vehicles that were not ridden. While the road surface was being improved, drainage moved to subsurface conduits that removed another unpleasant experience of traveling on the pavement by foot, bike or coach—unpleasant odors and soiling of garments.

Hauling and Speed

This wheel-and-pavement reduction of noise notwithstanding, the network and its users became the source of new loud sounds that would have to find further technological and management adaptations to abate—engine noise, noise due to speed, and horns. Motor engines grew progressively more powerful to attain higher speeds, and also to increase their haul capacity: from the 1920s Model-T's 22-horse power (hp) to the 1990s average passenger car's 200 hp (e.g., Toyota Celica), a tenfold increase in power has occurred in the span of a mere two generations. Trucks soon appeared that now command up to 2,000 hp, another tenfold power increase from the common cars. Engine power correlates with the noise it emits, though not proportionately. Except for developing a new type of engine, as we shall see below, so far there is no systemic adaptation that would alter this relationship. A management adaptation that cities introduced confines larger engines (transport trucks) to specific parts of the network and, in some cases, to certain times of day. This administrative measure, reminiscent of the Roman edict, reduces the number of residents who are directly exposed and the duration of exposure to this stressor.

The combination of engine power and speed manifests itself on expressways, highways and parkways. Residents living next to such thoroughfares experience high levels of noise annoyance. Physical adaptations have been applied to reduce the effect. Where they cross a city district, these roads have been fitted with 10–12 feet (3–4-meters) tall sound barriers that reduce the sound level reaching adjacent homes, although they do not eliminate it. An unintended effect of this transformation is the change in the acoustic environment on the road; it becomes an effective sound box that reinforces the sound within the right of way of the highway. Another type of noise-abatement measure that has also been widely adopted—the landscaped berm—is less effective than sound barriers but visually more appealing.

These noise buffers (or barriers) have appeared regularly in the design of new districts along major, and occasionally minor, arterials. This new network design element applies the lessons derived from the transformation of existing freeways and highways that were equipped with sound barriers retroactively, following insistent demands by citizens in their vicinity. It anticipates and resolves the tension in advance of traffic sound reaching volumes that breach the expected acoustic quality of the neighborhood.

This resolution has an unintended effect on the road space itself. Though large, open and often embellished with trees, the road feels alien, mostly devoid of people. The residents behind the sound barriers obtain the desired quiet, but people walking on the sidewalk get little visual stimulation or informal surveillance. A new friction point has arisen that demands

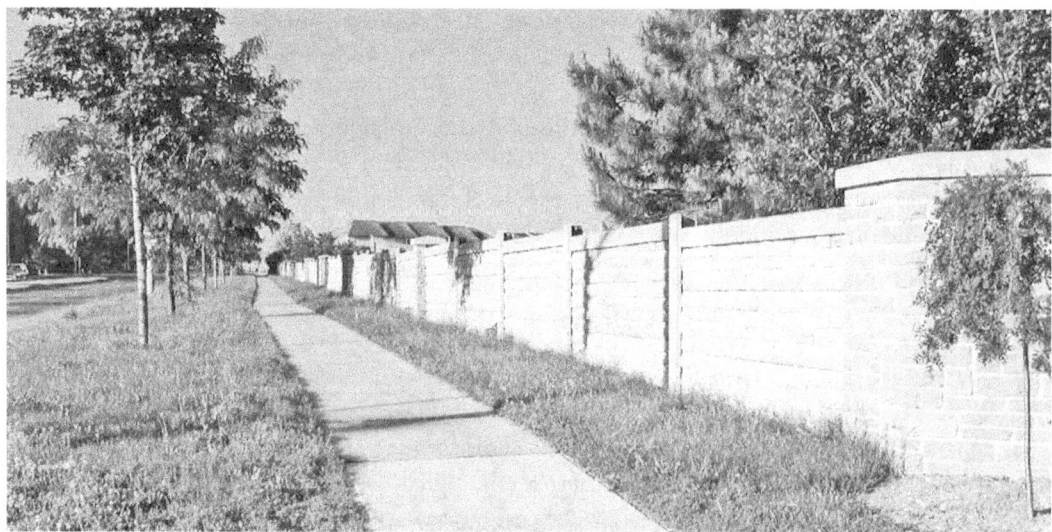

Adaptation with Side Effects: As road decibels increase with motorized traffic on higher-tier roads, few options are available to secure quiet. Mile-long sound barriers accomplish this task but create a sterile, unwelcoming landscape.

an appropriate adaptation. Network configuration, a subsequent topic, can influence the frequency and intensity of noise. A network layout that forces frequent stops will induce braking and down-gearing sounds as well as acceleration noise; both are above the normal operating level of engine sound. One adaptation for this inevitable occurrence, when the layout includes small block lengths, is the introduction of synchronized traffic lights, which promote continuous movement at a steady speed. Traffic lights, however, represent a substantial investment, and thus appear only on a few major arteries, leaving the majority of the city's intersections with simple stop signs, which, inevitably, induce the stop-and-go movement of motorized vehicles. This remains another noise-abatement issue to be resolved.

A network adaptation that unintentionally lowers noise levels in the city blocks adjacent to a high-speed road is the sinking or tunneling of a road. As we saw, speed and congestion pressures have brought about this change in the road network. It applies only to major roads that, if not sunk, would have dissected the city with detrimental development (and also social) outcomes.

Network system maintenance has evolved to become another source of high-level noise. Regular street cleaning and repair, unlike the previous manual removal of debris, now involves large trucks fitted with equipment that surpasses the sound safety threshold considerably. The nuisance is compounded by the fact that these trucks operate mostly at night so as to not cause congestion during the hours of high traffic.

Speed, a network-dependent element of movement, induces a proportional noise generation through the tire action on the pavement. This effect is most pronounced and observable on wet pavement. Cities have adopted regulations that limit speed according to a street's primary use with the intention of improving traffic safety. When observed, these limits invariably also reduce noise; observance, however, is at best spotty. Cities have introduced physical transformations of the network to reduce speed such as speed bumps and humps, also for the purpose of improving safety. Their effect on noise, however, is evidently counterproductive—noise levels rise. As this case shows, two network design requirements, noise reduction and speed reduction, can be conflicting, and they require a decisive resolution.

Horns, which were introduced for safety reasons, produce sounds that, in some cases, when close to the source, are in the injurious range of decibel levels. At the street plane they are extremely annoying, and within adjacent residences, offices or shops they can be highly disruptive. Horns are standard equipment on every vehicle and, in some high-traffic roads, their effect on the soundscape is devastating. Responding to this highly stressful condition, regulators introduced restrictions in their use, but, in general, these controls have been less effective than anticipated. Horns are generally used more frequently in dense traffic, essentially when a network is overstressed. As we shall see in the element size section, network design has responded to this congestion stressor and evolved to anticipate and accommodate growth in traffic volumes.

More disturbing than horns are the sirens of police and rescue vehicles. Though not exactly co-variant, the larger the population in a given area, the higher the odds that incidents will occur that require an emergency response. Ironically, it is also in densely populated areas that traffic flows are high; consequently, the response vehicles must wade through by sounding their siren warnings constantly.

Several of the above noise stressors are unavoidable and linked to the location of one's residence or business. Only a personal adaptation, moving (which some residents opt for), can deal with the source of the stress.

A decisive assault on noise is emerging from an unrelated development—electric and fuel-cell car engines (an *unplanned*, incidental noise-reduction solution). Their introduction has been driven by the quest to switch to sources of energy other than oil and, in effect, do away with the internal combustion engine that has dominated transportation for a century. The low sound levels of these engines come to rescue the city resident from an excess of noise and its detrimental effects on sleep, attention and socializing. Ironically, their sound level is currently judged to be so low as to generate concerns about traffic safety and a call for the installation of artificial sound-emitting devices in such cars—another case of conflicting design requirements that need resolution.[20]

The reduction of street traffic noise would also improve living conditions in central city districts, which have suffered the most from this stressor that is said to have contributed to their depopulation. The effect of this personal adaptation of centrifugal dispersal can be experienced in numerous city centers. The gradual reduction of resident numbers has produced contrasting experiences between day and night, and between present and past: bustling activity (and noise) during the day and hardly any noise or activity in the evening.

The noise stressor has been substantially reduced through unintentional evolution of pavement improvements, tire technology and traffic management. The personal adaptation of relocation has reinforced the noise-suppression effect by reducing the number of cars on specific roads.

Children at Play

For the majority of settlements' four-millennia history, children (more so than adults) owned the street. It has been the place of play, friendship, mischief and growing up. Whatever its size, it would instantly transform into a field or a stage for real or imaginary play. Perhaps with the exception of the main thoroughfare, with its range of benevolent and suspicious characters (and often literally packed with people), all streets were home territory for children. In the densely built and populated areas, the street was generally the only open space in the neighborhood.

With the emergence of motorized transport, including trams, buses and cars on the streets, most of the street network become off-bounds for children, practically and also legally. It became a punishable offense to play on the street. A new stressor surfaced, particularly for at-home resident mothers.

In the decades following the acknowledgment of this stressor, several adaptations were introduced: physical, administrative, design and personal. Many residential streets became one-way to reduce the traffic volumes and improve the safety of crossing. Other streets were closed to traffic at one end, while another set was fitted with speed bumps. These measures did have a positive effect in exiting neighborhoods,[21] but the street did not fully recover its original character of a play space. New neighborhood layouts introduced a non-permeable street network using cul-de-sac and crescent-type streets, citing the safety and play activity of children as a design criterion. The outcomes of such layouts are encouraging, as we shall see in Chapter 6.

From the personal adaptation perspective, many parents with young children decided to flee the busy central city streets to a place where there was much less traffic, particularly on cul-de-sacs, and open spaces for play, now regulated into existence by municipal governments for all new neighborhoods. Some even opted for the nearest old, yet-to-be-urbanized village, which retained to a large degree the atmosphere they themselves experienced as children.

Configuration and Shape

As we saw previously, road width is critical in accommodating the transport of merchandise, produce, people, troops, supplies and emergency equipment in a settlement. In some instances, it had to also accommodate temporary sellers' stalls, which might be the size of a wagon or a cart, and leave enough room for passing traffic. Both the functions of the street and speed have imposed their respective requirements on the network system, as we gleaned.

The configuration of the road network plays a crucial role in achieving speed: backtracking or making detours to reach a destination, for example, particularly when it involves carrying a load, squanders time and taxes people's endurance. Generally, networks responded to the need for reducing effort and optimizing time through their configurations.

Maps, discovered documents, and now aerial photos reveal a wide range of network configurations: regular and irregular, repetitive and random, geometric and haphazard. Some are adaptations to topographic constraints, others to transportation means, and yet others to a mystical intuition of a higher order (e.g., the Chinese "Holy Field" of nine squares). Some show a mixture of configurations that are set side by side, while others are overlaid; the latter, an overlaid pattern, is the case of central Paris, a key example of a network configuration that was adapted with specific, known objectives, which we will examine more closely later. The Paris case is unique for both the extent of its transformation and its well-recorded intentions and reactions.

STRAIGHT LINES

An early, conscious adaptation of network system configuration was the introduction of straight streets and street intersections at right angles. In addition to speed, which, as we saw, works best with straight lines for all vehicles, at least one other requirement that surfaces in all settlements, from small villages to populous cities, makes a straight street imperative: the need for a route for civic, military and religious processions (often indistinguishable, as worldly power has been mostly seen as an extension of the divine realm for much of history). A third need may have been incidental, casual, unofficial chariot racing, with the prevalence of chariots around 1500 BCE; not all cities had or could afford a hippodrome, as Rome and Constantinople did, and a street may have supplanted that role occasionally.

In Babylon, around 615 BCE, King Nabopolassar built a long straight road to honor the god Marduk.[22] Traveling to Babylon more than a century later (450 BCE), the Greek historian Herodotus admired the ordered, straight lines of the city's network. Several years earlier (479), Hippodamus oversaw the rebuilding of Miletus, which includes only straight streets in its plan; this was to become an enduring pattern. A third trigger for the adoption of straight streets may well have been the orderly and efficient subdivision of land for cultivation that, due to its simplicity, minimizes disputes about borders and simplifies the area calculation for tax purposes—reasons entirely unrelated to transportation (see Appendix). The straight street and the intersection of streets at right angles were repeated by the Romans throughout their empire for about 400 years.

While Greeks and subsequently Romans perpetuated straight streets and networks based on right-angle intersections in their new colonies, many preexisting settlements, such as the original parts of Rome itself, did not incorporate this geometry. Also, new settlements outside of or subsequent to the domination of Rome continued to grow by accretion without an overall plan.

New, whole-city plans did emerge in the Renaissance, and a small number of them were built. Their street network configurations inside the confines of the defensive walls fall into two basic categories: a checkerboard plan and a radial plan. Generally, in both cases, two intersecting main streets traversed the 2,600-foot (800-meters) city diameter and led to four gates. They have at least Roman-sized or larger widths for all streets, presumably because Renaissance thinkers admired the ancient Greeks and Romans and imitated their design ideas. By the 1700s, when the founding of many new cities in North America and other continents was in progress, there were several straight-line, whole-city plans both on paper and in physical form to draw inspiration from. As these plans of the Greco-Roman and Renaissance traditions were applied, with or without modifications, they became the built inheritance of many city centers worldwide and the de facto network for the circulation of pedestrians and all vehicles in subsequent centuries.

THE STRAIGHTENING OF PARIS—
BEARING THE GREAT CROSS

Paris of the mid–1800s had a different inheritance. Paris, a town that predated and endured past its Roman period, had all the characteristics of early organic settlements, such as narrow winding, twisting streets and alleys that changed direction frequently, included acute angles and at times came to a dead end—the bane of visitors and foreign or national troops.[23] As others have observed, early cities such as Paris, Edinburgh and London were "cities of fragments." These layouts did not follow an overarching pattern, as did most Roman, Greek and later Spanish cities or colonies. As we saw earlier, this random layout posed no difficulty to Parisian residents who lived within walking distance of most city functions. But as Paris grew more populous and into an economic, political and cultural center, and also the world's biggest industrial hub by 1850, the state could no longer control its disenfranchised and rebellious citizens, nor could the city function effectively in peacetime, when the cart, coach and wagon provided the transportation for its economic activity, the governing class and its military.[24] Baron Haussmann's transformation of Paris from 1860 to 1875 had do to with the size of network elements but also, and more importantly, with configuration. Coincidentally, as the adaptation of the street network began, the rail network appeared on the scene. Railroads also required straight alignments and had to be functionally integrated into the city's street plan.

Directed by the emperor and financed by the state, Haussmann's "piercing" (as it came to be labeled) created major north-south and east-west arteries—"la grand croisee" (the great cross)—and also several straight streets radiating from strategically selected "places" (squares). Working in an area of 12 square miles (32 square kilometers) (or a diameter of about 3.7 miles [6 kilometers]) and a population of about 1.5 million, the baron pierced new, wide, straight avenues amounting to 124 miles (200 kilometers) (of which 87 miles [140 kilometers] were new) in length.[25] He joined previously discrete, disconnected street segments into longer straight roads, many of which terminated at squares. Since squares functioned as secondary centers for public buildings, amenities and events, radiating streets produced optimal walking distances to them from the surrounding residential quarters. The new major through streets speeded up movement both into and out of town. This transformation eased the congestion and speed frictions of the layout it modified. In doing so, it established two principles of network layout that would be embraced by transportation planners a century later: hierarchy of streets and "arteriality."[26] Instead of a web of predominantly uniformly narrow streets having little or no directionality, a new configuration will have a specified range of street

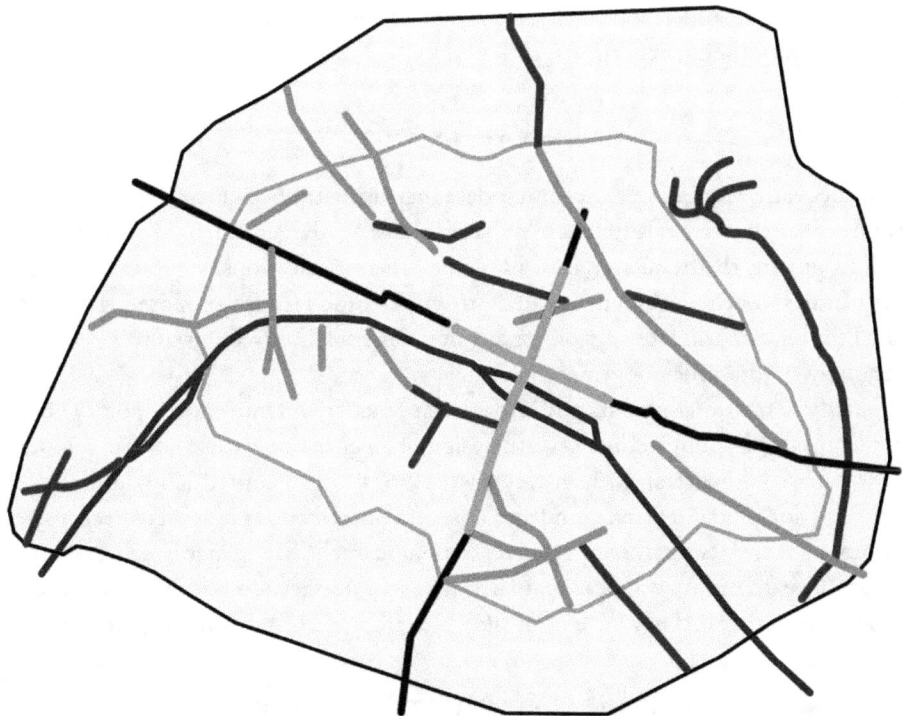

Painful, Unavoidable Surgery: Within a 10-km-diameter circle, Paris was pierced with new, wide roads to enable the movement of people and goods that had clogged its earlier arteries (the gray grades show the stages of the work).

widths and, at least for a fair number, a clear direction. An overall network of higher-tier avenues was thus established. These configuration rules are now enshrined in transportation engineering manuals as essential guidelines for a network system suitable for motorized traffic.

Just as a Roman city had the *Decumanus* and the *Cadro* as the principal streets of a 160-acre (64-hectare) colony (e.g., Timgad), and the Renaissance planned cities had at least two intersecting principal streets leading to the gates, contemporary cities also express the idea of road hierarchy by means of the size of the route and its location in the network system, now covering several square miles.

During the centuries that the movement speed was uniform across an entire network, that of hoof and foot, hierarchy of elements was based primarily on planned volume and function. High Streets and Main Streets carried far more traffic than neighborhood streets and also functioned as markets or as places for ceremonial events—a sufficient justification for their larger width and higher rank in the hierarchy.

When movement speed became differentiated and ranged from the hoof-and-foot pace to tram and car rates (themselves also ranging from a low 20 km/hr to 100 km/hr), speed was inevitably added to the volume and function criteria for ranking streets in the hierarchy. Once possible, speed became useful and necessary, and, consequently, one of the key design criteria for street networks.

In addition, twentieth-century practice reinforces the hierarchical structure by progressively restricting access to higher-tier roads by lower-ranking streets. And whereas the Roman city had three official street classifications, contemporary networks have at least six, as we shall see in subsequent sections.

HENARD'S SPIN

Another early adaptation to accommodate increasing traffic, which may have been entirely unnecessary in Greek, Roman or Arab city plans, was Eugene Henard's roundabout of 1877.[27] Recognizing the frequent failure of major street intersections due to the burgeoning number of carts, coaches, wagons and pedestrians, Eugène Hénard proposed the transformation of the regular grid intersection (or any multi-branch intersection) into a continuous, circular one-way rotational movement (a "rotary")

Henard's adaptation found its way into regular practice and into contemporary network design manuals. For example, the network design of an entire new town covering 34 square miles (88 square kilometers), Milton Keynes (f. 1967) in the United Kingdom, uses it at every intersection of major arteries and also at several intersections of local collector streets. The roundabout and its small-scale relative, the traffic circle, have experienced a resurgence in the last 30 years and now appear regularly at cross intersections of roads—a permanent physical transformation. They have been shown to improve traffic flow and safety.[28]

CERDA'S TRUNCATED BLOCK

Preceding Henard's idea and synchronous with Haussmann's work in Paris, Ildefons Cerdà drew a plan (1859) for a large extension of Barcelona. In that plan, supported by ar-

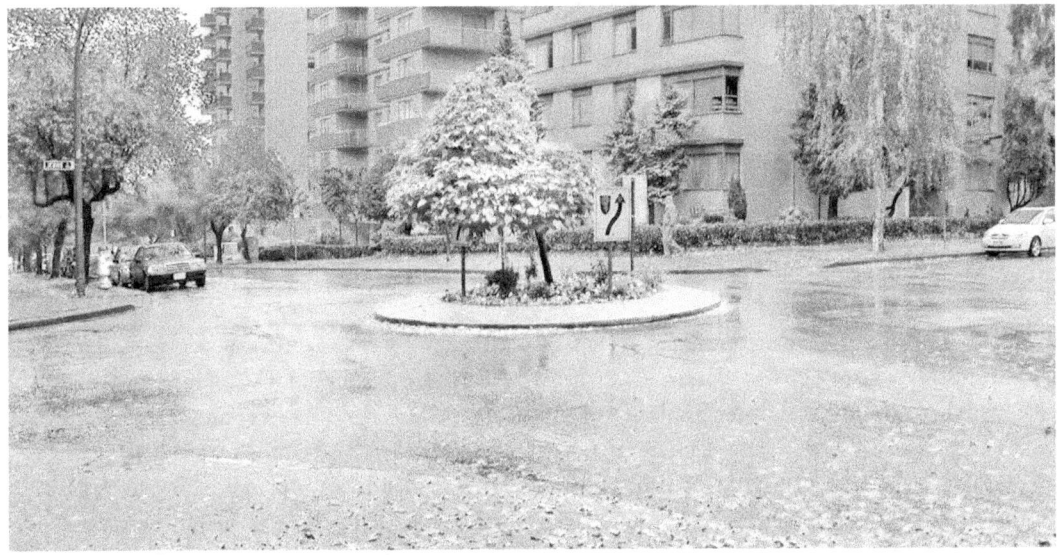

Double Adaptation: As the rigid grid geometry proved risky and ineffective, a small circle at the center provided relief by altering the movement geometry; straight ahead is no longer an option.

guments on the importance of mobility, he introduced streets wider than all previously known networks and far wider than Barcelona's medieval network. The narrowest dimension was almost twice as wide (66 feet; 20 meters) as the largest regulated Roman street (40 feet; 12 meters). The plan also included an entirely new geometric characteristic that had not been seen before—the truncated block. All city blocks in the plan and the buildings on them were chamfered for the purpose of accommodating the turning radii of carts, horse-drawn omnibuses and the as-yet-to-be-introduced urban railways. This adaptation, of enabling wheeled vehicles of substantial size to turn easily at corners by making adjustments to the intersection geometry (which allows vehicles to turn *before*, they reach the actual intersection), is now standard road engineering practice. Cerda's plan proved prophetic in that it can now accommodate vehicles of sizes far greater than he knew of or could have imagined. Coincidentally, the chamfered corners also anticipate the possibility of a traffic circle, an intersection safety device.

With Haussmann's and Cerda's plans, we arrive at the recognition, presentation and embodiment of fundamental adaptations to the inherited network configuration and its intersections: straight roads, a hierarchy of roads and turning radii for new vehicles. Henard's traffic circle adds a third adaptation to the conventional four-way intersection. More adaptations to networks emerged in the 1900s following the proliferation of motorized transport, which we will examine next.

New Network Configuration

As we saw under speed and shall see under safety, in spite of partial physical modifications and general traffic management techniques, the inherited city street network failed to provide safe, quiet and pleasant living conditions for its citizens, particularly for families.

The rapid population growth during the years spanning the 1900 mark, and the consequent increase of all types of vehicles (including motorized ones), made city roads congested, malodorous, noisy and dangerous. The general absence of greenery on the streets and the increasing smoke from the industrial and domestic use of coal (the only practical source of energy until the late 1930s) intensified the negative impression of an unhealthy, oppressive milieu.

NEW STREET TYPES

Enormous pressure emerged to modify the network for the purpose of providing the necessary attributes that sustain the citizens' health and well-being. One advocated option, which continues to influence planning to this day, was to build a new daughter city—the Garden City—independent and self-reliant, and based on railways, horse-drawn vehicles and walking as its primary means of transport. From its proponents came the conscious reintroduction, codification, and formal use of a preexisting street type—the cul-de-sac—that had previously appeared circumstantially in city networks but was temporarily banned due to its coincidental association with squalor and overcrowding. It was a renewed, purposeful adaptation of the street network to the double stressors of risk and noise disturbance.

The cul-de-sac and its relative, an equally exclusive local street type—the crescent (or loop)—became standard elements in new districts at the peripheries of growing cities and in new towns. Raymond Unwin (1863–1940) introduced the cul-de-sac in the Garden Suburbs of Letchworth (1903) and Hampstead (1906). His follower, Clarence Stein, applied it in Radburn, New Jersey (1929), as the dominant residential street type, thus rendering "Radburn" synonymous with its use. Most new development adopted it as a principal means with which to create peaceful, safe residential streets. For example, Milton Keynes (1967), a town built on virgin land, uses cul-de-sacs and loops extensively in its residential districts. The cul-de-sac now typifies the base level in the new hierarchy of streets: a street that is entirely local and at which all vehicle movement terminates. However, when it also forces the termination of a pedestrian or bicycle route, it creates a new tension—lack of path directness and the consequent trip elongation for these types of travel.

This limitation did not surface when the cul-de-sac network adaptation emerged unintentionally in existing urban districts that were primarily laid out as open grids, as we saw. In attempting to preserve the function of major arterials, certain streets were closed permanently at their junctions with the arterial, making motorized through traffic impossible, though foot and bicycle traffic were allowed to pass. Particularly suitable candidates for such modifications were streets intersecting with existing roads that became de facto major thoroughfares, such as, for example, roads that led directly to bridges and highway ramps. Such adaptations to the need for uninterrupted circulation altered the functional configuration of the existing network for motorists, though it remained virtually unchanged for pedestrians. The outcome was two coexisting operational configurations based on the same physical infrastructure for two distinct means of transport—a virtual network for motorized vehicles that did not match the physical infrastructure and one for non-motorized transport that did.

Also conscious was the application of the cul-de-sac concept in specific existing residential neighborhoods at the request of residents, such as in Berkeley, California, and Seattle, Washington. In these cases, it was safety and quiet that drove the adaptation, not traffic flow. In fact, traffic might have become more crowded at the periphery of such transformed neighborhoods, a fact that brings into focus, once again, the constant friction between the conflicting qualities that a network system must provide. An adaptation to an existing system cannot always meet all the requirements satisfactorily; priority must be inevitably assigned between them by the people who demand the adaptation.

The Radburn (1929) and the Milton Keynes (1967) plans incorporated another adaptation that resolved the risk between cars and pedestrians—grade-separated intersections of foot or bike paths with car roads. Though such separations had previously been sporadically used for railroad intersections, where the topography was favorable, these two projects made a systematic application of this separation type throughout their respective developed areas. During this 40-year period between the two projects, many idealized and unrealized plans appeared, showing a complete separation of the two basic networks—for cars and for

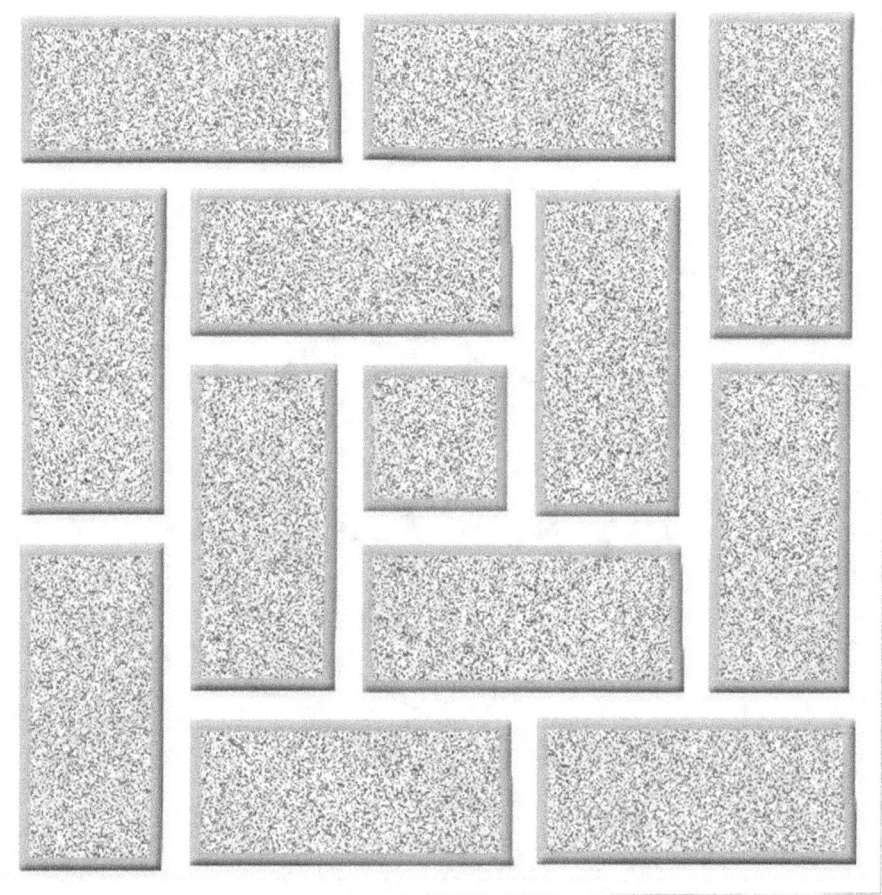

Sizing and Shaping a Neighborhood: A new configuration would discourage or prevent through traffic in a "sanctuary" of about ¼ mile. In this option, streets within the neighborhood end at a T-intersection.

pedestrians (e.g., Corbusier, Hilberseimer and Doxiadis). Though never realized in their entirety, modified components of these ideas would reemerge in the cores of existing cities, as we shall see. This idea keeps resurfacing and has made another recent appearance in a proposal for an entirely new network system. In this case, the separation is at grade with two co-extensive, non-intersecting networks for different modes and speeds.[29]

Grade separation also appeared as an adaptation to the speed requirement of the highest-rank road elements of the network—the freeways or expressways—intended for speeds over 37 miles (60 kilometer) per hour and reaching up to 60 (100) or more. Whether at the periphery of a settlement or crossing it, such roads could not sustain their expected performance with at-grade intersections at every 30 seconds of travel; average speed degradation would be too excessive, as would the risk of collisions. Inevitably, such grade separations brought about a historically new network element—the cloverleaf intersection, with all its variations of high-to-high and high-to-medium speed road connections. Certain built examples of these intersections are of astounding size and complexity, dwarfing the Roman viaducts and Egyptian pyramids in scale and parallel only to the enormity and complexity of contemporary subway networks, storm drainage systems, sewage disposal systems and power dams. All of

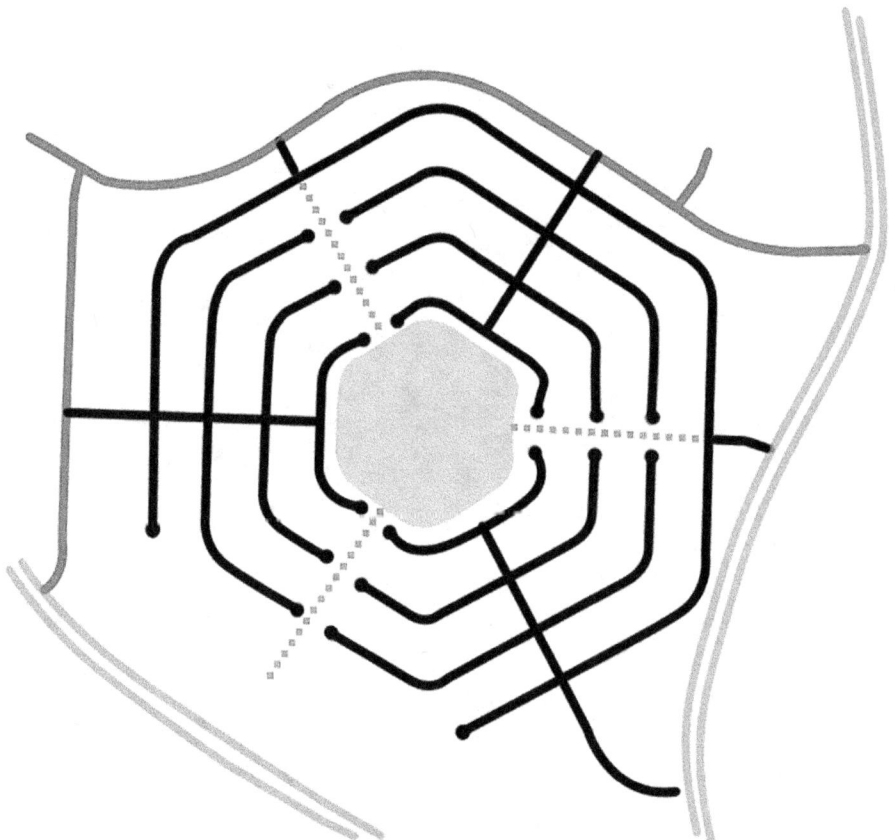

A Vitruvian Fused Grid: In an area of similar size to a polygonal Vitruvian walled city (160 acres), a contemporary neighborhood plan adopts the geometry and adapts it to the current imperatives: no through traffic, low speeds and independent pedestrian paths. A subdivision in Los Angeles.

these structures are the faces of a technological century in full blossom; they stun contemporary citizens and would render ancient ones speechless.

New Regional Street Types

The new 60 m/hr highway, unlike its Roman Appian remote ancestor, no longer admitted—in fact, forbade—any other users but vehicles capable of such speeds, about an order of magnitude higher than its predecessor experienced. These speeds turned the pavement of the common roadway into a "freeway" or "expressway," or, from an ancient cultural perspective, a breathtaking racetrack. Such transformation rendered any land adjacent to it entirely unsuitable for regular commercial uses or public buildings, as one might have found previously on main thoroughfares (or "High Streets").

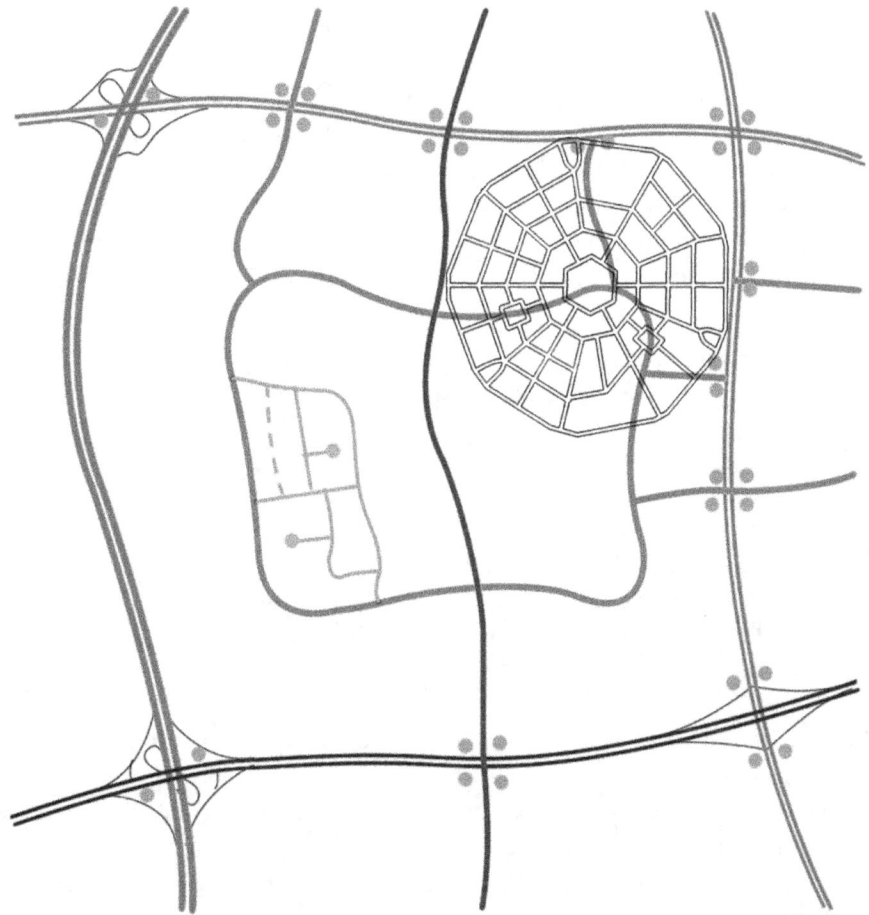

Shaping a New Network: Responding to 10-fold increases in speeds and distances, a scaled-up network emerges with differentiated components and a new organic structure—drastically different from the traditional endless repetition of blocks and streets into the horizon. For contrast and scale, a Renaissance ideal city plan is superimposed.

This change proclaimed that a new order of road network had been born that transcended the "town-on-the-crossroads" settlement concept. Major inter-city roads would no longer run through the center of settlements or be the locus of community activities and services. They were *in the service of* the settlement but not *part of it*. In this respect, they were very similar to railroads (also a new addition to movement networks), which traverse a town in a dedicated ROW but have no fronting uses on them.

In existing settlements the new order created an unavoidable friction. Because traditionally the widest and most direct streets crossed the town at its center, they were also the natural route for the new motorized regional traffic that traversed the town toward other destinations. But the volume and speed of this new traffic clearly collided with commercial and social activities of the main thoroughfare. A new dilemma faced these towns: traffic was desirable for generating commercial activity, but undesirable when it simply crossed the town. This conflict continues to be felt in small towns, whose inherited main streets are overwhelmed with regional traffic passing through. Some towns resolved this dilemma by introducing a bypass highway—not a uniformly positive adaptation.

Realistic road network diagrams that would apply to large districts appeared (circa 1958) that included most or all of the adaptations to speed, safety and tranquility that we examined. They included nine road types (or classes) and eight intersection types (see textboxes). Curiously, the diagram inadvertently conceals the differences between old and new intersections. On paper, they appear identical to the ones on earlier city diagrams, though they differ substantially on how they function. What is not observable in the diagrams is the time element for each component, which is the outcome of the corresponding speed on it.

• Freeway—Divided • Expressway—Divided • Major arterial—Divided • Minor arterial—Undivided • Collector • Local—link between streets • Local—loop or cul-de-sac • Public lane (garage access) • Bike paths (recreational or other) • Pedestrial paths (exclusive)	**Intersection Types** • Three-way, T • Virtual T of one to one-way • Four-way signed • Four-way forced right turns • Four-way with lights • Four-way with lights, limits • Four-way grade separated • Four-way clover leaf • Roundabout

Intersections could no longer be assumed to function in their natural physical state, as they did for all of previous settlement history. They hence had to be controlled by either a new geometry; a new physical arrangement; personnel who managed driver behavior; or a multitude of signs and signals that did the same. The critical intent in exercising control was to establish movement priority. A suitable intersection geometry adaptation for easy, natural control emerged—the three-way—which made movement priority indisputable. Numerous new districts incorporated it in their designs at an astonishing ratio of twelve three-ways to one four-way (less than 10 percent), compared to previous 100 percent four-ways. In other instances, a physical adaptation of the road itself—a continuous raised median that prevents cross movement—also transformed a normal four-way intersection into a three-way. With the full complement of signs and signals, a new network emerged that went beyond the physical geometry of blocks and buildings shown on drawings; this network had an invisible time element, the time assignable to control devices that prevented indiscriminate continuous movement, a natural occurrence in all previous networks. Time became part of a network design but remained indiscernible on layout drawings. However, space and time were integral parts of the design calculations for the network.

This new network diagram emerged to replace the Milesian, Roman and Renaissance prototypes. Essentially, it is still an open grid like its predecessor, but conceived on a far larger scale, a scale commensurate to the ten-fold increase in movement speed and number of trips. Even in its partial portrayal, the network organization covers an area about 10 times the size of Miletus and at least twice the area of imperial Rome or Constantinople.

At that scale, the diagrams show major roads with large curvatures (nearly imperceptible from the driver's seat), perhaps anticipating topographic elements that might need to be accommodated rather than subdued. For an entirely different reason—aesthetics—the diagrams show a predominance of curved street shapes for the lower classes of streets. This preponderance could simply be a reflection of a prevailing practice rather than the conscious imposition of a "model" for application or a necessary functional attribute. For circulation purposes, straight local streets are just as practical as curved ones, and just as suitable for the new diagram as long as they retain their "local" access function in the hierarchy and in practice. With the new diagram, there is a reversal of the path-dependent process of land development. Though still incremental and conditioned by property boundaries, development has to accommodate existing or planned higher-order road networks traversing or abutting a candidate property, not the reverse, as was the case in earlier networks where property boundaries conditioned the formation of a network.

Depending on the road class level, limited or no access may be available from a specific network element, be it a highway or a major divided arterial. This can be seen in the Barrhaven plan (see drawing in next chapter), where access to the developed area is restricted to every 1,300–1,600 feet (400–500 meters) from the three bounding major arterials. Every two of these access points represent the average diameter of a complete Greek or Roman colony—a mere residential neighborhood in the scale of contemporary development.

Another consequent reversal has occurred at the lowest level of network elements—local streets. In incremental growth settlements, such as villages that grew into towns, additions to paths and built properties emanated from the initial nucleus in small additions and the overall configuration of the network "system" was a work in progress—unpredictable and indeterminate. Conversely, in planned settlements, if the original nucleus had introduced a "system" or a "pattern" such as square blocks, for example, its incremental extension would be generally predictable. In the new "diagram" of districts, the overall configuration of major roads is more or less preconfigured and guided by decisions that supersede the local municipal-level authority. It is a given, expressing transportation logic at a district scale. By contrast, the network pattern that fills the area within these predetermined boundaries is entirely dependent on the developer's preferences, which vary according to vogue, taste and his interpretation of the purchasers' expectations. Consequently, adjacent districts that share the same boundaries of higher-order roads may exhibit entirely different characteristics in their layout of the intermediate and lower-scale network elements.

This discontinuity of patterns (or generative principles of layout configuration) between adjacent districts bestows an unintentional variety on the general area, but also creates uneasiness of navigation in visitors. Historically, it is no different from visiting distinct, picturesque, medieval towns or villages: each has a dissimilar layout and is invariably just as indecipherable as the other.

From a network user perspective, the critical aspects of the configuration are always directness of route, average travel speed, and safety. These characteristics are essential for each and every means of travel. From the resident's perspective, the network configuration should reduce risk and nuisances such as noise and impure air. The network geometry is simply a means to deliver these attributes, and imperceptible to a user who simply lives on a street, not an abstract diagram.

DA VINCI RESURGENT

In Henard's drawing for a roundabout, one can discern pedestrian crossings at a level below the road surface plane. This expansion of the street space below grade solves the conflict between the new size of the intersection that accommodates vehicles and the need for a direct pedestrian path across the street.

This concept is now a common adaptation to key, central-city intersections of major thoroughfares, as are the less convenient overpasses. Both adaptations to the car-packed pavement and overcrowded sidewalks have found a new expression in the plus–15 and underground walkway network systems. Toronto, Montreal and Chicago are prime examples of underground systems, while Minneapolis–St. Paul and Calgary exemplify the overhead plus–15 system. They are adjacent to the at-grade network but free of its obstacles and risk. They quickly became magnets for commercial enterprises. Interestingly, the below-grade networks and their extensions into adjacent buildings echo Da Vinci's (1452–1519) sketch of the multilevel city.

In fact, the area that such under/over-ground pedestrian networks cover is often equal to or larger than a typical 1400s city, as are their citizen traffic and economic output. In the Toronto case, an average 325,000 pedestrians per day flow through its system, which supports 1,200 retail, restaurant and business establishments. In the Montreal case, the underground network counts about 30 kilometers of passages and connects 10 subway stations, 2 railway stations and 2 bus terminals. On its route there are 1,700 businesses, 7 hotels, 200 restaurants and 1,600 boutiques (as of 1997), as we saw earlier.[30] This is far greater activity than any main street of an average town could boast; in effect, it is another "town" in the making. This adaptation to motorized traffic generated unforeseen opportunities and transformations, as well as a renewed appreciation for a circulation space devoid of vehicles and filled with the commotion of people moving safely at their natural pace.

As we saw under the speed and element size sections, Da Vinci's multilevel city has found two more contemporary expressions—subways and tunnel motorways. The first moves pedestrians and generally includes some city activity at each station, while the second allows motorists to exit at sparse, predetermined destinations of concentrated activity. Adding all three expressions of his idea, and incorporating the extensive underground parking in central districts, often many levels below grade, the rudimentary sketch of the 1400s is not far from an actual section of a contemporary downtown district.

Safety

As we saw previously, movement in the city areas where an inherited network predominated slowed to a crawl and also became dangerous. Crawl defeats the speed advantage of the new transportation means, and risk of injury added a new stressor in city living caused by its network system and the objects moving within it.

The perception and assessment of danger forced many adaptations in existing city districts: operational, physical, and personal.

As we saw, an operational measure—one-way traffic—had already been applied to minor roads to reduce congestion and improve flow since Roman times. Under specific conditions, the same measure could reduce traffic volume on a residential street and thereby lessen the risk to the people residing on it. This happens because the opposing traffic stream, which the street is actually capable of carrying, is removed. Lower volume and one-way traffic make crossing the street safer, as attention must be paid only to one direction. This operational measure is widely used.

Three physical changes, aimed at improving safety, were made to existing networks over time: street closures, traffic diverters and speed bumps. Street closures at one end eliminate passing traffic and restrict the volume of vehicles to those belonging to the residents on the street. In effect, closures re-create the cul-de-sac street type that was proposed by Raymond Unwin and already applied by him and his followers in the new, peripheral districts of cities. The closure invariably also reduces vehicle speed, as there is not enough road length in which to accelerate; the perception of the street is that of a harbor, a haven, the end of a trip.

Traffic diverters also prevent through traffic on residential streets, thereby reducing the number of vehicles on it. By means of a sharp, right-angle turn at the end of the residential block, a diverter invariably forces a lower speed on the vehicle, thus achieving a reduction in the odds of an accident occurring.

Reduction in speed is also the basis for the introduction of another physical adaptation to the network—speed bumps and humps (starting in the 1950s). They proliferated widely and are now permanent fixtures in many central districts of cities (but not entirely permanent, as in several districts residents demanded, and obtained, their removal). Speed bumps, however, are an incomplete adaptation: they create undesirable noise and driver discomfort, and, more critically, they reduce the speed of rescue vehicles. In spite of these flaws, they have emerged in newly built districts at the periphery, a reminder that the lessons of the last few decades of adaptations have not been fully translated into practical solutions; the evolutionary trial-and-error process is still ongoing with regard to accommodating the new transport devices in the settlement environment.

A fourth adaptation that emerged in the 1970s was the application of Eugene Henard's traffic circle on a much smaller scale. It has proven very effective in reducing collisions at cross intersections, where usually most occur. Unexpectedly, traffic circles also have been shown to enable a better flow of vehicles, a desirable side effect for the network as a whole.

A surprising safety adaptation emerged in central districts on busy arterials at mid-century. Where traffic is dense for most of the day, crossing of the street at random and at will, as was customary in a village, town, small city or residential area, could no longer be tolerated. Such crossing not only presented an enormous risk for the pedestrians attempting it but also created a huge disruption of traffic flow and raised the risk of collisions. A new physical modification appeared on these streets—fences. Fences were installed in the medians, where such existed, or on sidewalks across the same street, or on both. Just as traffic lights controlled the *time* of movement of pedestrians and cars, the fences controlled the *place* of pedestrian movement. In some cases, the most direct path between origin and destination for pedestrians became very circuitous, causing inevitable stress. Moreover, fences (whether crude or crafted) gave the street a displeasing resemblance to a camp or a corral, adding tension to the daily routine.

Personal adaptations to the actual or perceived lack of safety include modifications to the daily cycle of individual and family activities. The most prominent of these is the absence of social and play activity on the street. Children were the first to be withdrawn from the street and, lacking at least one good reason to be on the street (that is, child supervision), parents soon followed. In a self-reinforcing cycle, this personal adaptation became a typical, accepted pattern that emptied the streets of human presence, particularly residential streets.

A second personal adaptation, just as pervasive as the first, was the reduction in walking and cycling based on either motivation or permission. Children first were not permitted to walk or bike to school; parents were simply too concerned about their safety. Parents followed with their own avoidance of cycling or walking. Even short-distance destinations for shopping or recreation would be traveled by car, which was perceived to be the safest method, as comparative collision numbers confirm. The impact of these personal adaptations to risk on the road network was to increase traffic volumes, thereby increasing the risk to pedestrians and cyclists in a self-reinforcing cycle of decreasing safety.

All of these stressors and the adaptations to remove or alleviate them can be seen from the perspective of the collective culture we defined earlier: the sum-total of all activities that secure the survival of a group of individuals, be it a tribal clan, a city or an empire. From this perspective, several fundamental settlement functions involve transportation and its evolving means.

A settlement needs to be provided with food, water, energy, message transmission means, power for the production and movement of goods and raw materials, and the means of disposing waste. These are not elective "cultural" activities, as one might consider music or poetry, for example, but rather essential tasks on which the survival of the group depends entirely and constantly. Each of these would inevitably require some form of transport, and consequently paths, conduits, or channels through which transport could be carried out. The adaptations to the existing networks or the new complements to them that we examined in this chapter suggest a potential reconfiguration of the "system" that embeds them permanently in its structure.

4

A Contemporary Pattern

In the previous chapter we looked at how network system and personal adaptations have gradually responded to the stresses of changing cultures in cities. This ongoing process of adaptation continually responds to new stressors with novel mutations as necessary. This chapter will illustrate these adaptations as a context for the proposed pattern. It will explore the implications of these adaptations regarding the formulation of a *contemporary* pattern in abstract and practical terms. It will also highlight recent and current ideas about neighborhood and district network planning that supply some of the elements of the new network pattern mutation.

Space and Speed

As we saw in Chapter 3, when the population of a city increases and new means of transport proliferate, circulation space becomes progressively scarcer. As a consequence, movement speed and travel time reach unsatisfactory levels. This relationship between growth and movement space has been true throughout city history, from foot-and-hoof-served Rome, Paris and London to motorized New York, Tokyo and Shanghai centuries later. A corollary to this relationship is the law of congestion, which applies to all cities of all periods: more road space will attract more traffic; relief from congestion can only be temporary. In a city that continues to grow, people will always choose what appears to be a faster, more convenient route, causing it to become congested. The relationship between population growth and congestion is not unique to road traffic. Electricity network service degrades to "brown-outs" at times of unusual demand for heating and cooling by an increasing number of customers or abnormal weather conditions. On rare occasions, the water network will produce a trickle rather than flow at the spout end due to higher-than-usual demand. Similarly, Internet service comes to a crawl or is denied entirely when a specific destination site becomes highly popular. Increasing demand for service on any type of network will inevitably create degradation of service.

City dwellers will always attempt to limit the time allocated to travel and the effort it requires by way of available alternative means of transport. City authorities, for their part, will seek to enable the movement of people and goods by means of improving the transportation network and widening the choice of means. Continuing city growth, diversifying and emergent means of transport, and the immutability of built infrastructure all raise the question: What transportation network layout can best accommodate contemporary culture and perhaps anticipate future needs?

In attempting to answer this question, we focus on the configuration that shapes paths, ways, and roads on the surface, while recognizing that a contemporary metropolis cannot be fully served without below- and above-grade networks. It would also be ill served without air ways and both wired and wireless communications. In focusing on the physical surface networks, we recognize that shaping them may follow general rules for the large-scale elements while permitting variability on the small scale, as we shall see in this and subsequent chapters.[1]

Principles, Elements and Forms

In response to the above question, we survey the network adaptations to the changed means of locomotion and their size and speed, as we did in Chapter 3, and we extrapolate a number of principles, which are historically new. Along with these principles, we discern elements and forms of networks that emerged during the ongoing new period of mechanized transport. In many other fields, experimentation and specific solutions preceded the formulation of a general set of principles; it is the same with transportation networks.

HIERARCHY

As we surmised from Paris' transformation in the 1850s, a monumental and unequaled example of physical intervention,[2] the most prominent principle to emerge from practice is that of the *hierarchy* of roads: a hierarchy that corresponds to an expected speed and volume of vehicles and the consequent size and shape of network components. Following a century of transportation progress, contemporary manuals classify automotive roads into distinct categories according to total right-of-way width, number of lanes, lane width, expected travel speeds and vehicle volumes. Manuals also characterize a road's likely role in the network system, such as "distributor," "collector" or "access" road, even when this nomenclature is applied to existing networks that did not anticipate it or differentiate their elements (numerous networks have been laid out in the past in ever-expanding uniform grids, and with generally identical width dimensions). This classification and characterization is new and significant.

At first glance, these terms seem paradoxical when we realize that all roads are "connectors" between a certain origin and a chosen destination; nothing is collected or distributed, and both the origin and the destination on given streets are access points depending on the direction of the travel. These terms become meaningful only when understood in a context of "flow," a metaphor that applies to the movement of mechanized transport only (or fluids in other systems); pedestrians and quadrupeds, the ancestral units of locomotion, do not "flow"—they simply tread.

Up to the mid-nineteenth century, the range of city movement speed was inconsequential—from 2 miles (5 kilometers) per hour to about 6 (15); no insurmountable conflicts were present at this treading or trotting speed. With mechanization, the range widened from 2 to 50 miles an hour, a roughly ten-fold increase from the previous average (and, in the case of fast trains, an almost 20-fold increase). Since this dramatic increase, a critical threshold was breached that made it impossible and undesirable for every street to accommodate all speeds and volumes: in most existing districts it was physically unfeasible, due to their inadequate width, and in new ones it was theoretically incongruous, due to the increase in the

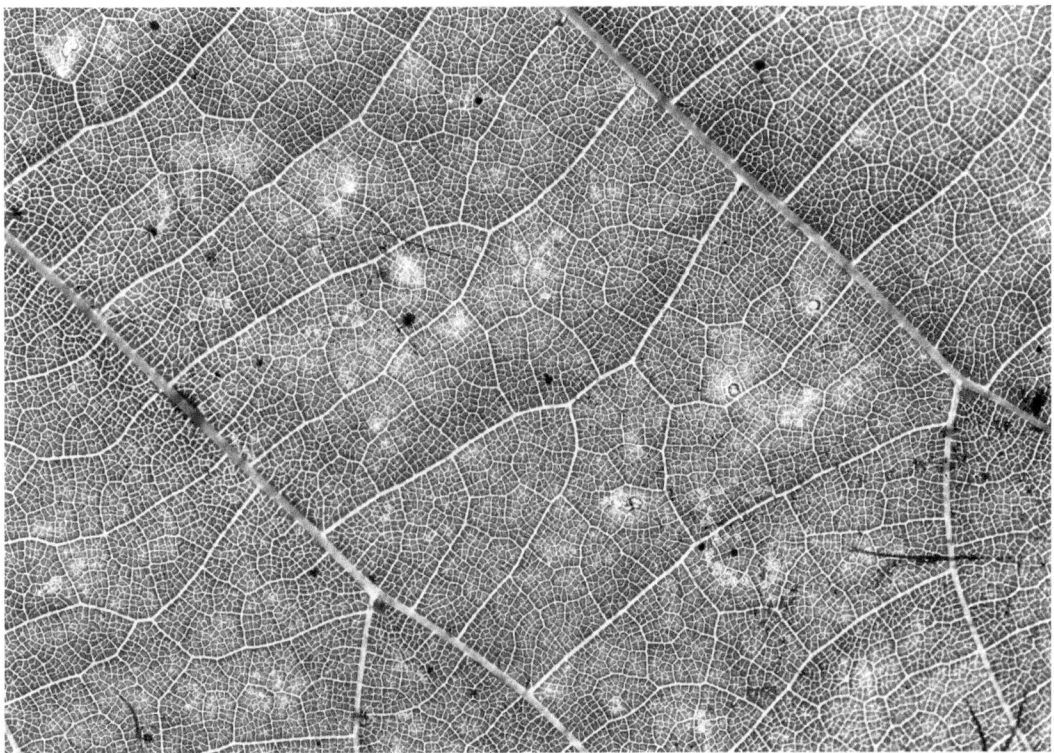

The Leaf Metaphor: The circulation system of a leaf shows a hierarchical and fractal organization of paths from the principal leaf-stem vein to three levels of sizes and lengths below it. Though not strictly dendrite, almost all vein connections are three-way.

points of movement conflict. Consequently, classification and class-specific design requirements became imperative and emerged as a new standard practice. This practice broke with the tradition in which all roads drawn on plans and laid out by surveyors were mostly undifferentiated and the overall configuration of many appeared to be a mechanical repetition of identical elements. This break initiated a new era of transportation network design. (We will later examine efficiency/inefficiency of land, and efficiency/inefficiency of movement.)

The emergent hierarchical classification was brought about by, and dealt primarily with, motorized vehicle movement, the root cause of the need for adaptation. Being focused on mechanized means, this new classification often omits preceding means that are still part of the movement system—bicycle and foot—an omission that it is seen by some observers as undermining the system as a whole. This lapse in the range of means, however, is not an inherent attribute of the classification system, as it may appear from some of its applications; the rigorous design requirements for the new modes simply overwhelm the network program agenda, to the detriment of the earlier ones.

Road classification and its underpinning principle of *hierarchy*[3] have been given new foundations by recent network theory. It was found that networks occurring in nature exhibit strong hierarchical structures that obey mathematical rules. In certain man-made networks (such as the Internet, for example), the same rules seem to apply. It is argued that if self-organizing systems tend to assemble in hierarchical structures, the emergence of road classification and its application in network design can be interpreted as an attempt at self-organizing, a natural adjustment. At least partial evidence of that argument is provided by the distribution of lengths by class, as we shall see later in this chapter.[4]

Just as in natural systems, the hierarchy of vehicular movement conduits must be expressed in a geometric pattern that renders the principle operative. Such a pattern will invariably have clearly identifiable and immutable characteristics, as we shall see in subsequent sections. It will also have a predictable structure, though its form may be variable as it adapts to accommodate specific district constraints. It is important and relevant to keep in mind that due to the ten-fold increase in speeds, the pattern itself will become recognizable only at a scale considerably above the familiar block and street, closer to a ten-fold size of preceding patterns.[5]

A relevant illustration of growth, speed and hierarchy of paths comes from another recent mobility development—the elevator banks in skyscrapers. As buildings grow taller, elevator cabs are classified by floor number range; correspondingly, the trip time is kept constant for reaching most floors by eliminating stops (i.e., intersections); they obey a hierarchy of speed by selectively excluding access to a predetermined set of floors.

Separation

One derivative characteristic of *hierarchy* is the rule of *separation* (i.e., access constraint) in horizontal and vertical space. A clear example of separation is the case of railways crossing a town: their speed and size require that extreme precautions be taken to ensure that nothing encroaches on the train's right of way. Rail transport is a radical departure from all conventional transport means preceding its invention. Though on wheels, like many others, it runs on especially laid tracks (i.e., railroads), has enormous horsepower, draws multiple coaches and develops immense inertia. It would be inconceivable for a train to function within a city district with street intersections at regular city-block 300-foot intervals. (Were it to stop, its size alone could block several intersecting streets.) Its stops are thus placed tens of miles apart. Just like railways, roadways intended for high-speed, high-volume and large transport vehicles require the same degree of functionality and protection. Without separation, vehicle size and normal operating speeds would pose enormous collision risks; alternatively, potential service degradation would exact financial penalties. In both cases, the presumed benefits of road transport would diminish.[6] The principle of hierarchy and the separation it requires can also be seen clearly in a leaf vein structure; it is not a uniform tessellated pattern of veins that covers the leaf surface, but rather a tiered structure.

In road network practice, separation would be made visible in a district to which it has been applied by the progressive reduction of access to higher-rung roads from lower-class roads. This, in turn, would be seen in the gradual reduction of intersections between certain classes and only at specified intervals. Vertical separation, a complement to the horizontal one, would appear at major intersections through the introduction of over- or underpasses.

Both principles of hierarchy and separation can be seen in the rapid evolution of the newest transportation networks in cities—elevators. Once a building exceeds 20 floors, the elevator cabs are grouped in banks that serve only one "community" of floors. Further differentiation occurs when the structure becomes taller and the elevator configuration dendrite: a main floor elevator leads to a lobby on a higher floor, from which a bank of elevators serves the community contained between two such lobbies. The highest-speed elevators intersect with the common lobbies only, not with specific floors. This rational, dendrite organization of elevator paths that divides paths by speed and extent of reach, and segments the building volume by sets of floors served by "highway" or "local" elevators, expresses the exact same objectives and constraints of mobility at the horizontal plane of earlier and recent city development. The floors are a "walkable" territory, a "neighborhood," while intra-neighborhood travel is best done by elevators. A significant difference, which bears on the configuration of a street network, is that the two modes, elevators and people on foot, never occupy the same path or cross paths. One might draw a parallel with the subways that deliver people to "floors" (i.e., districts) but do not intersect with people's paths. Once a skyscraper is seen as miniature version of a city with its invisible vertical transport means (and paths), the converse image of the city as very large building with its visible and invisible horizontal means and paths, each obeying similar organizational principles, appears realistic, even if somewhat surprising.

Frontage Restrictions

Extending the logic of intersections to interactions results in progressively limiting the fronting of commercial/public buildings on higher-tier roads. This is one case in which network design influences the use of adjacent land. The frontage restriction emerges naturally due to the inevitable risk of collisions on account of people crossing the road indiscriminately, cars turning into frequently occurring driveway entries, and bicycles claiming the same rights of access. This combined set of potential events would tend to produce either intolerable levels of collisions or unacceptable degradation of travel performance.

This incompatibility between traffic and commercial frontage is historically new and contrasts sharply with previous experience. The spontaneous emergence and ubiquitous presence of commercial space on earlier main arteries (High Street or Main Street) in pre-automotive centuries indicates a strong synergistic, symbiotic relationship. Conversely, the decline of commercial space near early thoroughfares in existing cities indicates an inverse relationship that points to certain critical thresholds: high volume of mechanized traffic and low availability of proximate parking stalls. When these thresholds are exceeded, they produce negative effects that deter the use of commercial facilities: in high-volume thoroughfares, walking space is rendered inadequate and unpleasant, and shopping becomes inconvenient; in low-parking-supply arteries, convenience may be compromised due to unavailability or long walking distances from stalls. Consequently, shop activity wanes and merchants or businesses move elsewhere—a familiar phenomenon.

Though not strictly a traffic flow issue, such negative influence would inevitably become a network design subject, where its effects are deemed undesirable. Solutions for existing districts have emerged and historical examples from pre-automotive cities also exist, and both can be integrated into a new contemporary model. We will examine these in subsequent sections.

River Islands

When the principle of hierarchy and its inevitable precondition—separation—are combined, the outcome is conceptually analogous to a river delta: a series of islands created by local streams (distributaries) of different widths and water flows. It suggests a nested hierarchy of streams according to water volume and the proportional size of the stream. Delta "islands" thus created are also nested. Each smaller island contains progressively fewer "rivers" until the smallest island has none; its perimeter streams define its size.

The delta analogy is useful for traffic networks to the extent that flow paths show a hierarchical organization that defines nested "islands." The resemblance starts with the city blocks, which were first defined by the paths surrounding them, generally of similar width and serving, for almost all of city history, slow-moving traffic of people and animals. Sets of these blocks can be seen as an "archipelago," where water is almost still most of the time.

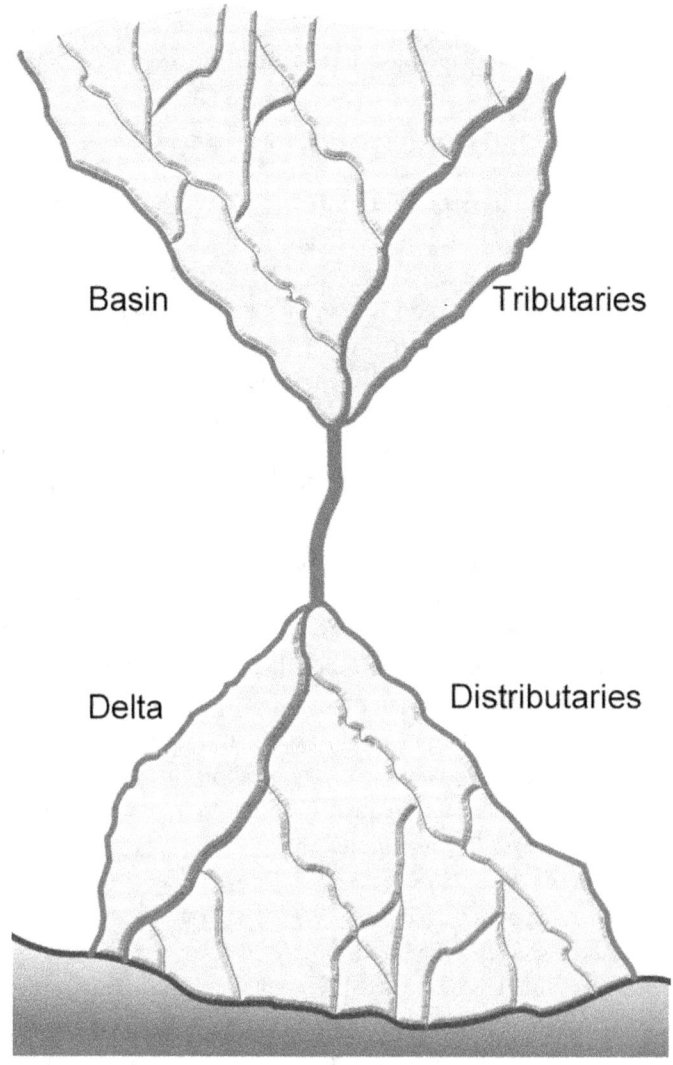

The Basin and the Delta Metaphors: Both these systems of water flows naturally form dendrite configurations with a nested hierarchy of paths and "islands." They are analogs for many flow systems: biotic, mechanical and informational.

The new element that the river delta adds to the still archipelago is the constant flow organized in hierarchical "distributaries," which follow the paths of least resistance in the landscape. If the naturally evolved flow configurations, such as the delta, leaf veins and bronchial tubes, produce nested islands of decreasing size, each circumscribed by a lower size and flow conduits, then it might be expected that the same geometric effect would inevitably emerge in a road network configuration for similar functional reasons; in fact, it did, albeit partially, at this time. Just like water, traffic has been shown to follow a path of least resistance, concentrating on wide thoroughfares, where they are available, to their fullest capacity. Where a bypass or an additional lane is introduced, they will also fill with traffic.

The largest "islands" created by the highest rank of roadways—provincial or state highways—could be city-size regions. Though such regions may be adjoining and forming a larger conurbation, they would be decidedly separated by very large streams of traffic and connected only by (highway) bridges, completing the analogy of the delta (e.g., a leaf's central and branching veins provide an example of separated regions belonging to the same leaf).

The city of Venice stands as a vivid representation of the island metaphor at a smaller scale: waterways define islands of habitation that are connected by bridges. The assembly of connected islands constitutes the entire "island" (or peninsula, more precisely) of Venice, linked to the mainland via a causeway. (Paradoxically, and a haven for pedestrians, Venice's dual network inadvertently excludes bicycles—a convenient, economical and safe mode in a car-less environment.) Many other cities, like Venice, relied extensively on the use of barges for the transport of goods—Paris in the eighteenth and nineteenth centuries, for example.

The converse image of the delta, also stemming from natural water flows (and a similar analogy), is the river basin. A basin's multiple origins of water follow paths toward the main river body, some of which are direct and others indirect. Tributaries merge with other tributaries of gradually diminishing number, but increasing in size, until a few meet the main river body that flows out to sea. Like the delta, it, too, has a loosely dendrite structure, with occasional "islands" forming between tributaries. An imaginary, abstract superposition of these two flow systems (divergent and convergent) would produce a nested hierarchical grid.

Hierarchy Revealed and Reviewed

The delta, basin, and bronchial structure analogies can serve as abstract functional diagrams in formulating and understanding contemporary, complex movement networks. If considered as archetypes or stencils, however, they have to be reinterpreted to account for the differences between the natural and biological flows they represent and the mechanical equivalent of motorized traffic. The former flow in one direction only toward a single ultimate destination. The latter—vehicles—crisscross the city to reach many varied destinations; origins and destinations are indistinguishable and interchangeable. A furniture store, for example, is a destination for manufactured goods and the origin for furniture delivery to homes.

Owing to this interchangeability of vehicle traffic origin and arrival points, a second important difference needs to be addressed in the application of an archetype (or pattern): cross-tributary (or distributary) connections. This difference requires a departure from the

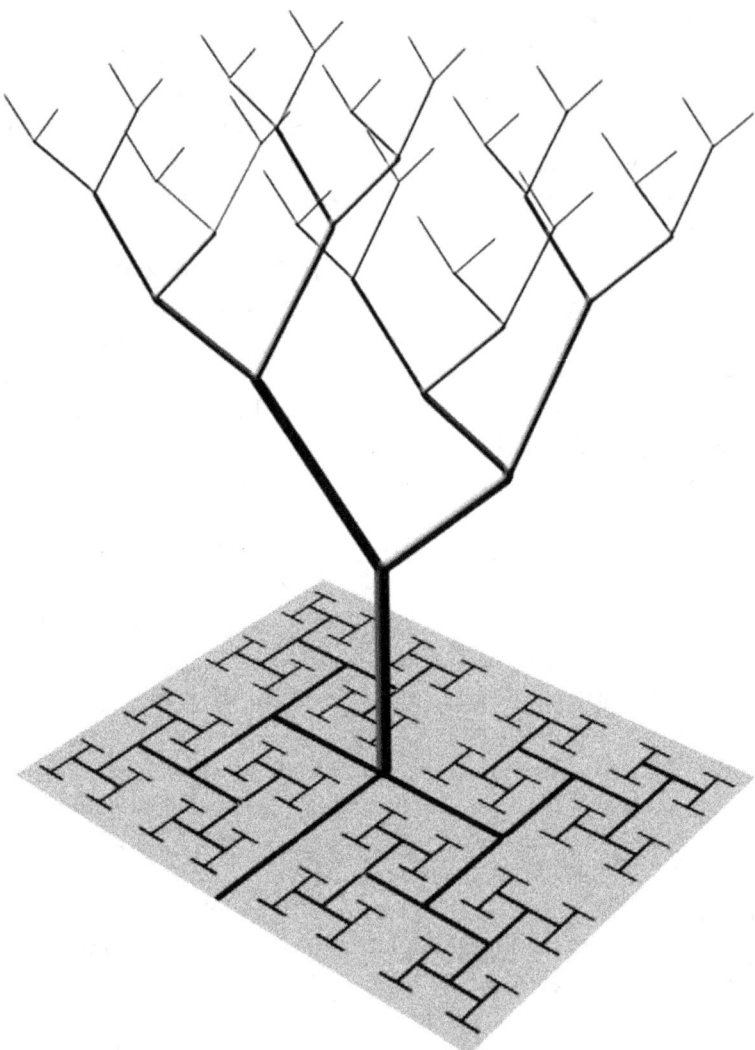

Tree Structure and Planar Projection: A tree's fractal hierarchy produces a dendrite path system when projected onto a flat plane. Though rational and orderly, it proves not as suitable for a city as its organic original is for a tree. This shows the limitations of transposing models.

strictly dendrite configuration of organic and natural systems—they preclude flows between branches at *any* level. And since all branching points are a Y-type (T-type or 3-leg) configuration, they create a condition that generates a severe problem: in a Y-type connection any blockage prior to branching could deprive all derivative branches from accessing a destination—a detrimental or even catastrophic condition in organic systems (i.e., blood clot). In transportation networks, such blockage could create severe stress, though likely transient, depending on the speed of reparation.

Out of these functional premises of hierarchy, separation and cross-district connections, emerge two principles for a contemporary network: "arteriality" and "filtered permeability." The former, already briefly discussed in previous sections, describes a necessary attribute of some of the roads in a system, and the latter the absence of arteriality in low-tier roads for automotive traffic in a graduated range of specified vehicle types (we might call it "capillarity"). Arteriality can be defined as continuity, or *uninterrupted continuity*, that accommodates intermediate and long-distance trips. Its absence would confine trips to local short-distance destinations. We shall return to this topic in subsequent sections.

Approaches to Hierarchy

Diagrams in the following two sections show contrasting approaches to establishing a hierarchy of roads: one entirely dendrite and the second an entirely homogeneous array of streets in perpendicular directions, with no terminal points. Aspects of both appear in historic and new city districts.

As we have seen, neither configuration meets all the requirements of a well-functioning contemporary layout. Modifications to each would be necessary to satisfy all mobility options and performance expectations.

DENDRITE TRANSFORMATION FOR ARTERIALITY

Layout A (see next page), a hypothetical, dendrite configuration in a fractal H progression,[7] would degrade pedestrian circulation: trip length between two nearby points could be lengthened by a factor of two or more due to the circuitry of the path. This trip elongation would render walking impractical and undesirable due to the disproportional effort involved in reaching a destination. To alleviate this crucial drawback, an extensive complementary network of pedestrian and bicycle paths would have to be introduced. These paths would link each cluster of streets (and blocks) to adjacent ones.

Layout A also produces a similar elongation for motorized travel not only by increasing the distance between points, a lesser concern when no physical effort is involved, but also by degrading speed through the frequent stops, turns and backtracking. Such speed degradation, unwelcome to motorists, would be altogether detrimental to public transit modes, rendering them inefficient and undesirable, particularly when combined with the pedestrian inaccessibility mentioned above. Public transit would also have to backtrack frequently in order to serve adjacent clusters of blocks—a further deterioration of its performance efficiency. It is worth noting at this point that the elongation increases in proportion to the level of hierarchy at which a trip is made.

To overcome this shortcoming, two of the higher-rank roads can be extended across clusters of streets and blocks as a first step. This type of modification can be extended to lower levels of the road hierarchy at will. With this transformation, the initial diagram loses its strictly dendrite structure and becomes a *hybrid* that combines low-level dendrite structure and a high-level, two-directional grid. If the extension of connections continues down to its lowest-level streets, it will eventually become identical to layout B (see page 89). At the first stage, some roads achieve arteriality; following subsequent extensions, all roads share this characteristic. As we shall discuss, this final transformation contradicts the principle of hierarchy, the starting point of this diagram, and renders the system operationally dysfunctional.

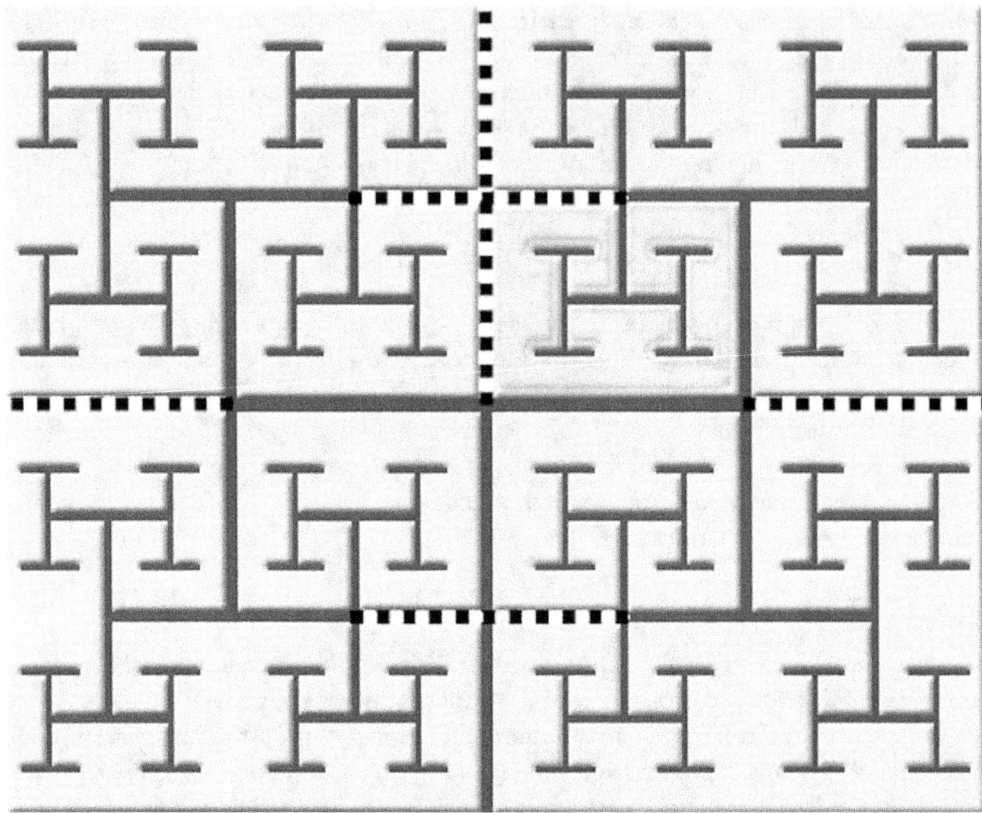

Layout A—Dendrite Plan Adaptation: Adding vehicular connections between homologous hierarchical segments (dotted lines) and pedestrian connections between the lowest-rank access streets preserves the organic logic of the dendrite structure and removes its disadvantages.

Open Grid Transformation for Arteriality

Layout B (opposite page) allows for unconstrained pedestrian and bicycle movement, not confined to predetermined paths; such movement can follow a desired line to a chosen destination. Though direct, the movement is interrupted frequently by crossing the entire hierarchy of roads, requiring repetitive waiting periods at intersections—signalized or otherwise. (In some extreme cases, crossing the highest-tier road, a multi-lane highway, for example, may be simply impossible.)

This frequent crossing is particularly disadvantageous for bicycles, which cover the distance between intersections in half the time (or better) clocked by pedestrians only to spend an equal amount of time or more at crossings. Consequently, the actual time spent in reaching a destination on a normal walking trip of a quarter-mile to half a mile (400–800 meters), or a proportionally lengthier bicycle trip, may be one and a half times (or even more) longer compared to an ideal, uninterrupted continuous walking movement, and proportionately longer for riding a bike.

To overcome this limitation, pedestrian and bicycle routes would have to continue uninterrupted under or over intersecting roads, an option that appears extremely impractical in this configuration. Alternatively, they can be separate and independent from vehicular streets and crossing mostly at grade, or above/below as needed. Such an option bypasses the complexity of designing intersections to satisfy all means of movement that have drastically different speeds.[8] A third option would be a distinct path system that may occasionally co-incide with the road network, avoiding many or most normal vehicular intersections. Such a version would turn the combination of the vehicular ways and pedestrian ways into a hybrid.[9]

Layout B frees motorized movement from the repeated turns and reversals of direction that characterize layout A, as well as the consequent speed degradation and trip and time lengthening. Yet, as drawn, the frequency of intersections that it creates, all of them four-way, would be detrimental to vehicle performance, more so than for pedestrians and bicycles for the simple reason that car travel time is measured in higher units due to its speed: time spent in deceleration, stop and acceleration at intersections equates to much greater distance "lost" than for other, slower means.

To surmount this weakness of configuration B, and render it fully functional for motorized traffic, layout modifications would have to be introduced so as to reduce the number of intersections. This can be achieved by selectively rendering certain intersections between

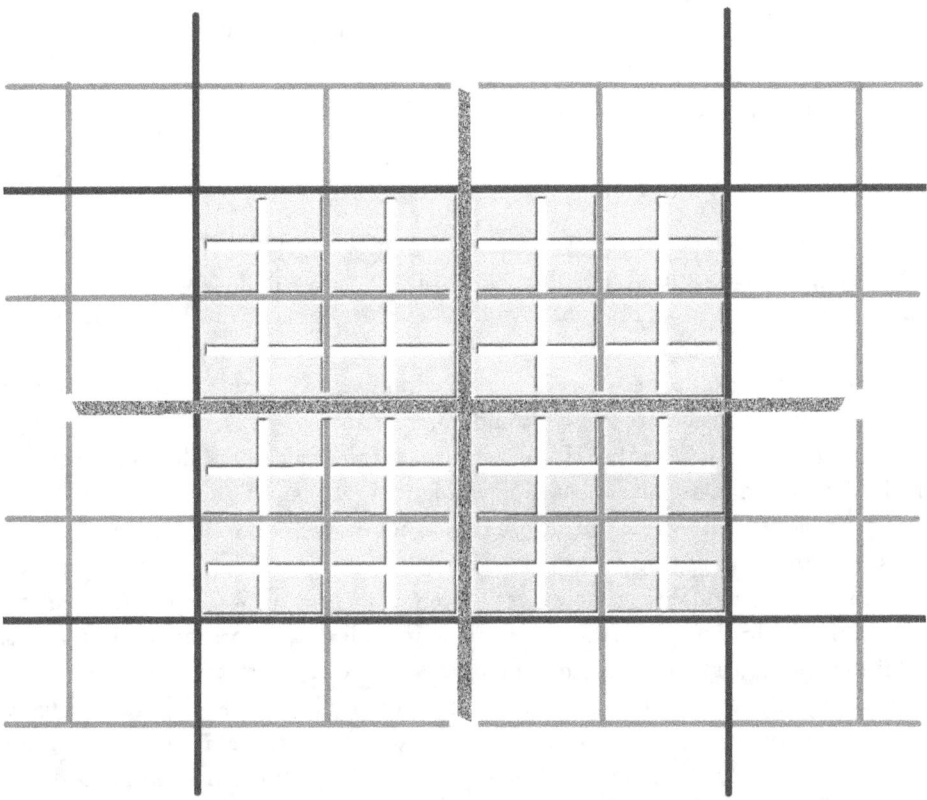

Layout B—Grid Plan Adaptation: Removing vehicular connections between dissimilar ranks of roads transforms the grid from an undifferentiated uniform structure to a hierarchical one with quasi-dendrite attributes. By retaining all the connections for pedestrians, it achieves an ideal fusion of paths.

chosen ranks of roads inoperable. To visualize this option, we choose the rule of allowable intersections between same and one rank up only—a tentative, experimental choice. (The actual choice would be made on the grounds of relative traffic volumes and expected speeds.) The resulting diagram has a quasi-dendrite and quasi–open grid configuration. In other words, it is a hybrid:

- The top two ranks of roads exhibit arteriality—continuous travel with interruptions only at large intervals: the higher the rank, the larger the interval.
- The two lower ranks of roads are local only. They are dendrite with cross rather than T-intersections (as we shall see, cross intersections can be replaced with T versions).
- Two sizes of nested islands are created; both are accessible by automobile traffic but not traversed by it.
- Depending on the size of the islands, public transit routes would be direct and continuous, with no backtracking.
- Pedestrian/bicycle paths are continuous within a large area and may become connected to adjacent districts by using under/over passes.

In addition to the suppression of intersections, other possible configurations can also reduce the number of intersections with main roads for improved performance:

a. Increasing block length
b. Turning most intersections to T
c. Ts, forced turn and merge (raised median type)
d. Introducing service roads

Increasing block length from 400 feet to 600 or 800 feet (120, 180, 240 meters) reduces the number of intersections proportionately for the roads running parallel to the blocks. In the perpendicular direction, roads of any rank will experience the same frequency of intersections as before. This solution provides only a partial answer to the issue of hierarchy and separation. It also makes pedestrian circulation within a district more cumbersome, though this defect could be easily rectified with mid-block paths.

In addition, turning most intersections from cross to T can reduce the number of upper-tier road intersections and give them an unambiguous movement priority.

The diagram titled "Sizing and Shaping a Neighborhood," shown in the previous chapter shows how arteriality can be maintained every five roads (or blocks) apart. Intersections with the peripheral roads are reduced, respectively, from four to two. In this diagram, these intersections are three-way and, therefore, they automatically give priority to the main road. In addition, the higher-rank road can be modified to force no intersection with the opposing stream of traffic by means of a raised median. It is theoretically possible to decrease or increase the distance between roads that acquire arteriality down to three or up to six (or more) roads. Such a potential change raises the question of what constitutes an appropriate distance, a question that will be discussed in the next chapter. Returning momentarily to natural systems, we observe that, almost without exception, all intersections of conduits, whether leaf veins, bronchial tubes or blood arteries, are three-way—a fact to keep in mind when configuring "capillary"-scale networks.

To buffer the effect of frequent intersections with roads that need to maintain arteriality, a parallel road on either side of the main can be introduced with which local roads intersect. At chosen intervals, its traffic is channeled to the main road using a merge lane. This is a common device in the design of the uppermost tier of roads—highways—and can be used for the lower one or two tiers. A well-known example appears in the Champs-Élysées' 10-lane arterial in Paris. The addition of a parallel access road creates the familiar layout of the multi-lane boulevard that can also be found sporadically in a number of cities, usually post-automotive, where both the need and the space to introduce them were present.

Scale is purposely not shown on the larger diagrams (layout A and B), which depict and explain the outcome of introducing arteriality and its twin of "separation." They are meant to indicate the process by which preconceived abstract geometric patterns that stand as proxies for circulation systems can be transformed to accommodate contemporary means of transport and their expected performance goals. Scale will emerge when additional factors come into play at the neighborhood level.

In completing these transformations, we realize that nature has evolved dendrite flow configurations for its animate and inanimate organisms, but these are not necessarily work-able stencils for motorized traffic flows. Yet the hierarchical structure of these configurations proves indispensable in designing a contemporary vehicular network. Other man-made net-works also follow hierarchical structures, as we shall see.

Similarly, we realize that one conscious human experiment in configuring a complete network, the Milesian model, proves unsuitable for motorized transport in its pure form, without crucial modifications. A studied fusion of the two, the natural and the man-made, the organic and the geometric, we argue, would likely produce a workable hybrid.

The Question of Street Width

As we saw in previous chapters, adaptations to relieve congestion and decrease travel time center on street width and street shape. Straight streets inherently enable speed, but their size may limit flow. Cities with a grid configuration, which usually implies straight streets, such as Charlottesville, Portland, Houston, New York, Sacramento and Salt Lake City and many others, display substantially different ROWs for streets: from 40 feet to 60, 80, and 120 feet (12, 20, 24 and 36 meters). Between the narrowest and widest, the size triples (as would the consumption of land for roads, a later subject). Assuming a theoretical equal amount of traffic in all four configurations, some of these streets may be congested, others will be well used and the rest underutilized. Also, as we know from traffic count surveys, even in the same configuration (and irrespective of street size), traffic volumes will vary, often by an order of magnitude, depending on their position in the system, making the low-volume streets appear oversized and vice versa. Constant width for all streets seems unjustifiable, but variable width, the rational option, requires a method by which to assign widths in appropriate proportions to a network's component streets.

As we saw earlier, larger streets will invariably attract more traffic, particularly when they connect distant destinations. But the exact amount of traffic will vary over time as the city experiences growth by expansion or densification, or both. Predicting growth in order to forecast future traffic volume is at best a speculative exercise regarding the amount and location of growth; even growth per se is subject to numerous economic and social elusive variables. Consequently, the question of arterial size becomes a question of potential future size and, therefore, in the absence of precise forecasts, of flexibility, adaptability. The location of an arterial, however, should not be a matter of speculation, as the hierarchy of elements will always require the same number of tiers, each of specific characteristics and, as we shall see, of recommended spacing.

The street size question that anticipates flow volumes leads us to the issue of hierarchy of sizes—widths and lengths. We have seen that widths can and should vary for flow efficiency and, invariably, land-use economy. Length variation is a less obvious case, unless one considers it in conjunction with hierarchy and separation. Theoretically, on a plan, all streets can be continuous indefinitely, whether straight, crooked or curved. However, because they would inevitably intersect with others, their arteriality attribute could be eroded on account of the degradation of speed. As can be seen in natural flow systems, lengths of conduits diminish along with the reduction in their cross-sections (see leaf image). These two attributes, length and width, are bound up with arteriality and separation and have to be factored in simultaneously.

For initial guidance in matching design to function, we revisit natural networks with full awareness of the differences we have already encountered between them and the networks for vehicle movement, such as the interchangeability of origin and destination and the multiplicity of probable destinations from any single origin.

One additional difference also limits the full applicability of natural models. Leaf veins, bronchial tubes and blood veins grow along with the organism until they reach their ultimate, final size. Then they and the organism stop growing; they reach a stasis. City street networks, by contrast, remain mostly identical to their original physical dimensions and shape during the city's growth; the network expands in total length, as the city does in size, but does not change in cross-section. Cities simply grow without a predetermined size limit; they do not arrive at stasis. Imagine a conventional pattern of a uniform grid in which all streets have the same width, in three versions, each with a different width. It conjures up the current question: If street widths are to be differentiated according to rank, what should be the relative proportions of streets having the same width?

Related questions would be about the range of street widths, the size of a district that would inevitably include all widths, and the frequency of occurrence of each in this all-inclusive district. Similar questions arise with respect to street lengths: How many length sizes and at what frequency?

Answers to these questions may be found in recent theoretical formulations and systematic observations such as the Pareto distribution and fractal analyses.

THE PARETO DISTRIBUTION

The Pareto distribution postulate, empirically derived and subsequently mathematically expressed, has been found to mirror faithfully a number of natural and social phenomena. In its simplest form, when applied to a road network system, it would suggest that 20 percent of roads will be long connections and 80 percent short, local connections. Extending this idea to traffic, it can be hypothesized that 20 percent of the roads will carry 80 percent of

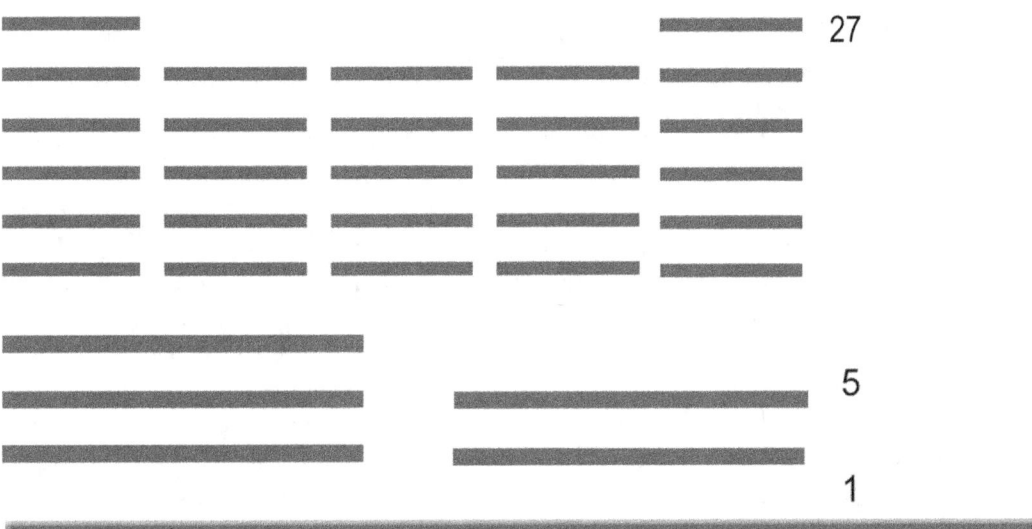

Observing Principles: Expressing the principle found in natural and man-made network systems: ratio of distribution of lengths—a system may not function well if it strays far from it.

the daily traffic volume. The same result, expressed as a converse relationship, would imply that 80 percent of roads will carry only 20 percent of traffic.

From this general proposition, it follows, at least theoretically, that 80 percent of a district's roads can be sized to dimensions commensurate with the lower traffic volume they would carry. In view of this preliminary conclusion, a uniformly dimensioned network, of which there are many built examples, would be inefficient and wasteful of resources. Traffic will always choose the most direct routes to a number of key destinations, and the remaining routes, though available, will be underutilized. The diagram titled "Observing Principles" expresses this distribution of lengths graphically (18 percent long, 82 percent short).[10] Knowing the ratio of lengths is only the first step toward a network configuration in which these lengths are part of a *system* and are defined *geometrically*, not simply by classification name. More precisely, if the longer lengths possess "arteriality" (i.e., continuity), as might be expected, the shorter paths should exhibit "locality" (i.e., discontinuity).

Discontinuity in terms of flow, when interpreted geometrically, can take several forms: (a) termination of path; (b) substantial change in direction, including reversal; and (c) severe path constriction (i.e., drastic reduction in size). There are no full-scale, implemented prototypes of such organizations in existing cities' repertoires, though there are partial examples of each of these concepts. The single large-scale example we have looked at so far is an abstract fractal construct that hints at the possibility of such a structure. Before looking at potential whole system geometries that might satisfy these requirements of length and width ratios, we briefly examine precedents that might show consistency with this distribution.

An analysis of the network of the city of Paris within the Peripherique, which includes Haussmann's wide and long boulevard incisions, shows that the street width frequency more or less follows a Pareto distribution, with only minor deviations.[11] It is worth noting that the pre–Haussmann Paris, even though it grew organically, would not reflect this distribution rule faithfully. Having grown organically and with several intermittent interventions, it has no graspable geometric order that can be held up as a prototype and as a visual counterpart to its mathematical expression.

Network systems that evolved in the contemporary, automotive era, now a century old, should show similar Pareto-type distributions of lengths, if they grew spontaneously by incremental additions and without a grand plan. Indeed, the pie chart—"Miles by Functional System"—shows that local streets, the lowest rank, represent 71 percent of the total U.S. urban network length, a value not far from the expected distribution. Moreover, allowing for imprecision in the definition of what constitute local and collector streets, the percentage could become even more congruent with the Pareto set, if the lowest two ranks were to be amalgamated.[12]

We also observe a similar but inexact match when looking at the amount of traffic carried by the respective road classes at the regional level: the lowest two tiers carry about 10 percent of the total volume. This disparity could be a sign of a welcome situation to the residents of neighborhood (lighter traffic), but it could also indicate dysfunctional higher-tier road elements.

Checking the lower scale of contemporary development, we find the following distribution of street lengths (allowing for idiosyncrasies within a range): arterials, 2; collectors, 14; locals, 60—very similar to the Pareto distribution in a plan of a typical subdivision. (See drawing titled "Hierarchy and Intersections in a Conventional Subdivision," page 96.)

Miles by Functional System: U.S. Total-Urban

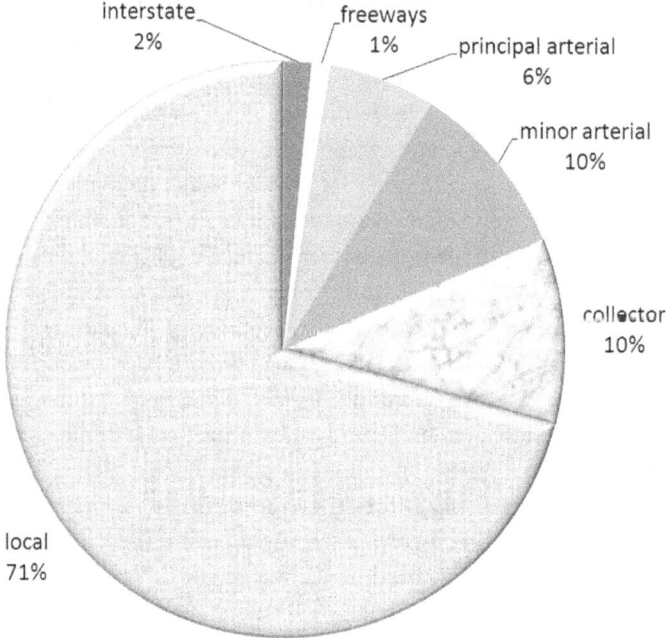

Distribution of Lengths by Road Class—U.S. Total Urban: The evolving road network system has naturally attained a state that closely approximates the Pareto distribution.

Daily VMTz by Functional System–LA, Long Beach, Santa Ana

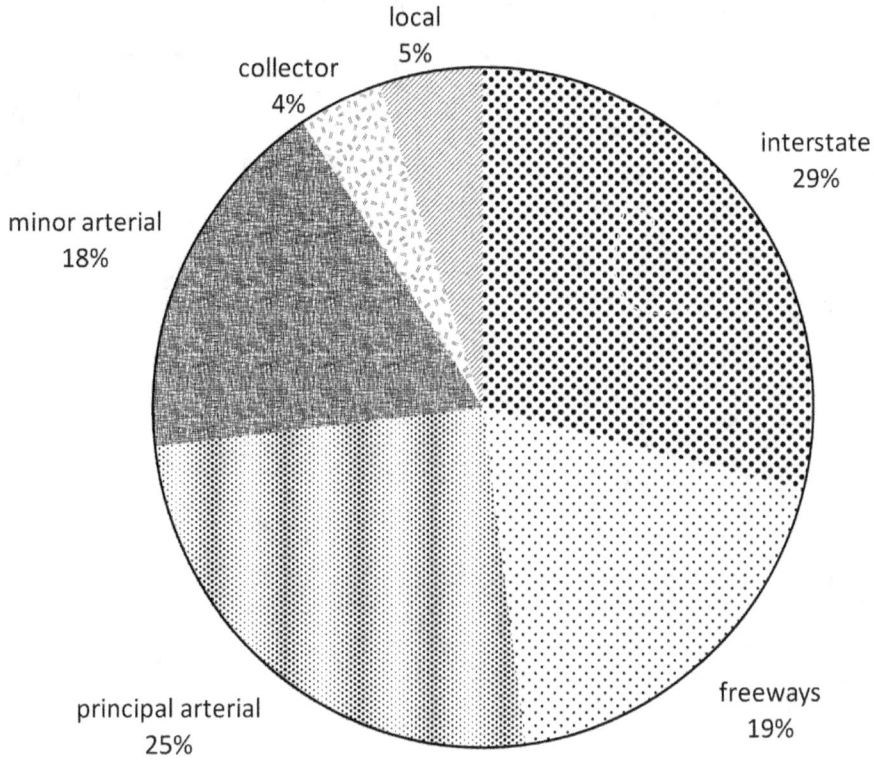

Miles Traveled by Functional System: The two neighborhood-scale streets, local and collector, in these districts carry about 10 percent of the total traffic volume, not reflecting the Pareto distribution precisely. It may be a sign of too dendrite a network structure or imprecise counting.

Clearly, the graphs and the quantities they represent deviate slightly from the ideal formulaic distribution. Deviations from the ideal may be expected due to several factors:

a. Certain phenomena, network elements and traffic distribution included, may not be amenable to high mathematical precision. The formula is observation-based, not experimentally derived; it therefore leaves room for variance. Moreover, the distribution of network sizes is derived primarily from natural dendrite structures that, as we saw, are dissimilar to traffic networks and, consequently, cannot be expected to precisely reflect them.

b. Definitions and categorizations of roads may vary between observers, thus affecting the accuracy of measurements—not an uncommon occurrence in non-physical sciences; much of the accuracy depends on what is measured and how.

c. Types of system configuration may obscure categorization. Some may admit traffic flows that deviate from the expected functional classification. Wider local and collector roads, for example, can be used to bypass clogged minor or principal arterials, thus distorting the distribution toward nonconforming results.

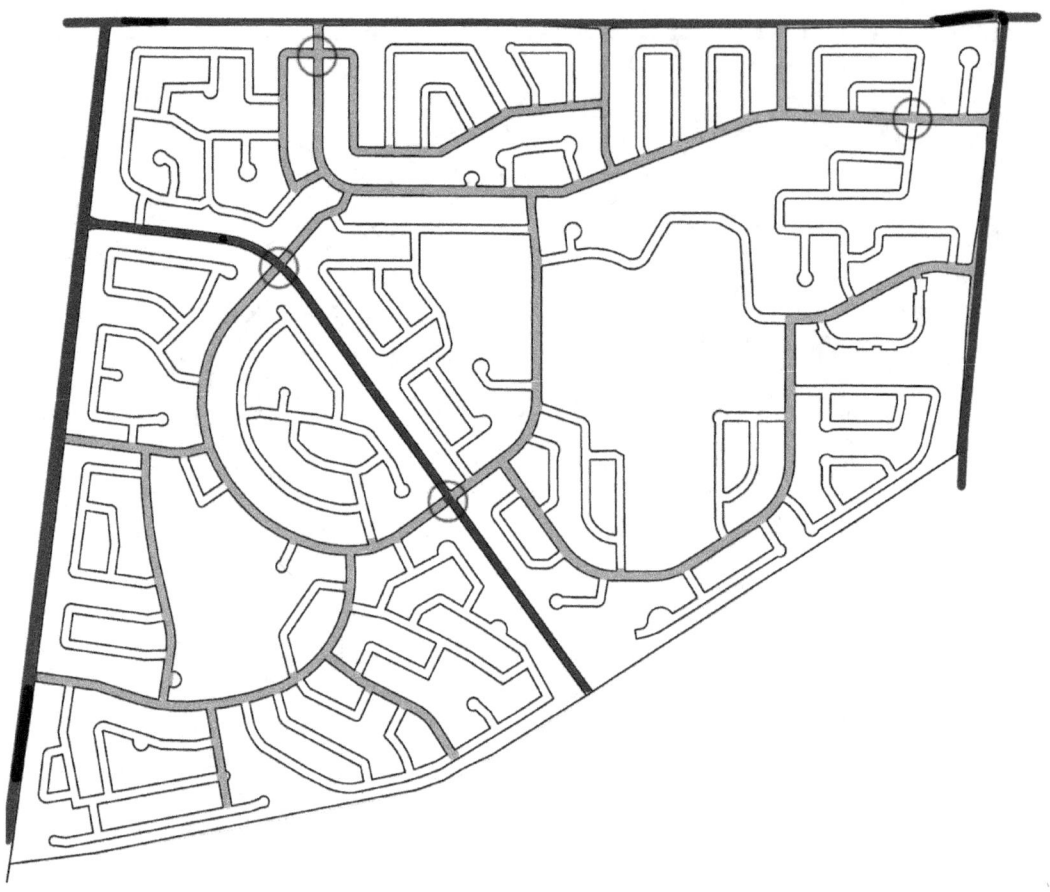

Hierarchy and Intersections in a Conventional Subdivision: Disregarding its random, idiosyncratic shapes, this 1970s subdivision exhibits a near–Pareto distribution of path lengths and a predominance of T-intersections analogous to the leaf structure.

This brief excursion to verify the correspondence of a theoretical proposition suggests that, allowing for some inescapable deviations, current road network systems conform generally to the distribution of sizes postulate. However, this general agreement at national, state and conurbation scales may not constitute sufficient direction for proposing a network model because:

    a. hidden in this agreement may lurk substantial disparities between districts that are smoothed out by the contrasting variances in individual values;

    b. the total network of regions, conurbations, districts and cities includes a patchwork of layout rules, often at odds with each other, that obscures the selection of the "correct" pattern; and

    c. all new contributions to city growth will generally be at the district rather than regional level, which implies that the highest tiers of the network would be given, predetermined, and therefore less amenable to adaptation.

This general congruence hides yet another fundamental observational flaw: it rests on counting the paths of mechanized traffic, leaving out walking and bicycling. Though presumed to often follow the same paths, pedestrians and bicycles are in a class of their own due to their speed and reach; often they do not mix either by prohibition (e.g., on freeways) or due to perceived lack of safety (e.g., on heavily trafficked main arterials).

This apparent agreement also ignores the contribution of subways to mobility within a city; should the rail-based subsurface mode be analyzed in terms of equivalent lane miles, the addition to the overall network system's length and width could be substantial, and its distribution among lengths could affect the frequencies considerably. It possesses arteriality and uninterrupted flow far superior to surface-based networks, and would require its own classification among them. For all these weaknesses of observation and omission, drawing concrete guidelines for the formation of an idealized network from the Pareto distribution would be a risky undertaking. However, we can use it in an advisory capacity, as it does have strong empirical foundations.

The principles that have emerged so far for the configuration of a network—namely, hierarchy, exclusion, and the distribution of sizes (lengths and widths)—apply well to mechanized surface transportation. Conformity to the inverse power law distribution, as validated by natural and unplanned human systems, may, with caution, also guide the generation of a contemporary network prototype for systems that deal with traffic flow.

However, neither the principles nor the distribution of lengths and widths are critical to a mathematical precision degree for pedestrian movement, as the pre-automotive history of cities shows. For foot and hoof movement, what matters most is directness of route and "level of service," a concept we will examine in the following sections.

As we saw in the transformation of the dendrite and open grid diagrams, it is possible to apply the principles of hierarchy, separation and the attendant arteriality to both. By applying these mechanized traffic principles strictly, however, the resulting system would tend to suppress route directness for pedestrians.

Two concepts, which were mentioned in passing earlier, need to be elevated into working principles for network configuration in general. Recent theoretical investigations have ventured in that direction. Both could be integrated into a contemporary network configuration that meets the performance criteria of both mechanized and active transportation. We will look next at the concept of "filtered permeability" and then the method of "level of service" evaluation for pedestrian movement.

Filtered Permeability

From the continuing adaptation of connectors to accommodate the evolving transport means, we see the inevitable assignment of exclusivity to certain modes on certain roads: railroads for trains; subways for underground trains; highways for automotive transport; and recently exclusive paths for bicycles. Also recently we have witnessed the creation of exclusive networks for pedestrians above grade (+15) and below grade. In the same vein, new bridges that span small city rivers are now built for pedestrians and bicycles only. All these exclusive right of ways, from highway to bridge, appear logical, self-evident, and are taken for granted. They are all connectors, each of a different variety for a specific mode and speed in response to the commonsense realization that not all modes can mix on all roads. Unlike other natural and man-made conduit systems, which carry only one type of "fluid," (i.e., water, air, blood, electrons and info-packets), roads accommodate a wide range of objects that are disparate in both size and speed. Consequently, the structural rules that govern these systems may not apply directly to the multi-speed, multi-size man-made system; after all, the entire city is a new "organic" system and its transport mechanisms very recent, in biological terms.

"Filtered permeability" is a logical extension of the exclusive dedication of connectors that responds to the disparity of means and speeds.[13] When applied systematically over a city district, usually at the neighborhood, foot-reach scale, it implies that a network can be laid out in a way that excludes certain modes (i.e., mechanized) from portions of it by giving the exclusive right to these portions to other modes (i.e., pedestrians and bicycles). This is already a fact with regard to certain transport vehicles—heavy trucks—that have designated routes in the city and are prohibited from traveling on other routes, even though it may be physically possible. From their viewpoint, a network that appears fully accessible it is not— by decree, not a physical transformation. Similarly, it is a fact, in certain cases, where extensive bicycle paths cover a wide city area, that they are entirely inaccessible to mechanized modes.

A similar approach would, by design, render portions of a network inaccessible to car drivers, giving preference to active transportation modes. Thus, again, what appears discontinuous for one mode is continuous for another; paths are available to one but not the other.

The diagram "Grid Adaptation for Arteriality and Active Transport" demonstrates this principle of exclusivity in its simplest form first and more elaborately in a second step. A grid network of about 200 by 200 feet assigns portions of every second street to pedestrians and bicycles. Cars can move in both directions as before; they simply "see" longer blocks in one direction. This initial transformation provides pedestrians with exclusive paths in one direction. It shows that while all north-south roads are accessible to vehicles from the periphery, only half of them are continuous; in other words, cars are "filtered out" at 10 intersections of five roads. (For the sake of simplicity, this diagram does not incorporate the necessary principles of arteriality and exclusion.)

A further development of this concept would create "islands" of pedestrian networks that encompass movement in both cardinal directions.

The lower diagram shows how a portion of the grid assigns certain parts of the network to pedestrian movement in both cardinal directions while at the same time incorporating the principles of hierarchy and separation and the resulting arteriality.

In this transformation, the hierarchy includes *local* pedestrian paths, the previously missing rung, and also *local* streets that change direction sharply and thereby lose their arteriality. The bounding streets of the island would be collectors or minor arterials in a complete system, depending on their position in the network. They maintain their arteriality.

Though the term "filtered permeability" is relatively new, the concept it expresses has already been applied variously in existing and new city districts. We introduce it in this chapter as an essential characteristic of a contemporary network, crucial in filling the missing rank in the hierarchy of connectors and the missing element in the distribution of sizes, down to the narrow footpath or urban through-the-building access path.[14]

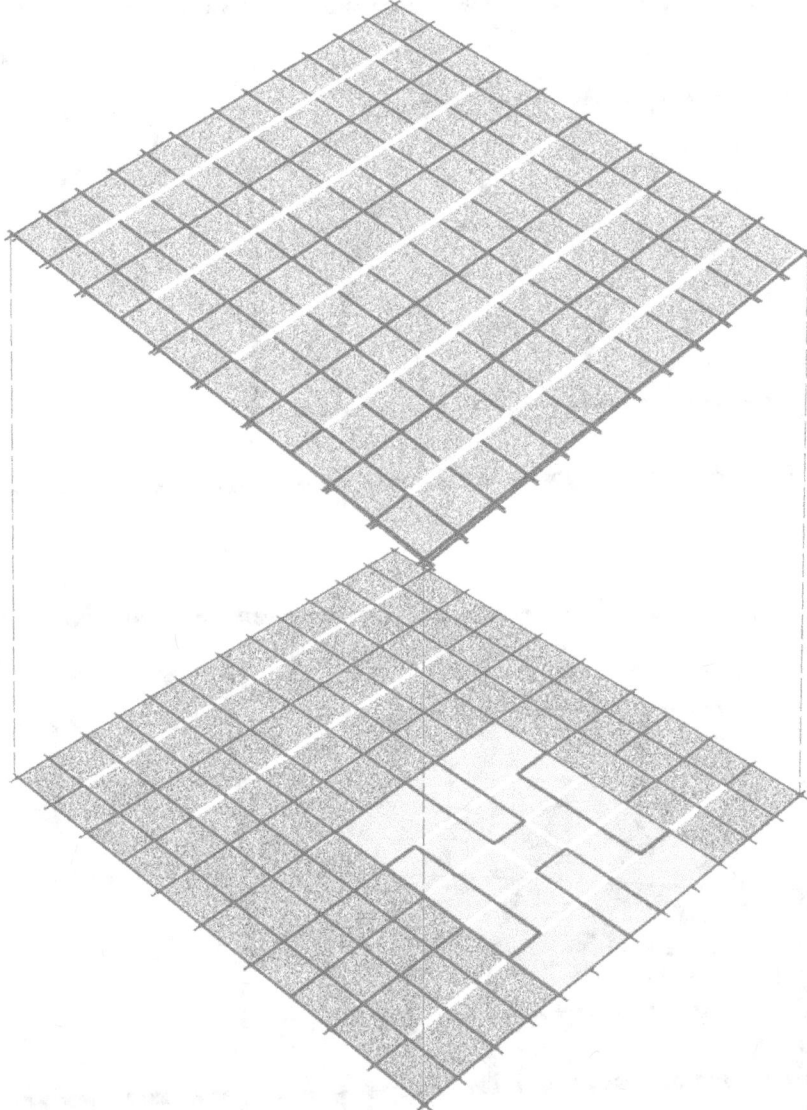

Grid Adaptation for Arteriality and Active Transport: Starting with a uniform grid, selected N-S streets become pedestrian (white). In the second step, a neighborhood excludes through traffic and transforms sections of previous paths to pedestrian paths.

Level of Service Method and Findings

Level of service (LOS) evaluation systems are already in use to judge the performance of signalized and non-signalized road intersections, measured in seconds of waiting (from 10 to 80). Pedestrian road crossing is one cause for the delay of automotive traffic at intersections, but from the pedestrian's perspective the reverse is true, particularly when crossing multi-lane boulevards; were it not for the traffic, pedestrians would continue on their trip uninterrupted.

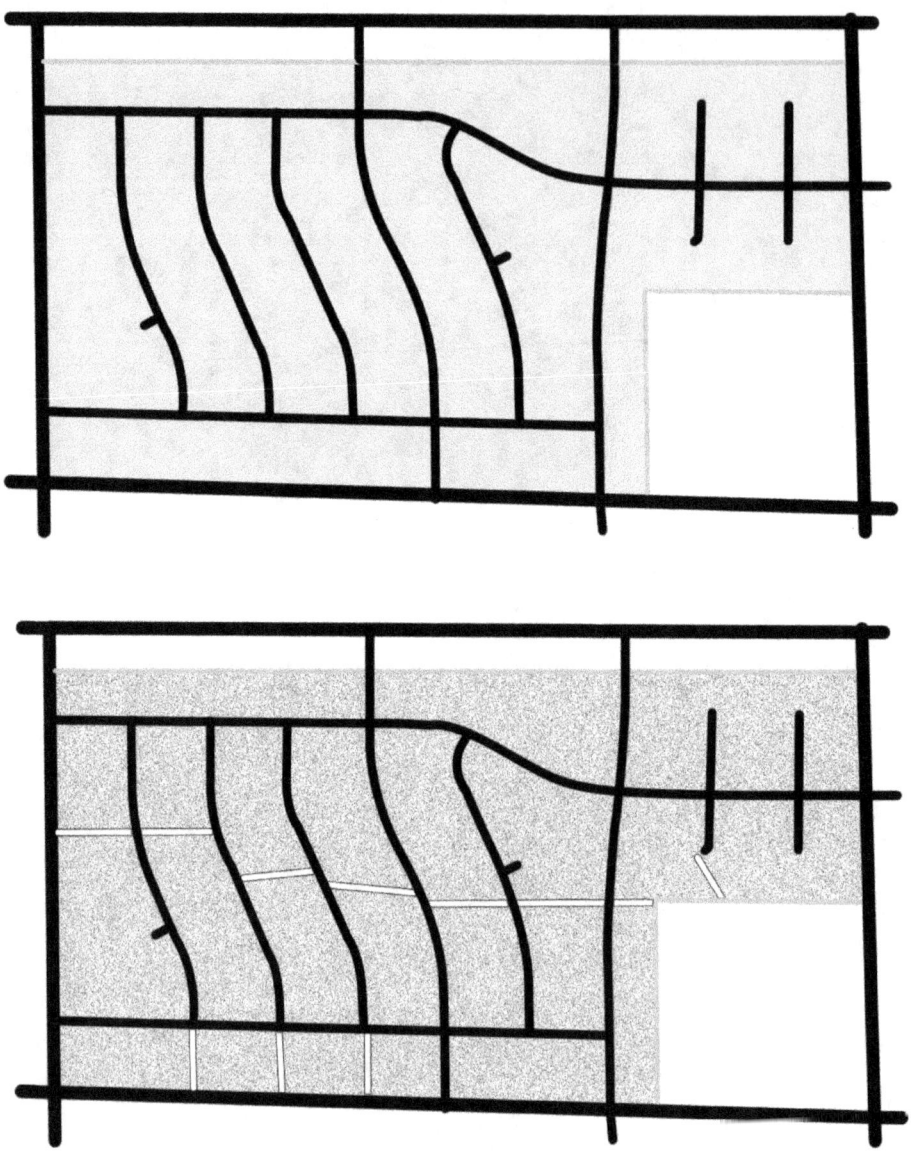

Adaptation for Pedestrian Connectivity—Level of Service: The addition of strategic pedestrian paths (white, bottom) to the original plan (top) improves pedestrian accessibility dramatically (original design by Amy Shackleton and Paul Stangl).

Intersection stopping is more crucial to vehicle movement than to pedestrians: decelerating, stopping, waiting and accelerating all degrade overall trip efficiency and waste fuel and shorten engine life. For pedestrians, it simply means loss of time (though safety is a major concern). When time *and* effort increase in reaching a chosen destination, a pedestrian is not well served.

New research proposes a method to evaluate when a pedestrian is served well by a district's network layout.[15]

As we saw in the previous chapter, foot and hoof cities had a radius of about ¼ mile to

1/3 mile (400–500 meters), a distance of a 5-minute walk to the center and a 10-minute walk to cross the entire town. This was the daily pedestrian reach—an area of about 250 acres (100 hectares). Walking usually meant exertion, especially when carrying water, fuel or goods—rarely a recreational activity. This is not the case with automotive mobility. A five-minute journey by car would cover a distance of 1.5–3 miles (2.5–5 kilometers)—that is, five to ten times greater than by walking and with practically no effort. The five-minute drive would shape a much different settlement than the five-minute walk: its area would grow from 250 acres (100 hectares) to as much as 25,000 acres (10,000 hectares).

While a few hours of leisurely walking would have been sufficient to take in most of an early town's 250 acres, it would take several days of constant walking to survey the new town of 25,000 acres—the equivalent of one hundred early towns, side by side. Such a multi-day stroll is an unlikely enterprise on foot; other means of travel would normally mediate a foot-based exploration.

This inevitable use of other means of transport, public or personal, to reach and explore many parts of the new, larger city on foot reintroduces the idea of pedestrian "islands" that emerged out of the principles of arteriality and filtered permeability. These islands, being primarily a pedestrian reach territory, should in principle exhibit a high level of service (LOS) for pedestrians.

The variety of configurations of early towns suggests the possibility that there may be an equal variety of configurations for the new "islands" or "villages" within the much larger city that could meet the requirements for pedestrian movement just as well as the old towns. The method that was devised to evaluate the pedestrian level of service of an island or district confirms this possibility. It is based on measuring the directness of a route from any house lot to the "island" perimeter and vice versa. Directness is measured as a ratio between the straight line distance and the actual path, which implies the relative amount of route elongation. The percentage of the lots that achieve less than a 1.6 elongation ratio defines the good level of service; the higher the value over 50 percent, the more pedestrian-oriented the island is.

The analysis shows that the shape of the network has little bearing on the LOS; a rectilinear grid can have just as low an LOS as a curvilinear network. It mostly depends on the size of city blocks and the presence of pedestrian paths. For example, in a 250-acre island (the size of an early town), a rectilinear layout with 800-feet-long blocks achieves 55 percent LOS, while a layout with 400-feet-long blocks reaches an 85 percent LOS.

The diagram titled "Adaptation for Pedestrian Connectivity" shows how the addition of strategically placed pedestrian paths within a non-rectilinear "island" can raise its LOS from 20 percent to 80 percent. It is worth noting, in the context of pursuing a contemporary network, that this layout represents a *hybrid,* a fusion between the all-roads-for-all-modes conventional practice and all-streets-for-two-modes in the pre-automotive era. This fusion dedicates specific parts of the network to one mode—pedestrians—which connect or merge with the remainder of the network.

We have now established the principles of hierarchy, separation, filtered permeability and pedestrian level of service (PLOS), and we have seen transformations of inherited and current network layout concepts that may incorporate these principles partially or wholly. As noted earlier, there remains a curious case of synergy and conflict bound up in the dual role of the arterial street as a thoroughfare for traffic and as a place for commerce and social activity. We return to this conundrum in the next section.

A Contemporary Thoroughfare

The ironic conflict between traffic that a vibrant commercial thoroughfare thrives on and traffic that degrades its potential for transaction activity takes us briefly back to the evolution of thoroughfares and transport.

Frontage restriction, or frontal access prohibition, is simply the final ironic outcome of this evolution, entirely antithetical to previous organic growth. The early main street was primarily a space between buildings, sometimes a gathering place and other times a marketplace, but always a main thoroughfare. There were no rules of movement, as the dominant group, pedestrians, moved spontaneously and erratically, each at their own pace and according to their interests, entirely unconstrained. When carts, carriages, jitneys and other wheeled vehicles, drawn by horses, proliferated in the seventeenth and eighteenth centuries, the first rule of movement appeared: wheeled vehicles would have to drive on only half the street in each direction—a strange rule when the other half may have appeared empty for much of the time (the emptiness of the "other side" is still evident today in rush-hour automobile traffic on some thoroughfares). The *divided* (but not separated) bidirectional high street was thus born. (Strict division of counter-flows is also present in all natural and man-made systems—for example, electrical and HVAC systems.) This first division was by edict only and it did not affect the free movement of pedestrians on and across the street; there were no physical changes to the street surface.

The division of the street became stricter, and it finally took the form of a physical barrier, first for cars, to prevent left turns, and then, more pronounced, to prevent pedestrians from crossing a thoroughfare indiscriminately (fences barring the crossing). Pedestrian movement became controlled and regimented; the more important the thoroughfare in a network system, the tougher the restrictions and the more prominent the barriers that were introduced. In addition to the median, the sidewalks were also fenced along the main thoroughfare to prevent rogue pedestrians from crossing during traffic gaps and jumping over the median barrier.

The unintended outcome of these progressive measures for protecting pedestrians and drivers from potentially injurious or lethal circumstances was the suppression of the commercial and social activity on the thoroughfare, now confined mostly to each of the two separated sides.

The median is a protector, a regulator and a barrier all at the same time. The lanes of traffic are potential carriers of customers and also of the risk factor in crossing; the more lanes, the higher the risk. This dichotomy of qualities in the same network element—the arterial or thoroughfare—has drawn constant attention, and at least one solution has emerged, which abolishes the median and routes the counter-flow streams of traffic on either side of a city block. The outcome is a shorter crossing distance, no median or fences, and a new block on which pedestrians can roam freely from store to service and to leisure activity without crossing a thoroughfare; they are *in the thoroughfare*, as they were in its pre-automotive stages.

Early sketches for this type of mutation of the main arterial appeared in theoretical speculations about its future by Kevin Lynch.[16] Precursors of this transformation of the arterial thoroughfare have appeared in the history of thoroughfares in existing city districts and, recently, in new developments.

According to historian Mark Girouard, the main street stores did not appear with the birth of a village or town. Market was an event, not a place, though it did take place at a specific spot in town where space allowed. And since it was a transient event, so were the stalls that were set up to sell merchandise. (A faint reminder of this transitory nature today is the "sidewalk sale.") As the frequency of market events increased, so did the permanency of the stalls; they became stores. The stores were in fact within the thoroughfare's right of way; other stores gradually emerged on either side of the street.[17]

Currently, a partial transformation can be experienced in certain central districts, where traffic is partly or entirely excluded from the arterial, thus converting two parallel city blocks into one, where the street becomes a space and a place and loses its character and function as a "route." Vehicular traffic is diverted onto streets parallel to the arterial, usually designated as one-directional flow. Many contemporary cities contain examples of this transformation of a thoroughfare, which has been baptized a "pedestrian mall" to denote the absence of mechanized traffic.

Another variation of an evolutionary transformation of an existing main street in small towns or cities is as follows: a two-way main street (thoroughfare) that carried all the traffic in town and through town is coupled with another to relieve the volume, congestion and exhaust fumes and to create a more congenial environment for shopping and socializing.

A conscious application of this new form of thoroughfare, where two one-way streets that constitute the main traffic through the town inscribe city blocks intended for commercial and public uses, has been applied in plans for new districts at the turn of the twenty-first century. They also found a theoretical, diagrammatic expression.[18]

The principles of a contemporary network configuration and the resolution of the dichotomy in the role of the main thoroughfare (arterial) that were reviewed in this chapter lead to the shaping of a network diagram that incorporates the sum of these ideas—the fused grid—the subject of the next chapter.

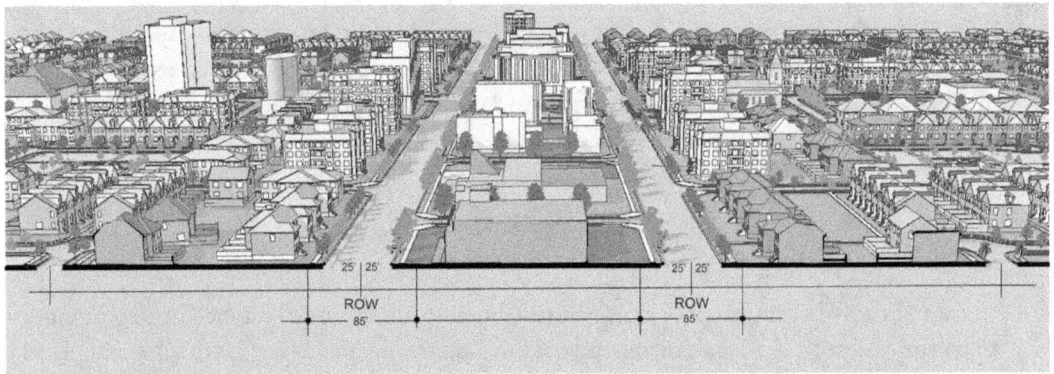

A Contemporary Thoroughfare: Similar to incidental one-way couplets in central-city districts, this is a planned arrangement for major boulevards that connect districts. The mixed zoning for the intervening block, combined with the abundance of commuters, will inevitably entice a range of appropriate uses.

5

The Fused Grid Design Process

"The street is an invention." —Spiro Kostof[1]

In the previous two chapters we discussed the reasons why the fused grid network model may respond well to contemporary issues of land use and transportation. We have summarized evidence in support of this contention, including persistent stresses of the street networks and their users, the multiplicity of adaptations to alleviate these stresses, and some recent thinking that opens the door to the formulation of a new comprehensive model. In this chapter, we illustrate the process by which fused grid neighborhoods would be designed, starting with the general diagram and proceeding to specific neighborhood scale configurations. Case studies in Chapter 7 will exemplify this process by looking at specific projects.

Simply put, a fused grid denotes a "fusion of grids," including a fusion of vehicular, non-vehicular and green space networks (or grids). This is not a novel concept in itself. And although grids are not a critical prerequisite, we suggest that in the pursuit of efficient use of land, essential for reducing the use of natural resources (of which land is one), a grid can be shown to be the most efficient organizing geometry. The novel element in fused grid model is the configuration of local streets that keeps non-local vehicular traffic on the perimeter; it uses discontinuous loops to manage local vehicular accessibility, promotes active transport across neighborhoods, overlays a restorative green space network within one-minute walking distance of every residence, and manages the safety and mobility for non-local vehicular trips via a perimeter network of roundabout controlled intersections and one-way arterial boulevards. A successful fused grid design can be defined by a number of expected positive outcomes when compared to traditional neighborhoods, as we shall see in subsequent sections of this chapter and in the following chapter, which provides corroborating evidence of its potential benefits.

We begin this design process description with a discussion of the supporting on- and off-road transport grid, including its orthogonal origins. We discuss design principles and steps to develop individual 40-acre (16-hectare) neighborhood network modules as well as 160-acre (64-hectare) district modules. These street networks are supplemented with a grid of green spaces that form part of the circulation system for active modes. Finally, we provide case study examples to flesh out these concepts.

Grids

Orthogonal geometry (appearing in settlement plans as a grid) has been and continues to be the easiest to use for drawing up buildings, surveying parcels of land, allocating land and laying out street networks. For a network, once the principal directions of the streets

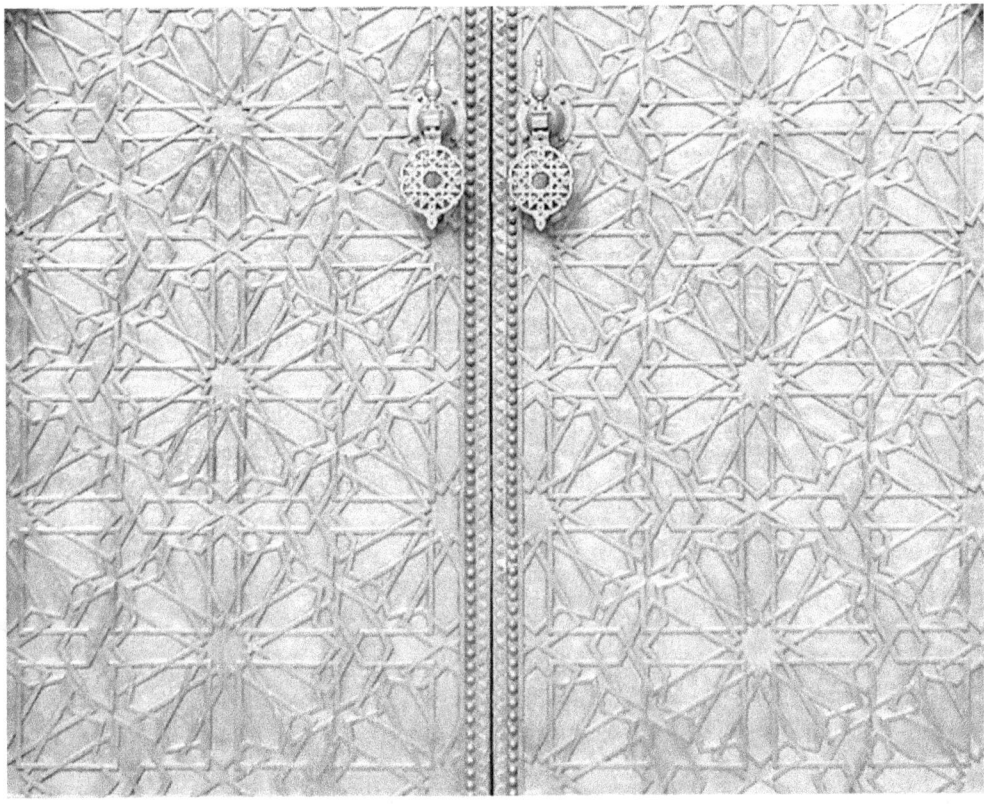

Ordered Complexity: Geometric shapes can vary from simple—a square—to very complex interwoven polygons, such as this pattern on a palace door. The order is obvious, but the generative method is not readily apparent.

have been set, the rest follows a repetitive set of steps that place streets and blocks of chosen sizes in horizontal and vertical arrays (or cardinal directions) that reach the periphery of a designated area for a new settlement or an expansion of an existing one.

Working with a pattern that incorporates not just precise geometry, as the simple grid does, but also more than one organizing principle, becomes more demanding both technically and in practice than the simple array of identical components. When a pattern includes several individual stencil components, as the fused grid does, the possible combinations increase, as does the complexity of application. Arab decorative patterns, for example, are visually intriguing and hard to decipher; yet they follow precise rules that produce a pleasing effect of order. With complexity also comes an increased level of freedom, as choices multiply. To exercise that freedom, familiarity with a range of options creates a solid launching pad—the purpose of this chapter.

Other rule-bound constructions, such as fractals or tessellated polygons, require mathematical formulae and, in some cases, computing power. Replication by simple observation would be taxing and likely unsuccessful, and space efficiency could be compromised.

From the era of the Greek colonization of the Mediterranean and the subsequent Roman conquests, new outpost cities were laid out according to an orthogonal geometric pattern. The same is true of the Spanish and English colonial cities in the Americas. Not only did the city layouts follow orthogonal geometry but the surrounding agricultural lands were also subdivided in rectangular parcels (quadrangular land subdivision dates to the Egyptian pharaohs, and even earlier). When these large parcels were apportioned, they became the property of a colony's new citizens. As a result of this land subdivision and the property rights thus enshrined, property boundaries became the de facto constraint on the size and the form of development well into the future existence of these cities and up to contemporary times.[2]

In this inherited context, it may come as no surprise that this rectilinear parcel geometry becomes a central element of the fused grid layout. It is a given framework for laying out a network of streets that complies with preexisting property boundaries, and, in principle, there is no strong reason not to follow it. Conversely, there are no compelling reasons to apply a different geometry. It is simple to understand and work with and, on the ground, very efficient to survey. Apart from these virtues, there are also *contemporary* reasons for following it: first, motorized traffic flows better on a straight road with long vistas; second, orthogonal (i.e., right-angle) intersections offer the best visibility conditions and are the safest compared to odd-angle intersections; and third, orthogonal shapes pack most efficiently, increasing land productivity. Conversely, as we have seen, contemporary higher speeds and four-way intersections can be disadvantageous—hence the need for proper management of local and through vehicular traffic flows, by means of network configuration and not necessarily by departing from orthogonal geometry.

As we shall see later, site topography and constraints may, in certain cases, demand other geometries. It can be shown that the principles of the fused grid model can remain intact under any geometry. There are plenty of examples of contemporary configurations that are set within large-scale orthogonal property limits that abandon orthogonal geometry within the given boundaries. These examples provide a rich vocabulary that can guide the designer's hand when dealing with non-orthogonal layouts. The best place to start, however, in order to gain proficiency in using the fused grid principles with flexibility under any and all site constraints, is with a geometry that is easily understood and drawn—the orthogonal plan. That geometry respects and reflects preexisting constraints of land subdivision and offers a practical path to optimize the layout results. Once familiar with the process of using rectangular layouts, the step to other geometries is easy to take.

The design of a fused grid layout starts with a substratum of an orthogonal grid that will guide the subsequent layers of streets, paths and open spaces of neighborhoods and districts. The dimensions of the grid can be uniform or variable in response to the market context of the lands subject to development. Certain districts may require wide and deep lots while others, where modest housing is to be built, may favor narrow or shallow lots. Similarly, blocks intended for large buildings such as apartment complexes or commercial and institutional uses will require generous non-typical dimensions. As a result, grid line frequencies can vary in both directions to accommodate the anticipated uses of land: the underlying grid would be non-uniform. It would be modulated according to market expectations and the developer's perceptions of client propensity for preferred lot sizes, house types and price ranges. However, it will nonetheless remain an orthogonal grid substratum.

Modularity

Using clues from the adaptations of existing settlements, planned new developments and numerous theoretical works, the fused grid model proposes a modular construction.[3] We are surrounded by modular constructions of all kinds: some invisible, such as the molecules that make up elements or compounds, and some visible, such as tree leaves and fruits (e.g., grape clusters). Some occur in nature, such as the cells of an organism, and others are man-made, such as quilt patches, floor tiles or computer parts. Modularity continues up the scale from atoms to galaxies, and from living cells to organs, to organisms, and to collections of organisms, such as a typical beehive or anthill. In all these examples, an assembly of individual elements assumes new properties that belong to the collective only, and not to its separate elements; the water "module," for example, has properties not found in either of its two constituent elements. A beehive is a functioning whole, with roles and routines, not an accidental assembly of individual insects. Consistent with this pervasive presence of modular constructs, the fused grid introduces modularity in the layout of neighborhoods and districts.

Founded cities, which we mentioned earlier, exhibited three levels of modularity in their plans: the lot and house, the block and street, and the whole city with its protective perimeter. In laying out colonies, blocks and streets were set out in a uniform repetitive sequence that terminated at the predetermined perimeter. The block dimensions were based on traditional, known house sizes. The city module, based on walking distances, acquired its functionality as a unit when certain blocks were given to city functions, such as the agora, theater, temple and forum. It has been documented that Roman castra (military outposts) followed this pattern of modular construction faithfully.[4] Cities did not expand; with some exceptions, they generally established copies of themselves—colonies—new modules elsewhere.

This three-level modularity is only one possible structure. One city—Savannah—supplies a unique example of an intermediary scale of modularity that was introduced with a social intention, a useful prototype to recapture in contemporary planning.[5] Its city blocks are assembled in groups of eight, four of which are residential, with four smaller ones for common-use buildings. The eight blocks are configured so as to create and surround a common open space. Thus an intermediary, repeatable cell of organization is created that exhibits unique properties not found in the block and street level of modularity. This eight-block repeatable unit could be seen as a "neighborhood unit" with a distinct, strong focal point— the open space—and its common trust lots and (public use) buildings as the first level of service and social organization. Although it is widely recognized that neighborhoods are more social than physical constructs, the presence of a physical structure has been shown to raise the probability of social network formation.[6] It is also understood that such bonds are aided by the presence of low-level services such as a local store, park bench, community garden, or playground. To the extent that a central square (agora, forum) functioned as the main and important social space at the village, town or city scale, its analog could replicate that role at the neighborhood scale. The fused grid adopts this intermediate scale of modularity to create "neighborhoods," each with a focal point and distinct boundaries.

The Savannah–like intermediate level modularity may be an essential and important attribute for contemporary city districts for four reasons:

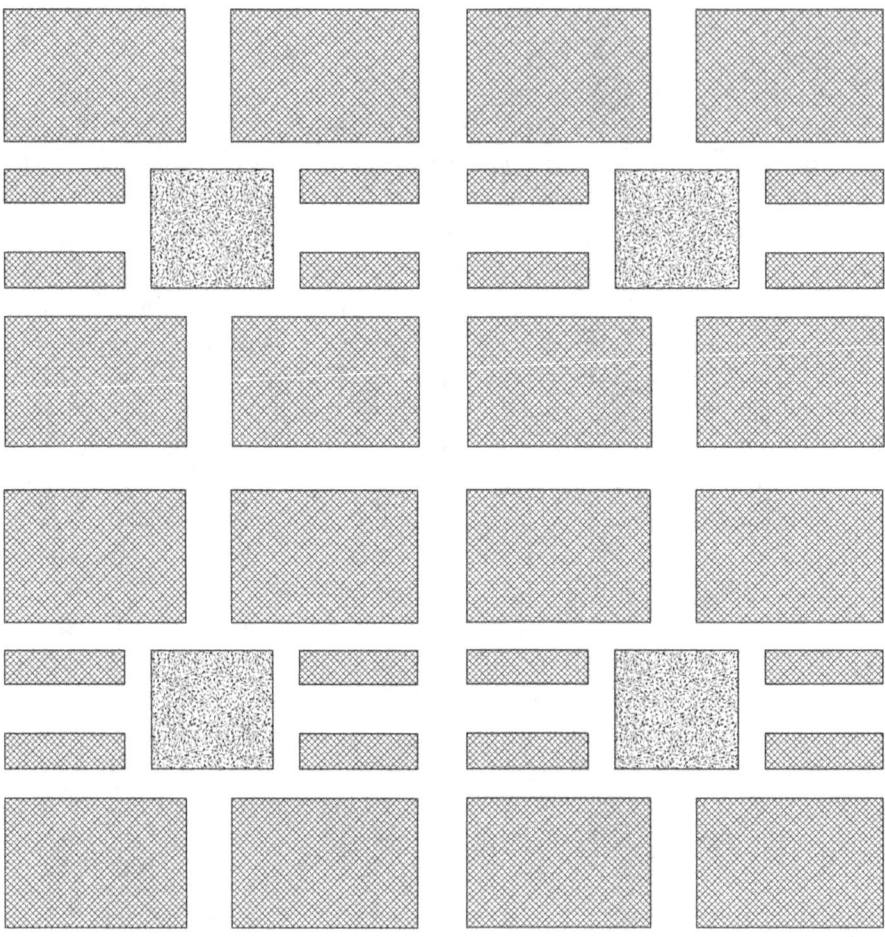

Middle-Level Modularity: Of all regular city patterns, Savannah's layout is the only one that is built of modular units larger than a city block—an assembly of eight with a common open space in the center.

1. Physical city boundaries have disappeared.
2. Administrative boundaries keep on expanding.
3. Social boundaries or identifiers have become meaningless or been repudiated.
4. Cities now expand to engulf other neighboring towns, imposing a redefinition of identity and of presumed affiliation or affinity.

In this fluid environment that cultivates anonymity and lack of association, a neighborhood milieu that supports familiarity could be seen as a constructive counterpoint. Moreover, a grid pattern facilitates contiguous modularity that provides for the most economic provision of civic services (i.e., sewer, water, refuse and emergency).

SIZE OF NEIGHBORHOOD MODULE

The optimal size of the neighborhood grid module results from two unrelated constraints:

1. the historically convenient walking distance of about ¼ mile (400 m); and
2. the more recent historical subdivision of land into ownership parcels in increments of 40 acres, "a quarter section" (16 hectares)—this latter constraint prevails mostly in North America.

Walking as a determinant of settlement size dominates land-use patterns in most early, inevitably pedestrian, cities. A large proportion of them had an approximate diameter of ½ mile to ⅔ mile (800–1000 meters) (a ten- to fifteen-minute walk across town). Walking to nearby destinations remains a criterion from antiquity to the present. This walk-based dimension, combined with the frequent presence of two intersecting main thoroughfares, divided early cities into four quadrants roughly ¼ mile (400 meters) on each side. The coincidence of land property parcels of that size today, particularly in the Americas, makes it simply a convenient choice for a planning module. However, other constraints, such as preexisting roads, streams, lakes and woodlots, could modify the size of the module to suit such special conditions, while the modular construction of the district would remain intact. Similarly, other equally unalterable conditions may lead to larger modules, and also maintain the modular construction of a district. A variety of module sizes can be created to suit a range of conditions, such as those described above.

Street Types

Streets, in their long history, have been recognized as wide or narrow, main or side, straight or crooked. These are cross-sectional and shape characteristics, not typological. As we saw in Chapter 4 when discussing the fused grid's theoretical foundations, key twentieth-century planners have sensed the need for and recommended new road types for local, residential streets: loops and cul-de-sacs. These may have varied morphological characteristics, just like all previous streets. What distinguishes them is their role in the network system—they are discontinuous or "local." Local is a typological characteristic, an *invention* that is derived from a hierarchical structure and its corresponding nomenclature.

As such, loop and cul-de-sac streets provide origin or destination points, but no connections between other parts of the network. These result in quiet and safe neighborhood environments, as expected by planners and residents alike and as experienced in practice.[7] This traffic impermeability advantage has a converse effect of lack of connectivity (but not necessarily, as we discuss below).

These new street types quickly became enormously popular, confirmed by house prices on cul-de-sacs being generally higher than those on through streets. Stemming from their widespread application, several valid criticisms emerged, including that they:

1. put pedestrians and cyclists at a disadvantage; and
2. provided only a single access into and out of neighborhoods, creating traffic congestion and safety concerns where they intersect with arterial two-way roads.

In response to these valid criticisms, refined versions of these street types evolved over time—the connected cul-de-sac and loop (or crescent). The refinement consists in differentiating between vehicular and pedestrian permeability: connections between these new types of

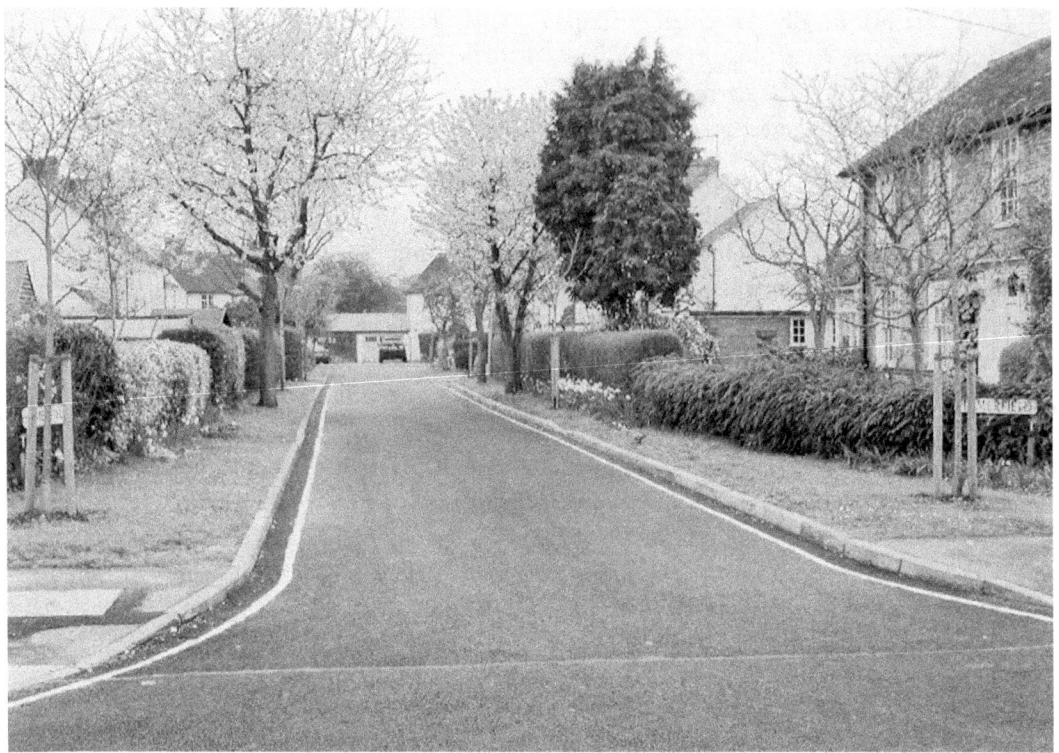

The Classic Cul-de-sac: A short, narrow, terminating street as envisaged and applied by R. Unwin and his followers (photograph Welwyn Garden City).

streets are exclusively active transport routes. For this new attribute of connectivity, planners have renamed the cul-de-sac a "thru-de-sac." An alternative to its other common name, "dead end," has also been coined—"live end" (alluding to play and social activity). As for the loop, an appropriate name for the new version has likewise been proposed—"loose loop." Whatever the name, their essential new attribute is that they connect to each other with paths unavailable to motorized traffic. Their capacity to connect beyond their apparent end has been officially recognized in certain jurisdictions by the installation of traffic signs indicating visually the presence of a path for pedestrians or bicycles, or both.

The second presumed weakness, which is in fact their advantage, is highly dependent on the size of the neighborhood, the configuration of its street network and the length of the cul-de-sac or loop. It points to the usual tendency to overdo an element that is seen to deliver positive outcomes. In other words, a disciplined and judicious use can eliminate these presumed weaknesses, as we shall see in the next chapter. The fused grid introduces such discipline, based on the modular construction of neighborhoods.

The exact shape of the "through-de-sac" and "loose loop" can vary, and both can be used singly or in combination within a neighborhood. They can also form mutated versions that combine the two types into one assembly, which is then used to form a neighborhood. The diagram titled "Five Basic Street Forms" shows the local street types and their mutations both in isolation and in combinations, always in reference to the neighborhood boundary at which they terminate.

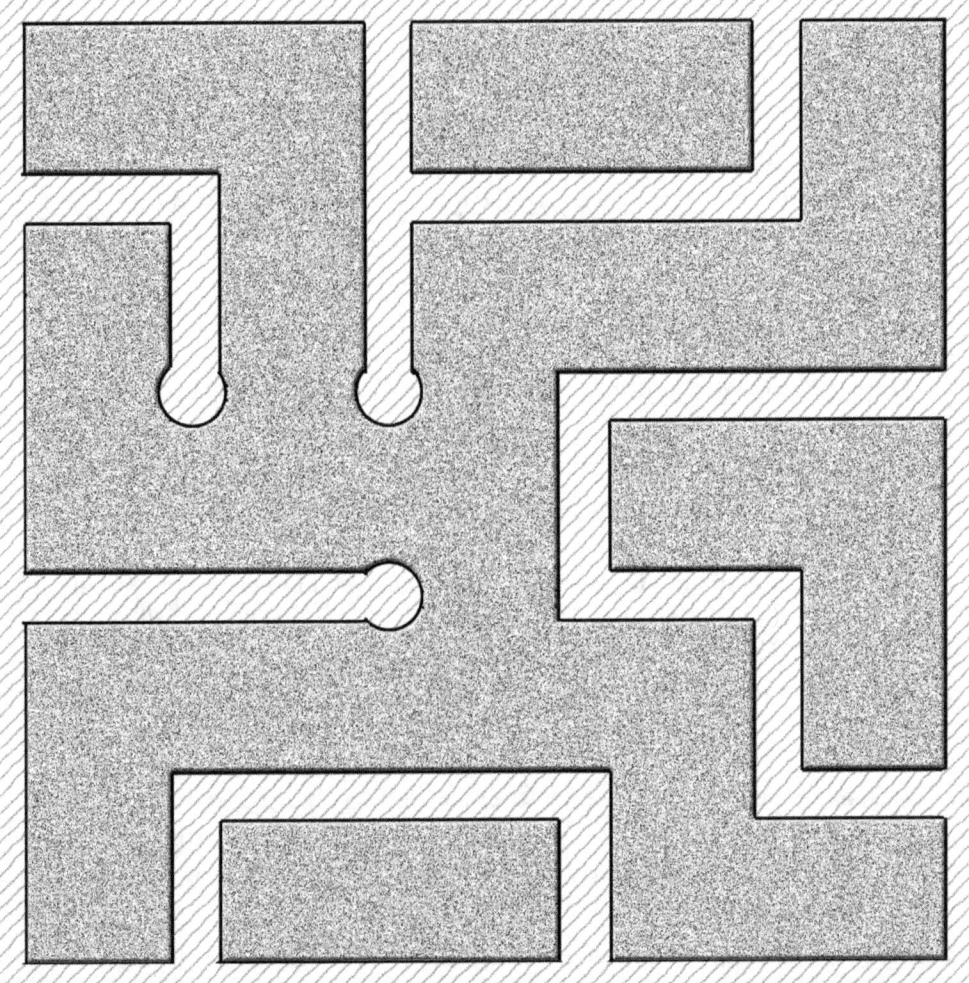

Five Basic Street Forms: Non-through neighborhood streets return traffic to the road of origin and are either loops or cul-de-sacs, or else a combination of the two. Their geometry and shape can vary.

The Design Process

Having many street and neighborhood configurations in hand, we can look at the method of joining streets and blocks to construct neighborhood modules of variable sizes. We introduce the design process with a short discussion to confirm vocabulary and process assumptions and lexicons for practitioners—planners, engineers, developers, decision-makers, and so forth. Six major steps involved in most design processes are listed below. While many permutations exist for this basic design process, we assume that they will be followed with necessary adjustments made to suit particular design and regulatory practices.

The main steps encountered in any design process include the following:

- Problem definition—market opportunities, community values, project goals
- Data collection—site, regulatory, stakeholder, decision-maker

- Analysis—brainstorm concepts, design refinements
- Consultation—evaluation criteria, weights, scores
- Recommendations—budget estimates, regulatory approvals, final designs
- Construction—monitoring, maintenance, measures of success

Assuming this generic design process, the fused grid equivalent adheres to a set of overarching principles, which then flow into prescriptive design steps, first at the neighborhood level and finally at the district level.

Overarching Design Principles

The overarching design principles that permeate every fused grid module, regardless of module size, are as follows:

1. **Filtered permeability**. Neighborhoods are so constructed as to prevent (filter out) through traffic but enable (filter through) complete human-powered accessibility to all their parts.
2. **Paths match the mode**. Connector types correspond to travel modes and can be independent or combined, as long as filtered permeability is fully maintained within the neighborhood module.
3. **Focal point, common space, crossroads**. Every neighborhood has a focal point that acts as a crossroads; pedestrians crossing the neighborhood would ideally pass through that space.
4. **Taming speed**. As posted speeds are frequently ignored, it is up to the street geometry to tame car speed to less than 30 km/hr through self-reinforcing and safe street design configuration. Short street lengths and turns, along with tailored widths, achieve this taming effect.

These principles are expressed diagrammatically in the drawing titled "Shaping a Differentiated Network."

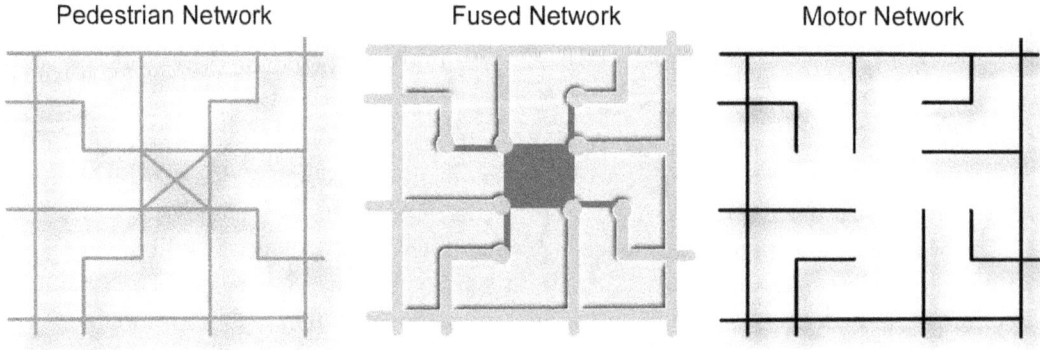

Pedestrian Network   Fused Network   Motor Network

Shaping a Differentiated Network: A network that reflects the relative capacity and speed of movement of two modes—a fused grid—equalizes the travel choices while improving a neighborhood's ambiance.

With a basic vocabulary of *local* street types in hand, the four principles of organization, and the underlying orthogonal geometry, the stage is set for the design of neighborhood modules.

Neighborhood Modules

One approach for beginning the fused grid design process at the level of a 40-acre (16-hectare) neighborhood is modifying an underlying schematic grid through elimination of street segments. The drawing titled "Four Steps to Fused Grid" demonstrates the progression from a regular, uniform grid to a fused grid through that process. The result is a neighborhood module that exclusively uses loops (connected loops).

These diagrams show only the road network structure. Completing the fusion process requires the addition of green space and active transport path networks.

Neighborhood Design Principles

Independent of the typical recurring interfaces described in the previous section, site conditions may impose restrictions on the size and shape of a neighborhood. We have already seen a few configurations that are based on the optimal size of 400 by 400 meters, and many more are possible and have appeared in other publications

However, simple dimensional limitations—property size; preexisting municipal land-use allocations; adjacency to existing highways; abandoned rural right of ways; and natural features—will often necessitate the layout of neighborhood cells with overall dimensions that are neither optimal nor square, nor even orthogonal. These modified, irregular cells can also abide by the principles of organization that preserve the essential, positive characteristics of a neighborhood. What they all have in common is a set of design guidelines:

1. Whatever its size, a neighborhood module will always have a discernible, defined perimeter that borders on, or connects to, a transport corridor of a rank higher than a local street.[8]
2. Vehicular streets emanate from the neighborhood core and always head out toward the perimeter; they never cross, and always protect, the core. Their intersections

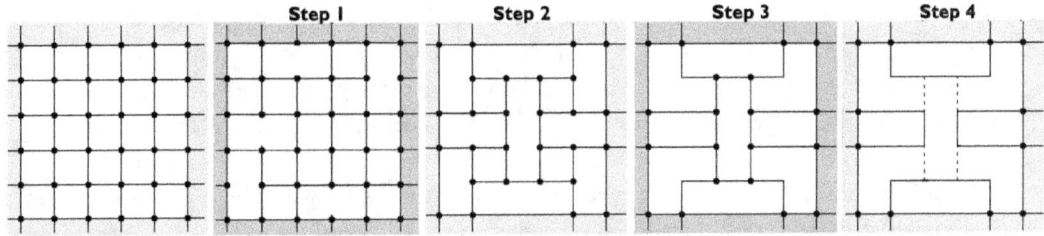

Four Steps to Fused Grid: Starting with a regular grid, the gradual elimination of selective street segments yields, in this case, four loops and four foot paths (dashed lines) that connect the entire neighborhood. This four-step process can give rise to a variety of configurations.

with perimeter streets are generally three-way and may be controlled by round-abouts or right-in/right-out physical restrictions.

3. There are no vehicular intersections within the neighborhood, unless unavoidable; only paths intersect or merge with streets. If intersections must occur within the cell, they are always three-way and controlled by traffic circles.

4. An open "community" space is set at or near the core of the neighborhood, with smaller restorative space opportunities dispersed throughout, such that no home is beyond a 60-second walk of green space. Streets and paths emanate from and connect them all. The open space partakes in and completes the pedestrian circulation system; it functions as a virtual crossroads. The working image is that of a hub with spokes.[9]

5. Two types of streets, in a variety of shapes, are used within the neighborhood: loops and cul-de-sacs.

Context-Sensitive Design

Starting with a regular, repetitive, essentially abstract grid demonstrates the method of forming a stencil for a repeatable neighborhood module. To create a module within a specific development site context, the same process can be followed, but with input from the site conditions and the marketing intentions of the developer. An exurban or suburban development for affluent home buyers, for example, will modify the underlying grid to permit deeper lots (e.g., 120–140 feet), while the redevelopment of a site at the urban fringe, such as a disused airport, or a more central site, such as abandoned rail yards or port docks, may be more amenable to smaller lot depths (e.g., 80–100 feet). In the latter case, the land may not subdivided into lots for individual ownership units due to its high cost; only apartments (condominium or rental) are economic alternatives. Large sites that span the gamut of market demand by virtue of their locations may have a combination of lot depths. Each of these cases of development requires special block dimensions suitable for the planned buildings. Yet the network configuration can retain all the principles stated above. (Case Study 2, Stuyvesant Town, shows a site with only apartments.)

Another factor that will affect the underlying grid frequency and its dimensions is street width, because consecutive parallel streets add to the total module dimensions. Street width is typically controlled by traffic engineering standards, which in turn are tabulated in municipal regulations. These leave room for change subject only to proper professional engineering judgment and/or municipal council dictums. Emerging influences—complete streets, safety,[10] climate change—are shifting the traffic engineering design focus from traditional vehicle priority to active transport (i.e., mobility and safety of vulnerable road users) priority. This shift in priority will provide planners and engineers, who would be applying the fused grid neighborhood design principles, with the necessary flexibility to adjust street widths, functional classes, and other design attributes, while continuing to meet professional best practices and regulatory goals. Case studies in Chapter 7 will further illustrate this design variability and flexibility.

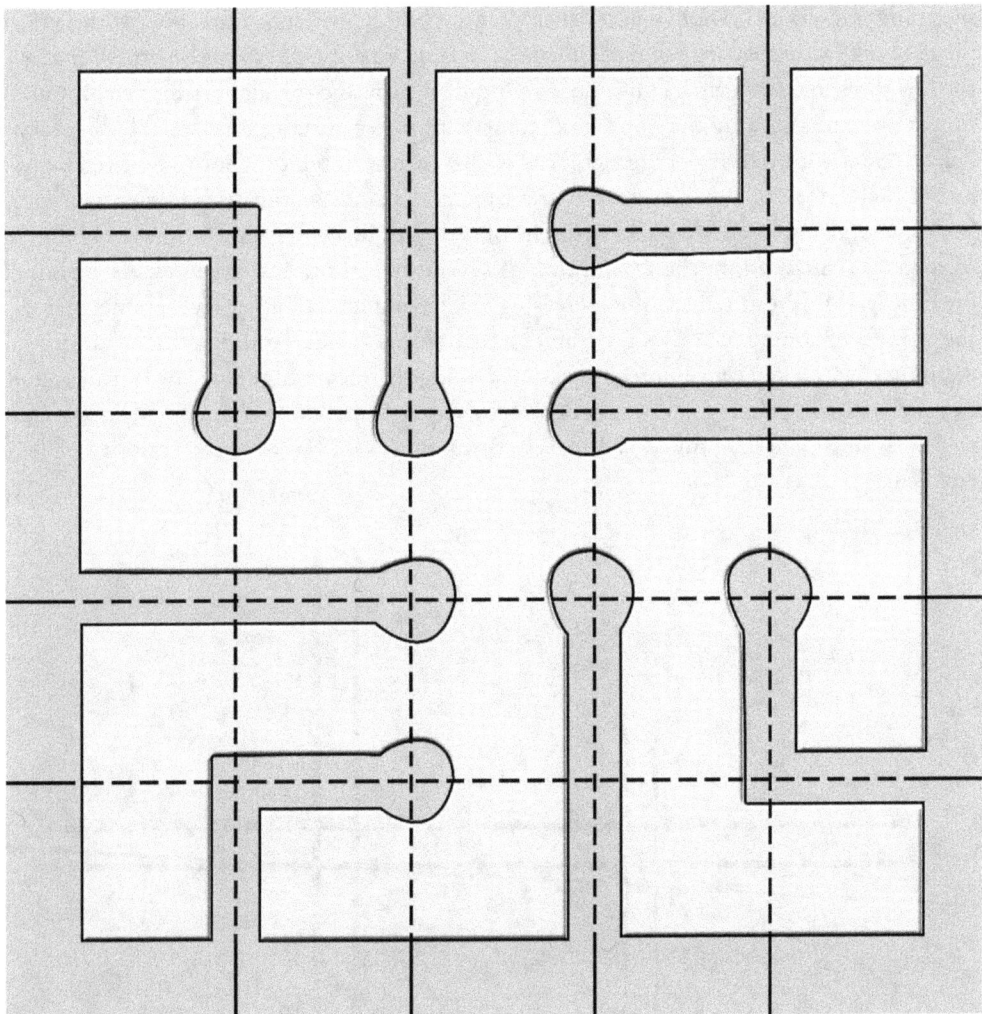

Geometric Foundation: The basis of all neighborhood layouts is a grid (dashed lines). It determines block dimensions through its frequency and imparts legibility to the whole plan. The streets are drawn on top of it.

District Design

When a development site of several 40-acre (16-hectare) neighborhood modules approaches 160 acres (64 hectare), the district-level modularity comes into play, and the design process must consider the regional road network context as well. The site may already have regional roads crossing it, in which case the fused grid neighborhood modules would have to accommodate them. Where such roads do not exist, the layout of the modules will generate them.

A 160-acre (64-hectare) area would normally include four optimal-size neighborhoods, each 16 hectares in size. This area, could, at reasonable densities (e.g., 10–12 units to the acre), generally accommodate sufficient residents and employees to warrant a basic level of shopping and services. Though unit density cannot be designed into a street network a priori, the network can anticipate it and complement its functionality. Ten to twelve units per acre is the low threshold for having convenient shopping nearby and for supporting a viable public transit system, assuming the household composition also sustains a reasonable *population* density. Such unit density can be achieved with a variety of building forms or, preferably, a mix of them, none of which imposes extraordinary demands on the network configuration.

The drawing titled "Nested Hierarchy of Network Elements" shows how the hierarchy of roads is structured on the assumption of several neighborhood modules. As explained previously, this layout reflects the increasing traffic volume on higher-level connectors and the affinity of commercial uses for traffic. It also shows the determining role of transit accessibility by the adjacent built-up areas in shaping the location of efficient transit routes. Transit routes in existing and newly developed districts are currently planned to match as closely as possible the ¼ mile (400-meters, 5-minute) walk limit for the majority of their residents.

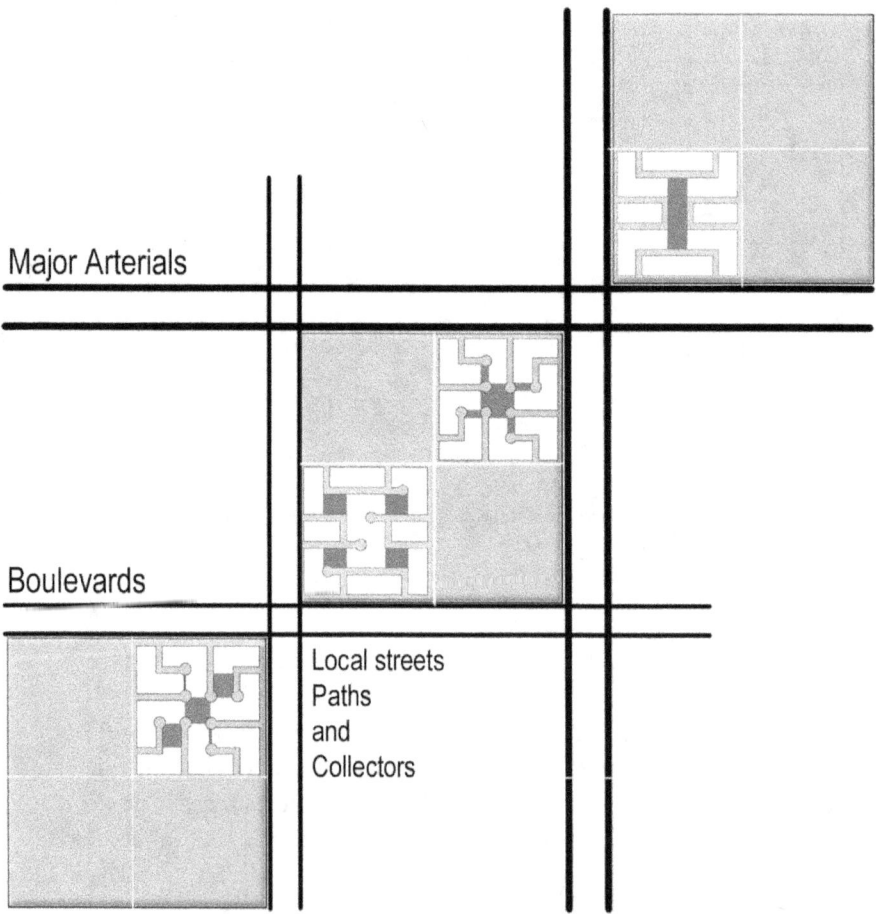

Major Arterials

Boulevards

Local streets
Paths
and
Collectors

Nested Hierarchy of Network Elements: Each class of roads forms a progressively larger grid, from collector (white) to minor boulevard (thin black) and major boulevard (thick black), and on to the freeway or highway. Local streets (grey) form a virtual grid of capillaries.

DISTRICT DESIGN PRINCIPLES

The district structure is more than an assembly of neighborhood cells. At this larger scale of organization, new formative principles apply, related to arterial roads, directness of route and synergy of land uses. All three relate to the contemporary means of transport and commerce.

Arterial is a functional road classification (or a typological attribute) that implies linkage to long-distance destinations. Just as in other circulation systems, natural or man-made, a main trunk (or artery) feeds several branches (veins, vents, circuits, capillaries), so does an arterial road. It is a major supplier of an entire system on which all lower-level connectors depend. Capillaries, vents, phones and sockets are termini of a system, while arteries (or conduits) are the intermediary channels leading to them.

From the overall system perspective, arteries can evolve distinct characteristics that separate one from another. On the basis of these characteristics, they range from the highway down to the collector, forming a set of distinct types, each with its own design specifications. In the fused grid model these road classes can be found outside the 40-acre (16-hectare) neighborhood cell, which is a terminus point or, metaphorically, a region of capillaries.[11]

Directness of route implies that the major supporting road network will connect origins and destinations between neighborhoods within a district as efficiently and safely as is feasible. This performance attribute is a prerequisite for a well-functioning transit system and for the delivery of goods, services and emergency response. To achieve directness of route, as well as speed of people and goods transport, a grid of arterials and collectors is created. Along the district perimeter, an arterial grid is a unique attribute of urban circulation systems that differentiates them from all natural and other man-made systems; these natural systems are typically dendrite in structure, meaning each class of element size branches off to a lower class size, and it does not connect with its homologous class of circulation elements. Two main branches of a tree, root system or heating system do not interconnect, as we saw.

By contrast, in the fused grid transportation system, the district perimeter arterial routes interconnect to achieve full and direct access to all city districts. They also connect with the collector roads within each district (which complete the perimeters of each neighborhood), thus forming *nested* hierarchical grids. This exceptional interconnectedness is justified on the grounds that, unlike in natural distribution systems, origins and destinations within a city and its districts are multiple and also reversible, while the need for speed remains constant. For example, a cheese factory is the terminus of the supply route of several farms' milk output, but also the origin of a distribution network of the factory product to several neighborhood stores. Placing the factory at the end of a dendrite network would be disadvantageous to the delivery of its products to multiple outlets in the city.

Arterials accommodate traffic flow. Commerce and institutions depend on traffic for profitability and prosperity. The vitality and viability of any main street results from its being a *main* thoroughfare—that is, it connects many parts of a district and, frequently, other nearby communities. As culture transitions from foot and hoof to automobility, businesses sprout and thrive on roads in proportion to the traffic they carry. This relationship can be observed in the gradual transformation of uses along roads that changed roles in a district's transportation network from minor road to a key arterial. Typically, the houses that flanked such a street became shops, restaurants, barber shops, spas, lawyers' offices, and so on, displacing the residential function of the original buildings. This observable change can be anticipated and channeled in order to preserve the value and the desirable attributes of residential districts. In the fused grid district design, one-way arterial couplets, or arterial boulevards, are divided by a block of space that is directly associated with them and would be most amenable to public uses such as commerce, education, recreation and others. In our contemporary context, traffic equals mostly private auto traffic, which translates to profitable, thriving businesses.

However, too much traffic can also have negative consequences in supporting business and services. For example, a high-speed road with a heavy traffic load not only is not conducive to fronting businesses, but access management policies by city traffic authorities would also prohibit access to and/or zoning for land uses that generate high turning-in/out volumes, which may result in worsening traffic safety conditions. Access restrictions for commercial enterprises needed to support the local community are analogous to urban passenger and freight railway corridors that are typically fenced off, effectively dividing the community and discouraging active transport.

This conflict between speed of movement and commercial uses is a strictly contemporary phenomenon; up to the end of the nineteenth century, all traffic on any street moved at a pace of around 5 km/hr, no different from a brisk walking pace, with plenty of latitude for interaction with the surroundings. A contemporary conflict requires a contemporary solution. In the fused grid network, the historic more-traffic-is-better-for-business relationship is preserved while also promoting local resident traffic on foot and bicycles, through conveniently shorter trip distances and safer intersection and crossing treatments.

Design Steps for a District

The sequence of steps described in this section assumes a clean slate, starting a new town or a very large (i.e., 2 by 2 miles [3 by 3 kilometers] district on previously undeveloped land—a rare instance. We make this assumption in order to demonstrate the applicable principles of network organization.

These principles are not entirely new and can be discerned in a number of existing districts that have evolved in recent decades. Appearing as modifications and adaptations to preexisting conditions, they become difficult to conceptualize. For this reason, they are abstracted here and made visible in diagrammatic form. They relate to the frequency of network elements at the district scale and to the shaping of *nested* grids, as follows:

1. A ¼-mile (400-meter) grid of collectors
2. A ½-mile (800-meter) grid of minor arterials (arterial boulevards)
3. A one-mile (1,600-meter) grid of major arterials (arterial boulevards—B)
4. An approximate 2-mile (4-kilometer) grid of highways (not shown in the diagram)

Parenthetically, we use the term "arterial boulevard," a blended term that may seem redundant. However, its use may be justified on the grounds that an arterial may not always have the design attributes of a boulevard and, conversely, a boulevard may not always be an arterial road. The combined term expresses the intention that these thoroughfares exhibit both attributes. "Boulevard," due to its Parisian origin and cultural connotation, conjures up the image of a complete street, a welcoming place of strolling, cycling, and exchange that most arterials lack. Allowing for these attributes to emerge is only the first step based on the network configuration. This step will inevitably be complemented by growth and land-use policies that permit a range of land uses and higher densities, topics beyond the scope of this book. By constructing a network that is derived from and responds to changes in the transportation and business culture, it is expected that the built environment will follow suit, as it normally does.

The highway grid concerns us here only to the extent that it provides access to the district as a whole either from other districts or from out-of-region origins, such as airports or regional or national parks. Most new districts would rarely exceed a two-mile (4-kilometer) dimension and, in general, would *follow* the construction of a highway, which would enable access to them. Highways fall outside the planning domain of local civic authorities and, consequently, the bounds of this chapter. They come into focus here because they may inevitably border a district to be developed. In that case, the district's network design would require specific solutions for the area in the immediate vicinity of the highway. Precedents of such solutions exist and can be drawn upon to consider and adapt to the fused grid network as needed.

The next two levels down in the district hierarchy are nested grids at half-mile and one-mile (800-meter and 1,600-meter) frequencies, respectively, of arterial boulevards. Constructing nested grids of sequentially higher-capacity roads is simple and familiar. Their simplicity lies in their orthogonal geometry and regularity. Their familiarity likewise stems from their presence in most large metro areas that span distances greater than 6 by 6 miles (10 by 10 kilometer on side), even though in a form slightly different from the schematic representation of them in the fused grid diagram. The new and distinguishing feature of the fused grid arterial boulevards that sets it apart from a traditional, conventional grid is the cross-section of the roads at the district level of hierarchy. These arterial boulevards are divided not with the usual concrete (sometimes fenced or landscaped) median, but rather with buildable commercial space in the form of average or purpose-sized city blocks (see image in previous chapter).

As explained in Chapter 4, this is an inevitable and desirable evolutionary adaptation. It can be seen in its nascent and evolving form in existing city roads. It progresses from a yellow dividing line, which separates opposing streams of traffic on normal busy roads, to a raised median that disables random left turns, and, finally, a full barrier that also prevents cyclists and pedestrians (and service/emergency vehicles) from crossing. These functional characteristics are identical, in principle, to those of a city block, whether built upon or not (conceptually, a very large median). Replacing the median with a city block appears to be a logical next step. This transformation can also be seen clearly in small cities where the original Main Street and a street parallel to it have been converted to one-way streams and now function as an "arterial boulevard." Examples can be found in large cities, too, but are harder to identify because, being a transformation of an existing network, they mesh with it and are almost imperceptible. Yet, on closer observation, one can discern on colored maps one-way couplets that constitute major thoroughfares linking to important bridges, highways or ports. However, this structure becomes unnoticeable on a satellite photograph (e.g., Google Earth) that misses the transportation expression of the road system.

The size of the intermediary blocks framed by the arterial boulevards would reflect the location of the new district and its regional context. For the purposes of constructing an initial diagram, the intermediary block dimensions can be set at about 200 and 300 feet (60 and 90 meters), respectively, for the next two levels of the network hierarchy. These dimensions can be adjusted as the district design progresses toward a final plan. Once these overarching nested grids of arterial boulevards have been constructed, we return to each 800-meter district and apply carefully chosen neighborhood modules.

The ¼-mile (400-meter) grid of collector roads (minor arterial boulevards for higher-density developments) that provides access to four neighborhood cells is nested within the ½-mile (800-meter) arterial boulevard grid. This collector grid connects between the ½-mile grid and the neighborhood local discontinuous streets. At this collector-local road intersection, it also fuses with the pedestrian and bicycle paths, providing a link across perimeter arterial boulevards to the contiguous set of four neighborhood cells. In this non-vehicular guise, the ¼-mile collector grid *is* continuous and doubles as pedestrian- and bicycle-friendly streets. If given appropriate dimensions, it can provide flexibility to accommodate future increases in traffic by becoming a continuous multimodal route, without infringing on the impermeability of the neighborhood unit.

Friction Points and Modifications

Having constructed the overall district grid, it becomes apparent that the simple, indiscriminate placement of neighborhood modules within it could generate friction points. Friction could be encountered due to:

- intersections
- access to second-tier arterial boulevards from properties facing it
- denser forms of buildings and their access and parking requirements
- driveways and parking for all types of properties
- bus stops and commercial loading zones
- pedestrian/bicycle routes, crossings, and turning lanes on collectors

ROUNDABOUT NETWORKS

All of the above items are traditional friction points, regardless of the underlying land-use and transportation system. Intersections are generally regarded as the largest cause of congestion and crashes in cities, therefore warranting careful attention in the design process. Anticipating this stress, one of the distinguishing features of fused grid design is the extensive use of roundabout networks that naturally support and optimize the aforementioned one-way arterial boulevard networks. This would include mini-roundabouts at collector/local and local/local intersections, and roundabouts at collector/arterial and arterial/arterial intersections. Roundabouts naturally lend themselves to the transitions necessary for turning at the major intersections of one-way couplets, as well as the lesser arterial/collector intersections. A full traffic engineering capacity analysis would be required for design details to ensure that each component roundabout and road link works properly in concert with the fused grid system.

Adaptations to the layout of neighborhood units are also needed when bordering on minor arterial boulevards. Again, adaptations to resolve these conflicts exist in traditional neighborhood layouts, and may be applicable directly or with modification. For example, back lanes are one approach that obviates the need for driveways off of boulevards, a dominant contributor to congestion and collisions.[12] A second approach is access roads or lanes, separate from the boulevard itself, between the boulevard and the fronting properties. These two options resolve partially the conflict of access to properties. A common, functional but severely criticized option is to back the buildings on to the boulevard (back-lotting) and provide access to them from a street internal to the neighborhood cell. This practical option resolves the frequent access conflict but creates inhospitable spaces, as we saw before. It should be noted here that the divided boulevard, which ameliorates movement and preserves the attributes of a neighborhood, would make back-lotting unnecessary in most instances.

The divided boulevard, which is incorporated into the fused grid model, eases the extremity of the conditions that cause friction, thus reducing the necessity for drastic solutions such as long, uninviting, and sometimes foreboding barriers. It reduces the total traffic volume to which properties are exposed. Though the total regional/district traffic passing through remains identical, the decisive separation of the two streams reduces the visible and audible traffic by half. The other half is virtually invisible due to the intervening block of district-based land uses. Hence, traffic noise is considerably attenuated due to the increased distance and the intervening obstacles such as buildings and vegetation.

The divided boulevard system also removes a number of conflict points that usually cause erratic driver behavior, which occasionally leads to collisions. This removal of conflicts would result in smoother traffic flow, devoid of sudden stops, prolonged waits and aggressive speeding.

The emergence of these conflicts at the district scale emphasize, once again, that the fused grid model should be conceived as a complete system, not as an assembly of individual components. The whole-part relationship of a pattern (or a functioning organism) comes back into sharp focus.[13] To achieve district functionality, the relationship of each part of the system to others would have to be resolved at the design stage in full anticipation of the operational phase.

Being systemic, the conflict relationships described earlier will appear persistently. As we saw in Chapters 3 and 4, such conflicts are inevitable when the inherited network of the city was originally based on foot and hoof transportation and now is asked to accommodate greater volume and higher-speed, motorized transport. In new districts these conflicts can be reduced or eliminated through a contemporary network design adapted to contemporary transport modes. Developing generic adaptations for recurring interfaces between neighborhoods and arterial boulevards would complete the district scale pattern.

The descriptions and diagrams in the next chapter focus on these potential conflict situations. Based on the nested grid structure, each neighborhood cell would have two of its sides bordering on:

- Level B arterial boulevards (high density) or collector roads (low and medium density),

- Level A arterial boulevards, or
- Level A and B, respectively, on two adjacent sides.

Layout solutions and rationale for each of these conditions of adjacency deserves careful engineering analysis that exceeds the scope of this chapter.

Expected, Characteristic Benefits

The fused grid network model is proposed as a means of alleviating known frictions, stresses and disadvantages that inevitably emerged from city growth and the evolution of transport means. Based on observation of the negative effects of old or current widely practiced models, the proposed network is expected to deliver the following characteristic benefits.

On the transport front:

- Active transport as the highest number of trips inside the neighborhood
- Shorter times and distances for walking/bike trips across the neighborhood versus driving
- Lower number of motorized trips
- 60 percent fewer road collisions (i.e., ped/bike/car), including those on perimeter roads
- Shorter home-based shopping trip distances
- Five-minute walking time to a corner store and to transit stops

On the health and well-being fronts:

- Increased sense of security by residents walking/biking/playing in neighborhood
- Increased sense of ownership and maintenance of neighborhood green spaces, including community gardens
- Healthier residents, with restorative green space within a one-minute walk from home
- A greater sense of community, as measured by social interaction frequency

These benefits can be anticipated, but not claimed, without evidence. In the following chapter we present substantial evidence to support this expectation.

6

Research Evidence on
Key Expected Outcomes

Having looked at the reasons for the fused grid model's emergence, as well as its geometry and key organizing principles, in the preceding chapters, this chapter will discuss whether the model would work in practice, and whether it would produce expected, desirable outcomes.

Common to all innovations is the fact that implementation usually lags behind their introduction, often raising normal doubts about their workability. Such is also the case with the fused grid. Since its first publication in 2003, three Canadian municipalities have approved subdivision plans based on the model and a fourth has introduced policies that encourage its implementation. As of this writing, the first two plans are under construction. Full build-out and occupancy will take the normal 4-to-6-year period. As a result, comprehensive field research of the model's effectiveness cannot be done until these or other communities are fully built and occupied.

In lieu of full in-situ validation, this chapter presents inferential evidence of effectiveness based on theoretical studies of key elements that make up the fused grid model (e.g., land efficiency, safety, VKT, active transport, well-being and so on). Where available, we also provide in-situ validation studies of key elements of the fused grid that are found in existing communities (e.g., cul-de-sacs, open spaces, pedestrian-only paths, and others). This partial validation of components in something other than a full-scale system application provides a glimpse of the effects and their trends. As new research is completed on the fused grid model as a whole, the current evidence will be supplemented by its results. For the time being, we have surveyed work in all related disciplines and provide here a distillation of their findings. These findings rest on sound, up-to-date science and analytical methods.

It is now possible, using new, sophisticated analytical tools and computational power (only recently available), to project real-world data and established assumptions onto any network concept, and then examine the network's performance in regard to a single isolated element (e.g., traffic flow, modal split, and so on). In addition, a growing body of research in the applied sciences (transportation engineering), natural sciences (environmental), social sciences (economics, psychology), and health sciences (public health) can provide inferential evidence for aspects that are based on field research. This is the territory that we navigate here.

This chapter covers a range of relevant research that provides evidence in support of the key elements and, where available, the complete system of the fused grid model. For clarity, we divide the evidence into separate topics, reflecting the streams of current research, under the headings *social*, *economic*, and *environmental*. Inevitably, the groupings may at times appear arbitrary, as a number of the issues under each category straddle disciplinary boundaries. Ultimately, what matters is the evidence itself, its strength and relevance. Readers can pass their own judgments on its reliability and can refer to the listed original papers for an in-depth appreciation.

Social

One definitive descriptor of social fitness is "health," often a subcomponent of an overarching, if somewhat less tangible, concept of "quality of life." Though both terms may be viewed as subjective at first glance, they can be dissected into measurable determinants or variables. Health, in its most general sense, is defined as an absence of causes of illness and disease, and it has been the primary concern of settlement planners since the birth of the profession. In fact, the very existence of planning regulations rests explicitly on the grounds of maintaining the health and safety of a settlement's citizens. Four elements of contemporary neighborhoods are known to influence the health of residents: air quality, safety, noise and green space. We present studies on these four determinants, plus two others that are becoming increasingly more visible—social interactions and crime—that fall suitably under the quality-of-life rubric.

AIR QUALITY

Impure air is the largest contributor to premature deaths and impaired living due to its negative influence on heart or bronchial functions. In 2008, for example, there were an estimated 21,000 premature deaths attributed to polluted air in Canada; slightly more than 10 percent of these were caused by short exposure to air pollution.[1] Similar conditions and effects occur in other countries.[2] The long-term effects can also be serious, particularly for children. A related study concludes, "Children living in areas with poor air quality have been found to have reduced lung function growth that places them at risk for future respiratory illness."[3] Another study, also focusing on children, states, "Children who live near high traffic areas (20,000 cars passing per day) may be six times more likely to develop childhood leukemia and other cancers,"[4] linking health impact to traffic circulation and network design. Alternative approaches to current network design may be required to reduce exposure to polluted air.

Although nonpoint sources, such as oil or gas HVAC systems in buildings, contribute significantly to a district's air quality,[5] most of it originates in vehicle traffic, the most direct and highest contributor to air pollution impacting air quality in a residential district. Empirical evidence[6] suggests that the production of noxious gases from car engines correlates with the following factors, which result in an increase per kilometer output:

- short trips
- traffic volumes
- stop-and-go traffic
- below-optimum speed travel

Invariably, the health and well-being of children, adults, and seniors are affected more when they live, walk or bike near heavy traffic. Taken together, solutions for reducing the production of noxious gases and exposure to them should:

- discourage or displace shorter car trips
- enable smoother traffic flow
- plan for moderate speeds and fewer stops
- separate people from traffic to the greatest extent possible

Two studies based on comparative analysis of neighborhood designs, and a third that was based on travel diaries, suggest that the fused grid model would accomplish these objectives.

A traffic engineering team[7] looked at three typical street layout designs superimposed on the same built-up site and used CORSIM, a prevalent traffic analysis software, to model traffic flows in each one. Results showed that, of the three, the fused grid exhibited the following trends:

- Vehicle delays of up to 32 percent less than conventional suburban cul-de-sac models
- The lowest traffic volumes within neighborhoods
- The lowest increase in neighborhood traffic for corresponding increases in density, at up to 52 percent less than the conventional suburban cul-de-sac models

In other words, lower delay times translate to more efficient travel, and therefore lower gas

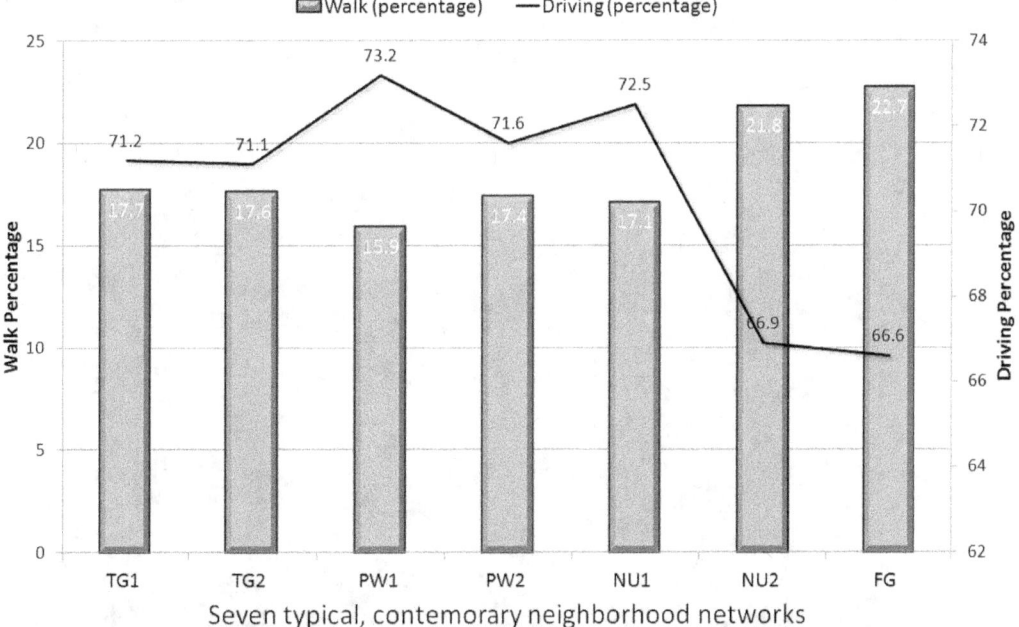

Comparative Values for Walking and Driving Shares in Seven Networks

Walking and Driving: Comparison of the amount of driving and walking predicted for seven types of neighborhood layouts: TG1 and TG2 (traditional grid); PW1PW2 (postwar suburban development); NU1NU2 (New Urbanist Development); and FG (fused grid) (original design by Xiongbing Jin).

emissions, while relative lower traffic volumes within neighborhoods imply lower exposure to pollutants within the daily walking environment.

A theoretical study[8] compared travel behavior in seven neighborhood layouts that were taken from existing city neighborhoods. The researcher used Agent Modeling to analyze the relative incidence of a travel mode and trips per mode in each of the seven neighborhoods. Out of all seven, results indicate the highest level of walking and the lowest level of driving in the fused grid model. Regarding exposure to emissions, the same study showed that pollutant concentration was occurring at the periphery of the fused grid neighborhoods, away from the frequently used pedestrian circulation paths and where the majority of homes were found, as shown in the drawing titled "Concentration of Pollutants." It also confirmed that the key variable responsible for these positive effects was the presence and strategic placement of dedicated bicycle and pedestrian paths.

An empirical study[9] used resident travel diaries in three neighborhoods, one of which had bicycle/pedestrian-only shortcuts to destinations, a key element in a fused grid layout. The data analysis revealed a potential 23 percent reduction of neighborhood vehicle kilometers traveled (VKT), and an 11.3 percent increase of home-based walking trips, both of which suggest a corresponding decrease of emissions within the neighborhood. These VKT reductions within neighborhoods benefit all residents, especially those on foot and bicycles.

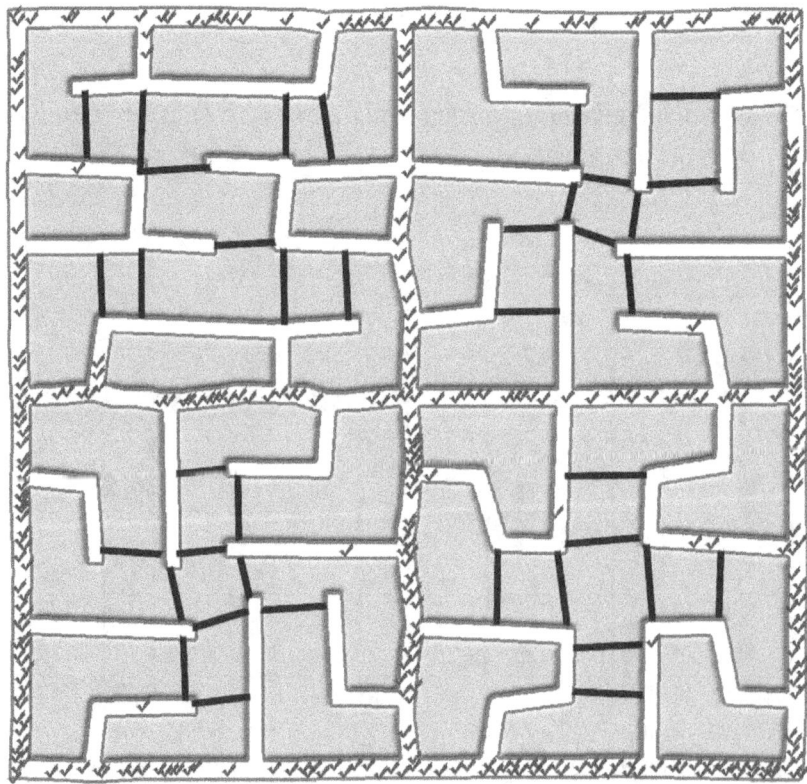

Concentration of Pollutants: Study results show that pollutants are concentrated at the periphery of each of the four neighborhoods (tick marks point to the location and density of concentration) (original design by Xiongbing Jin).

The neighborhood street layouts of the fused grid result in, all else being equal, about three-quarters of all houses facing internal streets and, consequently, being exposed to lower levels of emissions.

RECREATION AND PHYSICAL ACTIVITY

Consumer surveys indicate that the choice of a place to live is strongly influenced by the desire for "a good place to raise a family." Motorized transportation steers the more vulnerable road users (i.e., bicyclists and pedestrians) out of their traditional realm—the street—and onto sidewalks. Simultaneously, streets become off-limits as recreational territory for children of all ages.

Observation of children's general behavior has shown that children will spontaneously use any space for play and construct imaginary worlds to suit a game. Parents, however, often feel uneasy about street play and habitually will not let their children, particularly young ones, play on it, often overestimating the risk from passing traffic. Moreover, some cities explicitly prohibit play on the street for liability reasons, even if a street is located in an isolated area with infrequent traffic.

University researchers looked into the differences in the amount of play that occurred on two types of streets: permeable streets ("non-cul-de-sac") and impermeable streets (a.k.a. cul-de-sacs or "dead-ends").[10] Results confirmed persistent anecdotal observations that cul-de-sacs are more frequently the loci of play than other streets. In addition, the duration of

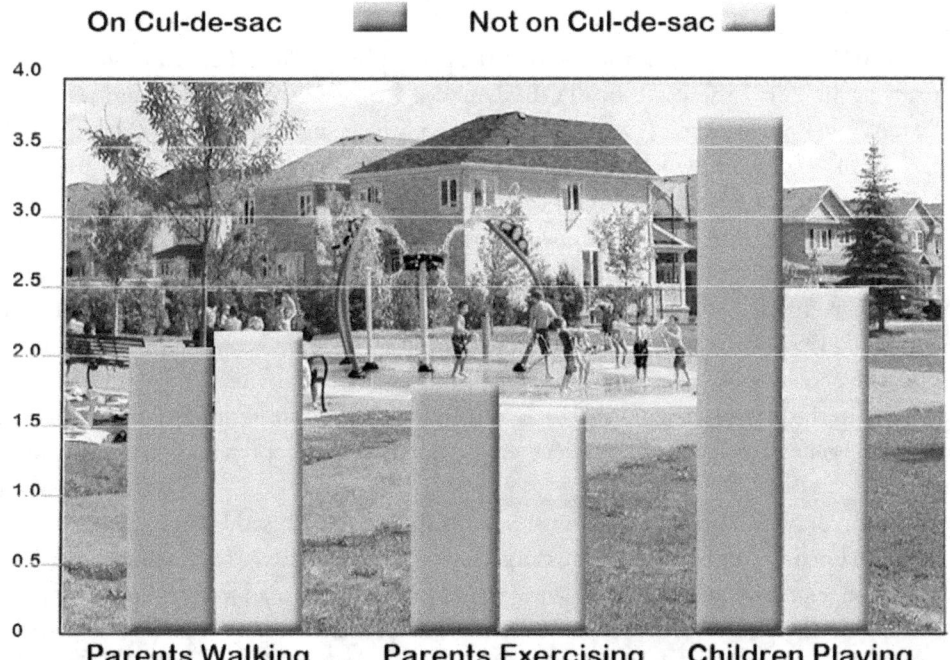

Street Type and Exercise: A 50 percent difference was found in the amount of time children spent outdoors playing between the cul-de-sac and non-cul-de-sac streets (original design by Susan Handy).

play is also greater. This finding provides indirect confirmation that the systematic inclusion of non-through streets, such as cul-de-sacs and loops, in the fused grid model would increase the odds of spontaneous children's play on the street. Given that cul-de-sacs typically experience very low traffic volumes, exposure to emissions would also be minimized, as the previously mentioned study indicates.

TRAFFIC SAFETY

This section looks at safety strictly from the perspective of traffic deaths and injuries, both of which curtail an individual's life or full participation in society by limiting his/her abilities or faculties, either transiently or permanently. Though individuals may be free of illness following a collision, their participation in society may be constrained by virtue of collision-induced disabilities. Moreover, collisions and resulting disabilities have an impact on not only the individual but also his immediate social milieu, such as family, relatives, employment, and support services.

Though not strictly a health condition, the presence of limitations is a quality-of-life issue that resembles those of a chronic disease, and for that reason safety is highlighted in the context of social issues.

The World Health Organization has labeled injuries from collisions as one of the top ten epidemics worldwide, forecasting (according to current trends) that it will rise to third worst by 2020 unless drastic action is taken (WHO, 2012). The death and injury toll worldwide (over 1 million and 50 million, respectively, in 2004 alone) is unsettling when compared to other causes, particularly in developing countries. The U.S. death toll in 2009 from collisions totaled about 34,000, and collisions were the leading cause of death for children aged 3–14 (USDOT, 2011). Despite the fact that the per-capita number of collisions has been on a steady decline since the 1940s in all OECD nations, the current frequency and severity of collisions remain unacceptably high, not to speak of the economic burden, which totals 2–5 percent of GDP worldwide. The public benefit resulting from motorized transportation is being diminished by its social and economic burdens.

Collisions between cars do not always result in injuries or fatalities. Cars hitting pedestrians and/or bicyclists, however, invariably result in serious injuries. In Canada, for example, there were an average of about 400 pedestrian deaths and 14,000 injuries per year in a ten-year period (1992–2001). The young and the old (under 15 and over 65) represent a disproportionate percentage of these numbers. In looking at deaths and injuries of pedestrians, we find a counterintuitive statistic—that walking is the most dangerous mode of travel per mile. As with the general collision figures, the young and old are over-represented in these collision statistics.

Road safety analysts typically consider collisions to be caused by one or more of the three fundamental components of the transport system—the driver (e.g., vehicle operator), the vehicle (e.g., car), and/or the driving environment (e.g., road and its configuration). There is overwhelming evidence that the driving environment—road design (e.g., lane width, number of lanes, median type, and sidewalk width) and network layout (e.g., intersection type and frequency, one- or two-way flow, and road alignment shape)—is a contributing factor in 30 percent of collisions. Vehicle failure accounts for at least 10 percent of collision contributing factors, and is an incidental, uncontrollable occurrence. However, by far driver error dominates as a contributing factor in over 95 percent of collisions, and, as such, it provides a second area that neighborhood planners and engineers can control through neighborhood designs that encourage less driving. Simply said, taking the driver out of the car and onto sidewalks and bicycles removes 95 percent of contributing factors. Moreover, neighborhood designs that increase the physical separation between these active travel modes and vehicles will further remove another 30 percent of contributing factors. The Dutch Sustainable Road Safety Research Institute has been encouraging exactly this form of community planning and design since the mid–1990s, and it has seen road fatalities drop by over 60 percent, from over 2,000 to under 700 nationally, since that time (2013 Fact sheet).

Safety studies on key elements fall into two general areas: first, cross-sectional studies that analyze existing neighborhoods with differing street types and network patterns; second, before-and-after studies that analyze existing neighborhoods in which streets were retrofitted to alter vehicle circulation patterns.

Early evidence of a relationship between network pattern and collision emerged[11] that showed at least one order-of-magnitude difference in collision frequency between open grid network patterns (generally rectilinear) and limited-access suburban patterns that use predominantly 3-way intersections (usually curvilinear) and cul-de-sac road patterns. Though the study was criticized for methodological weaknesses, more rigorous research confirmed these findings, although with moderated ratios.

Eran Ben-Joseph compared police collision records from neighborhoods with distinct road network types.[12] His analysis showed a clear benefit in using cul-de-sacs and loops for reducing collisions. Neighborhoods with grid road patterns recorded a trend of two to three times the collisions that were observed in neighborhoods with loop and cul-de-sac patterns. This study was also criticized for its methodology, but its results were later found to be consistent with newer findings.[13] These early studies provide partial inferential evidence that the use of cul-de-sacs and loops in the fused grid, along with the predominance of 3-way intersections, would improve traffic safety.

The second stream of research involves before-and-after safety studies of retrofits to existing neighborhoods. A seminal study[14] examined the results of the transformation of a neighborhood—Five Oaks—in Dayton, Ohio, that was initiated for security reasons. The neighborhood's street layout was transformed from a traditional grid to a series of branching cul-de-sacs. Gates were used at key intersections to restrict through traffic while allowing complete pedestrian circulation. This transformation resulted in a 36 percent reduction in traffic volume and a 40 percent reduction in collisions.

Extensive traffic calming with beneficial traffic safety effects was implemented in Seattle, Washington, in the early 1990s. One program in particular entailed the installation of small traffic circles at the center of four-way intersections. The results from the monitoring of 32 intersections over a five-year period show an impressive average of 89.8 percent reduction in collisions and a similar reduction in injuries. The proven positive effect on safety and on street life quality has spurred the installation of over 1,000 traffic circles in Seattle over the last 30 years.[15]

Similar transformations occurred in Vancouver, British Columbia, in the early 1980s. These involved a variety of physical traffic calming changes, such as closures of intersections

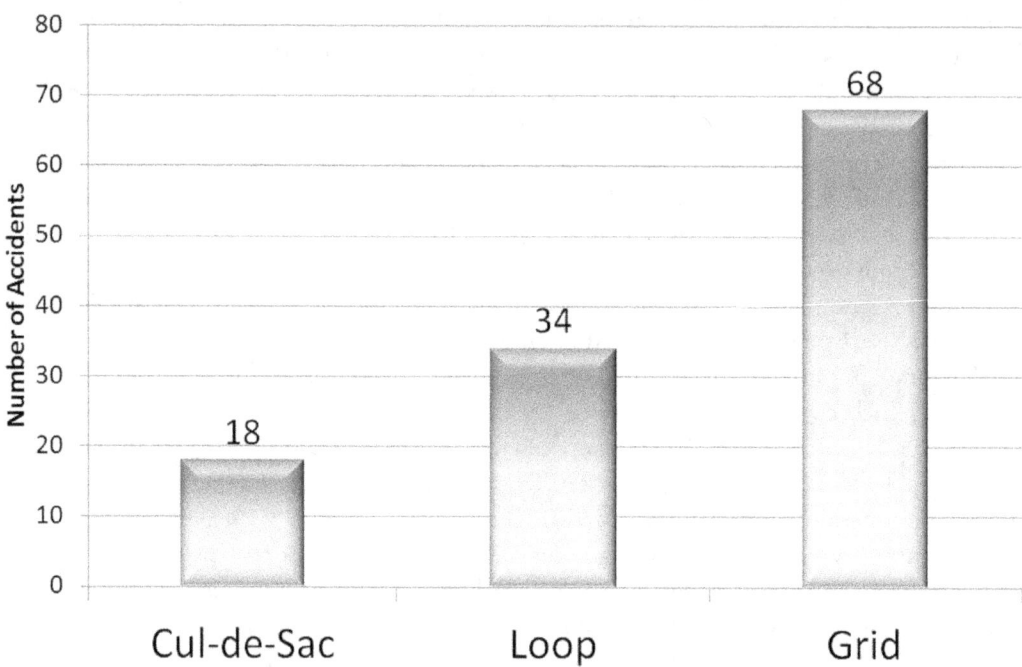

Cumulative Collisons over a 5-year Period

Comparing Collisions by Street Type: Cumulative data show the cul-de-sac as being the safest street type and the traditional grid as the least safe (original design by Eran Ben-Joseph).

(virtual cul-de-sacs), traffic circles, diagonal diverters, forced-turn islands and one-way designations. Post-transformation statistics for Vancouver's West End neighborhood show an 18 percent reduction in the frequency of collisions.[16]

These successful transformations of Five Oaks, Seattle and Vancouver in response to traffic and other growth pressures suggest that the conventional grid, with its four-way intersections, is a suboptimal pattern for safety. Modifications that restrict through traffic, create virtual cul-de-sacs (without limiting pedestrian movement), and manage the flow at intersections can deliver substantial reductions in collisions and injuries. The fused grid model, which explores similar design devices in neighborhood layout, may, based on the above evidence, be expected to produce similar outcomes.

Examining the built environment from a similar safety perspective, a team looked at the city of San Antonio, New Mexico, to identify factors that could be linked to reductions in collisions.[17] It found, among the many significant influences on collisions, that 4-way intersections are associated with increased total and injurious collisions, while 3-way intersections have no effect on total or injurious collisions. It also corroborated the above-mentioned modeling study that pointed to a sizable increase in collisions associated with the grid.

A stream of research proactively analyzes city- or region-wide, geo-coded data to discover collision trends in relation to network layout patterns, road designs and patterns of land use. The first research looked at collision data stemming from the Vancouver region and drew strong correlations between street layout patterns and frequency of collisions.

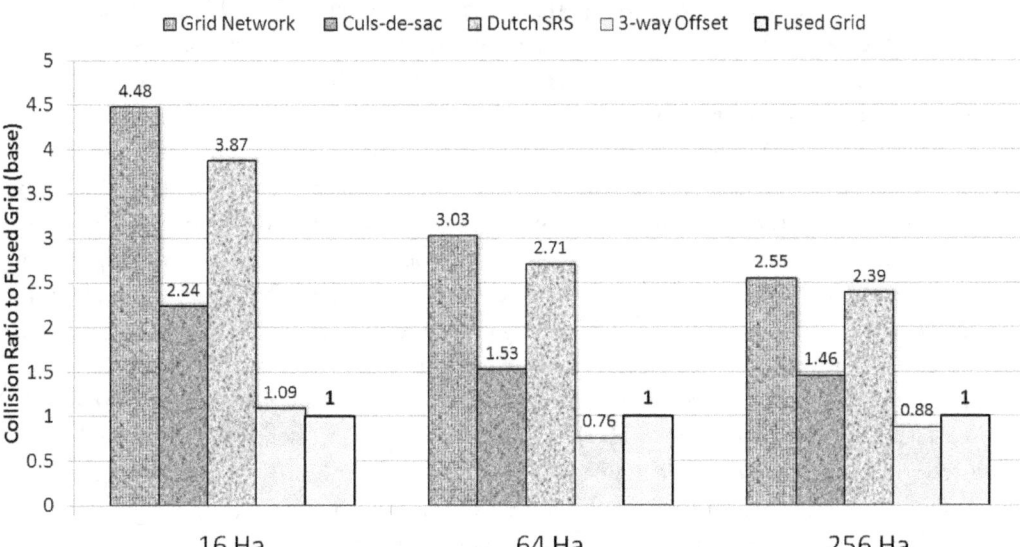

Frequency of Collisions: Comparison Among Five Types of Layout Patterns

Comparing Collisions by Network Type: Five network types applied at three different scale districts (40, 160 and 640 acres) yield consistent results: in all cases, the fused grid and the 3-way Offset types remain substantially safer than the other three alternatives.

Based on these findings, and with the addition of traffic data from Ottawa, Ontario, a second-step study examined the potential outcomes of two new layout patterns: the fused grid and the 3-way offset. The analysis showed that the new layout patterns could reduce collisions by over 60 percent compared to traditional layouts. The bar chart titled "Comparing Collisions by Network Type" presents summary collision statistics for five layout designs based on this analysis. Given that the fused grid model has fewer intersections overall, 80 percent of which are 3-way, these modeling studies confirm its potential on-the-ground performance.[18]

All the collision-related studies, which span a 60-year period, provide inferential evidence of the safety advantages of network patterns that use predominantly 3-way intersections, with cul-de-sacs and loops, at the neighborhood scale. The avoidance of four-way intersections in neighborhood network planning is essential. Moreover, the most recent theoretical study concluded that the fused grid model offers optimal safety outcomes. However, now that it has been confirmed, at least tentatively, that the fused grid model increases active-mode trips and reduces automotive ones, research that includes adjustments to mode choice in the safety evaluations would be a natural next step in refining its full, exact positive impact.

Noise

Unwanted, disturbing sound has been part of city living from early to contemporary cities. The stone paved streets, on which iron-rimmed chariots and carts were drawn by iron-shod horses for at least two thousand years, were extremely noisy places. In Rome, the patricians and the equestrians escaped to the periphery or even outside the city walls to avoid the clamor. Medieval and Renaissance cities experienced similar conditions. Not only street noise but also neighbor-generated noise was ever-present because of crowded conditions and poor building construction, as we saw in Chapter 2.

In the twentieth century, noise has reached unprecedented levels of intensity and diurnal duration. The pervasive use of mechanical devices for work, pleasure and transport (including power tools; construction equipment; trains, trams, buses, motorboats and airplanes; music equipment, television and radios) accumulates to produce a disturbingly loud environment. This plethora of sound sources has created a pool of constant waves varying in intensity and degree of intrusion, to the point that "calling noise a nuisance is like calling smog an inconvenience. Noise must be considered a hazard to the health of people everywhere," as Dr. William Stewart, a past surgeon general of the United States, put it.[19] And according to the World Health Organization (WHO), "Excessive noise seriously harms human health and interferes with people's daily activities at school, at work, at home and during leisure time. It can disturb sleep, cause cardiovascular and psycho-physiological effects, reduce performance and provoke annoyance responses and changes in social behaviour."

Research has documented both the extent of intrusion and the range of its negative impact. The most pervasive and persistent noise comes from traffic, the source of about 75 percent of all noise annoyance. For example, exposure to noise in Paris, as mapped by a city specialty team, puts 15 percent of residents at high health risk and 37 percent at moderate health risk; all these residents experience levels between 60 and 75 decibels for extended durations.

In the United Kingdom, research on noise suggests that 2 in every 100 deaths from heart disease may be caused by stress attributable to noise. One study from Canada finds that 1.8 million people aged 15 and over are highly annoyed by traffic noise.[20]

Within residential neighborhoods, one of the key sources of noise is car traffic. Research shows that "low-level but chronic noise of moderate traffic can stress children and raise their blood pressure, heart rates and levels of stress hormones."[21]

The level and duration of traffic noise depends on speed and on daily volume, respectively. Both of these variables increase with the degree of arterial function of a street or, stated differently, the degree to which a street is used as a through road link by the entire network to reach cross-town destinations. Higher-functioning arterials inevitably generate increased noise and potential negative human health and environmental impacts.

Noise intensity can be reduced at the source by distance or by a barrier. Noise duration can be limited through the type and volume of traffic that is allowed on a street. Buses or trams, for example, usually cover a large segment of the 24-hour cycle. Some stores remain open all 24 hours of the day attracting traffic. Both of these examples extend the duration of potential annoyance.

From these facts and relationships, it becomes evident that in order to reduce the intensity and duration of noise that affects neighborhood residents, road network layout and land-use allocations in a given network need to be responsive to these facts.

Design insights can be gained by looking at noise maps recently developed by some European cities. For example, a visual inspection of the noise map of Paris reveals patterns that can also be found in other maps. These are as follows: (a) the farther away from the city center, the quieter districts become; (b) major and minor arteries are the places with the highest decibel readings; (c) the farther away from an artery, the lower the noise levels; (d) streets that are purely local (i.e., one or two blocks long) show very low levels of noise at or below the threshold level of annoyance; and (e) parks, particularly local parks not bordering on arterials or main streets, exhibit the lowest decibel levels that are non-disruptive.

Based on these recurring patterns gleaned from data of cities in operation, at least two general rules can be extracted for reducing noise impacts on residents: (1) A district should be organized in distinct, small enclaves that preclude through traffic. (2) A road network should have a hierarchical structure (similar to a leaf-vein pattern) in which traffic is channeled according to volume and type.

Though noise abatement is a relatively new requirement for network design, and clearly external to the main functions of a network, its implications for network layout coincide with the main criterion of rational organization of traffic flow.

As we saw in Chapter 5, a fused grid district plan comprises neighborhood cells within which streets become vehicular termini, preventing any through traffic from using them as alternative routes to non-neighborhood destinations. Consequently, the volume of traffic equals the number of street residents. Car speed is restrained by the short length of each street segment, never more than 500 feet (160 meters). In this manner, volume and speed, the two major contributors to noise, are restrained. The nested hierarchy of roads also channels progressively heavy and constant traffic to higher-rank roads, leaving large districts in between at relative peace. Moreover, the splitting of the traffic streams into one-way pairs, with an intervening space between them, puts a distance and a shield between the noise source and the residential district, a feature that further attenuates noise that would otherwise reach the residences in the circumscribed district.

From these network organizing principles and their congruence with the observed levels of noise in current cities, it can be inferred with some degree of confidence that the fused grid network will procure low-noise-level habitat areas for the majority of residents.

GREEN SPACE

Removing stressors in a neighborhood such as traffic noise, air pollution, and safety concerns is significant in abating tension, but not sufficient alone to support a sense of well-being. We turn our attention to another important element—nearby nature opportunities and green space. Prominent planning figures at the turn of the twentieth century understood intuitively the importance of nearby nature in improving population health. It was a central theme of the garden city movement and became a strong feature of all garden cities that were planned and built. Raymond Unwin showed how a transformation of the dreary by-law street type of city block development could provide individual and collective gardens for neighborhood residents without sacrificing economy and profit.[22] At the time, their beneficial effect was proclaimed based on intuition. It was not until mid-century and later that population health and clinical research produced strong objective evidence of the beneficial effects of natural settings on health and well-being. It has since been unambiguously shown by several studies that there is a strong association between the enjoyment of nature and the health of a city population in general.

A large epidemiological study looked at mortality and morbidity among four income levels in relation to their access to green, open space. The study examined about 360,000 deaths in a population of roughly 41 million. While it confirmed that wealthier individuals were generally healthier than those with lower incomes, it made another remarkable discovery: all groups, irrespective of income, showed an improvement in health in proportion to their access to green space, and the differences in health status between income groups who had equivalent access to progressively more green space, shrank, favoring the lowest socioeconomic group with the highest morbidity the most.[23] In simple terms, everyone benefited from access to green space, but the lowest income group benefited the most. These striking results, based on an exceptionally large population sample, confirm unambiguously the health-related benefits of green space and suggest its importance as an element in neighborhood layouts, not only in order to reduce health disparities between income groups but also to promote general health and well-being.

A second epidemiological study in the Netherlands examined the health of 17,000 people in relationship to the presence of green space in their surroundings.[24] It found that residents of neighborhoods with abundant green space are, on average, healthier. This correlation was clearly evident in the general population, but it was more pronounced among seniors, housewives and low-income people. Also significant was the correlation between health and the total amount of green space, even though, in some cases, part of it was located at a distance of one to three kilometers from home.

A third study took place in Tokyo, which is known for its high population density.[25] This was a longitudinal study that followed a group of 3,000 70-year-old citizens over the

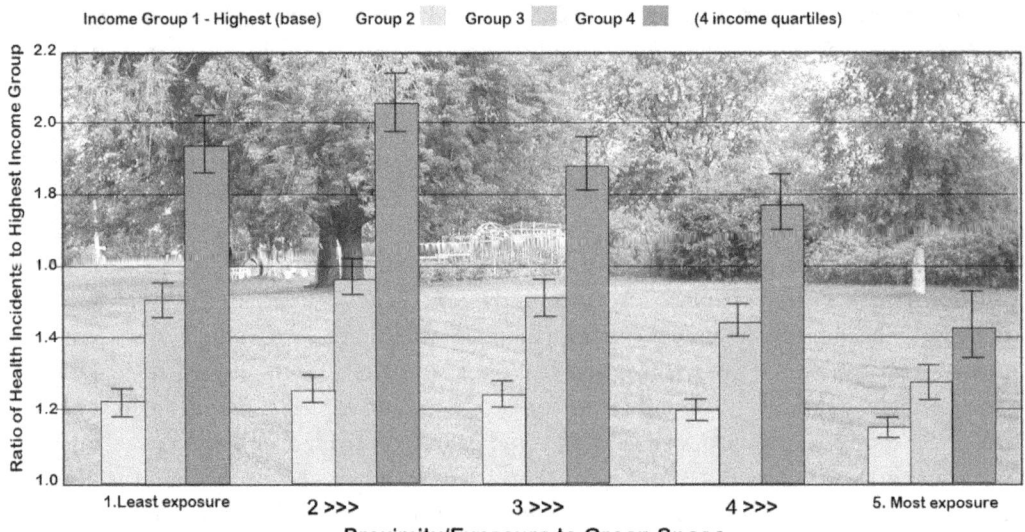

The Effect of Exposure to Green Space on Health and Health Disparities

Income Group 1 - Highest (base)   Group 2   Group 3   Group 4   (4 income quartiles)

Ratio of Health Incidents to Highest Income Group

Proximity/Exposure to Green Space

Health and Proximity to Green Space: As the availability of nearby green space increases (from left to right), the frequency of ill health among three socioeconomic groups (3 bars) decreases, as do the differences between them (original design by Richard Mitchell).

course of five years. The presence of relatively plentiful green space in a neighborhood correlated with a lower mortality risk. This correlation was stronger in a sub-sample of elderly people with few physical disabilities.

A recent study (2013), using data from 10,000 individuals, attempted to determine the connection between urban green space and well-being as well as mental distress. The research found that people living in urban areas with more green space, on average, showed lower mental distress and a higher sense of well-being.[26]

While these three studies provide sound evidence of the potential general health benefits of the presence of green space in urban settings for the population at large, other research looked at specific demographic groups, such as age, occupation, socioeconomic status and unusual health conditions or symptoms. Though these studies vary in their degree of scientific rigor, they all point to the potential benefits of nearby nature, including:

- Nature has a positive effect on recovery from stress and attention fatigue. People in highly stressful occupations, such as caregivers or hospital nurses, can shed much of their stress by being or walking in natural settings. Encouragingly, this effect can occur even when the exposure to nature is brief.
- Nature has a positive impact on mood, concentration, mental fatigue, self-discipline and physiological stress.
- Hospital patients who have a view of nature through their windows show faster recovery rates, which can be attributed to stress reduction in the absence of other explanatory mechanisms.
- Parents of children suffering from attention deficit disorder report improvement and fewer attention problems when the area of play is in natural settings.
- Green spaces may enhance the potential of creating and sustaining community interaction and social networks.
- The presence of green spaces nearby may encourage walking and other physical activity.[27]

Research has also been conducted to study the size of the green space needed to realize its beneficial effects. Urban land costs are a central consideration in development; consequently, land allocation to green space must be done judiciously and with good justification. A survey of residents showed that "what was valued here are not greenbelts and urban parks; residents are expressing intense satisfaction with small pieces of nature, with the views of some trees and shrubs."[28]

The evidence regarding the positive impact of natural settings on general health and well-being suggests that they ought to be a regular part of neighborhood and district layouts. Consistent with these findings, the fused grid incorporates green space as a key structural element. As such, these green spaces may enhance their inherent potential effects by enabling residents to have daily contact with nature and each other.

Social Interaction

While traffic noise may trigger annoyance and consequent psycho-physiological effects, the presence of traffic itself impacts another sense of well-being—the sense of belonging, or, more importantly, the "sense of community" that emerges from social interactions among neighbors.

Starting with the landmark 1981 book by Donald Appleyard, *Livable Streets,* many researchers have examined the relationship between traffic volume and local social networks centered on the street. Appleyard established the inverse relationship between traffic volume, frequency of social interaction between neighbors, and the extent of acquaintance. In the three streets that were examined, traffic volumes ranged from 2,000 veh/day to 8,000 veh/day and 16,000 veh/day, respectively. Observed social interactions ranged, in inverse proportion to traffic, from 3 friends and 6.3 acquaintances to 1.3 friends and 4.1 acquaintances, to 0.9 friends and 3.1 acquaintances, respectively, per resident on the facing blocks.

A team in New York looked at four neighborhoods with streets that carried 1,000 veh/day (light), 2,000–3,000 veh/day (medium), and 5,000 veh/day (heavy) on each of three streets for every neighborhood. It found significant differences in the number of friends-per-person between streets with light and heavy traffic. The difference ranged from double to quadruple in almost all cases.[29]

A study in Birmingham, England, tried to replicate Appleyard's work in a city with a socio-cultural context distinct from that of California. It was hypothesized that these cultural differences may influence behavior and therefore outcomes. The UK results were remarkably

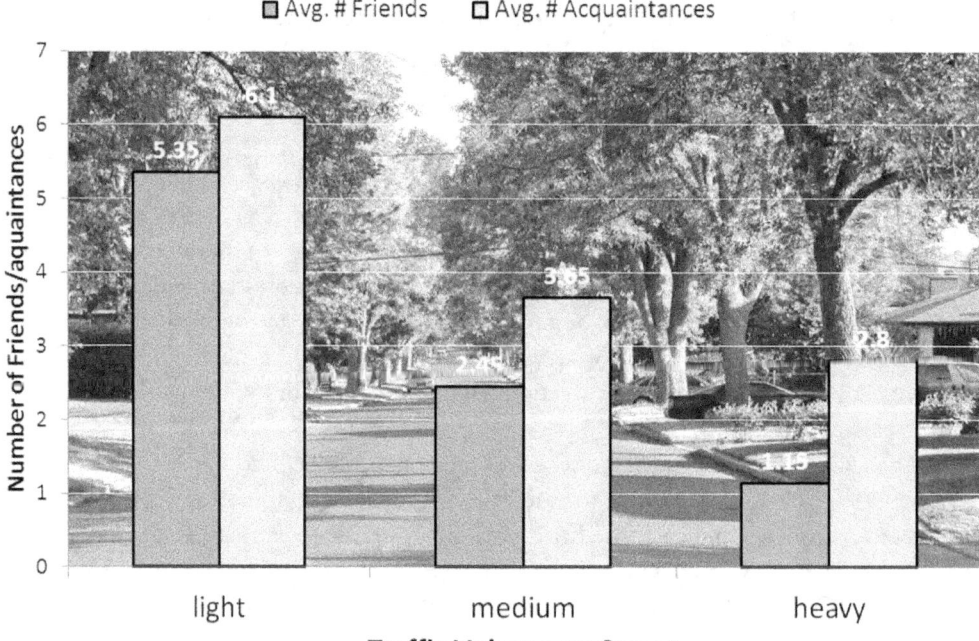

Average Number of Friends/Aquaintances per Person on Three Streets

☐ Avg. # Friends   ☐ Avg. # Acquaintances

Traffic Volume and Social Contacts: Three streets with light, medium and heavy traffic volume (from left to right) yield social contact numbers (friends and acquaintances) in inverse proportion to the amount of traffic.

consistent with the earlier studies. The chart titled "Traffic Volume and Social Contacts" shows that the respective social activity is convincingly higher for the corresponding lower traffic volumes. The number of friends doubles with each reduction in traffic volume, and an analogous trend is observed for the acquaintances. The most "social" of the three streets is a cul-de-sac, which had the lowest traffic volumes, confirming previous observations about the sociability of cul-de-sacs.[30]

These studies, taken together, suggest that any network layout that restricts traffic on residential streets can be expected to intensify social bonds on the street. As we saw in the previous section, the fused grid model exhibits the lowest traffic volume on local streets out of all other current network layouts. Consequently, it might be expected to generate a friendly, sociable environment.

CRIME

It is widely recognized that crime and related antisocial behavior originates in communities with a predominance of underprivileged persons of certain socioeconomic characteristics, including some, if not all, of the following: lack of education, unemployment, and clan divisions. These are the strongest determinants of antisocial behavior. As such, to reduce crime, civic authorities usually target socioeconomic conditions as a priority. Changing the physical structure of neighborhoods is often a supplementary step. Nonetheless, it is still relevant to know how different neighborhood models function under more or less comparable socioeconomic conditions, and whether the street network, traffic, building type and land uses influence the incidence of crime. The most convincing evidence could only come from results following the transformation of a neighborhood's physical attributes, especially its street network.

The Five Oaks community retrofit was one such physical transformation. This rare experiment, intended to make the community less prone to criminal activity, showed that certain layout elements assist in reducing antisocial behavior by mediating a greater sense of "ownership" of common spaces. After the modifications to the street network, violent crime fell by 50 percent and overall crime by 26 percent, in contrast to a 1 percent increase in the city as a whole. From a neighborhood design perspective, the changes to the network reduced car permeability—also termed filtered permeability—while maintaining full pedestrian connectivity. This meant that many streets were accessible from one point of entry only, which was also the exit point. Shortcuts through the neighborhood became practically impossible; only local, recognizable traffic would enter the streets.[31]

While the Five Oaks experiment studied a smaller troubled neighborhood with a relatively homogeneous socio-cultural mix, a larger study found analogous results across a more diverse community. Using a large crime database of over 13,000 burglaries and over 6,000 robberies in a district of 263,000 people, an extensive multivariate analysis[32] concluded that the elements that constitute a safe residential environment are as follows (quoting):

a. Flats are always safer than houses, and the wealth of inhabitants matters in both cases; the wealthier the residents, the more infractions.

b. Density is generally beneficial but more so at ground level.

c. Local movement is beneficial, but larger-scale movement is not.

d. Relative affluence and the number of neighbors have a greater effect than either being on a cul-de-sac or being on a through street.

e. Simple, linear cul-de-sac streets with good numbers of dwellings that are joined to through streets tend to be safe.

f. Residential areas should be permeable enough to allow pedestrian and bicycle movement in all directions, but not vehicles. The over-provision of poorly used vehicle permeability is a crime hazard.

While building form and social aspects may not always be within the community designer's jurisdiction, network permeability, cul-de-sacs and local movement appear entirely congruent with the structure of the fused grid:

1. This layout provides local vehicle access, but restricts through traffic to neighborhood perimeter.

2. Cul-de-sacs and crescents are short and give off-road active transport routes to an open grid–structured network.

3. Local movement on foot and bicycle is facilitated and encouraged.

Consequently, the above evidence suggests that the fused grid network would provide safe, secure living environments, all else being equal.

Economic Issues

Developer and municipal economic perspectives on land development generally have the most influence on planning decisions. Developers seek to build viable projects that meet customer demand while maintaining profitability that sustains their business. Municipalities seek to maintain services while minimizing ongoing expenditures, thereby lowering taxes and rendering the municipality attractive for investment. Reducing infrastructure expenditures supports these missions of both main participants in the land development process. These direct cost reductions, however, have to be balanced with other external societal needs, including accessibility, traffic flow, safety, emergency response, walkability and environmental impact.

Traffic safety and air pollution, which are quality-of-life issues, also have substantial economic implications and are influenced by street network layout, as we saw in Chapter 4. However, these two external costs do not affect the profitability of a development or municipal expenditures because they are borne by higher levels of government and society as a whole. For this reason, they are often overlooked in land development feasibility analyses. They are indirect costs, external to the development and its balance sheet. While this section deals with network infrastructure optimization from a design, placement and maintenance perspective, it also provides a brief review of these "external" costs for context.

LAND USE EFFICIENCY

Developers look for efficiencies in the use of land with an eye to increasing housing unit yields, which can raise a project's viability. At the same time, they pay attention to marketability with specific market groups in mind, as customer demand contributes to profitability. The amount of buildable land, lot yields and "curb appeal" all determine project viability.

Two elements affect the amount of buildable land: road dedication and green space dedication. While minimum ratios for green space dedication are regulated (e.g., area per capita, or a percentage of net developable area), road dedication is based on performance-based requirements (e.g., road class types, level of service, accessibility and so on). These requirements differ among developments depending on the size of the municipality, the location of the development within the urban boundaries, and municipal standards. Consequently, road space is more variable, negotiable and amenable to neighborhood design exploration, so long as access and mobility requirements are addressed as part of traffic impact assessment studies for the proposed neighborhood. As a result, the ultimate proportion of land to be allocated to streets in a given development is unknown at the outset of the planning effort; a range between 25 percent and 40 percent is typical, a wide range that leaves considerable latitude for optimization. These percentages apply to vehicular streets that are assumed, erroneously, to be the only type in community development.

In laying out a network, design parameters that affect the proportion of land that is dedicated to right-of-ways (ROW) are lot depth, street width and block size; these are mostly unaffected by the geometry of the network. Whether a street is curved or straight, whether the blocks are orthogonal or not, for every increase in a street's width, a proportional percentage increment of land is used up for that street.

Lengthening building blocks increases the developable land area, as fewer cross streets are introduced. Similarly, the block depth has a positive relationship with buildable land; the deeper the block, the further the streets are set apart and the smaller the portion of land they occupy. When the two factors, depth and length, are combined, the resulting block area is also indicative of the efficiency of land use; the larger the block area, the more

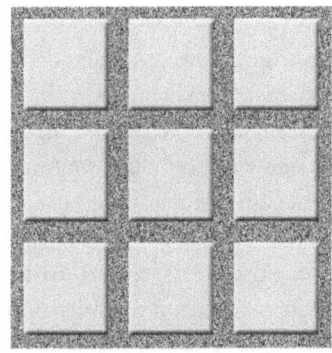 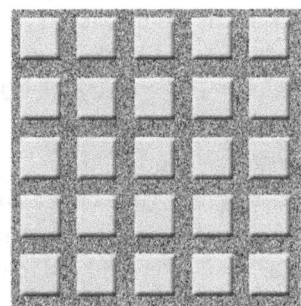 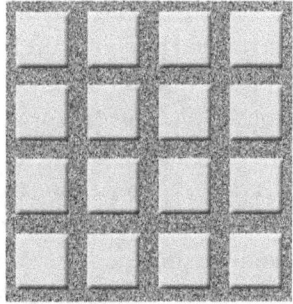

Sacramento	**Portland**	**Houston**
Block: 330 by 330 feet	Block: 200 by 200 feet	Block: 250 by 250 feet
Street Right of Way: 80 feet	Street Right of Way: 60 feet	Street Right of Way: 80 feet
Land portion for streets:	Land portion for streets:	Land portion for streets:
35.2%	**40.8%**	**42.6%**

City Block Size and Land Taken by Roads: The larger the blocks, the smaller the proportion of land used for right of ways (ROW). Street width can trump this rule, as in the case of Houston.

efficiently land is used. However, large blocks introduce inefficiencies when only their perimeters are occupied with buildings, causing the housing unit count per land area to drop.

Three city layouts demonstrate the variability in percentage of land absorbed by streets and illustrate the reasons for this variability. Sacramento has the largest block of the three. Block size determines the density (or frequency) of streets and, consequently, the percentage of land they consume; the fewer the number of streets per square mile, the less land they take up. Portland, by contrast, has the smallest block size of the three and uses a larger percentage of land than Sacramento, but slightly less than Houston, which has a larger block size—a surprising result. The latter difference is explained by the second factor that affects street land use: street width. Houston's ROW width, at 80 feet, is 30 percent larger than Portland's (60 feet). The cumulative effect of the wider streets thus counteracts the advantage of its larger block.

With these simple correlations in mind, the table of land use for road infrastructure in three alternative layouts shows that the conventional subdivision layout uses the least area of land for roads, followed by the fused grid layout, with an almost identical ratio, and by the grid-like layout that consumes about 28 percent more in lane-kilometers.[33]

Table 7.1: Street Density and Intersection Density in Three Layouts

Street Layout Type	Intersection Density (intersections/ha)	Street Density (lane-km/ha)
Conventional Suburban Cul-de-sac	0.48	0.35
Traditional Neighborhood Design	0.87	0.46
Fused Grid	0.51	0.36

Another way to look at land used for road infrastructure is via intersection and street density. Both are symptomatic of the frequency at which streets occur and, therefore, the probable consumption of land. The higher these two densities are, the more land is allocated to streets. Table 7.1 shows the relative densities for three alternative layouts for the same existing subdivision.

Conventional suburban cul-de-sac subdivision layouts minimize the use of land for streets and maximize the buildable land. Road infrastructure expenses represent the bulk of upfront costs for land development; for that reason, developers pursue its reduction assiduously. The outcome of this pursuit is also confirmed by the same study, which compared the infrastructure costs of these three layouts. The fused grid occupies the middle ground between the conventional cul-de-sac subdivision design and the traditional grid-like neighborhood design. All these tabulations present a clear picture of the direction for optimizing land-use efficiency—away from the traditional grid and toward the conventional subdivision layout, but with caution, as we shall see.

By knowing the influence of block size and street width (or street density and intersection density), it becomes relatively simple to arrive at an optimal layout from the perspective of reducing infrastructure costs. The conventional layout has the lowest capital costs for roads, followed by the fused grid (12 percent higher) and the neo-traditional (grid) layout (46 percent higher).

Focusing on a single key element's cost for arriving at a district layout, however, may create an imbalance with respect to other key elements, such as traffic flow, traffic safety and pedestrian/bicycle mobility; the first two have economic implications of considerable magnitude, while the third is primarily an issue of health and quality of life. All three, however, affect the residents of a district and are experienced as inconvenience, discomfort, anxiety and risk. The marginal gains for increases in block size follow a negative exponential trend, and, conversely, the disadvantages increase exponentially. A balance point needs to be identified.

USERS

Having analyzed the land-use efficiency of three common types of layouts, it may be necessary to also check their performance with respect to users, including safety, access, and mobility. It would be counterproductive to develop a plan that reduces infrastructure costs without regard for delays and collisions or for alternative transport options such as biking and walking.

For traffic movement, the number and type of intersections play a significant role. However, their frequency or the ratio between types is not regulated or listed in general practice guides. Importantly, rules that apply to vehicular movement may not apply equally well to pedestrian or bicycle circulation; as a result, rules about one mode may not serve the others well.

Unlike the land-use efficiency aspect, it is nearly impossible to gauge the mobility characteristics of a plan through simple observation, without the use of computational models. As we saw previously, analyses of on-site collision data show clearly that four-way intersections increase collision incidence. This fact, combined with the higher infrastructure cost of the layout with the greater number of four-way intersections, renders this layout least desirable from a user perspective. Its high frequency of vehicular streets becomes a double disadvantage. To distinguish between the remaining two layouts, the conventional and the fused grid, we turn to the question of facilitating movement and access.

Access, often measured by delay, provides additional economic and user criteria for judging layouts. The chart titled "Network System Delay in Five Density Scenarios" shows the comparative trip delay—network-wide—for the three typical layouts. The economic cost of user delay, though external to developer and municipal costs, is substantial. In a site-specific IBI study,[34] it was calculated to equal or even exceed the annual lifecycle costs of building and maintaining the road infrastructure! Despite its substantial monetary costs, delay is experienced predominantly as loss of time, inconvenience and frustration by residents of a subdivision. Its monetary value does not show up on any specific ledger. Nonetheless, it cannot be dismissed out of hand, considering its magnitude.

By this criterion, traffic delay, the most infrastructure-efficient plan is the poorest performer. The delay costs incurred by the conventional cul-de-sac layout are 12 percent higher than those of the fused grid, while the traditional neighborhood plan (grid-like) registers a 15 percent higher delay. Under two increased-density scenarios ("transit" and "downtown"), the fused grid layout generates 25 percent and 35 percent lower delay costs, respectively, compared to conventional suburban cul-de-sac layout.

Pedestrian mobility, the third user-related criterion, is mentioned here first because of its potential impact on health, and second because of its potential, if small, contribution to the reduction of air pollution through the avoidance of short-distance car trips, which, as

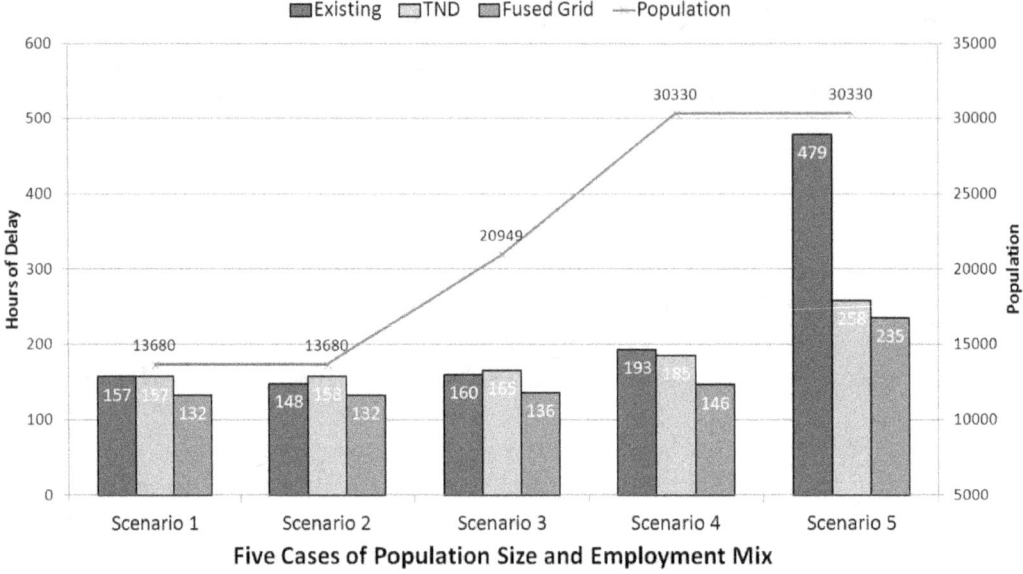

Network System Delay in Five Density Scenarios: In all population and employment density scenarios, the fused grid shows the lowest trip delay times. The Conventional Suburban pattern (Existing) shows exceedingly high delay at center-city level of densities (original design by Brian Hollingsworth).

we now know, are the most damaging. As we saw earlier under air quality, the fused grid has potentially the highest walking percentage and the lowest driving percentage of seven commonly used alternative layouts, including the conventional subdivision plan.

In summary, the fused grid would entail 12 percent higher annual lifecycle costs for infrastructure with respect to one of two alternative layouts. However, it would outperform both alternative network systems, particularly the conventional one, in terms of critical economic and user-related criteria: traffic safety, traffic delay, and pedestrian mobility.

GREEN SPACE

Green space is the second key layout element that affects net developable land area and, therefore, project economics. As a regulated dedication of land, the green space "loss" on the development ledger guides developers to dedicate the minimum green space percentage required by law.

There is a large body of scientific research regarding the positive influence of green space on the well-being of residents, and particularly on seniors and children, which we examined earlier. However, the cost issue of concern to developers (as an opportunity cost) and to the municipality (as a maintenance burden) remained unanswered until recently. The issue of whether green space can be justified purely on economic grounds, aside from its other recognized health benefits, has gradually been resolved. Site-specific research has supplied some notable and surprising answers. With caution, these findings can be extended to other sites.

The most notable of all findings relates to the values of real estate that has views of water.[35] Such views, depending on their directness, can add 8–59 percent of value to the property. The value of properties that actually front a lake can be as much as 126 percent higher than the base price. Similarly, a study that examined properties near a riparian corridor found 2.4–6.0 percent increases depending on the distance from the corridor, with the highest value corresponding to about 200 feet (60 meters) of distance.[36] Another study looked at property values near a golf course. It found a general 5 percent increase in value.[37]

The most comprehensive study[38] looked at a range of developments and attempted to determine the potential profitability of a project based on the sum total of all property value increases near the open space. It quantified the monetary value of open space to both a developer and a municipality. It also identified the relationship of price premiums and distance from the park and calculated the total value of all price increments within a development. The results showed that a developer would earn more than the value of the dedicated green space removed from buildable area. Similarly, the municipality would recover the construction and maintenance costs for the green space through increased property taxes due to higher real estate assessments. Moreover, size and location of green spaces can affect these earnings. Their level would be largely proportional to the number of properties that are within 500 feet (150 meters) of the open space that yields an estimated 10–15 percent price premium.

Values of properties beyond that range also increase, but at a rate diminishing rapidly with distance. From an economic perspective, two small parks that satisfy the distance requirement are preferable to a large one that does not.

These research findings suggest that the systematic inclusion of small to medium-size parks within an average 500-foot distance from all homes in the fused grid neighborhood module can be fully justified from an economic viewpoint.

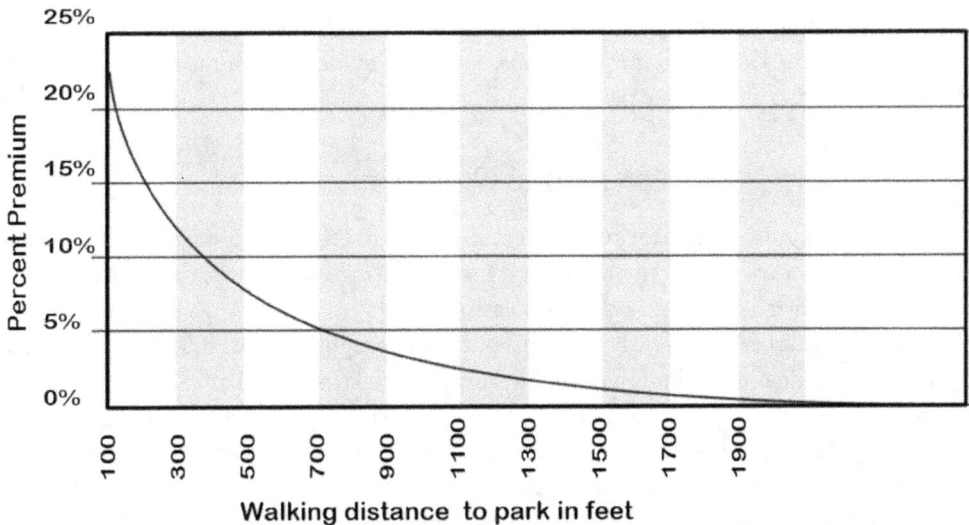

Influence of Proximity to Park on Property Values: A location up to 600 feet from a park properties can gain from 5 to 20 percent in value.

Environmental Issues

All land development impacts the natural landscape and disrupts ecosystems in the transition to human settlements, but these impacts can be minimized through careful design. Of all transitions, the change from a natural to a built environment has the largest impact. Green space is reduced, and buildings, asphalt and concrete take over. Moreover, new residents add to the community's ecological footprint with their normal consumption patterns.[39] And since over 75 percent of our contemporary living routines still depend on fossil fuels, new residents will also inevitably contribute more air, water, and greenhouse gas pollution. The designers of new neighborhoods and districts can reduce their ecological impact in two ways: first, by increasing the use of permeable surface treatments to absorb and completely eliminate rainwater runoff; and second, by increasing accessibility for pedestrians and bicyclists, which gives at least a competitive advantage to making local trips on foot or by bicycle versus driving personal vehicles.

HYDROLOGY

Key elements that decrease surface permeability include the most influential, such as buildings and roads. One research project attempted to quantify the relative surface permeability of three alternative site plans for the same location.[40] The analysis considered roads, rear lanes, building footprints and sidewalks. Results showed that the impermeable areas of the three layouts ranged from 34.7 percent for the fused grid option to 35.8 percent for the conventional suburban layout, and to 39 percent for traditional grid patterns—small but measurable differences. Streets were the single most influential factor in the amount of water runoff. They accounted for an impermeable surface of up to three times that of the building footprint. Of the total impermeable area in the three layouts, the portion attributable to streets ranged from 48 to 65 percent, with the fused grid having the lowest amount. The fused grid model achieves this favorable environmental impact outcome through its reduction in street length and the systematic use of open spaces as key elements of the layout to provide off-road pedestrian and bicycle paths.

GREENHOUSE GAS EMISSIONS

Direct and indirect evidence suggests strong potential for the fused grid model to increase the number of trips taken on foot and bike, and, correspondingly, to reduce local car travel and thereby greenhouse gas (GHG) emissions.

As we saw earlier, an extensive trip diary study of neighborhoods based on geo-coded trips to local destinations found that neighborhoods with layouts similar to a fused grid configuration increased home-base walking trips by 11.3 percent in comparison to the traditional grid. Its 10 percent increase in relative pedestrian connectivity is associated with a 23 percent decrease in vehicle kilometers of local travel.[41]

A modeling study, also mentioned earlier, compared seven neighborhoods of distinct, though typical, street network layouts for the daily travel patterns, including the amount of walking that occurred. The test set of network patterns included two versions of the traditional grid, two versions of postwar cul-de-sac suburbs, two versions of a modified grid, and the fused grid. It found that neighborhood designs similar to the fused grid exhibited considerably more walking activity. The lowest amount of walking was found to happen in one of the postwar conventional cul-de-sac subdivisions. Using it as the benchmark (100) for comparison, the two traditional grids registered 111 percent, the second cul-de-sac subdivision registered 109 percent, one modified grid neighborhood 108 percent, the second modified grid 137 percent, and the fused grid 143 percent as much walking. In terms of the total distance walked, the fused grid registered 23 percent more distance walked than the benchmark cul-de-sac layout, and it also had the lowest number of local car trips.[42]

The fused grid anticipates the location of convenient (i.e., within walking distance) shopping and amenities at the periphery of the neighborhood. Moreover, any part of the fused grid neighborhood is a five-minute, ¼-mile (400-meter), walk to the periphery, and a ten-minute, ½-mile (800-meter), walk across the entire neighborhood (assuming four quadrants of 40-acre neighborhood modules). Closeness of all local destinations for walking and bicycling—school, shopping, services—is a key element in the design of the fused grid modules. The same structure, based on ¼-mile (400-meter) intervals, coincides with current practices for transit route location. Consequently, the street network pattern, the anticipated land-use distribution and the location of urban transit stops are all conducive to walking and bicycling.

The volume of GHG emission is affected not only by amount of car travel but also by the flow of traffic. Low speeds and short trips contribute significantly more GHGs than normal arterial travel at optimum speeds. Improved accessibility for active travel modes lowers car travel and GHG generation. Smooth traffic flow, or, in traffic engineering terms, reduced trip delay, also reduces GHG generation attributable to the residual local trips that are made by car. As we saw earlier in this chapter, under normal urban density conditions of 36 people per acre (90 per hectare) or 40 people per acre (101 per hectare), including jobs within the community, the fused grid experiences 30 percent and 35 percent less delay than the two alternative layout patterns, respectively. This suggests that emissions attributable to less than optimal traffic flow conditions would be lower in a neighborhood laid out in a fused grid pattern.[43]

LIMITATIONS IN REDUCING ENVIRONMENTAL IMPACT

It must be recognized that a new neighborhood and its social, environmental, and economic impacts, whatever its layout model, will always inherit and be heavily influenced by the larger context and culture of the community in which it is built. The neighborhood location is largely predetermined; land is developed where it is available and ripe for development. Location will predominantly affect the mode of travel to work. Similarly, the building intensity of development will follow market rules of land economics and proximity; a layout can anticipate, but not dictate, population density. Many of these factors, such as location, development intensity and proximity to other uses, could play a decisive role in shaping the residents' travel habits and, consequently, the total environmental impact of the new neighborhood. Any network layout will be subject to these limitations; using the one with the potentially lightest footprint is a step in the right direction.

Summary

The value of the fused grid neighborhood model rests on the systematic application of key design elements that optimize neighborhood quality of life and health benefits and, ultimately, within the limitations discussed above, will contribute to lowering community environmental impacts.

On a more general level, this book has traced indirectly the evolution of transportation systems and alluded to their impact on the city form and on the quality of life of their citizens. Through a vast patchwork of intentions and realizations, we see a steady increase in the range of benefits that citizens derive by living in cities. Through the constant tension between stressors and adaptations, whether physical at the city scale or personal, adaptations and mutations have occurred that render city life ever more desirable—hence their constant growth. This book offers one such adaptation, which resolves known contemporary stressors and may even contribute to their attraction.

7

Case Studies of Applications and Designs

In the previous chapters we described a sequence of steps by which the fused grid network model can be applied, and we presented inferential evidence of its potential benefits. This chapter will illustrate how this model has been employed for specific sites and what benefits could accrue from its application. As discussed elsewhere, these are the early years of the model's application and, consequently, there are only few examples, particularly of fully built and occupied sites. As a result, in situ analysis of the model's functional aspects is not possible at this time. However, even from the first steps toward full implementation, there are sufficient data to draw tentative conclusions of the model's potential utility.

The four case studies presented in this chapter attempt to glean insights into the process of application, the issues surrounding it, and outcomes either in evidence or expected. Interestingly, one of the applications that predate the initial publication of this model—Stuyvesant Town—demonstrates that the principles of the model can be found in other projects independent of its structured configuration.

The presentation sequence proceeds from projects that have been designed and built or are being built, such as Saddlestone and Stuyvesant Town; to projects that have been approved and anticipate construction, such as the Stratford expansion; and to projects that have been designed, proposed and await further action, such as Kelowna.

Saddlestone, which is located at the periphery of the City of Calgary, Alberta, is the first district to move from conception to construction. Stuyvesant Town, now more than sixty years old, is a mature neighborhood in the heart of a metropolis—New York City—on Manhattan Island. When seen together, these two case studies provide evidence of the flexibility of the model both in its configuration and in its potential application to diverse urban settings. The Stratford expansion provides evidence of a municipal government process by which new models can be introduced and applied on a large scale. The Kelowna, British Columbia, case study provides lessons to be learned from the retrofitting of an existing predominantly single-family residential neighborhood.

Given that the following case studies are not post-construction, post-occupancy research with exacting methods, criteria and metrics, their structure and content vary according to the nature of each project, available data, the history of the project, and the context of its implementation. They provide a tableau of the issues, processes and potential outcomes that come into play when applying the fused grid model.

Case Study 1—Saddlestone: A Connected, Walkable, Safe Neighborhood

INTRODUCTION

Saddlestone is the first application of the fused grid street network model that was spurred by a developer's initiative. Following a presentation of the model to a workshop audience, a Calgary developer—Genesis Land Development—approached the speaker and requested collaboration for the implementation of the model on a site on the northeast edge of the city. After finalizing the draft layout plan in 2004, the developer confirmed the business case for the proposed layout by comparing it to previous developments of similar size and setting (see table 1 following). The plan approval process of the city, lasting about three years, and an intervening downturn of the local housing market, pushed the construction schedule into 2009. At the time of this writing, over one quarter of the 160 acres have been constructed and inhabited. This part, as do each of the site's four quadrants, includes a central neighborhood park.

LOCATION

The site is located in Calgary, Alberta, a dynamic city that is experiencing rapid growth. It is found at the northeast edge of the city, north of 80th Avenue NE and west of Stony Trail NE highway. The site borders the Taralake community to the south and the Saddleridge subdivision to the north and west.

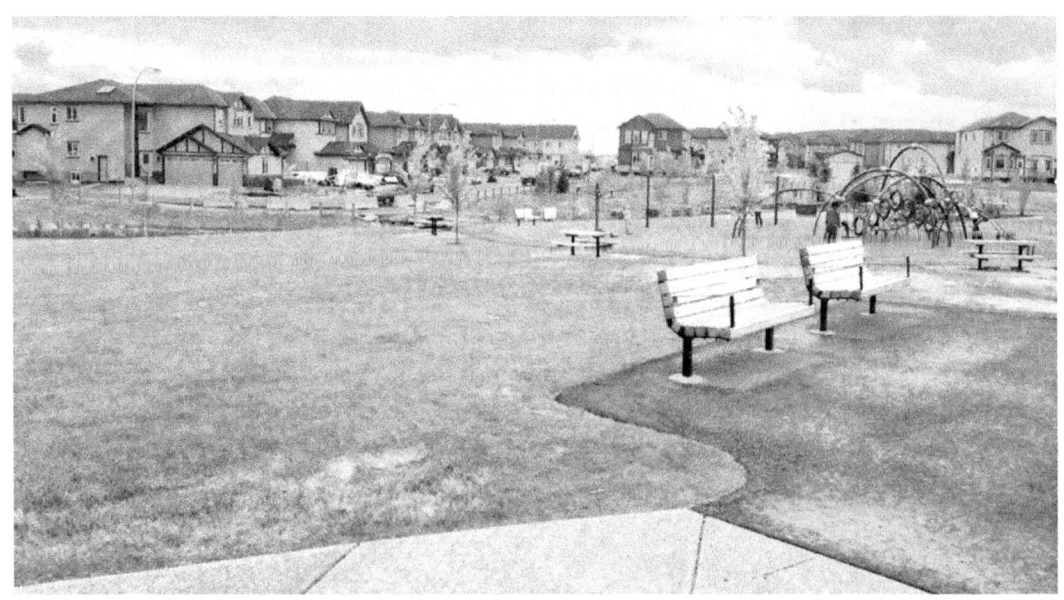

A View Looking Across the Central Neighborhood Park: Still in the early stages of construction, the Saddlestone neighborhood displays its emphasis on pedestrian movement and children's play.

CHALLENGES AND OBJECTIVES

The design challenges in laying out the Saddlestone plan were similar to those of any other suburban subdivision: infrastructure efficiency, affordability, walkability, connectivity, safety, low environmental impact, and delight. The first two design objectives are prime considerations for the developer who seeks to sustain a viable business and build profitable projects. They are also important for any municipality, since they reduce ongoing lifecycle costs and help house a wide range of families. The remaining design priorities are important from the future resident's perspective. When met, they provide a functional, comfortable and enjoyable milieu that residents favor.

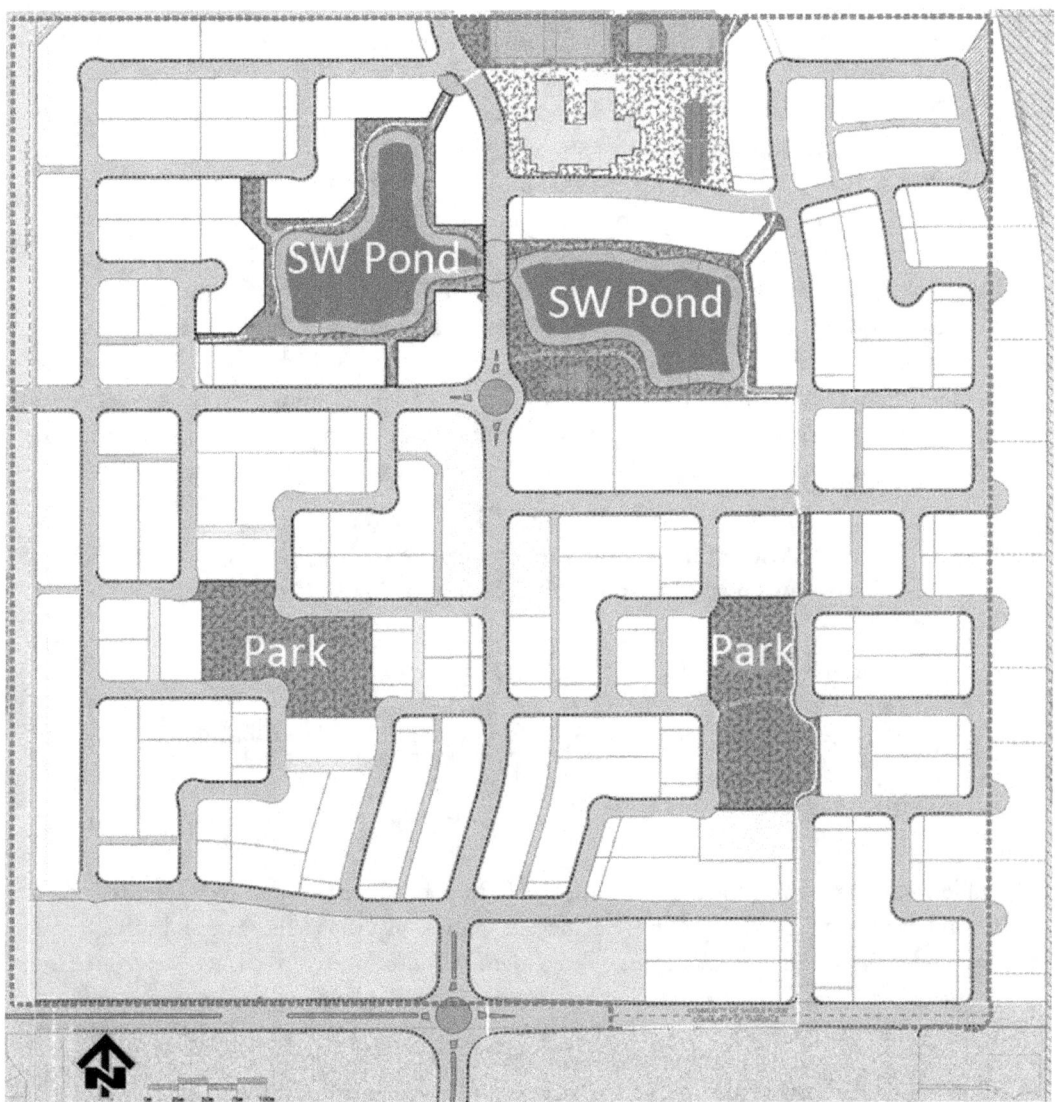

Site Plan of the 160-Acre District: The district is made up of four neighborhoods, each with a focal open space that acts as a connecting hub, recreational space and rainwater management device.

Infrastructure Efficiency

Infrastructure matters because it represents the major capital outlay for the developer and a key accounting element in pricing the homes, after land. For new homes to be competitive and offer affordable, entry-level shelter to the influx of new families, infrastructure costs have to be equal to or lower than what conventionally has been achieved in previous developments or by the industry at large.

As we saw in Chapter 6, theoretical analyses of the fused grid model predict slightly higher costs of infrastructure than conventional suburban development: a 6 percent increase in annual lifecycle costs (ALC) and a 12 percent increase in capital costs. However, they also predict a 14 percent reduction in ALC and 23 percent reduction in capital costs compared to what grid-like, neo-traditional suburbs exhibit.[1] These analyses were based on diagrammatic representations of typical layouts in one case, and on a 1970s conventional subdivision overlaid with a fused grid plan in a second study.

The Saddlestone subdivision is the first test of the previous theoretical results. As the comparative figures in table 1 (below) show, the developer's own analysis proves consistent with the predictions, and even betters them. In this case, the fused grid layout reduces infrastructure costs even in comparison with conventional suburban development that has so far been the epitome of efficiency. The new layout results in fewer roads and more developable land. Though the differences are small and this is only one instance of comparison, these results demonstrate convincingly that the fused grid layout model is at least as efficient, and perhaps more so, in controlling infrastructure costs than what hitherto has been the most efficient method of laying out new subdivisions. Based on this efficiency, the model adds a competitive edge to the house prices and widens the range of families that can obtain shelter. In addition, it keeps future municipal outlays for servicing the infrastructure in check.

Table 1: Comparison of Infrastructure Areas Allocated to Five Development Components Between Conventional Suburban and Fused Grid Layouts

Measured Item	Taralake (Existing)	Saddlestone (Proposed)	Difference in percentage points
Total Area	64.78 ha	64.24 ha	
Roads	15.72 ha (24.3%)	13.5 ha (21.0%)	-3.3% roads
Development	36.27 ha (56%)	36.94 ha (57.5%)	+1.5 % development
Municipal Reserve	5.4 ha (8.3%)	7.1 ha (11.1%)	+2.8% open space
Water or Pond	3.4 ha (5.2%)	3.1 ha (4.8%)	-0.4 % water surface
Public Utility Lots	3.99 ha (6.2%)	3.6 ha (5.6%)	-0.6% PUL

Table 1 compares two adjacent communities in the same district: one already built and the second proposed (at the time of the calculation). Given that the analysis and tabulation were done by a seasoned developer, keen on improving his fiscal outcomes as well as reputation, they can be relied upon for accuracy more than theoretical speculation or analyses conducted by a disinterested party.

Connectivity and Walkability

It has been shown through detailed analyses of plans that most recent and current suburban developments have low connectivity and thereby inhibit walkability.[2] This uninten-

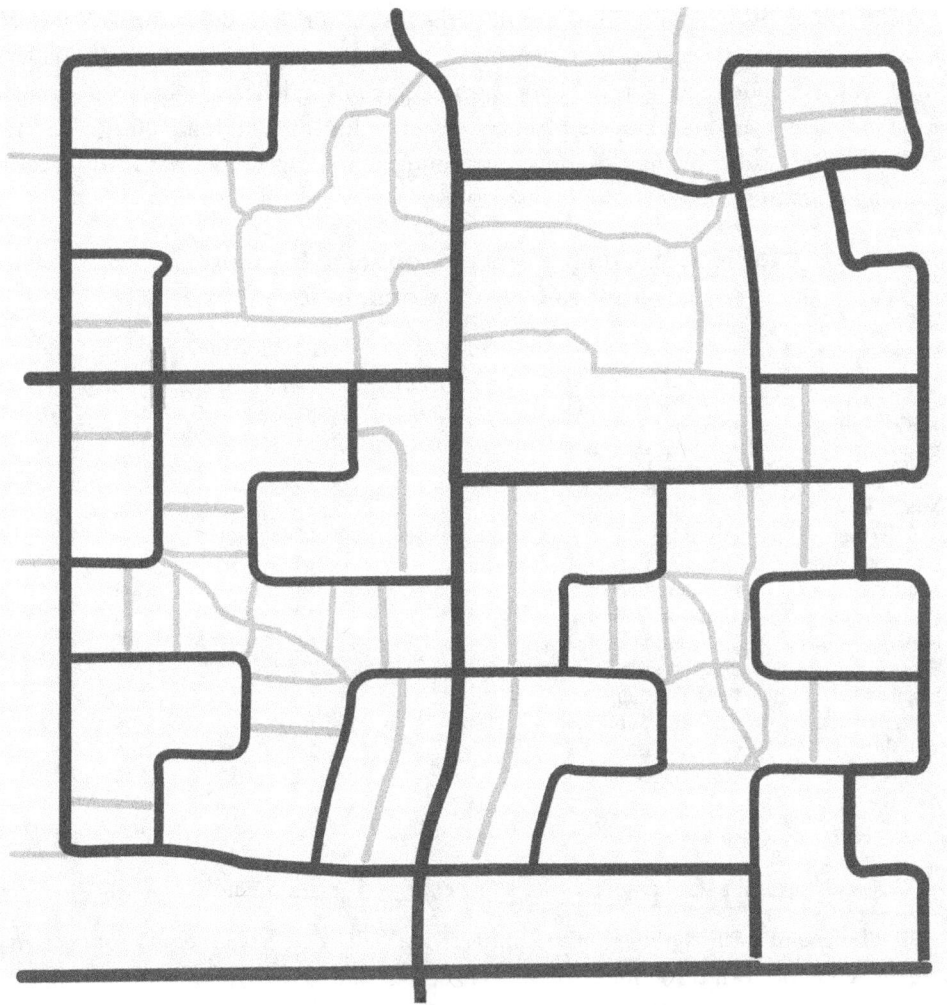

Pedestrian and Car Circulation: Roads (black) serve each neighborhood but do not cross it. Pedestrian paths (grey) supplement the streets and connect the entire neighborhood.

tional negative outcome can be attributed to the quest for land-use efficiency by means of reducing road costs, which has resulted in very long blocks and less frequent intersections. In addition, the preference for the cul-de-sac street type, a proven favorite of community residents, inadvertently disadvantaged pedestrian directness of route. Moreover, the tendency toward curvilinear street shapes further exacerbates route directness. The ultimate, undesirable combined effect of these traits is to limit choice of travel mode by discouraging walking and biking.

As we saw in the above section and chart, the fused grid model maintains or improves the efficiency of land achieved by conventional subdivisions. Consequently, it might be expected that its connectivity will be as low as (or lower than) that of conventional subdivisions. Contrary to expectations, early theoretical analysis showed that while it maintains land efficiency, it in fact improves on connectivity in general and, most importantly, on pedestrian connectivity.

Saddlestone, its first application, provides the first acid test of the theoretical results. The City of Calgary did a connectivity comparison of 13 communities shown in table 2 (below), which included Saddlestone. The comparison was included in an advisory document that was intended to assist developers, planners, city planning staff and community advocates in understanding and applying the concept of connectivity. (The table was rearranged in descending order of score for clarity of discussion.)

Table 2: A Comparison of Connectivity Scores of Thirteen Calgary Communities

Community	Type of Layout	Street Connectivity Index	Active Mode Connectivity Index	% of ROW Residential Streets/Alleys
Killarney	Classic Grid	2	2	31%
Hillhurst	Grid, long blocks	1.7	1.7	19%
Mount Royal	Grid, mixed shapes	1.7	1.7	28%
Saddlestone	**Fused Grid**	1.6	1.7	21%
Garrison Woods	Grid-like (TND)	1.5	1.6	25%
Acadia	Grid, modified	1.5	1.5	28%
Somerset	Conventl Suburban	1.4	1.5	23%
McKenzie Towne	Conventl Suburban	1.4	1.5	21%
Ogden	Grid, mixed shapes	1.4	1.4	26%
Haysboro	Grid, fragmented	1.4	1.4	25%
Tuscany	Conventl Suburban	1.3	1.5	24%
Temple	Grid, modified	1.3	1.4	30%
Chaparral	Conventl Suburban	1.2	1.2	26%
Average		**1.5**	**1.5**	**25%**
City Targets		**1.4**	**1.6**	

Table 2 reveals several useful associations, some expected and some not:

1. The layout with the maximum connectivity, Killarney, has an equal connectivity score for both travel modes. This is expected due to the fact there is no differentiation between roads for vehicles and paths for pedestrians or bikes. It shares this characteristic with six other community layouts.

2. Killarney's high connectivity comes at a high infrastructure cost: 50 percent more road area than the next highest connectivity score communities of Hillhurst and Mount Royal. A high ratio of land for roads implies not only more road infrastructure but also opportunity costs attributable to land that becomes unavailable for development. Moreover, as was mentioned in Chapter 6, the classic grid imposes invisible (and high) costs in terms of traffic safety.

3. Two communities stand at the average for street connectivity and the majority—seven—fall below average. This statistic confirms the perception that most networks of conventional subdivisions built recently and being built currently are not sufficiently interconnected.

4. Six communities (Saddlestone, Garrison Woods, Somerset, McKenzie Towne, Tuscany and Temple) show a surprising, new result in which the active mode connectivity is higher than general street connectivity. This higher score implies that the layout includes separate, distinct paths that are intended exclusively for walking

and biking, suggesting that there is a sound alternative approach to achieving high active mode connectivity.

5. Three communities fail to meet the recent targets set by the city for both active mode connectivity (1.6) and street connectivity (1.4).

6. Similarly, eight of the thirteen communities (including the three indicated above) do not meet the target for active mode connectivity (1.6), and only four surpass it.[3]

7. The fused grid layout, Saddlestone, has the second highest score (1.7) for active modes after Killarney, and the third highest score for street connectivity. That score surpasses the city's target for street connectivity (1.6 vs. 1.4). Significantly, it achieves these levels of connectivity with the second lowest percentage (21 percent) of ROW for streets.

It is worth noting that communities which share nomenclature (grid, modified grid and conventional suburban or curvilinear) produce inconsistent outcomes. This implies that connectivity outcomes are not intrinsically linked to the shape of streets or blocks, whether rectilinear, curvilinear, crooked or fragmented. It is the overall network system (or pattern) that has the greatest influence. The fused grid system produces consistently high values.

This analysis confirms the theoretical expectations of the fused grid connectivity performance and its infrastructure efficiency in practice.

Traffic Safety

Evaluation of traffic safety in the new neighborhood must follow the full built out, when resident travel patterns have been established. However, analytical studies that are mentioned in Chapter 6 predict a significant advantage in terms of collision reduction.[4] These studies assign by inference low safety scores to the Killarney grid-type configuration, and they predict considerably higher traffic safety performance for the fused grid configuration. Given that the Saddlestone layout is fairly faithful to the schematic fused grid model, its safety performance is expected to match the theoretical predictions and confirm the inferences drawn from communities that share some of its morphology.

Delight, Satisfaction

As with traffic safety, resident surveys can only be meaningful only once the neighborhood is built out and fully occupied, and following a few years of residency. Inferences from other communities that share some of the fused grid's characteristics, such as no through traffic and quiet, common open spaces nearby, suggest a high probability that the neighborhood will be well liked. Most residents have a direct or indirect view of open space, which is within a one- or two-minute walk from any house in the neighborhood.

A particular source of enjoyment may also be the fact that parks act as hubs or crossroads for the pedestrian circulation within the neighborhood, not simply as destinations. As cited research has shown,[5] this feature, combined with the absence of through traffic, increases the odds of forming casual acquaintances and friendships, which strengthen the sense of belonging. This effect in turn has a positive influence on the degree of satisfaction with the neighborhood.

Environmental Features

The centrality of the open space that each neighborhood is endowed with offers the potential for it to be used as a stormwater management feature. Saddlestone took up this opportunity and incorporated two types of storm management techniques: raingardens and ponds (two of each). Raingardens, a relatively new approach, maintain a walkable, green surface throughout the open space, but have constructed substratum layers with a high absorptive capacity. They have proven to be one of the most effective ways of retaining rainwater on site and substantially reducing stormwater runoff. By using ponds and raingardens, Saddlestone exploits the potential inherent in the fused grid to reduce the environmental impact of a new neighborhood.

Walking Distance to Transit

As laid out, the Saddlestone neighborhood places 90 percent of homes within a five-minute walk of a bus stop and the remaining 10 percent within a maximum of seven minutes. While residents have excellent access to bus stops, transit buses also trace a direct, short travel path through the neighborhood, thereby improving trip times. These two features can encourage the use of public transportation, thus potentially reducing the degree of reliance on automotive transport.

Conclusion

This case study offers the first pieces of evidence from a partially built example of the fused grid network model. The positive picture that emerges so far produces grounds for confidence in the model. A comprehensive analysis of its performance upon completion of the entire 160-acre district will yield more insights into the various aspects that characterize a good neighborhood. For the time being, its performance in key areas of importance to a developer, a municipality and the ultimate user—the residents—offers ample evidence of its well-above-average positive outcomes.

Case Study 2—Stuyvesant Town: An Urban Oasis Amid Asphalt and Concrete

Introduction

City plans of previous times and different places can express similar ideas, principles and intentions, but they may not have a common name. Often a generic name is applied in retrospect when similarities are deciphered. Such is the case of the Stuyvesant site plan. The plan was conceived and built in the late 1940s by a team[6] that was inspired by the ideas of the garden city movement. The goal of giving prominence to nature, which is gradually receding from the city, resulted in a layout that could now be easily named a fused grid. Coupled with the renewed emphasis on natural settings is the dominance of pedestrian networks on the site, key fused grid characteristic. Though built half a century before the new model emerged, it stands as a prime example of the concept. Moreover, it provides evidence of the

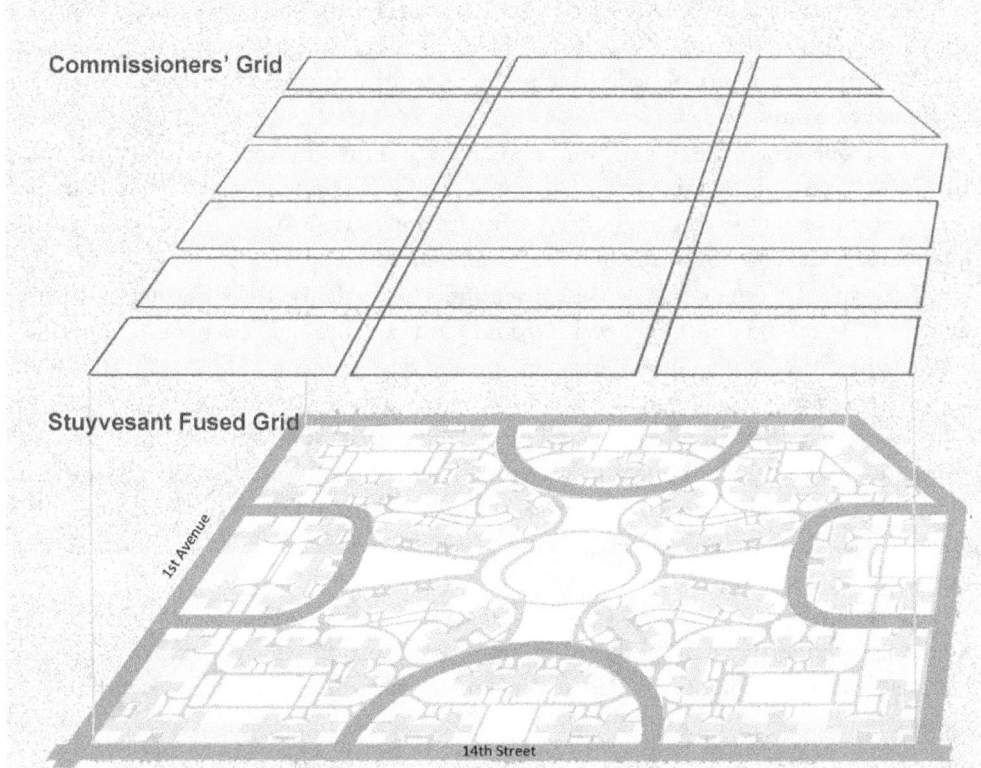

Alternative Layouts for the Same Site: Seven streets of the original New York grid were replaced with four crescents and numerous pedestrian paths. This choice transformed the area into an urban oasis.

flexibility of the new model: unlike the Saddlestone development (case study 1), which is built at the periphery of a city, Stuyvesant Town is found in the center of a throbbing, heavily populated metropolis—New York City. Evidently, the model adapts to both a city-center urban environment and a suburban milieu at the periphery—a key reason for being presented in this set of case studies.

LOCATION

Stuyvesant Town occupies the area between 14th and 20th streets and between 1st and Avenue C on the east end of Manhattan Island, bordering on the East River. Its central location would suggest high real estate values, which may also be amplified by the proximity to the river. This explains the high density of the development.

THE STUYVESANT TOWN LAYOUT

The Stuyvesant site plan replaced 18 blocks of the 1811 Commissioner's Manhattan grid and occupies about 80 acres (32 hectares) of land in a perfectly rectangular block (except for one truncated corner). Its size is about twice that of a typical 40-acre neighborhood module, a standard structural component of the fused grid network. Yet, at that double scale, it displays one of the fourteen schematic network layouts: four looped roads (crescents) enter and exit the site from its four sides but do not intersect. The entire site is then connected with an extensive network of pedestrian paths, wide for frequent, main routes and narrow for secondary routes.

The looped-road–based neighborhood layout has found many imitations, variations and reinventions since that time, primarily at the periphery of cities. One example, a variation conceived and built following on the heels of Stuyvesant Town, is Wildwood, a neighborhood in Winnipeg, Canada, consisting of single-family houses.

This type of configuration was unconventional for its time and a daring departure from the then 100-year-old grid, which was introduced to expedite land speculation.[7] It was also in tune with the emerging modes of financing and development. While in the 1800s city land was transacted in small increments for houses, townhouses or walk-up tenements in slow progression, with the advent of the railway, subway, elevator, and particularly the large corporation, land could be bought in large parcels and developed in short order. Stuyvesant Town, among other developments, represents this momentous leap in technological and financial clout. Rather than following an old planning order, its builders had the necessary foundation to create a new one.

As we shall see in what follows, the advantages of the Stuyvesant layout include efficiency of land use, connectivity and walkability, active transport, fitness opportunities, noise reduction, clean air, restorative ambiance, community cohesion and a reduced environmental impact.

Efficiency of Land Use

The new plan replaced seven grid vehicular roads with only four. On this basis, approximate comparisons of infrastructure elements can be made (not counting the perimeter roads in either case), as seen in Table 3.

Table 3. Comparison of Land Allocation for Roads Between Stuyvesant Town and the Commissioners' Grid

Layout Type	Stuyvesant Town Plan (Fused Grid)	Commissioners' Classic Grid	Difference	Percent Increase
Linear feet of road	5,316	12,870	7,554	242%
Total ROW area at 60' width (in acres)	7.3	18.3	11.0	250%
Area of site allocated to street ROWs (%)	9%	23%		

As can be seen from these figures, the Stuyvesant plan has less than half of the Commissioners' plan in linear feet and in right-of-way area for streets. As a percentage of the total site area, the difference is even more striking, with the former taking up 9 percent of the 80-acre site and the latter 23 percent. The 11 acres that are thus extracted from the road system are reallocated to other uses, such as greenery, a central square with a fountain, sports fields, playgrounds and a swimming pool. The infrastructure efficiency not only reduces capital expenditures on a feature of negative value but also provides opportunities for investment in elements that contribute to improved quality of life.

Connectivity and Active Transport

The 80-acre area within the perimeter roads can be crossed on foot in five minutes in the north-south direction, and in about seven in the east-west direction. For such short distances, there is hardly a need for motorized transport when visiting friends, relatives, and schoolmates or attending community events on the site. The extensive network of paths that link the various parts of the site has distinct advantages over normal street network: (a) The paths are more direct, as the network includes convenient diagonals and cut-offs that are impossible in the classic grid. (b) They preempt waiting time at what would have been intersections of busy streets, thus shortening the trip duration and allowing for a continuous, uninterrupted pace. (c) They remove the perception of risk and the undercurrent of apprehension that is normally associated with regular vehicular streets. (d) They shed the noise and odors experienced on streets, instead providing a green canopy and green surroundings in every direction. Walking to destinations such as convenience stores and services at the periphery is not only more efficient, due to the directness of route, but also pleasant. The central square that dissects and connects the crossway paths also offers a momentary stop to those who need a short rest. The neighborhood provides an exceptional pedestrian environment. Partial evidence of its low reliance on automobility is the level of car ownership: whether owning or renting, Stuyvesant Town residents have 0.3 cars per occupied unit versus 1.1 cars for homeowners and 0.4 cars for tenants in New York City as a whole.

Active Living

Walking to destinations within the neighborhood and to the perimeter—a palpable choice—is only one aspect of the active living enticement of its structure. The presence of sports grounds enables residents to take up athletic activities within a few minutes' walk from their places of residence. The location of a basketball court, tennis courts and a swimming pool within sighting distance of pedestrians crossing the district forms a visual magnet and a stimulus to participate and engage in such activities. Moreover, children and young adults living in this neighborhood are more likely to walk and find enjoyment in sports activities.[8] This early involvement builds a lifelong affinity for sports and affords strong social links.

By rejecting the dominance of roads, the fused grid site plan of this neighborhood reintroduces the activities that streets supported up until vehicular traffic occupied them—play and socializing.

Restorative Ambiance

Common city streets offer stimulation, distraction and tension, but rarely, if ever, relaxation or restoration. In central districts not only are pavements full of cars, sounds and smells but the sidewalks are also packed with people and messages from a plethora of disparate sources, from storefronts to billboards. This crowded, overstimulating environment overwhelms the senses and the brain, a condition that naturally seeks the opposite: rest and relaxation. Intuition leads central city residents to seek parks and natural settings where they can relax and recharge themselves amid natural sights and sounds, such as trees, flowers, waterfalls and birdsong. Usually, this implies a trip to a neighborhood or district park, another

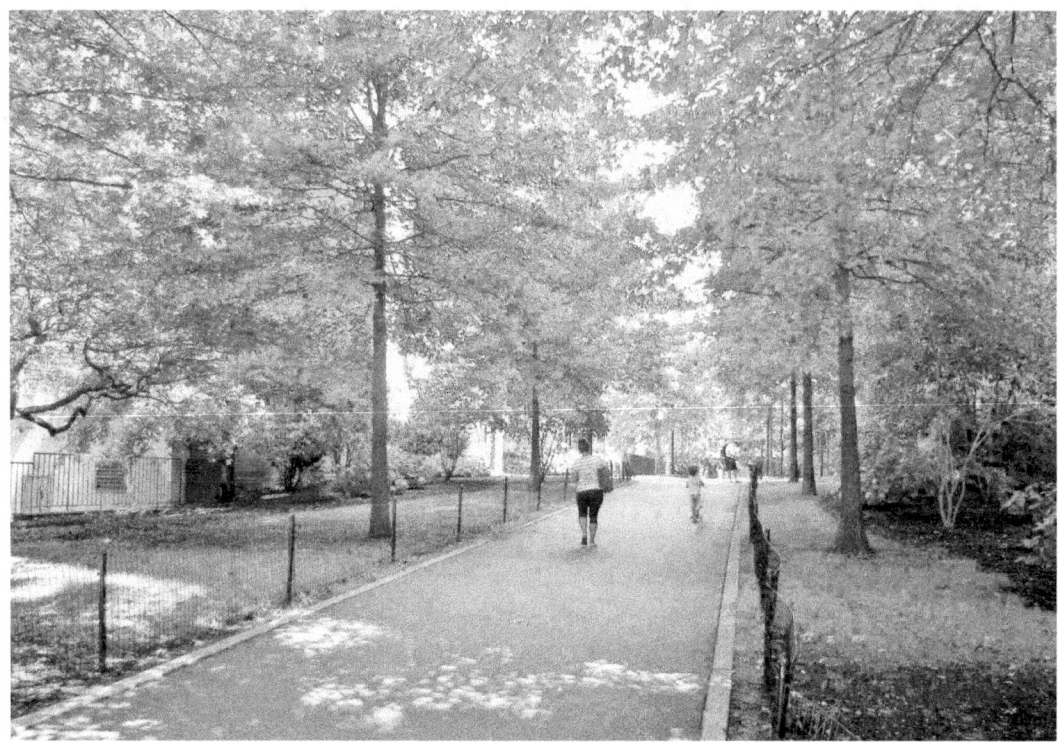

Restful, Delightful Streets for People: One of several paths that cross the neighborhood, canopied over by trees, creates a peaceful and enjoyable ambiance and removes all apprehension about accidents.

added effort. The Stuyvesant layout, having dispensed with the tension-filled streets, turns the entire area into a natural setting. Rather than going to a park, this layout enables residents to walk through a park daily either on their way to a destination or on a recreational stroll. As we saw in Chapter 6, daily contact with nature accrues significant health and well-being benefits for residents.[9]

Sunlight and Sky Views

Layouts for cities that predate the elevator inevitably presumed a building height between two and five stories, the limit of available building technology for most of history. At this range of height, and in all but the narrowest of streets, ample daylight can reach the lower floors, and, in many instances, sunlight also enters the front rooms. In such an arrangement the view from the ground-floor window includes a swath of sky. However, with the advent of the elevator and the structural capability for large and tall buildings, this original relationship to sunlight changed. Framing the same street that anticipated 2- to 5-story buildings, there now stand 10- to 20-story buildings. In New York's grid, where streets and blocks run east-west, the inevitable arrangement of buildings along the streets automatically prevents lower-level units from ever receiving sunrays in their rooms and from having sufficient levels of daylight. This is always the case on the south side of the street and, depending on building heights, also on the north side. Thus, the view from windows of lower floors encompasses only buildings and no sky. Sunlight has long been associated with better health and well-being.[10] Access to sunlight is automatic in low-density suburban settings, but achieving it in high-density districts requires bold, unconstrained planning. The Stuyvesant plan, by departing from the rigid grid geometry, is able to position its tall buildings freely, with more space between them than the conventional 60-foot ROW would dictate. In this freer arrangement, daylight is ample on all floors and sunlight can reach all levels at some point during the day.

Absorptive Surfaces and Environmental Impact

Streets and buildings remove absorptive surfaces from a site and, when combined, are the largest contributors to rainwater runoff. As we saw above, this site plan removes 11 acres (or 14 percent of the site area) of impermeable surfaces, such as street pavement and sidewalks, from what would have been the regular New York grid. This reduction becomes a positive contribution to the onsite rainwater absorption capacity and the reduction in rainwater runoff. In addition to the surface, the presence of an extensive tree canopy, uncommon in central cities in general and not found in the regular city blocks of New York, has several other positive environmental impacts: it reduces building energy consumption, increases stormwater absorption, reduces rainwater runoff, absorbs CO_2, intercepts particulate matter and other pollutants and improves local air quality.[11]

These multiple effects of the tree canopy, when combined with absorptive ground, plus the reduction of motorized travel on site, lower the environmental impact of Stuyvesant Town in comparison to the standard New York block arrangement. In addition, the necessarily high population density of the site supports public transit use, which further contributes to lowering this development's environmental footprint.

Clean Air

City air becomes impure or even hazardous to breathe on account of many sources of pollution, but more prominently due to the vehicular traffic. Vehicle exhaust is proximate, immediate and concentrated, particularly when traffic crawls. As we saw in Chapter 6, living next to an artery with heavy traffic can amplify the risks of breathing impure air. Though polluted air moves freely and cannot be compartmentalized, its density of concentration can vary locally and regionally. Like sound, as the exhaust air disperses, it mixes with other, cleaner air, resulting in lower concentrations. By removing seven through streets from the 80-acre site, pollution that would have resulted from traffic that would have traversed them is eliminated. In addition, to some extent the perimeter buildings shield exhaust dispersal into the neighborhood. The presence of ample greenery, especially large trees, acts to some degree as an air purifier, as research has shown,[12] thus further ameliorating air quality within the neighborhood.

Noise Reduction

Of the 35 residential buildings, less than half stand on the periphery by the streets and avenues that frame the site; the remainder are situated over 150 feet from the periphery, where attenuation due to distance, blockage and intervening foliage removes most of the noise's power to annoy or disturb. The six central buildings in particular are more than three hundred feet from the road and so positioned as to deflect whatever sound reaches them.

Unlike the soundbox effect of a regular street framed with tall buildings,[13] which reinforces street noise, this placement abates and disperses sound.

Community Cohesion

In an era of secular individualism, one might expect little or no identification with or sense of belonging to an artificially inscribed geographic area. Yet Stuyvesant Town has exhibited continuing resident involvement in staging and participating in community events. They have published a community newspaper for over sixty years. Residents also showed exceptional activism at the time of a financial crisis that threatened to erode their say in the future of the community. Residents asked for and were given the right to submit a bid for the acquisition of the entire property from the original owner—a paradigmatic show of community cohesion.

COMMENT ON THE ARCHITECTURE OF EFFICIENCY

Having reviewed all the benefits resulting from the Stuyvesant Town fused grid plan, a common, frequent point of criticism deserves attention: its plain, unimaginative architecture. Thirty-five almost identical blocks, clad in the same red brick, occupy the site. It seems as if they were mass produced, not hand crafted. And indeed they were mass produced. Built by a large insurance company, these buildings were not intended as civic monuments or a display of class distinction; they simply represented another business opportunity for the corporate investors. In that respect they are no different from the Levittowns, with the endless repetition of typical models along residential streets, or the veteran's housing built by many national governments after the war.

Before these corporate and government undertakings, Shakers and other social groups built humble, unadorned, identical simple houses, which are today admired for their simplicity and functionality. None of the above efforts to build houses or housing lay claim to architectural laurels. Their builders aimed to house families for a rent they could afford, and they have met this goal: good, modest, humble dwellings.

In the same vein, efficiency and frugality have produced in recent times affordable, identical cars for millions of families or identical shoes and jeans to dress entire generations. Designer cars, shoes and clothes are still available, for a price, as are spectacular condominiums on stunning sites. There is plenty of room for simplicity in a city; it wears work clothes here and a wedding dress there.

CONCLUSION

This case study highlights two important points: that the fused grid model can be applied to urban settings with equally beneficial outcomes as in a suburban milieu, and that its application can produce considerable benefits in terms of land-use efficiency, connectivity and walkability, active transport, fitness opportunities, noise reduction, clean air, restorative ambiance and community cohesion. It has been said that a good place for kids is a good place for everyone. Stuyvesant Town provides proof: it has a much higher percentage of families with children (36 percent) than the average in New York City (22.7 percent). Such a statistic shows that a central city district can be a good place to raise a family, if laid out as a fused grid.

Case Study 3—Stratford, Ontario: A Plan for a City Expansion

INTRODUCTION

A rare opportunity arose when a coincidence of events occurred. The City of Stratford, Ontario, was in the process of developing a plan for the newly annexed 300 acres to the north of the city when the fused grid model made its first appearance (2003) in the professional press. The city's planning director called for a presentation of the model that resulted in a three-year collaboration and consultation. The outcome of the collaboration was a staged, considered process that led to the adoption of a secondary plan for the new district that fully incorporates the fused grid network model.

The process entailed several staff meetings with all the applicable city departments (planning, infrastructure, traffic, parks and maintenance). It required input and agreement in principle for each of the elements of the new plan from every department. Public meetings were also a standard and necessary part of the process, at which all stakeholders were invited to voice their views and ideas about the future plan.

When all of the steps were completed, the council was faced with a choice among three plans that underwent a detailed evaluation against a predetermined set of priorities and criteria. The approved plan was the first fused grid secondary plan[14] to be adopted by a municipal government, three years after its first appearance in the public domain.

LOCATION

The area to which the new plan was applied is the northeast corner of the Stratford boundary. It is located east of Romeo Street N and Mornington Street (HWY 119) and north of Devon Street. The site is traversed by an existing 2-lane country road (#37), Vivian Street, at the northern end of Romeo Street, thus creating two distinct site segments.

Stratford is a small city west of Toronto with about 30,000 people—a population only slightly larger than that of the 80-acre site of Stuyvesant Town (see previous case study). Its primary industry is tourism, centered on its Shakespearean theater; however, it also has some manufacturing, and there is a growing population of retirees from nearby urban centers.

THE PROCESS

The consultant's planning team was instructed to prepare alternative study site plans for discussion, analysis and evaluation. Each of these would be representative of a contemporary approach to laying out a new district. Of the range of approaches indicative of current trends, two were chosen as the basis for designing alternative plans: the conventional suburban, characterized as "warped parallels" or "fragmented parallels" in planning literature,[15] and the fused grid model. The traditional grid approach as it appears in the core of this nineteenth-century town was not attempted.

Discussions with city departments and the consulting planners led to the development of a third alternative, also a fused grid, which addressed some of the concerns with the original version. These issues are worth noting because they bear on the question of respecting local market contexts, habitual practices, developer priorities and politics:

- Size of lots: In a small-town, semi-rural context, there is little land pressure and buyer expectations tend toward owning larger-than-average city properties.
- Perimeter road: A residential street may not abut on a development site's boundary. A developer expects double-loaded streets to minimize infrastructure costs. From its perspective, the city prefers not to give the impression that adjacent farmland is ripe for development. For these two reasons, perimeter roads are usually set at least one lot depth back from the site boundary.
- Sequence of development: Because the annexed land belongs to several owners and development is likely to occur incrementally over an extended period by many developers, each separate developer would want a double-loaded street at the boundaries of his parcel. Consequently, no planned road should fall on or next to a farm property line, even though adjacent land has already been slated for development.
- Twinned roads with commercial/institutional services in between: This emergent planning device was seen as inappropriate for this small town and, in particular, its periphery. It was reasoned that providing ample new commercial space might counter the rejuvenation efforts at the struggling city center.

These pragmatic, contextual constraints shaped the final fused grid plan, named a "hybrid."

Discussions also revealed another municipal concern about the efficiency of park maintenance: a number of small parks, it was argued, would cost more to maintain than a larger one of the same area. This general argument of economies of scale applies to many operations except in efforts to improve quality of life, as we shall see in the subsequent discussion.

The Plans

The first plan is a conventional suburban design. Its distinguishing characteristics are very long blocks (particularly at the perimeter), partially curvilinear shapes, and a highly idiosyncratic road configuration. The first is driven by the intent to minimize road length (and thereby infrastructure expenditure); the second is usually based on the desire to create a picturesque effect; and the third is an outcome of the first two and also, albeit indirectly, of the absence of any overall organizing pattern or model. In this plan, more intensive land uses and community functions were all centered in one part—at the intersection of the regional arterial roads. Park land was dispersed throughout the community to provide proximity to residents within walking distance. Typical of this approach is also the resultant virtual barrier to future connections with contiguous areas.

The alternative plan that emerged out of the consultative and participatory process is a modified fused grid that addresses or resolves the issues associated with the first fused grid

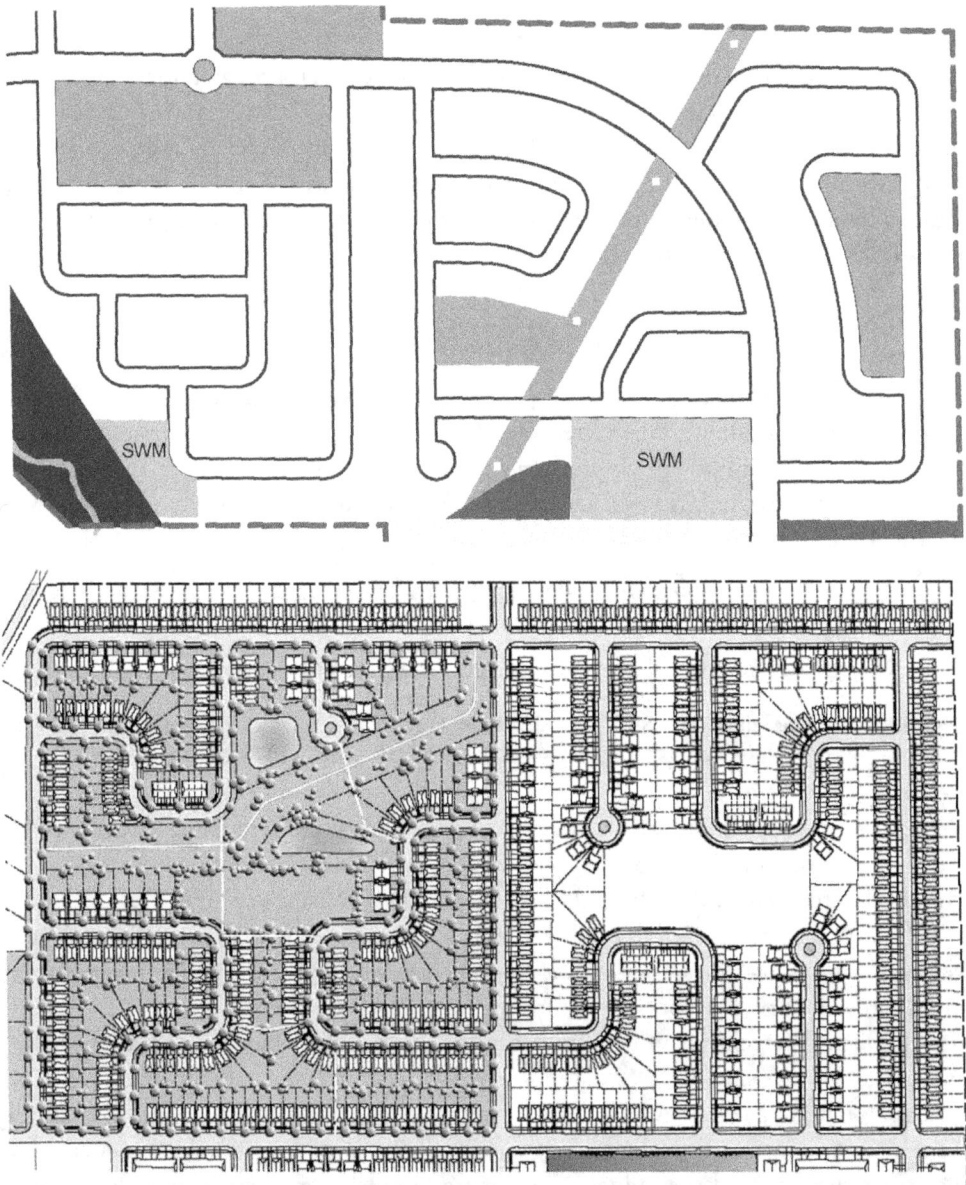

Top: Alternative Plan Approach One—Conventional Suburban: A segment of the layout shows the typical characteristics of this approach—very large blocks, curvilinear, and idiosyncratic network forms lacking an intelligible order. *Bottom:* Alternative Plan Approach Two—Fused Grid Model: A segment of the layout shows the typical characteristics of this approach—defined neighborhoods, non-through streets, and a central open space in each that enables pedestrian connections (original design by Chris Pidgeon of GSP Group, Inc., Kitchener, Ontario, Canada).

draft, mentioned earlier. It also accommodates topographic constraints, natural features and preexisting land uses.

Reflecting the structure of the model, it introduces a medium-sized (about 1,300 feet, or 400 meters), overall orthogonal grid of collectors that divide the site into seven distinct neighborhoods, ranging from 30 to 50 acres (12 to 20 hectares), with one incidental, smaller exception. The local streets within each neighborhood are loops or cul-de-sacs, characteristic of the fused grid. These do not traverse the neighborhood and follow an underlying, smaller grid spaced at about 260 feet (80 meters). Each neighborhood has a central open space that serves as a hub for footpaths, also a notable characteristic of the model. Its collector network anticipates linkages to future development to the north and east of the site at eight strategic points. Higher-level community uses for the entire site are placed along the main artery, which links it to the rest of the city.

EVALUATION

To conclude the design process and enable a choice to be made and approved by the city council, the consultants were tasked with doing a thorough evaluation of the alternatives based on three agreed-upon principles: efficiency, quality and environmental impact. These were further defined, criteria were developed for each and metrics for each criterion were identified, where possible.[16]

Table 4. Principles and Criteria

	Efficiency	*Quality*	*Environmental Impact*
Criteria	Net developable land	Walkability/connectivity	Protection of eco-elements
	Saleable frontage	Proximity to open space	Stormwater management
	Percentage of land for ROW	Access to transit	Car travel reduction
	Enabling future growth	Tranquility	Active mode increase
		Traffic safety	

Efficiency was understood as productivity, profitability and reduction of emplacement and lifecycle costs, and it was focused primarily on land and infrastructure. Metrics for a set of derived criteria are uncomplicated and presented in the discussion of the results.

Quality was interpreted as quality of life, a vague concept that encompasses health, well-being and, sometimes, social equity and inclusivity. Metrics for the developed set of criteria are at best proxies for what future on-the-ground sociological research can identify as the residents' perception and experience of the actual environment and an assessment of their status of well-being.

Environmental impact was defined as preservation of sensitive ecosystems, including the site's environmental features (such as watershed, creeks and rivers), the optimization of absorptive surfaces, and the reduction of car travel on site or to city-center destinations. Metrics for this set are simple for some criteria (yes/no type), complex for others (measuring impermeable surfaces without buildings); and, for a few, impossible (measuring travel mode share without residents).

ANALYSIS AND RESULTS

The analysis driven by the above criteria (listed in Table 4) and metrics was based primarily on quantifying relevant elements for each layout and comparing the results. No weighting was applied to the three principles or to any of the criteria. It became increasingly evident to the process participants that, lacking a rigorous set of precise criteria and metrics and working only from conceptual schemes, these comparisons would be simply indicative of the *potential* of a plan to deliver purported benefits.

Efficiency

The efficiency comparison in Table 5 shows that the fused grid has 2.5 percent less developable land and 3.2 percent more linear feet in roads. By contrast, it has 3.8 percent more saleable frontage, most likely attributable to the longer road length, as the two are usually covariant.

Table 5: Comparison of Two Alternative Plans with Regard to Three Criteria of Efficiency

	Net Developable Area, acres (hectares)	*Net Saleable Frontage, feet (meters)*	*Road Length, feet (meters)*
Conventional Suburban	205 (83)	58,100 (17,720)	51,509 (15,700)
Fused Grid Hybrid	200 (81)	60,300 (18,370)	53,150 (16,200)

The slightly lower road length of the conventional plan is an expected result from research that has emerged since this evaluation exercise took place.[17] It found a 4 percent difference in total road length between a conventional suburban layout and a fused grid alternative. The difference in this case is also corroborated by an analysis of block length distribution in the two plans. The conventional layout has 52 percent of its blocks in the range of 300–900 feet, as compared to 73 percent in the fused grid layout. Conversely, the conventional plan has 41 percent of its blocks in the 900–1,800 feet range, as compared to only 11 percent in the fused grid layout, an almost fourfold difference. Based on this substantial overrepresentation of large blocks in the conventional plan, its lower total road length can be easily inferred; the larger the blocks, the fewer the intersecting streets, and, therefore, the lower the overall street length. This is evidenced indirectly also by the total number of blocks in the respective plans: 44 versus 53, a 20 percent increase in the fused grid over the conventional plan.

Another incidental factor to the lower road length of the conventional plan is the complete absence of links to future adjacent development, as opposed to five in the fused grid plan, a lacking attribute that would not only constrain future development but also generate negative traffic conditions in both the old and the new district.

Longer, fewer blocks come with disadvantages. As detailed in the Calgary connectivity guide, few of the typical suburban plans meet the city's connectivity targets, which are significantly below an exemplary case.[18] These and other disadvantages are illustrated by Table 6.

Quality of Life

As we saw, the fused grid plan has more blocks but, counterintuitively, fewer road intersections (Table 6). This can be explained by the fact that many blocks terminate at an open space where there are no intersecting roads. This explanation also applies to the higher (almost double) number of path intersections (14 versus 27), as a large proportion of these occur at the open spaces that form the hubs of the six fused grid neighborhoods.

Table 6: A Comparison of Elements of Quality
of Life Between Alternative Plans

	Loop & C-D-S	# of Blocks, Road (intersections)	Path Intersections	Distance to Parks, feet (meters)
Conventional	19	44 (155)	14	1,509 (460)
Fused Grid Hybrid	23	53 (150)	27	623 (190)

The impact of the large blocks, which reduce connectivity, is also felt in two other quality-of-life metrics: distance to parks and distance to transit stops. These two distances are, on average, (a) 1,509 versus 623 feet to parks, the lower figure being for the fused grid plan, less than half of the alternative; and (b) 951 versus 700 feet to transit stops, a reduction by a quarter. These figures speak to a more pedestrian-friendly, highly connected and enjoyable environment. The superior connectivity of the fused grid has been confirmed with more rigorous calculations by the City of Calgary, as we saw in the Saddlestone case study. The lower distance to parks is attributable to the fused grid structure, which integrates park space in each neighborhood module. It was ultimately conceded that quality of life should take precedence over an unspecified increment in park maintenance cost, as the primary reason for introducing parks at all was for the citizens' health and well-being, a basic municipal goal. Proximity to parks has already been shown to correlate strongly with frequency of use.

A proxy for the tranquility criterion is the presence of cul-de-sacs and loops, as evidenced by consumer preference studies and the commonsense outcome of excluding through traffic. The fused grid plan offers 20 percent more opportunities for a peaceful living environment than the conventional suburban plan. Other research has shown that these streets types engender higher levels of social interaction, as compared to through streets, as we saw in Chapter 6.

A final, but important, comparison that centered on a quality-of-life criterion, road safety, rests in this analysis on the number of T-intersections, which have been shown in early empirical research to produce safer neighborhoods.[19] The comparison shows that the conventional design exhibits a larger number of T-intersections (50 versus 42) and a higher ratio of 92 percent versus 84 percent of the total intersections, respectively. Since the comparison of the two layouts is based entirely on a simple known fact and did not involve any other computations, it can be seen as indicative but far from conclusive. Were it to be a definitive metric and taken to its logical conclusion, it would imply that the safest network is the one in which nearly 100 percent of intersections are three-way—arguably a dysfunctional system with no direct routes to short- or long-distance destinations. Resolving this conundrum, research of greater depth and analytical rigor has emerged since the Stratford initiative, and it points to the fused grid as the safest among five configurations, with roughly 80 percent of its intersections being three-way.[20] This is an inferred threshold ratio that will have to be reexamined and confirmed or modified by further research.

As with the case of reducing road length, the pursuit of a single device to an extreme, such as T-intersections, can be counterproductive. Research that postdates this analysis,[21] shows that typical suburban layouts perform poorly in terms of traffic flow by comparison to the fused grid and, under certain conditions, are less effective even than the traditional grid. Finding the exact balance point both theoretically and empirically, rather than by trial and error, is a task that remains to be undertaken.

Environmental Impact

Both layouts incorporated existing woodlots that were considered important. They both protected a drainage creek within the site and created a buffer zone along the river, which frames one edge of the site. In addition, both plans included stormwater management ponds. All these measures were designed into both plans, as they were municipal requirements for that site. The surprise in this attempt at integration of these elements was how easily the fused grid incorporated them. Often seen as a "system" or "pattern" that implies inflexible application, it has shown that it can maintain its organizational principles and still accommodate local constraints.

A frequently used criterion for judging a development's reduced environmental impact is the split in travel mode choice. Higher-than-average active transportation and transit use indicates a positive direction. Conversely, higher car use is a negative sign. In this case, where occupancy of the site is decades away, the only basis for comparison is the degree to which each plan is judged to be conducive to or would encourage alternative modes to the car. On these grounds, the fused grid would be more advantageous than the conventional plan, as it displays higher connectivity and shorter distances to transit stops. These two attributes, plus strategically placed parks, have been shown to increase walking and encourage the use of public transit. Similarly, a second measure of the potential for active modes to gain prominence is the degree to which a plan discourages car travel. The fused grid plan makes it easier to walk throughout the neighborhood than drive by shortening the walking distance and elongating the driving trip. Since the plan acts as a positive reinforcement for walking and a deterrent for driving, it holds the potential to shift the balance of the modal share, other things being equal.

Conclusion

The Stratford planning exercise offered the earliest opportunity for the fused grid model to be compared with other prevailing approaches to site plan layout. It was also the first attempt by a municipal government to usher in a new concept through an exacting institutional process.

The study revealed clearly the limitations of doing a performance evaluation of a district based exclusively on plans: many real-life indicators are inevitably excluded and proxies for them become the basis of the analysis—a poor substitute that weakens the validity of the results. It also exposed the lack (at least at the time) of reliable methods and theoretical grounds by which to evaluate the plans. Symptomatic of this absence is the dominance of simplistic judgments based on high/low numbers alone, as in the cases of reduction of road length, T-intersections and park size. In isolating the elements of a neighborhood to be judged individually, it is degraded conceptually into a coincidental assembly of parts rather than a system with interacting components.

Within these limitations, the fused grid shows its resilience as a system and provides evidence of its potential to raise efficiency, improve quality and reduce environmental impact.

Case Study 4—Pandosy: Retrofitting Existing Neighborhoods in Kelowna, BC

Introduction

One of the most common questions that arises at conferences when speaking about the fused grid is whether it can be applied to *existing* communities. There seems to be no obvious reason why it could not. This case study is about an existing neighborhood, which also happened to be within the author's neighborhood, a fortunate coincidence for the city. It conveniently allowed an opportunity for intense, hands-on planning, design, and learning for city staff, and for UBC students.

Location

The site is located in Kelowna, British Columbia, a medium-sized city and one of Canada's hottest real estate markets. The neighborhood is bordered on the south by Kelowna's

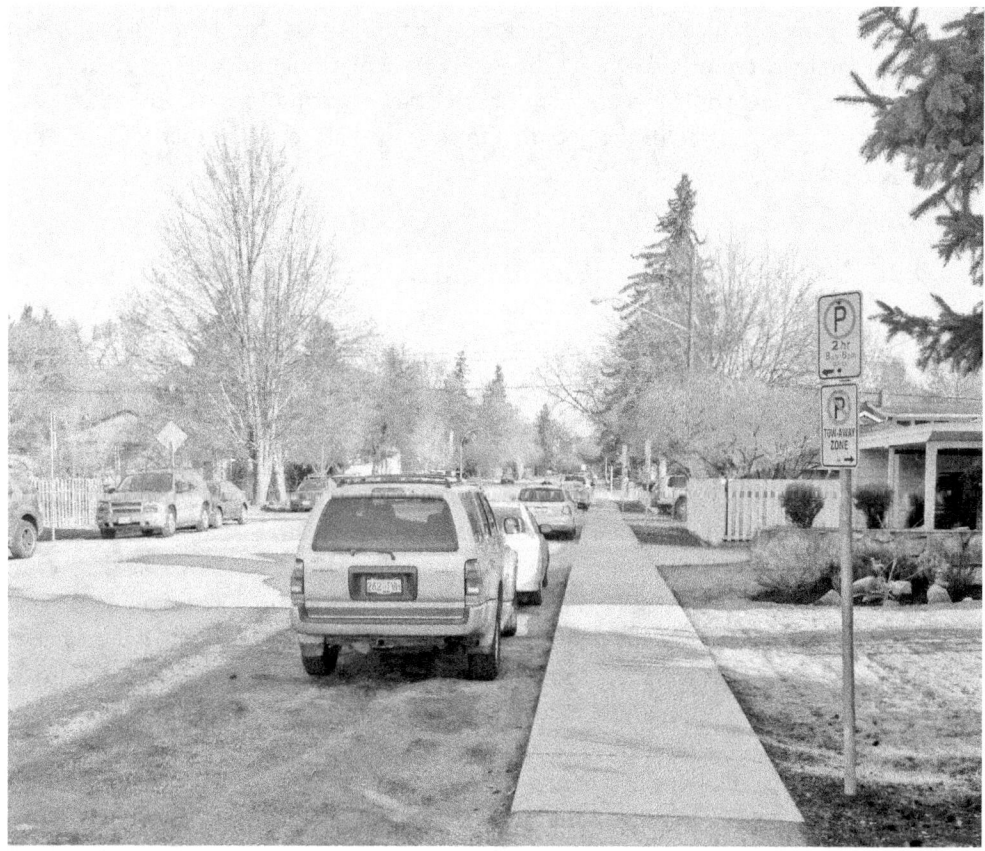

Pandosy Neighborhood: View of congested on-street parking across from hospital on Long Street.

General Hospital (KGH) precinct, on the west by Okanagan Lake, on the east by a major arterial road (Pandosy Street), and on the north by a collector road (Park Street). This neighborhood has an active residents' association that has been complaining to the city for decades about persistent through traffic shortcutting and on-street parking caused by KGH, as well as associated road safety and resident quality-of-life impacts.

DESIGN CONTEXT

The City of Kelowna recognizes that densification of its existing neighborhoods is inevitable. In correlation with its 2030 Official Community Plan, Policy 7.4.1, the city is exploring all potential enhancements that will contribute to maintaining its quality of life as it grows. This area is expected to have a significant increase in residential redevelopment and densification within the next 20 years, and it currently houses a varied population demographic in what have been designated as heritage homes built in the last 50–100 years. The defined boundary is located in between major trip-generator zones, such as the Kelowna General Hospital, downtown, and waterfront locations.

The current street layout is a mixture of grid and cul-de-sac networks. These traditional networks give minimal priority to pedestrians, as there are numerous discontinuous sidewalk routes in the neighborhood. Consequently, residents or patients looking to venture north toward popular destinations such as the downtown core or transit routes, or, most especially, seniors just out for a stroll and/or dog walk, are directed along the vehicle networks that provide no opportunity for refuge or sitting to interact socially with their neighbors. By applying a fused grid retrofit, the new network would prioritize the pedestrian and bicyclist networks by reducing their kilometers traveled and implementing green spaces of refuge throughout the neighborhood. In order to reduce unnecessary vehicular traffic, nonessential roads to the vehicle network would be closed. Three fused grid design alternatives were proposed—mild, moderate, and extreme—with the ability to be executed as a three-stage process leading from mild to extreme if and when opportunities arise.

DESIGN PROCESS

There were four main steps in the design process, including: (1) preliminary design, (2) traffic impact analysis, (3) consultation, and (4) final design. Three preliminary design options were brainstormed by looking at ways to safely overlay internal access (road) needs, active transport (pedestrian/cyclists) needs, and restorative (green space) needs. A series of internal road closures were proposed to direct through vehicles to the perimeter, while allowing vulnerable road users (seniors, children, cyclists) to travel through the neighborhood with more comfort and less traffic. Determining which roads to close, and which routes would support active transport, relied on identifying major neighborhood trip generators. Although a centralized green space was desired, in keeping with fused grid principles, pre-existing home locations required a more dispersed green space design, using opportunities presented by road closures and vacant lots. However, these disparate green spaces were linked through pedestrian- and bicyclist-friendly networks, allowing complete access throughout the grid.

Second, for each design option, a traffic impact analysis was performed to assess resulting impacts on the supporting main road network, such as left-turn level of service, intersection delays, and lane capacity. Traffic volume data was supplied by the City of Kelowna as well as intersection counts performed by UBC engineering students. In addition, location and service information regarding underground utilities and legal properties was gathered. The third (consultation) step involved a limited public review, as the city had not confirmed the budget or timing for this retrofit. It therefore only involved a peer review by UBC faculty and students and city staff, and was used to generally verify whether the designs met fused grid principles, using the fifteen criteria described below. Fourth, this review led to several design changes, including the decision to integrate all three preliminary designs into the final design, as escalating versions of the same general elements—mild, moderate, and extreme. The mild and even moderate designs included features that could be implemented quickly, while the extreme design included more innovative, first-time measures, such as a number of street closures and the creation of new residential lots.

Consultation Criteria

To better inform designers, the consultation surveys used fifteen evaluation criteria from three basic parameters, including efficiency in the use of land, infrastructure and services; quality of life; and environmental impact, minimizing risk to residents and adverse effects on the natural environment. The three proposed designs were critiqued with the objective of identifying the "best" design. The features of the "best" design were examined and, if possible, incorporated into the final design. To that end, respondents were asked to rate how well each of the three preliminary designs addressed the following criteria.

1. Minimizing Percentage of Land Area Used for Roads

Less roads and more green space is desirable and an important aspect of the fused grid.

2. Minimizing Municipal Costs to Build and Maintain

Economic feasibility is important when proposing retrofits. While this question was originally directed more toward the city officials who would be reviewing the design, it still had value and was critical to evaluate. Public perception of whether the benefits of the fused grid retrofit outweigh the cost is critical to long-term implementation programs.

3. Reduce Walking and Cycling Time/Distance to Amenities

Originally this criterion was titled "transit service and walking distances to bus stops," but was revised due to the fact that the goal of a fused grid retrofit was not just to decrease the distances to bus stops, but rather to reduce walking and biking time/distance to all amenities.

4. Traffic Flows That Don't Overload Intersections

It is important that the designs do not create further problems, such as overloading the intersections. While this would be a difficult question for the general public to answer, understanding their perceptions was critical.

5. Maximize AT Connections to Adjacent Neighborhoods

Originally, this item was titled "opportunities for providing service extensions to future urban growth areas." This was revised and simplified as to not confuse the audience. This question would be used to determine whether the retrofits fit into the surrounding area. The City of Kelowna has emphasized promoting active transportation by increasing active transportation corridors. For example, the proposed corridor on east-west Glenwood Avenue would create a key link to the city's north-south Ethel Street bicycle corridor east of Pandosy Street.

6. Maximize Net Developable Area

This question was important in determining how the public viewed each proposal as efficiently utilizing the selected area to its full potential. The closure of Long Street between Royal and Glenwood Avenues, generating two residential lots, was an example of capitalizing on the developable area.

7. Increase Neighborhood Tranquility

Respondents were asked to rate how the addition of traffic features such as road closures, or any other installed infrastructure, achieved the goal of vehicular traffic calming.

8. Increase Restfulness

This addresses the proposed raised crosswalks and other infrastructure installed in order to allow a pedestrian to travel with comfort and safety when crossing vehicle networks.

9. Increase Opportunities for Direct Views of Open Space

The addition of green space and the reduction of pavement is more aesthetically pleasing, and the opportunities for users to enjoy these areas were evaluated.

10. Increase Ease of Accessibility to Recreational Park Land

This evaluated the user's ability to access the green spaces, measured as the average distance to residential uses.

11. Increase Vehicular Safety

The implementation of three-way intersections (converted from four-way intersections) was evaluated for the perceived effect they will have on safety.

12. Increase Pedestrian Safety

The new pedestrian and bicycle network was analyzed for its "friendliness" to all demographics, and whether it was perceived as being an improvement in safety, particularly for children, as measured by the number of road crossings needed to walk to community uses.

13. Enhancement of the Natural Habitat (Woodlots, Watercourses, Floodplains and Wildlife Habitat)

Typically road construction results in the destruction of natural habitats. The fused grid aims to reverse this process by restoring green spaces. The designs were evaluated for their ability to enhance and restore nature.

14. Reduce Impact of Traffic Noise

Traffic noise has been shown to have a major negative impact on the environment and residents. The designs were evaluated to determine what features were preferred in reducing traffic noise through reduced traffic.

15. Reduction of Vehicular Traffic Volumes and Emissions Within the Neighborhood

Respondents were asked to rate each design according to their perception of how the design would reduce traffic on (i) internal roads and (ii) perimeter roads.

DESIGN MEASURES OF EFFECTIVENESS

The Pandosy Fused Grid Neighborhood Retrofit Project remains to be built, so no results for its success or failure are available. However, the designers did endeavor to recommend the following measurable criteria, or "metrics," for reference when the project proceeds:

A. Verified through traffic counts
   1. Decrease vehicle kilometers traveled (VKT)
   2. Increase use of active transport (AT) modes, including walking, biking, and transit
   3. Decrease on-street parking violations by nonresidents
   4. Increase neighborhood safety
B. Verified through pre-/post-construction observations and resident surveys
   5. Increase public health (hospital visits, obesity, active living, quality of life)
   6. Increase sense of community
   7. Determine net cost to build (after allowing for revenues of new residential lots)
C. Verified through modeling, augmented by field testing
   8. Decrease emissions (using VKT and AT results, with field test verifications)

COST ESTIMATE

Also, the designers did prepare at least preliminary estimates of the final design, which assumed that the retrofit would occur in three stages. The schedules of quantities were cumulative, such that each design incorporated the cost of the previous design. The first stage, referred to as the mild design, was estimated to cost roughly $1.4 million (in 2013 dollars). The second stage, moderate design (built on mild design elements), was estimated at $1.75 million. The third stage, extreme design, which incorporated mild and moderate elements, was surprisingly estimated at only $1.2 million, due to its creation of new residential lot revenues from road closures.

MILD DESIGN

The main features of the mild design are:

- Glenwood Avenue and Long Street park creation, by closing a section of Glenwood Avenue to create a three-way intersection

- Multi-use corridor along Glenwood Avenue, the first stage of an AT corridor
- Traffic circle installed at the Cadder Avenue and Long Street intersection to calm traffic
- Raised crosswalks installed along the grid perimeter

MODERATE DESIGN

The main features of the moderate design are:

- Glenwood Avenue AT corridor completed from Abbott Street to Pandosy Street
- Creation of the Glenwood Lot Park main green space
- Pedestrian/bicyclist refuge median island installed on Pandosy Street at Glenwood, to convert it to a right-in/right-out intersection and allow for safer AT corridor crossings
- Long Street AT corridor installed, running north-south between Park and Royal Avenues

EXTREME DESIGN

The main features of the extreme design are:

- Long Street closed at Burne Avenue
- Creation of Long Street Park at Burne Avenue
- Long Street closed between Royal and Glenwood Avenues
- Creation of two new residential lots, with a 3-meter AT corridor on the east side (the feasibility of these lots was explored and utility hook-ups were found to run east to west, which would allow for the lot creation without requiring utility relocation)

LESSONS LEARNED

As discussed, it is difficult to measure the results and impact of a retrofit, especially in the planning phase. The mock public consultation process was the largest indicator available regarding the perceived acceptance of each design. A consultation with the public and city officials would have been required for proper feedback, but the mock consultation still provided valuable input for improving project design, especially the integrated progressive design implementation staging. In that regard, given the economic benefits of the closure of Long Street between Royal and Glenwood Avenues, it should be transitioned to the first phase so that the new residential lot creations could help to fund overall project implementation.

CONCLUSION

The purpose of the fused grid model has been to move away from vehicle-oriented travel and toward more active travel modes (e.g., biking, walking, taking the bus). By closing off sections of a grid from vehicular traffic, the volume of traffic shortcutting through neigh-borhoods can be drastically reduced. In keeping with sustainability, using green spaces such as parks to replace the areas where pavement used to exist creates a more aesthetically pleasing and restorative environment. Furthermore, utilizing these green spaces as locations along commuting routes for pedestrians and cyclists provides a safer alternative to traveling along-side vehicles. The addition of green spaces can have a significant effect on a neighborhood, as research has shown that they contribute to a neighborhood's health and level of social in-teraction. The overall goal has been to create a safer, more comfortable network of AT routes and green spaces for residents and visitors that diversify the land use, promote health, and link the public to popular destinations such as schools, waterfronts, hospitals, and downtown shopping areas.

Appendix: A Speculative Investigation into the Origins of Orthogonal Layouts

"The street is an invention."—Spiro Kostof

The question of the origin of rectilinear layouts for settlements, and of orthogonal grid plans, persists, and the answer remains elusive, although some explanations have emerged. But to this date all have been predominantly conjectural. This appendix will seek to add another hypothesis to the existing set in the hope of charting a new path toward answering the question.

Previous Approaches

Some studies look at "origin" from geographical and historical perspectives and attempt to determine the location of the first instance of rectilinear layouts and the probable routes of their dissemination.[1] This approach neglects the possibility that such layouts might have appeared spontaneously in several places more or less synchronously or at different times without cross-fertilization between cultures, for which there is some evidence. It also leaves out the reasons and process for its genesis, which is the central quest of what follows.

It stands to reason that a cultural idea, an invention, which satisfies needs or intentions, could be reinvented several times when and where these needs and intentions are present. There are several examples of that phenomenon occurring, such as, for example, language, math and geometry, calendars, mythology and so on. These inventions, now seen as routine components of any human group, have emerged in cultures continents apart and at various times.

Another approach to deciphering the genesis of rectilinear grid-like settlement layouts looks at potential motives of rulers or leaders who may have adopted this geometry as a means of controlling the population under their command or, conversely, of democratizing and distributing power. The historical record provides scant and inconclusive evidence for both possible intentions: it suggests that orthogonal geometry (or grid-like plans) might have been used at different times and places to serve either of the two contradictory purposes—control or shared power.[2] The contradiction notwithstanding, a fundamental conundrum remains: It is difficult to see how a configuration might have been chosen for the first time for an effect, benevolent or otherwise, that had not been previously experienced, particularly at a time (around 2500 BCE) when new settlements must have been an infrequent occurrence. And since the historical record leaves room for both motivations, it would seem that, if the decision was based on intuition rather than experience, both choices could be right or wrong. That an orthogonal layout might have been used for these purposes after its invention is probable, and some inferences can be drawn from the historical record to that effect. We are, however, still left with the question of its origin and the factors that lead to the "discovery."

A third conjecture relies on "common sense," suggesting that people prefer to move in straight lines, barring obstacles.[3] Naturally, then, it is argued that those entrusted with laying out new settlements would choose a rectilinear geometry. However, the historical record of cities before and *after* the emergence of the rectilinear grid includes numerous settlements that did not apply this geometry. For those networks that preceded this "invention," it may be argued that the simple logic of the straight line had yet to become apparent; for those that followed, other explanations would be necessary.

Apart from these unfruitful excursions, pressure for a different explanation comes from the general observation that natural networks rarely, if ever, exhibit straight lines or uniform orthogonal patterns. Water, for example, follows a path of least resistance determined by a basin's topography. Natural patterns of circulation systems in biota (fauna *and* flora) exhibit dendrite hierarchical structures that can be seen as unified, due to their congruence with fractal laws, but not repetitive or uniform. Some "organic" settlements bear a strong resemblance to natural patterns of circulation that led to the coinage of the term, but we do not know whether the resemblance is a coincidence or the outcome of similar underlying laws, and, if so, what these laws are. In any case, though the similarities are many, significant differences can be seen on closer examination.

Determinants of Urban Form

As context for our quest, it should be mentioned that there are major and rich sources on the determinants of urban form, two of which this exploration draws heavily from. In the third edition of his seminal book,[4] A. E. J. Morris includes a list of sixteen determinants of urban morphology, along with brief explanations of how each affects the overall form of a city. These are presented not as a theory, as the author states, but simply "as a structured basis for analysis." Most of the sixteen are self-evident formative influences, such as *topography*. But one determinant in the set, "the gridiron," though easily seen as having a major effect on urban form, is so fundamental a form giver that it often supplants the term *urban form*; as such, it begs for its own determinants. The list also includes *urban mobility* as a determinant of urban form. Curiously, unlike the *gridiron*, which is described as a form giver, urban mobility is given the role of urban form modifier to the extent that it affects a preexisting form either moderately or with radical (and presumably negative) outcomes. Yet a street network system, which has been created to serve available transportation means, pedestrians, pack animals and wheeled transport, is the essential configuration of the city, giving it its characteristic form. Every preexisting form takes its character from its street transportation network. Transportation also shaped cities on coasts and rivers and cities with canal systems (e.g., Venice). Similarly, transportation gave Paris its current form under Baron Haussmann, who invasively restructured the old network and its "dysfunctional" form.

The second source is an expansive, encyclopedic overview of cities in history that is hard to surpass in breadth and detail—the two *City* books by Spiro Kostof.[5] These two books refer to many influences on urban form, directly and indirectly, in distinct chapters or references. The author tackles the grid head on in a full chapter. We draw extensively upon his analysis to decipher our question of the factors that gave birth to orthogonal planning and its outcome, the grid. The author himself asks the rhetorical question "Who invented the grid?"[6] only to dismiss it as unnecessary or redundant.

Several actual and presumed reasons for the use of the grid are woven into the text:

a) The equal distribution of land, parceling and selling real estate[7]
b) The most practical way to plan new cities[8]
c) The simplest way of making order in any given landscape[9]
d) Freedom from antecedent constraints[10]
e) The unimpeded flat topography of new chosen sites[11]
f) Egalitarianism (dismissed on the grounds of contradictory proofs)[12]
g) Mass or resident control[13]

Curiously, one potential reason for choosing an orthogonal network—transportation— is absent from the list.

Kostof goes on to express a resounding endorsement of the grid by quoting J. E. Vance: "Perhaps it is indeed time to stop condemning the grid plan out of hand as 'dull-witted, unaesthetic, and somehow speaking of a lower use of man`s intellect,' and to see it rather as 'one of the great *inventions* of the human mind'"[14] (emphasis added).

Yet these indisputably good reasons still leave the original question regarding the instance of its first application unanswered. *However great an option may be, it has to be created before it can be chosen.* We venture to explore the somewhat different question of not who, but rather how, the invention of orthogonal planning came about.

Seeking the Source

This quest is justified from the perspective of considering the grid as one "invention" out of many that propelled civilization forward; these are solutions that become embedded in the collective "social intelligence." Practical inventions are generally motivated by seeking a solution to a nagging problem but are preconditioned by the available level of technological know-how. For example, one cannot "invent" an iron head for a spear unless iron, fire and the tools to shape it are available. The bicycle took four millennia to conceive after the invention of the wheel. Throughout history humans dreamed of flying, and even tried to do so, but to no avail until the right techno-culture emerged. Cell phones are impossible without micro-transistors. From this perspective, anything that has been invented must be understood as emerging from a need, a purpose and from a technological context that makes it possible. This also holds true for the rectilinear geometry and the grid of city plans.

Triggers for a New Perspective

A portion of non-rectilinear networks, both past and more recent, can be explained as a response to topography, as the paths traced on hills and slopes would invariably have to conform somewhat to the variability of the terrain. Nonetheless, topography, it seems, has not always been a key determinant; there are plenty of examples of settlements—ancient and recent—with a rectilinear layout on hilly sites, even a preeminent one attributed to the "father" of the orthogonal grid—Piraeus—constructed on a topography demonstrably unsuitable for orthogonal geometry. Contrasting with the forced application of the grid on unsuitable territory are settlements on even, plain ground that did not follow a grid plan even after its introduction and spread. These defy the intuitive common sense of straight walking and require a different explanation. Even more puzzling is the undoing of grid patterns, for which the logic is presumed to be self-evident, in several cities after the Alexandrian and the Roman military commanders had left.[15]

Apart from the undoing of an established grid, there are instances of discontinuity from enshrined theory and convincing examples of subsequent settlements several times in history: Hindu texts have proclaimed its geometry and provided exact, "canonical" diagrams since 1000 BCE, but no cities have emerged in Hindu-dominated land that follow these instructions, with only one exception—Jaipur, founded more than two millennia (1727) after the scriptures appeared.[16] Discontinuity is also found in the case of Mohenjo Daro—there have been no further replications of its rudimentary grid.[17] In Europe a similar phenomenon occurred at the end of the classical period.[18]

We also glean from Kostof's analysis that the grid is not a necessary condition for a town's purposes to be served; it is simply a convenient way to start out on new land.[19] Any plan would meet these purposes.

It seems that the topography determinant can yield to other needs, reasons or intentions, and that the incontestable logic of orthogonal planning can be overridden or set aside for other purposes. Also, the gaps between theory and practice and the discontinuity in its application have yet to be fully understood, if we presume it to be "one of the greatest inventions of the human mind." After all, other great inventions have endured and advanced continuously.

The Way of the Machine

Contrasting the lack of uniformity and rectilinearity in *natural* systems, and providing a hint for a potential fruitful direction for inquiry, is the converse observation that straight lines and uniformity are the "way of the machine." The laws of physics, to which machines are subject, tend to produce visible outcomes that have near-perfect rectilinear shapes or mathematically precise curvatures. Examples are found in snowflakes (a crystalline structure) and soap bubbles (a tensile structure). These laws can be seen as determinants of form (or shape) of physical objects. But it can also be true of organisms in the case of mechanical action, such as fish swimming or birds flying (a streamlined body, for example, depicts the forces acting on the fish during motion, while aerodynamics shape the wings of birds and bats). What, then, of urban form and, more particularly, its circulation system?

A loaded donkey, one of the first pack animals (first appearing around 3500 BCE), when climbing a slope, will follow the path of least effort. In a plan, this path will appear as a sinuous, zigzag, arbitrary line, seemingly irrational to its human master. In a 3-D depiction, however, it becomes fully rational and comprehensible: the donkey's path consists of straight, gently sloping segments with sharp turns in between, a path much like a mountain climber would trace, and for the same reason—to moderate the expenditure of energy per unit of time. The human climber and the donkey can both be seen as expressing the simple physics of a machine, a pattern of energy use of which the visible manifestation is the donkey's path; the steeper the climb, the sharper the angles of the zigzag. Whether an animal, a human or a mechanical device attempts this trip, all will follow the same rule: climb rate proportional to the instantaneous power output.

This type of physics also becomes observable on flat land under other power-demanding situations—for example, when turning a loaded cart and when plowing. As we saw in Chapter 1, at least in the case of one settlement (Salt Lake City), it was recognized in advance of laying out the streets that a team of four oxen pulling heavy cartloads would have difficulty turning. This awareness translated into a specification for street width. The difficulty has to do strictly with the length of the ox-team-and-wagon assembly, compounded by the heavy load and by the fixed axles of the four-wheel primitive carts. Performing the turn in a narrow space would be close to impossible, since it involves having to back up the entire team and loaded cart, perhaps more than once, as the case may be. For such a hybrid machine, a combination of animated and mechanical elements, a straight line from origin to destination is

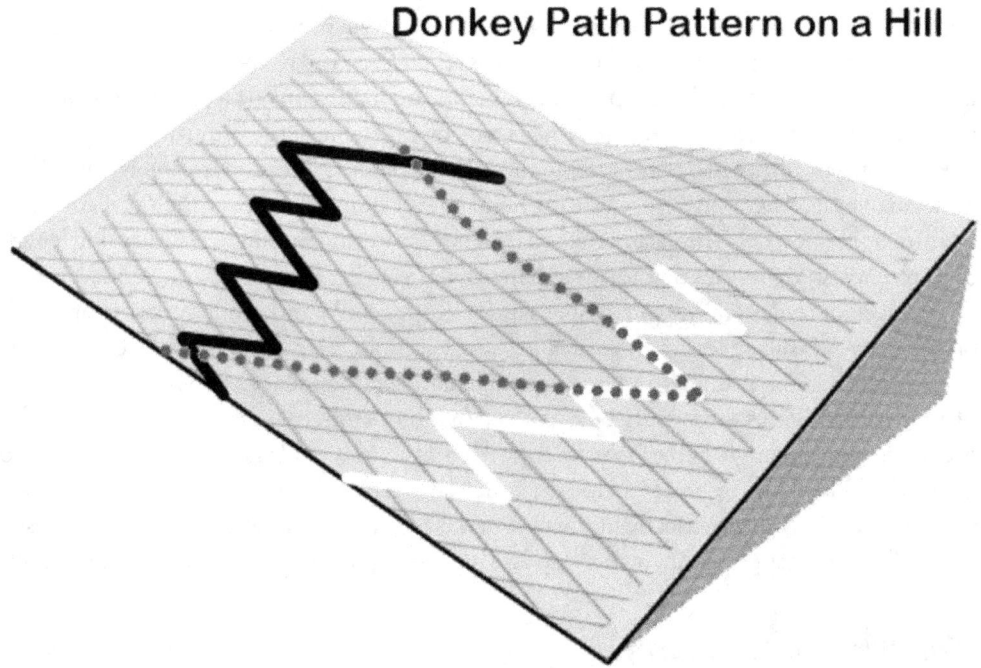

Donkey Path Pattern on a Hill

Paths on a Hillside: Whether short or long, straight segments conform to the energy per unit of climb physical limitation. The total path comprised of zigzags seems irrational in planar projection.

the least-effort, least-time, ideal path. Turning would require a large radius, which was provided for in this specific city plan.

A similarly hybrid machine, the bovine and plow, is even more bound by physics to a straight-line direction. The mechanics of the plow demand that it move in the exact direction of the pulling force, an imaginary straight line between the bull's yoke and the plow share (or chisel). Deviation from that line requires more energy, is unwieldy and slows the progress of work. Adding a second bull (a regular practice),[20] so as to increase plowing speed, makes the movement in straight line even more imperative.

Based on the physics of plowing, a cultivation field shape would be less than optimal from an ergonomic perspective unless it accommodates the movement of a plowing team. As images of freshly tilled land suggest, and early documents recommend, the optimal way of tilling is clearly the least-effort shape—a straight line.[21] From there, the leap to a layout of land parcels for cultivation is predictable. If agricultural land on a flat plane was exploited to yield a large harvest, it would be customarily parceled in shapes that render tilling, when using animal traction, most efficient. It takes no theory to plow a field; the bull leads the way.

Rudimentary Line Geometry

Humans, hoe in hand, cultivated land before they "invented" animal traction for about two millennia between 5500 and 3500 BCE. Several types of animals, including bovine, had been domesticated in the sixth millennium BCE, but the ard plow dates only from about 3500 BCE. During this human-powered period, agriculture was practiced in Mesopotamia, the Near East and Egypt on small and medium scales. At these scales (about an acre), planting, tending and harvesting is generally done in an orderly progression, which implies the organization of a plot in regular lines and segments. Even today, in areas where plows are impossible to use, such as the rice paddies on plains and mountain terraces, seeds are planted in straight rows, not randomly. The same is true of vegetable gardens in rural homesteads; every plant type lines up in a straight alignment. This simple linear arrangement must have been aided by another universal, enduring human invention—the rope, which preceded cultivation by about six millennia and the ard by ten.[22] From straight line and measuring length to a group of straight lines that forms a shape and measuring area, another invention is necessary—geometry (literally, "to measure land"). Ropes could and did have knots or marks on them for measuring length. Measuring an area accurately can be complicated unless the shape is rectangular. A crude, and perhaps sufficient, measurement can be made if the sides of plot are parallel, as they would be if plowed by a bull-and-ard method. For precise measurement, the right angle had to first be conceived as an idea, and then a technique for it to be drawn on land had to be devised. When the state (monarchs, and royal servants) owned most of the land, it was critically important that it be measured accurately for tax purposes, tenure fees, transfer to private ownership and amends for incurring damage to a property.[23]

The Birth of Geometry

Around the middle of the fourth millennium BCE, there was a sudden flowering of momentous discoveries that propelled civilization onto a new level of existence and achievement. Among them: the ard (3500 BCE), pack animals (3500 BCE), written language (Sumer 3500, Harappa 3500 and Egypt 3200 BCE), the wheel (3200 BCE), the calendar (Egypt 3100 BCE), and geometry (Babylonia and Egypt 3000 BCE). (The preceding dates are rounded off to give a general sense of progression.)

As might be expected, there must have been a vibrant synergistic effect between these discoveries. The ox-drawn ard triples the area and yield per worker,[24] creates a surplus, spurs trade and wealth, and, indirectly, frees up time for exchange of ideas and tinkering. Pack animals transport and deliver produce in quantities much larger than manpower can provide, saving labor and time. Writing brings the potential for knowledge transmission, codification, record keeping and civic management, and, importantly, reflection. The wheel becomes a wagon and a chariot, both of which are a means of effortless transportation of even larger quantities of goods and people; they also morph into instruments of conquest of neighboring states. During this period of agricultural revolution and multiple inventions, the human population increased exponentially, almost analogous to its increase after the Industrial Revolution.[25]

Geometry, emerging at the end of the fourth millennium (about 3000 BCE), an era of transition, intense activity and growth, may appear at first as an idle intellectual pursuit. Evidently, it was not only not superfluous to these developments but also inexorably tied up with them, and, in fact, born from them.

The brief and approximate chronology of inventions provided above suggests that geometry lagged behind the invention of the ard by at least 500 years and the wheel by 200 years. It also came 500 years after the use of pack animals and 1,000 years after the domestication of oxen. (The dates and number of years given above are only indicative of the sequence and spans, not an accurate account.)

As many sources note, the factor that ushered geometry onto the cultural stage was the cultivation of land and its division and allocation for ownership or tenure.[26] For as long as cultivation was practiced by individual village households, plots were located in land adjacent to the periphery of the village in whatever part had been cleared. But when it became a communal enterprise supervised by the city-state, particularly in the regions where city-built canals were used for irrigation (as was the case in Sumer and Egypt), cultivation became regulated and individual plots were contiguous and, inevitably, rationalized in shape. It is natural to expect that repeatedly measuring plots and their potential subdivisions would, over time, give rise to a more exact method that would develop into "geometry."[27]

At this point a question emerges that is central to the exploration of this chapter: If organized, regulated cultivation preceded geometry by several centuries, how was the fertile land divided into regular contiguous plots?

One speculative explanation is that the first geometer was a bull drawing an ard. Surviving evidence from the Middle Ages supports the inference that plowing drove the creation of land measurement units. The standardization of the *furlong*, which is called an "acre's length," is such an instance.[28] The furlong-acre rectangle has a 1:10 ratio of sides that reduces the significance of the error in the accuracy of the angles at the narrow ends; a slight deviation from perpendicular lines would still yield an area number within acceptable error margin. Long, narrow fields let more farmers benefit from river inundation or canal irrigation. They are also easier to plow. For these two practical reasons, they were a prevalent form.

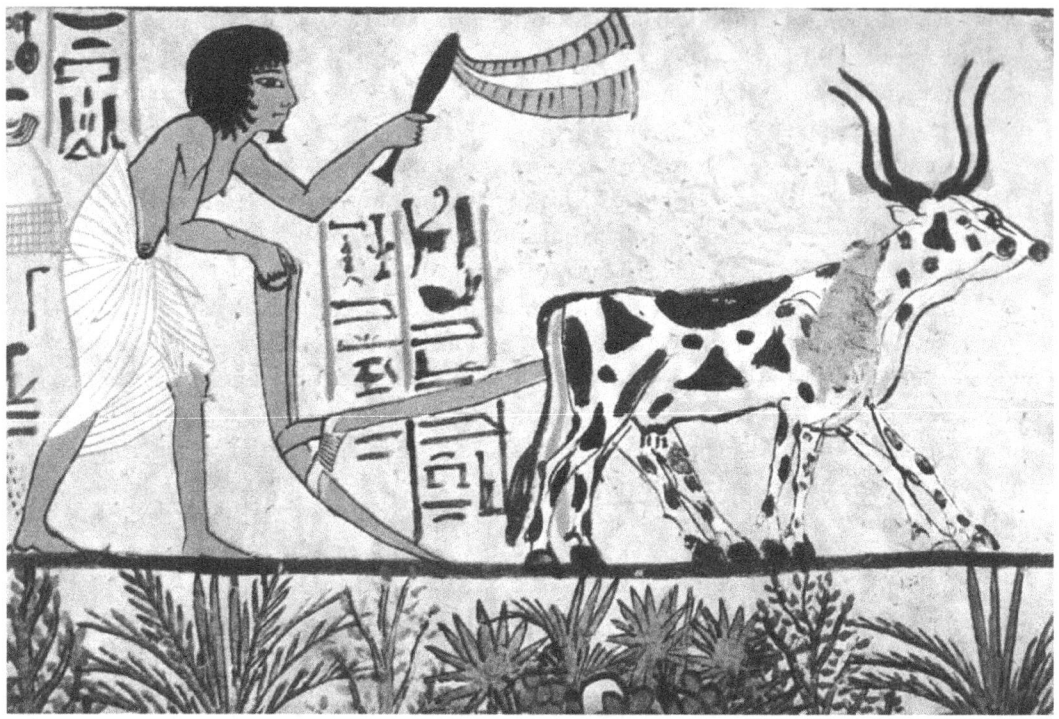

The Bull and the Ard from Egyptian Drawings: Wikimedia.

Though debatable, it stands to reason that in any culture dominated by organized agriculture as its main occupation and source of nutrition, health and wealth, its tools and practices would influence other realms of activity—thus the creation of land measurement units based on plowing.[29]

Additional evidence for the primacy of the bull-and-ard mechanism of arriving at rectangular plots without geometry, thereby providing the ground *for* geometry, comes from the examination of the method of plowing land with the ard, which evidently leads to squarish, if not exactly square, plots.[30] Moreover, in analyzing the method of cultivation using animal traction, we arrive again at the strong influence that practical factors, such as the method of harnessing the oxen and the hardness of soil, would have on the shape and size of plots.[31]

Elsewhere in the historical record, we find evidence of the connection between the bull—the master geometer—and the laying out of a new city.[32] Nothing speaks more strongly to the importance and reverence of a practice than its elevation into a ritual.[33] The Etruscans, whose ritual of using a bull-pair to plow the perimeter of a new city was adopted by the Romans, may themselves have brought the ritual to Italy from their ancestral lands in the Near East. Current DNA evidence suggests that, when migrating, they also brought cattle with them.[34] Based on that evidence, the lineage of orthogonal planning stops at the bull-and-ard (plow) mechanism via the surveyors who planned Roman cities and, before them, the Greek surveyors who laid out the Greek colonies and, before them, the Egyptian and Mesopotamian surveyors (rope stretchers) who measured and recorded land parcels.

In addition to the division of land into orthogonal parcels, another common agricultural practice produced paths between parcels. Originally, perhaps intended only for human passage to reach and transport crops, these paths might have been an unplowed land strip sufficiently wide for walking on (i.e., 3 feet). But as pack animals and, later, carts came into use, all in the momentous 500 years of the fourth millennium BCE, these strips may have been widened to accommodate the new modes of transport. Remnants of the practice of leaving a strip between farms can still be found in English towns. Depending on the size of the parcels and the resulting frequency of access paths, the outcome would be a roughly orthogonal net of land and paths, even with some discontinuity between paths. Though different from streets and building blocks in size and proportions, this net projects the idea of orthogonal planning for settlements. Given that for most of the history of settlements streets were unpaved and that, in early settlements, most streets were no wider than an arm's stretch, the translation of one system, fields-and-paths, into another, buildings-and-streets, would be quite plausible, if not natural.

Rudimentary Testing of Premise

Allowing for date imprecision, speed of innovation spread and adoption, and other cultural factors unknown or indecipherable, the premise of the bull-and-ard as a master geometer of settlements can be tested by looking at cities whose founding preceded or followed the invention and application of the ard and animal traction. This exploration could be an extensive study on its own, particularly if the sample were to include several examples from each of the regions where early settlements appeared. The purpose of this section is more modest: to look at a few examples of pre- and post-ard cities and compare their path networks in that light.

CATAL HOYUK (c. 7500 BCE)

This settlement dates from about 7500 BCE and was inhabited for almost 2 millennia, until roughly 5700 BCE. It is considered primarily a hunter-gatherer community with some minimal planting and a few domesticated animals. The settlement has no streets at all and its residents accessed their houses from the rooftops. In this extreme case, the question of an orthogonal settlement plan is obviated. On the basis of the absence of agriculture and animal transport, Catal Hoyuk would be expected not to show any rectilinear planning, and the absence of streets may imply that even the street had not yet emerged or been "invented" as a concept. The agglutinated house units and the roof access to them could be interpreted as a "cave-in-the-open"—a familiar form of refuge in earlier times transposed and reconstructed on the ground.

ERBIL (c. 6000 BCE)

Erbil (or Arbela), established at least two millennia before the ard and many centuries before large-scale cultivation, is clearly an "organic" city whose streets show no tendency toward any formal geometry. A.E.J. Morris describes it as the archetypal organic form: "[the aerial photograph] illustrates a close-knit cellular urban morphology, evocative of biological sections, which not only epitomizes the organic growth form of ancient history but also provides the direct link between the Sumerian cities of Mesopotamia and those of the Islamic urban culture."[35] Again, in this case we see a chronological connection between the city's form and the emergence of animal traction–based agriculture.

Ur (c. 3700 bce)

Ur dates from about 3700 BCE and was also inhabited for roughly two millennia, until about 2000 BCE. As a settlement, it spans the pre- and post-ard periods of cultivation, and it covers the era of the emergence of the wheeled artifacts (shown in the Standard of Ur). Due to its absorption of these cultural transitions, it should be expected to show evidence of non-rectilinear, non-orthogonal layouts with a later mix of orthogonal plans. The early residential area of Ur exhibits an agglutinated housing, much like Catal Hoyuk, with the important difference that now paths lead to the entrances of larger courthouses. The streets meander in various directions, showing no geometric rule of orthogonal order, and some come to an abrupt end. However, "[a]s recorded by Woolley, its layout [of the *temenos* district] was much later than that of the Isin-Larsa housing area and dates from Nebuchadnezzar's reign (c. 600 BCE) when the generally unplanned arrangement of the area was *reorganized* along rectilinear lines."[36] Here we have some evidence of "urban renewal" (in our terms), where the old order gives way to a new one that is based on the now-prevalent concept of orthogonal planning.

Babylon (c. 2200 bce)

Babylon, a magnificent city by all accounts, is an exemplar of orthogonal layout. Herodotus and other visitors were impressed with the orderly arrangement of streets, canals, and buildings.[37] Resting on level ground, its perimeter fortified wall was a nearly perfect parallelogram. All of these features speak of the command of geometry and mastery of orthogonal surveying. This is consistent with its founding date, which the ard and animal traction predate by more than a thousand years, geometry by about a thousand and, the four-wheel cart also by a thousand. It is reasonable to speculate that, being a wealthy, trading city-state, Babylon might have relied on both carts and pack animals (apart from plentiful human labor) for the transportation and distribution of agricultural produce and other goods. The generous width of its main streets might be interpreted as evidence of at least moderate use of the new mode of transport. Moreover, the foundation of Babylon coincided with the invention of the chariot, mostly an implement of war, but also often a form of personal transport and, on special occasions, a processional vehicle pulled by two or four horses. Straight, wide streets serve these modes of transport best, and Babylon's layout could be interpreted as an expression of that knowledge.

El Lahun (or Kahun) (c. 1835 bce)

Kahun was built as a special function town, much like a mining town in the modern era, and had a similar fate after its mission was accomplished. It was abandoned 150 years after its founding. It had a perimeter wall, inscribing a parallelogram, and a second wall separating the worker's district on its west side, which occupied about a quarter of the total area. The layout of the town followed precise orthogonal geometry, as did the houses of the workers and all other buildings in it. Two main streets serving the separate parts of the town were six times as wide as the streets serving the blocks of the agglutinated housing units. All this confirms the mastery of geometry and surveying that was into its second millennium of development by the founding of the town. As for the reason behind the rigidity of the plan and the relentless repletion of house plans, efficiency (that is, production efficiency) is the most reasonable explanation—the way of the machine.[38]

El-Amarna (c. 1353 bce)

El-Amarna presents an intriguing departure from contemporaneous walled-in cities of the Euphrates area, such as Babylon. Situated on the west bank of the Nile, it extends linearly for about 7 kilometers and has a varied width of 800 meters to 1500 meters. Built hastily for a political objective, it was abandoned about 40 years after its founding.[39] The rapidity of its construction might suggest a preexisting master plan. However, what excavations have unearthed is a rather loose arrangement along the seven-kilometer road, with some of the buildings in the center following a rectilinear arrangement with respect to the main road, whereas beyond that limited area it appears as a laissez-faire arrangement of blocks, buildings and streets. One might characterize it as a hybrid of a planned district and organic growth. Contrary to this lack of overall geometric order, its builders erected a perfectly square district for workers, the streets and buildings of which followed an exact orthogonal geometry. This walled encampment, in contrast to a sprawling city, demonstrates that the knowledge of and tools for orthogonal planning were available and used. It also suggests that if the city's layout did not follow a similar overall plan, as El Lahun did, it was clearly a conscious choice, or an inevitability, the reasons for which have yet to be understood. The length of the road between the two outer limits of the city is surprising for an era dominated by foot and hoof transport, raising another question of city functionality.

The case of El-Amarna clearly demonstrates the capacity for orthogonal settlement layout in a post-ard, post-geometry and post-wheel era, but it leaves the intriguing question of the departure from the orthogonal geometry in the main part of the settlement unanswered, at least for now.

Discussion and Apologetics

This appendix has tried to investigate the origins of orthogonal plans in settlement layouts. It traced a speculative path to the techno-culture of agriculture based on animal traction and the ard (and its subsequent improvements). In so doing, it did not answer some questions that surfaced along the way—for example, the discontinuity of its use in many cases and the undoing of its application in others. These questions belong to another, future (and more comprehensive) study.

In this adventurous expedition in the shifting sands of time, the vacillating interpretation of ancient texts and archeological finds, we bring no special skills. We do not specialize in archeology, Egyptology or classical studies. We relied on the work of many specialists, some well known and others toiling in academia or on excavation sites, trying to pin down an ultimate interpretation of what has been unearthed. Consequently, there may be errors of accuracy and misinterpretation in the facts or views presented here. The nature of this investigation is experimental and speculative. Its findings are presented only in the hope that it will trigger a critical review of what is known and more investigative fervor in directions not previously taken.

Chapter Notes

The following notes are included here rather than incorporated in the main text for the following reasons:

(a) To illustrate facts or historical context that relate to or have influence on network use and its constraints, though in themselves they are not network attributes or functions (e.g., population, animate power, refrigeration).

(b) To include more detailed descriptions and a wider range of examples than warranted in the main text—for example, the listing of city populations and densities.

These additional data and commentaries, when listed separately, permit the text to focus more precisely on network issues without diverting attention to other secondary, even if related, facts.

Preface

1. "In the analysis of cities, there is a lot of pseudo-science, some of which I am probably committing myself. Fixed rules of cause and effect are difficult to come by. From Mumford to Jane Jacobs to Andres Duany, a whole lot of ham-handed maxims are spoken that often have a half life of less than a decade or two. These rules in time take on the sepia and absurd tone of solemn pronouncements by orthodox Marxist economists." Alex Marshall, *How Cities Work: Suburbs, Sprawl, and the Roads Not Taken* (Austin: University of Texas Press, 2000), 99.

2. Stephen J. Gould writes, "Gross flouting of procedure and conscious fraud may often be detected, but unconscious finagling by sincere seekers of objectivity may be refractory. The culprit in this tale is a naive belief that pure objectivity can be attained by human beings rooted in cultural traditions of shared belief—and a consequent failure of self-examination." Ironically, Gould himself fell prey to the same weakness. See http://www.wired.com/wiredscience/2011/06/gould-morton-revisited/, extracted December 30, 2013.

Introduction

1. This notion and distinction has been lucidly articulated by Stephen Marshall: "The evolutionary perspective still allows cities to be interpreted as 'organic,' without this interpretation being burdened by the limitations of the city-as-organism metaphor. In a sense, the evolutionary perspective liberates the organic interpretation of cities from the corporeal constraint of the organism." "Urbanism in Evolution: New Urbanism and Beyond" (essay on UCL website).

2. Ibid.: "A city may be 'organic,' but this does not mean it is an organism. A city is not corporate: it is not a finite, self-contained whole, constituted by parts that support the functioning of the whole, such that that the purposes of the parts are subordinate to the purposes of the whole. Also, a city is not in equilibrium: it does not have an optimal 'balanced' state, which it must maintain in the face of change. Finally, a city is not developmental: it does not, like an organism, develop progressively from birth to maturity; it does not grow and unfold like a seed growing into a tree, that however unique and unpredictable in detail, has a typical and predictable characteristic overall form. The three facets relating to corporate whole, state of equilibrium and developmental process are interlinked, and these make sense together in the case of an organism, but not, it is argued, for a city." Also, "In essence a generative process tells us what to do, what actions to take to build or revitalize buildings, rather than detailed drawings that tells us what the end-result is supposed to be." Besim Hakim, "Generative Processes for Revitalizing Historic Towns or Heritage Districts," *Urban Design International* 12 (2007): 87–99, and "Julian of Ascalon's Treatise of Construction and Design Rules from Sixth-Century Palestine," *Journal of the Society of Architectural Historians* 60, no. 1 (March 2001): 4–25.

3. As Rybczynski explains, change, whether physical or administrative, becomes imperative and inevitable: "The past is part of the city's charm but it exacts a price in terms of efficiency, convenience and endless maintenance. An old city is like an old car: it still runs, it will get you there, but it doesn't have the safety features, conveniences and efficiencies of a newer model." Witold Rybczynski, *Makeshift Metropolis: Ideas About Cities* (New York: Scribner, 2010).

4. The 2013 Nobel Prize in Physiology or Medicine was awarded jointly to James E. Rothman, Randy W. Schekman and Thomas C. Südhof "for their discoveries of machinery regulating vesicle traffic, a major transport

system in our cells" (Nobelprize.org, retrieved October 30, 2013).

5. A preeminent example of this misapplication of metaphors is found in the quest to understand the functioning of the human brain. From the Pavlovian conditioned reflexes (dog training) to the Freudian and Jungian subconscious, all failed to produce a full explanatory model. The emergence of computing provided a simple software/hardware metaphor, but it still leaves just as many unanswered questions about the brain's operation.

6. Alex Marshall sees elitism and class bias in such characterizations: "Another way to look at the Keats-Kunstler axis of criticism [of contemporary suburbs] is that the intellectual classes have had a snobbish aversion to granting the middle and working classes what the rich have enjoyed—space, a decent-size home, privacy, and an abundance of consumer goods that the suburbs could deliver more cheaply." Alex Marshall, *How Cities Work: Suburbs, Sprawl, and the Roads Not Taken* (Austin: University of Texas Press, 2000), 102.

Chapter 1

1. A supreme example of projection is seeing and naming constellations in the night sky filled with millions of randomly positioned stars.

2. "Tool Module: Chomsky's Universal Grammar," http://thebrain.mcgill.ca/flash/capsules/outil_rouge 06.html: "Universal grammar, then, consists of a set of unconscious constraints that let us decide whether a sentence is correctly formed. This mental grammar is not necessarily the same for all languages. But according to Chomskyian theorists, the process by which, in any given language, certain sentences are perceived as correct while others are not, is universal and independent of meaning"; Marc D. Hauser, Noam Chomsky, and W. Tecumseh Fitch, "The Faculty of Language: What Is It, Who Has It, and How Did It Evolve?" http://www.chomsky.info/articles/20021122.pdf.

3. Jane Jacobs, *The Death and Life of Great American Cities* (New York: Random House, 1961). In a similar vein, Alex Marshall writes, "What forces produce our streets, neighborhoods, towns, cities and regions, and the shape they take? And can we control them? To proceed without understanding is to almost guarantee ill-conceived and unwanted results." *How Cities Work: Suburbs, Sprawl, and the Roads Not Taken* (Austin: University of Texas Press, 2000), x. Marshall also cautions about replication without understanding: "If we want to revive or create urban places, we have to look at the underling systems that produced these places, and less at the design of the places themselves" (xviii).

4. Referring to a book source, a Wikipedia article states, "The streets are relatively wide, at the direction of Brigham Young, who wanted them wide enough that a wagon team could turn around without 'resorting to profanity.'" See "Salt Lake City," http://en.wikipedia.org/wiki/Salt_Lake_City, quoting William E. Hill, *The Mormon Trail: Yesterday and Today* (Logan: Utah State University Press, 1996), 26.

5. Besim Hakim, *Arabic-Islamic Cities: Building and Planning Principles* (London: Kegan Paul International, 1986).

6. Besim Hakim, "Julian of Ascalon's Treatise of Construction and Design Rules from Sixth-Century Palestine," *Journal of the Society of Architectural Historians* 60, no. 1 (March 2001): 4–25.

7. "As scholar Joan Ramon Resina writes 'The xamfrà [chamfer] is the palpable sign of Cerdà's subordination of living space to movement' (*Barcelona's Vocation of Modernity* 22)." Quoted at http://urbanculturalstudies.wordpress.com/2012/03/23/city-planning-101-ildefons-cerda/, retrieved January 4, 2014.

8. "In about 615 BC King Nabopolassar built a long, straight processional road in Babylon to honor god Marduk. Such grand processional avenues, or Kingsways, were to reappear in various cities throughout history (Haverfield, 1913). Herodotus described the streets of Babylon in 450 BC as laid out in ordered straight lines." M.G. Lay, *Ways of the World: A History of the World's Roads and of the Vehicles That Used Them* (New Brunswick, NJ: Rutgers University Press, 1992), 13.

9. G. Cullen, referring to the straight street, writes, "The spec-builder's layout produces a never ending prospect suggesting 'I am a bird of passage.'" Invoking the curvilinear or crooked streets, he writes, "Projecting buildings give enclosure and a sense of individuality; a sense of belonging. 'I live here.'" Gordon Cullen, *Concise Townscape* (London: Architectural Press, 1971).

10. Spiro Kostof, *The City Shaped: Urban Patterns and Meanings Through History* (Boston: Little, Brown, 1991), and *The City Assembled: The Elements of Urban Form Through History* (Boston: Little, Brown, 1992).

11. "Alexander's bible-like book includes Pattern 159, 'Light on Two Sides of Every Room.' Alexander's axioms are presented as do-it-yourself guide, which is the outcome of exhaustive and allegedly incontrovertible empirical evidence." Paul Andersen and David L. Salomon, *The Architecture of Patterns* (New York: W.W. Norton, 2010).

12. Ibid.: "So why the silence on patterns? There are a number of reasons: first, dissatisfaction with the previous architectural conceptions of them; second, their everyday association with superficiality and planned obsolescence; third, the ambiguity of the term pattern; and fourth, the uncritical and one-dimensional use of them in design."

13. "[P]attern is the means through which the world at once communicates and materially interacts with itself. Pattern is at once the empirical and the abstract." Sanford Kwinter, introduction to Andersen and Salomon, *The Architecture of Patterns*.

Chapter 2

1. "As it grows, a city requires larger and larger [as well as longer] roads. A network is always driven to adjust its communication infrastructure towards an inverse-power hierarchy. This is the reason why the mediaeval city—with short-range pedestrian connections—could not survive unchanged." Nikos A. Salingaros, "Connecting the Fractal City," keynote speech, 5th Biennial of Towns and Town Planners in Europe, Barcelona, Spain, 2003.

2. News item (with photos of people wearing masks) condensed: "Smog has choked China's northern city of Harbin, Heilongjiang province, forcing schools and

highways to shut and disrupting flights. PM2.5 levels, were above 500 micrograms per cubic metre on Monday morning; the limit set by WHO is no more than 25 micrograms per cubic metre." http://www.bbc.co.uk/news/world-asia-china-24579101, retrieved October 21, 2013.

3. Eric Morris, "From Horse Power to Horsepower," *ACCESS*, no. 30 (Spring 2007): 2–8.

4. "Parallel with this urban growth was the development of transportation. Human transport was the first known means of carriage and movement—men carrying bundles—as depicted on the 'standard' of Ur (2500 BC.) and a large vessel borne on a pole between two bearers as shown on an alabaster relief from Khafaje in Sumer, dating from about 3000 BC. Then followed the use of animals as beasts of burden; their domestication may have been accomplished as early as 5000 BC." Noe V. Ilano, "A Study of Population Density of Ancient, Medieval and Modern Cities in Relation to Transportation," Master's thesis, Massachusetts Institute of Technology, 1961, pages 3–4. In addition, "The first historical evidence for this [use of beasts of burden] is found in a relief from Beni-Hasan in Egypt, dating from 1900 BC, depicting the arrival of the Canaanites with their pack assess laden with children and tribute. In general, by the 2nd millennium BC, most of the domestic animals used today for carrying or pulling purposes were known in the Mediterranean area and probably in many parts of the world—the ox, the donkey, the horse, the camel, the elephant, and possibly the mule" (4). The Latin vocabulary preserves the distinction between a settlement, where all transportation is done on foot—"op-**pid**-um," or town (i.e., small city)—and "urbs" (city), where the settlement size requires a mix of many modes.

5. "Land transportation by means of crude wheeled was more limited in its use. Its handicaps were many: both wheels attached solidly to the axle with only the latter revolving, not only hard on making corners, but also a serious source of wear to the rim of the wheel; an inefficient method of hitching an animal to a vehicle, causing limited pulling power and requiring the use of more animals than ordinarily needed to pull a load, given a better harness ... no breaking mechanism was provided for downhill travels; a most hazardous undertaking especially with a heavy load on a rainy day. Because of these shortcomings, transportation of goods on land was done mostly by pack animals." Ilano, "A Study of Population Density," 5.

6. *General Note on Horses and Cars*: The Chinese believed the horses of Ferghana, called *argamaks*, had divine origins. They saw them as "heavenly horses" that could be ridden to the "land of immortals." In a similar vein, the Celtic tribe of the Gauls worshiped Epona, a goddess of horses, who became also a goddess in the Roman pantheon. According to legend, Epona was born to a white mare impregnated by a man, Fulvius Stella.

- Similarly divine origin has been assigned to the Arabian horse (born of the South Wind) by God in Islamic lore, who is said to have exclaimed, "I create thee, Oh Arabian. To thy forelock, I bind Victory in battle. On thy back, I set a rich spoil and a Treasure in thy loins. I establish thee as one of the Glories of the Earth ... I give thee flight without wings" (quote from Wikipedia).
- A horse's divine or supernatural power is also expressed in the persistent superstition, one of

many, that iron horseshoes and horse skulls can ward off malevolent spirits and protect households from them.

- It is easy to see the strong psychic, mystical bond that developed between man and horse in early oral societies—nothing short of worship. This worship could not be made more apparent than in the act of one of history's greatest figures—Alexander: after naming a number of cities that he founded "Alexandria," after himself, he also named one city after his horse: Bucephalia. It is also evident in the fact that early horse owners were found interred with their horses in their graves—a quasi-religious practice, reminiscent of the pharaohs' customary burial entourages.
- In the twentieth (secular) century, a similar strong emotional attachment between the personal car and its owner emerged—affection for an inanimate, unresponsive mechanical object that appears strange, even abnormal. It becomes easier to understand when the actual and symbolic similarities between horses and cars are compared: speed (flight without wings), power (and implied wealth), virility (inexhaustible running and speed), independence (no place boundaries), and, in many cases, a means of survival (getting to a job or providing a service). "She," the car, emerges as a personified beloved.
- As with the horses above, some early car owners asked to be (and were) buried with their cars, expressing a transcendental affinity for them.

7. The population size of most large preindustrial cities in Europe (c. 1050 CE) ranged from 15,000 to 90,000 people, very similar to the walled cities in ancient Greece and the Roman Empire, with few exceptions. For example, around the year 1050, six well-known walled cities had the following populations: Florence, 15,000; Paris, 20,000; Cologne, 21,000; London, 25,000; Naples, 30,000; and Rome, 35,000. Data from table 1 in J. Bradford De Long and Andrei Shleifer, *Princes and Merchants: European City Growth Before the Industrial Revolution* (Cambridge, MA: National Bureau of Economic Research, 1993). Also, "The ancient city of Miletus under the Romans Grew to be a city of 80,000 to 100,000 inhabitants. Its area within the walls was 88 ha (220 acres)." See A.E.J. Morris, *History of Urban Form: Before the Industrial Revolutions* (New York: John Wiley, 1994).

8. "[T]he main Phoenician cities never grew much larger than 40,000 people." Joel Kotkin, *The City: A Global History* (New York: Random House, 2007). In addition, Kotkin points out that "even by the third millennium, the powerful metropolis of Ur may have been no more than 150 acres (60 ha) and accommodated roughly 24,000 people." According to M.G. Lay, "Roman town size was restricted to about 700 × 500 m to ensure that all points were within hearing distance, particularly of the defensive walls (Mumford 1961). Plato gave a human thrust to this criterion by suggesting that the size of his ideal city would be such that all citizens could be addressed by a single voice. A more practical criterion was the need to restrict the length of the walls, which were expensive to build and maintain." *Ways of the World: A History of the World's Roads and of the Vehicles That Used Them* (New Brunswick, NJ:

Rutgers University Press, 1992). In the book *London*, Robert O. Bucholz and Joseph P. Ward also note, "We are now within the Roman walls of the old city.... This area of just **330 acres** is the core of the city of London [the 1500s], although the Lord Mayor's jurisdiction extends beyond the walls and indeed over the Thames for a few acres in every direction." *London: A Social and Cultural History, 1550–1750* (Cambridge: Cambridge University Press, 2012).

9. In *The City*, Kotkin notes, "As Plato would later observe: 'every city is in a natural state of war with every other, not indeed proclaimed by heralds but everlasting.'" Interestingly, planners owe the Milesian model, which is attributed to Hippodamus, to the sacking of the city by the Persians.

10. City wealth and the potential for personal affluence continue to attract people, as a modern example shows: "Singapore is one of only a handful of countries to have managed [to become wealthy] in the past half century. A colonial outpost now has the third highest average income in the world. Singapore has more millionaires per capita than anywhere else in the world. One in six households are in the millionaire club. They come to this city-state by design. The government offers low taxes, raising their revenues through a property tax on the expensive, multi-million dollar houses of the ultra-rich. In return the rich spend—boosting the local economy's shops, restaurants and even a Universal Studios. A key reason that expats are attracted is the quality of life." Linda Yueh, BBC, http://www.bbc.co.uk/news/business-24606989, downloaded October 21, 2013.

11. The same reliance on human labor continued until the Industrial Revolution: "To do the many menial tasks of a household, servants were employed. In 1695, 575 of households in a two-parish sample had at least one servant" (Bucholz and Ward, *London*, 75).

12. Joel Kotkin writes in *The City* that "most Romans lived in slum-like dwellings. There were twenty six blocks of insulae or apartment houses for each private domus. Despite the legislation of the Caesars, many apartment buildings still creaked, sometimes collapsed, and all too often caught fire." London was just as dangerous in the 1500s: "The reasons for London's deadly demographic profile should be obvious from a look at the city in 1550: the population density in London's core was 100 persons per acre in 1550, rising to about 200 by the time of the Great Fire in 1666. Many of these people were housed in ramshackle, multistoried, timber-frame-and-plaster constructions crammed into narrow alleys and small courtyards, with the corollaries of overcrowding, disease, crime, and structural collapse" (Bucholz and Ward, *London*).

13. Examples of city densities, both ancient and medieval: Rome's density peaked at 322 p/acre in 350 CE (similar to New York's around 1900), and varied from 142 to 72 (as well as 50 during its imperial era). Babylon and Ur showed similar densities within their respective walled areas around 600 BCE: 160 p/acre. Alexandria peaked at 308 p/acre in 100 BCE, and Athens went from 33 p/acre in 500 BCE to 77 p/acre in 150 CE. Of the medieval cities, Paris reached 277 p/acre in the 1300s and registered 112 p/acre in the 1850s, while London went from a medieval density of 49 to a density of 106 p/acre in 1377.

14. "Indeed, between 1563 and 1665, London experienced six major outbreaks of plague, each of which killed between 3 percent and 20 percent of its population. Less spectacularly, London's overcrowding and location along a sometimes foul river bred all sorts of other diseases that kill one just as swiftly, for example, diphtheria, dysentery, influenza, measles, scarlet fever, smallpox, sweating sickness, tuberculosis, typhoid fever, typhus, and whooping cough" (Bucholz and Ward, *London*).

15. The growth of cities appears unstoppable: "Urban development is very much an issue of our times and one that is inextricably linked to roads and streets. The recent nature of the issue is seen by considering the proportion of the world's population living in towns and cities: 1885, 3 percent; 1965, 30 percent; 1985, 50 percent. If villages are included, still only 20 percent of pre-nineteenth population lived in any sort of urban area" (Lay, *Ways of the World*). This dramatic expansion of cities can be contrasted with the evolution of the English urban scene: "During the early modern period, most people did not live in cities: perhaps only 10 percent of the English population in 1550, a little over 20 percent in 1750. Most lived in relatively small cathedral cities, county seats, and market towns like Salisbury, Hampshire; Dorchester, Dorset; or Richmond, Yorkshire. Compared to London, these were not really very urban at all: a thousand or so people living in just a few streets huddled around the Cathedral or market square only a few yards from the open fields" (Bucholz and Ward, *London*).

16. "Understanding mobility begins with the biological: humans are territorial animals and instinctively try to maximize territory. The reason is that territory equates with opportunities and resources. However, there are constraints to range—essentially, time and money.... According to Zahavi, since ever and in contemporary societies spanning the full range of economic development, people average about 1 hour per day traveling. This is the travel time budget." Jesse H. Ausubel, Cesare Marchetti, and Perrin Meyer, "Toward Green Mobility: The Evolution of Transport," *European Review* 6, no. 2 (1998): 137–56.

17. "Began in 1817 at the urging of Gov. DeWitt Clinton, the 350-mile canal opened the entire upper Mid-west to shipping, and cemented New York City's role as transportation hub for the nation, and the country's greatest city." Alex Marshall, *The Surprising Design of Market Economies* (Austin: University of Texas Press, 2012), 134. In addition, "Before the [nineteenth] century was through, [the United States] would have expended an enormous amount of blood and treasure to construct by some estimates, more than 400,000 miles of railroad tracks crisscrossing the nation (of which only 150,000 remain)" (137).

18. Quoted by several authors, a Roman poet and commentator named Juvenal writes, "What sleep is possible in a lodging? The crossing of wagons in the narrow winding streets, the swearing of the drovers brought to a standstill, would snatch sleep from a sea-calf or the Emperor Claudius himself." In ancient Rome, the problem was aggravated by Caesar's edict to ban circulation of carts during the daytime. The same ban was gradually extended to many major cities of the Empire.

19. "The rushing locomotives brought noise, smoke,

grit, into the hearts of the towns: more than one superb urban site, like Prince's Gardens in Edinburgh, was desecrated by the invasion of the railroad." Lewis Mumford quoted in Alex Marshall, *How Cities Work: Suburbs, Sprawl, and the Roads Not Taken* (Austin: University of Texas Press, 2000), 50.

20. Recent studies in Paris provide evidence that about 50 percent of residents are exposed to mildly or seriously injurious levels of noise. (See Chapter 6.)

21. Railway noise continues to be a serious nuisance—a compromise in quality of life for many citizens. Some also see it as a threat to economic development: "That [residents uniting against noise] is especially true when those whistles and horns blare day and night in neighborhoods, killing sleep and the potential for much-needed economic development. 'You have rail traffic sounding off at 2 a.m. and 4 a.m. anymore, like clockwork,' Loveland Mayor Cecil Gutierrez said. 'If we're going to add and increase the density of the housing in the downtown area, which is one of our goals, then how do you deal with that train horn noise in the middle of the night?'" Article in the *Denver Post*, December 8, 2013.

22. Street space in the growing urban centers was scarce: "This reminds us that London's streets were contested territory where the innocent pedestrian had to negotiate horses, carts, mud, pickpockets, drunks, brawls, beggars, barrels being rolled into taverns, porters bearing heavy loads, craftsmen working at their benches, criers and urchins hawking everything from broadsides to brooms, and housewives standing arms akimbo in their doorsteps judging—and sometimes insulting—all who dared enter their neighbourhood" (Bucholz and Ward, *London*).

23. Aristotle (b. 384 BCE), when he criticized the Hippodamian grid, wrote, "But for security in war [the arrangement is more useful if it is planned in] the opposite [manner], as it used to be in ancient times. For that [arrangement] is difficult for foreign troops to enter and find their way about when attacking." Aristotle, *The Politics*, 335–323, translated by T.A. Sinclair (New York: Penguin, 1962), Book VII, section xi, 422. The fifteenth-century architect Leon Battista Alberti suggests that maze-like networks with dead-end streets may have been used intentionally in antiquity for defense purposes: "The Ancients in All Towns were for having some intricate Ways and turn again Streets [i.e., dead ends or loops], without any Passage through them, that if an Enemy comes into them, he may be at a Loss, and be in Confusion and Suspense; or if he pushes on daringly, may be easily destroyed." Leon Battista Alberti, *Ten Books on Architecture* (1485), edited by James Rykwert (New York: Transatlantic Arts, 1966), Book IV, Ch. V, 75. In addition, "Such cities were a web of narrow streets, all below 2.5 m in width and barely permitting the passage of a packed animal, let alone a wheeled vehicle. The randomness of the network was a useful tool in defending the city against invaders who had penetrated the outer wall." Mumford 1961, quoted by Lay in *Ways of the World*.

24. "Because the medieval city developed haphazardly, the old Roman grid street pattern [of London] has been distorted" (Bucholz and Ward, *London*).

25. This resulted in rectangular-grid road layouts with "more roads having excessively steep grades in Iowa

than in Switzerland" (FHA 1976) and, in South Australia, roads "being marked indiscriminately over impossible acclivities or precipitous ravines" (Lay, *Ways of the World*, 11). Also, "Milesian planning was well used by William Penn in his development of Philadelphia, as matter of course rather than forced colonization. The effect was widespread: the 65 × 110 m street grid adopted in downtown Chicago was not that different from the 35 × 115 grid in ancient Pompeii. Through all this time, Milesian planning bravely maintained its tradition of ignoring local topography as in the alignment of the streets on the hills of San Francisco."

26. Eric Dumbaugh and Robert Rae, "Safe Urban Form: Revisiting the Relationship Between Community Design and Traffic Safety," *Journal of the American Planning Association* 75, no. 3 (Summer 2009); James Sun and Gordon Lovegrove, "Research Study on Evaluating the Level of Safety of the Fused Grid Road Pattern," External Research Project for Canada Mortgage and Housing Corporation (CMHC), Ottawa, Ontario, 2009.

27. Most visited metropolises between 2006 and 2008 by number of visitors: London—43 million; Paris—35.8 million; Bangkok—31.4 million; Singapore—29.9 million; Hong Kong—27.5 million; New York—24.7 million; and Dubai—20.2 million. See *DK Eyewitness Books* (London: DK Publishing, 2011). The corresponding city population numbers give a sense of the load of the potential traffic generated by visitors.

28. We get one example of the frustration from being unable to find your way from a general: "George Washington said 'the [English] roads ... are amazingly crooked to suit the convenience of everyman's fields and the directions you receive from people are equally blind and ignorant'" (Lay, *Ways of the World*, 11).

29. "For newcomers [London was] a stunning experience. For starters it was so vast that not even the most experienced coachman or porter could know all its streets, not least because they were not signposted nor the houses numbered until the 1760s" (Bucholz and Ward, *London*). And not only visitors lose their way. Sometimes even long-time residents can become lost under unusual conditions: "The last serious kind of mishap was that which overtook the sorry heroes of Petronius' story, who, leaving Trinalchio's table very late and slightly 'merry,' lost their way for lack of a lantern in the rabbit warren of unnamed, unnumbered, unlit streets and reached home barely before daybreak." Jerome Carcopino, *Daily Life in Ancient Rome* (New Haven, CT: Yale University Press, 1941).

Chapter 3

1. Howard Baldwin, "Wireless Bandwidth: Are We Running Out of Room?" Computerworld.com, January 25, 2012, http://www.computerworld.com/s/article/9223670/Wireless_bandwidth_Are_we_running_out_of_room_?taxonomyId=15&pageNumber=1.

2. Ebenezer Howard named the city attractions and disadvantages in the now renowned "three magnets" diagram of 1898. As attractions, he offered social opportunity, places of amusement, high money wages, chances of employment, costly drainage, well-lit streets,

and palatial edifices. Under disadvantages he listed the following: closing out of nature, isolation of crowds, distance from work, high rents and prices, excessive hours, fogs and droughts, foul air, murky sky, slums and gin places, and army of unemployed. Surprisingly, "distance from work" emerged as a disadvantage in the English industrial city even though it was highly concentrated and centralized.

3. Quoting Mumford: "Roman town size was restricted to about 700 × 500 m to ensure that all points were within hearing distance, particularly of the defensive walls (Mumford 1961). Plato gave a human thrust to this criterion by suggesting that the size of his ideal city would be such that all citizens could be addressed by a single voice. A more practical criterion was the need to restrict the length of the walls, which were expensive to build and maintain." M.G. Lay, *Ways of the World: A History of the World's Roads and of the Vehicles That Used Them* (New Brunswick, NJ: Rutgers University Press, 1992).

4. Densities of core and inner-city areas of American and Canadian cities show substantially lower densities, and the trend appears to be toward further dedensification: Vancouver—5,258 p/sq km 4,014 p/sq/ km; Montreal—7,128 p/sq km, 6,413 p/sq km; Toronto—7,627 p/sq km, 6,413 p/sq km; Boston— 6,328 p/sq km, 3,121 p/sq km; Philadelphia—7,912 p/sq km, 4,842 p/sq km; and Houston—1,159 p/sq km, 2,438 p/sq km. Pierre Filion, Trudi Bunting, Kathleen McSpurren, and Alan Tse, "Canada-U.S. Metropolitan Density Patterns: Zonal Convergence and Divergence," *Urban Geography* 25, issue 1 (2004): 42–65. (Copyright © 2004 by V.H. Winston & Son.)

5. At the birth of the automobile, many contemporaries held the bicycle and the horse in much higher esteem than the newcomer: "Fishman, although himself skeptical of any coming big change, recalls the scholar who around 1900 predicted that the automobile would never go far because it couldn't match the utility of the bicycle." Alex Marshall, "The Future of Transportation, and Thus Our Cities," blog article, posted on September 24, 2007.

6. Ibid.: "But better roads did not happen overnight. In 1922, 80 percent of U.S. roads were dirt and gravel." (Bicycles became the driving force for road improvement.)

7. Envisioning the potential of railway travel, Oliver Evans, an American inventor, said, "The time will come when people will travel in stages moved by steam engines from one city to another, almost as fast as birds can fly, 15 to or 20 miles an hour.... A carriage will start from Washington in the morning, the passengers will have breakfast in Baltimore, dine at Philadelphia, and sup in New York the same day" (from remarks delivered in 1813). Quoted in Alex Marshall, *The Surprising Design of Market Economies* (Austin: University of Texas Press, 2012). In addition, "Within a hundred years of the above mentioned date, railroads will be born, flourish and start declining in importance. The railroad period of cities and countries started around the middle of the 19th century and lasted about 100 years. The preponderance of rail transport started to decline with the emergence of the automobile in all its varieties around 1920. The following figures show the current and peak length (in parentheses) of railway lines

in selected countries: U.S. 224,800 (409,200); Germany 42,000 (58,300) and UK 16,300 (34,000)" (rounded last digits).

8. Jerome Carcopino, *Daily Life in Ancient Rome* (New Haven, CT: Yale University Press, 1941), 57.

9. "[T]echnological progress over time, through a decrease in the costs of transport and telecommunications, has led to a modification in the nature of cities and relaxed the constraints preventing their growth. Historically, we can distinguish first the pre-industrial cities whose growth was mainly limited by the costs of agricultural supplies. In their case, we will speak of a tyranny of distance." Gilles Duranton, "Distance, Land, and Proximity: Economic Analysis and the Evolution of Cities," *Research Papers in Environmental and Spatial Analysis*, no. 53 (Department of Geography & Environment, London School of Economics, January 1999).

10. A study for the Lincoln Institute of Land Policy concludes:

- The average built-up area densities of cities the world over declined from 144±12 persons per hectare (p/ha) in 1990 to112±9 p/ha in 2000.
- Average built-up area densities declined in 75 out of the 88, or 6 out of 7, developing-country cities in the global sample between 1990 and 2000.
- Average built-up area densities declined in all 16 cities in land-rich developed countries and in all 16 cities in other developed countries between 1990 and 2000.
- There was no significant difference in the average rate of decline in built-up area densities in cities in the three regional groupings.
- On average, mean built-up area densities in this universe of cities declined at an annual rate of 2.01±0.4 percent during this period.
- At present rates of decline, average built-up area densities in all three regional groupings can be expected to be halved in approximately 30 years.

Shlomo Angel, Jason Parent, Daniel L. Civco, and Alejandro M. Blei, "The Persistent Decline in Urban Densities: Global and Historical Evidence of 'Sprawl,'" © 2010 Lincoln Institute of Land Policy, working paper.

11. The following cities have introduced congestion charging (year in parentheses): London (2000), Stockholm (2006), Singapore (1975), and Milan (2008). Others have or are considering it: New York, Manchester, Edinburgh, and Hong Kong. Information was retrieved from http://www.govtech.com/transportation/ Does-Congestion-Pricing-Work-Infographic.html. Also, we read elsewhere, "In contrast, many megacities in developing countries seem almost unbounded spatially, and many policy interventions have failed. Schemes such as Mexico City's even-odd driving days (where vehicles with license plates ending in odd numbers cannot be operated on certain days, and vehicles with even numbers cannot operate on other days) have not reduced the relative benefits of traveling by car." Mark Kutzbach, "Megacities and Megatraffic," *ACCESS*, no. 37 (Fall 2010).

12. Jeff Byles, *Rubble: Unearthing the History of Demolition* (New York: Three Rivers Press, 2005).

13. Lay, *Ways of the World*.

14. Montreal has 29 kilometers of underground passages, for example. Original walled settlements of about

64–80 hectares registered lower network kilometers. See Pieter Sijpkes, McGill University, and David Brown, McGill University, "Montreal's Indoor City: 35 Years of Development," paper presented at the 7th International Conference of Underground Space, Montreal, 1997.

15. "Horses killed in other, more direct ways as well. As difficult as it may be to believe given their low speeds, horse-drawn vehicles were far deadlier than their modern counterparts. In New York in 1900, 200 persons were killed by horses and horse-drawn vehicles. This contrasts with 344 auto-related fatalities in New York in 2003; given the modern city's greater population, this means the fatality rate per capita in the horse era was roughly 75 percent higher than today. Data from Chicago show that in 1916 there were 16.9 horse-related fatalities for each 10,000 horse-drawn vehicles; this is nearly seven times the city's fatality rate per auto in 1997." Eric Morris, "From Horse Power to Horsepower," *ACCESS*, no. 30 (Spring 2007): 2–8.

16. "Studies on [traffic] lane widths report mixed results, with some studies finding wider lanes are safer, and other finding wider lanes are more dangerous. In general, lane widths appear to have a 'U' shaped relationship with crash performance, with crashes decreasing until lane widths reach roughly 11.5 feet (3.5 m), and increasing thereafter." "Built Environment and Traffic Safety," presentation by Reid Ewing, Department of City and Metropolitan Planning, University of Utah, based on a paper of the same title, published in the *Journal of Planning Literature* (May 29, 2009).

17. News reporting: Los Angeles has synchronized all of its 4,500 traffic lights in an attempt to keep vehicles moving: "In the meantime, Quan says, the synchronized signal program is putting up some pretty impressive numbers, even if the average driver isn't noticing them. It has reduced the drive time on several major LA corridors, for example, by about 12 percent." Another article states, "Estimates show that this Program has saved motorists, on an annual basis, $218 million in vehicle costs, 14.8 million travel hours, 18.7 million gallons of fuel, and 7,700 tons of pollutants to date. Travel times were reduced by as much as 24 to 29 percent." CBS, May 26, 2013.

18. Alan Boyle, science editor, "Hyperloop Revealed: Elon Musk Foresees Rapid Transit in a Tube," NBC News, August 12, 2013: "The Hyperloop would send travelers through low-pressure steel tubes in specialized pods that zoom at high subsonic speeds, reaching about 760 mph (1,220 kilometers per hour). That compares with typical speeds of 110 mph (for U.S. systems) to 300 mph (in China) for high-speed rail travel."

19. Lay, *Ways of the World*.

20. According to an article on Wikipedia, "The Pedestrian Safety Enhancement Act of 2010 was approved by the U.S. Senate by unanimous consent on December 9, 2010" (http://en.wikipedia.org/wiki/Electric_vehicle_warning_sounds).

21. Ewing, "Built Environment and Traffic Safety."

22. Lay, *Ways of the World*.

23. Persigny, minister of the interior in 1852, wrote, "The street of Paris were so congested, circulation had become so difficult that upon seeing on one hand such a rapid increase in the population and on the other hand the animated spectacle of the rue de Rivoli, so success-

fully opened, everyone was clamoring for new openings, new connections, but without so much preoccupation for the means to achieve them." Stephane Kirkland, *Paris Reborn: Napoléon III, Baron Haussmann, and the Quest to Build a Modern City* (New York: St. Martin's Press, 2013), 70. Furthermore, "The day when a carriage could race through the historical center of the Right Bank, straight from the place de la Concorde in the west to the place de la Bastille in the east, was within reach in 1854."

24. A Londoner wrote, "Paris strikes a stranger as still more bustling and noisy than London, as the streets being narrower and hack vehicles more used in proportion, the circulation gets sooner choked up and the rattling over the stones of the carriages is still more deafening, being within so confined a space; hence also the confusion is greater." Ibid., 23.

25. Byles, *Rubble*, chapter on Haussmann's demolition work.

26. "Arteriality: The manifestation of strategic continuity in networks, in which each route must be connected to another route of the same tier or higher tier." Definition from the glossary in Stephen Marshall, *Streets and Patterns: The Structure of Urban Geometry* (London and New York: Spoon Press, 2005).

27. Peter Wolf, *Eugene Henard and the Beginning of Urbanism in Paris, 1900–1914* (The Hague: International Federation for Housing and Planning, 1968).

28. "A major U.S. study conducted by the Insurance Institute for Highway Safety (IIHS) evaluated the changes in motor vehicle crashes following conversion of 23 intersections from stop sign and traffic signal control to modern roundabouts. This study estimated reductions of approximately 40 percent for all crash severities combined, 80 percent for all injury crashes and 90 percent for fatal and incapacitating injury crashes.... This study found that there were statistically significant reductions in delay; queuing and proportion of vehicles stopped at all the study sites after the installation of a modern roundabout." Eugene R. Russell, Srinivas Mandavilli, and Margaret J. Rys, "Operational Performance of Kansas Roundabouts: Phase II," Kansas State University, Manhattan, Kansas, May 2005.

29. Mark Delucchi and Kenneth S. Kurani, "Can We Have Sustainable Transportation Without Making People Drive Less or Give Up Suburban Living?" *Journal of Urban Planning and Development* (June 2013).

30. Pieter Sijpkes, McGill University, and David Brown, McGill University, "Montreal's Indoor City: 35 Years of Development," paper presented at the 7th International Conference of Underground Space, Montreal, 1997.

Chapter 4

1. "It is necessary to allow both self-generation of urban fabric on the small scale, as well as deliberate intervention on the large scale. This is in fact a central problem of urbanism—the competition between top-down imposed design, and bottom-up self-generated design." Nikos A. Salingaros, "Connecting the Fractal City," keynote speech, 5th Biennial of Towns and Town Planners in Europe, Barcelona, Spain, 2003.

2. "During his seventeen year reign, 27,500 build-ings were demolished.... By his own account, Hauss-mann later said that over the course of seventeen long years, he dislodged 350,000 people and their various factories, shops and taverns." Jeff Byles, *Rubble: Un-earthing the History of Demolition* (New York: Three Rivers Press, 2005). In addition, to build the compli-cated rue de Rivoli, 423 houses were demolished and the bill increased by 63 percent. See Stephane Kirkland, *Paris Reborn: Napoléon III, Baron Haussmann, and the Quest to Build a Modern City* (New York: St. Martin's Press, 2013).

3. "Hierarchy: A kind of constitution where there is a clear (especially, asymmetric) ordering of types, as in pyramidal or dendrite structures. The term 'hierar-chical' effectively implies the possession of either arte-riality or access constraint." Stephen Marshall, *Streets & Patterns: The Structure of Urban Geometry* (London and New York: Spoon, 2005), 293.

4. An implicit, though obscure, recognition of the need for hierarchy also appears in an ITE document quoted by Marshall (above) and others: "While TND street networks do not follow the same rigid functional classification of conventional neighborhoods with local, collector, arterial and other streets, TND streets are hi-erarchical to facilitate necessary movements." ITE Transportation Planning, *Traditional Neighborhood De-velopment: Street Design Guidelines* (Institute of Trans-portation Engineers, 1999). In addition, "Haussmann's intervention in Paris, on the other hand, can be ex-plained by fractal scaling. When Mediaeval Paris had grown beyond a certain size so that its narrow streets could no longer support traffic, it became necessary to add structures on a new, larger scale. Thus, it became necessary to destroy some urban fabric in order to cut longer/wider streets into the city" (Salingaros, "Con-necting the Fractal City").

5. "Recent investigations into the connectivity of urban form ... lead us to conclude that a functioning urban fabric—a living neighborhood—is connected by paths that obey an inverse power-law distribution. The most successful urban regions all over the world are found to have a great range of connections, from foot-paths, to bicycle paths, to low-traffic roads, to through roads, up to expressways; in decreasing number. Urban connections may sometimes be characterized by their width rather than their length. The data comes indi-rectly from measuring the fractal structure of urban connective networks, which implies an inverse power-law distribution according to both the length and width of individual paths (corresponding to the intensity of traffic flow)." Nikos A. Salingaros and Bruce J. West, "A Universal Rule for the Distribution of Sizes," *Environ-ment and Planning B: Planning and Design* 26, no. 6 (1999): 909–23.

6. A table from the *Access Management Manual* of 2003 shows that from the lower threshold of 20 points per mile to the next two thresholds of 40 and 60, crash rates increase by 92 percent and 147 percent, respec-tively, in an undivided road. For a divided road with a non-traversable median, the increases of crashes for the same thresholds are 75 percent and 134 percent, respec-tively. However, the divided version has on average about 70 percent fewer crashes than the non-divided (calculations by author based on numbers in reference).

"Built Environment and Traffic Safety," presentation by Reid Ewing, Department of City and Metropolitan Planning, University of Utah, based on a paper of the same title, published in the *Journal of Planning Litera-ture* (May 29, 2009).

7. The drawing for an H-type fractal progression was redrawn from M. Batty and P. Longley, *Fractal Cities: A Geometry of Form and Function* (London and San Diego: Academic Press, 1994).

8. C. Alexander, S. Ishikawa, and M. Silverstein, with M. Jacobson, I. Fiksdahl-King, and S. Angel, *A Pat-tern Language* (New York: Oxford University Press, 1977), pattern 52.

9. Clarence Stein's plan for Radburn, New Jersey, includes underpasses that connect adjacent neighbor-hoods.

10. Diagram redrawn from Salingaros, "Connecting the Fractal City."

11. Under the section "Fractal Analysis of the Parisian Street Network," we read, "The second graph shows the results obtained with the pedestrian network. The result is prominent: the indicator of deviation from the Pareto distribution drops to 0.17. This result con-firms that Paris road network follows a fractal scale of hierarchy, from the pedestrian network to the Hauss-mannian boulevards." Serge Salat, Françoise Labbé, Car-oline Nowacki, and Gila Walker, *Cities and Forms: On Sustainable Urbanism* (Paris: Hermann Editeurs des Sci-ences et des Arts, 2011).

12. USDOT Federal Highway Administration, Highway Statistics Series, Section V: Roadway Charac-teristics and Performance, 2006 (http://www.fhwa.dot.gov/policyinformation/quickfinddata/qfroad.cfm).

13. S. Melia, "Filtered and Unfiltered Permeability: The European and Anglo-Saxon Approaches," *Project* 4 (2012): 6–9.

14. Alexander et al., *A Pattern Language*, pattern 101 (Building Thoroughfare).

15. Paul Stangl, "The Pedestrian Route Directness Test: A New Level-of-Service Model," *Urban Design In-ternational* 17, no. 3 (2012): 228–38.

16. Michael Southworth, with Tridib Banerjee, *City Sense and City Design: Writings and Projects of Kevin Lynch* (Cambridge, MA: MIT Press, 1990; paperback edition 1995).

17. Mark Girouard, *Cities & People: A Social and Ar-chitectural History* (New Haven, CT, and London: Yale University Press, 1985).

18. Peter Calthorpe, *The Urban Network: A New Framework for Growth*, 2002, last accessed from the Calthorpe Associates website January 2014, http://www.calthorpe.com/publications/urban-network-new-framework-growth.

Chapter 5

1. Chapter epigraph by Spiro Kostof in *The City Assembled: The Elements of Urban Form Through His-tory* (Boston: Little, Brown, 1992).

2. "This most useful term [*cadastre*] refers to the pattern of pre-existing man-made rural property bound-aries, regional routes, drainage ditches, and so on, over which an organic growth settlement expanded, or which

had to be recognized in the planning of new urban form. From the earliest times, as soon as land came into individual ownership, the boundaries were 'legally' protected and could be changed only by autocratic action or democratic intervention." A.E.J. Morris, *History of Urban Form: Before the Industrial Revolutions* (New York: John Wiley, 1994).

3. "Based on our observation of historic cities from different cultures, and the work carried out by Italian morphologists ... we propose that the maximum edge length for a sanctuary area [i.e., protected neighborhood] (the area between major thoroughfares) is governed by a surprisingly small *400-meter rule*," and, further on, "from our studies and that of other authors it seems that the natural limitations of pedestrian movement in time (manifested in the 5 min walk) are fundamental to community formation." Michael Mehaffy, Sergio Porta, Yodan Rofe, and Nikos Salingaros, "Urban Nuclei and the Geometry of Streets: The 'Emergent Neighborhoods' Model," *Urban Design International* 15, no. 1 (2010): 22–46.

4. "Every camp was constructed according to the same master plan; although natural features were sometimes made part of it, ordinarily it was pitched on reasonably flat land and constituted a fort without rivers or cliffs to aid in its defense. It was square; each side was 2,150 feet [655 meters] long and had a gate." R.M. Haywood, *Ancient Rome*, quoted in Morris, *History of Urban Form*.

5. Colonial settlements also used modular units, but in this case motivated more by political effectiveness rather than military efficiency: "The city grid [Savannah's] was organized into wards, each with its own square measuring some 315 by 270 feet (96 by 82 m). 'Ward' of course is a political term. The plan was the blueprint of a political system. Ten freeholders formed a tything; four tythings made up a ward whose political officer was the constable. The tythings were grouped in two rows of five house lots back to back sharing a lane or alley.... The ward unit was repeatable, and Savannah extended its primary pattern unvaryingly into the 19th century." Spiro Kostof, *The City Shaped* (Boston: Little, Brown, 1991), 96.

6. "In the final analysis, neighborhoods are created by the social networks, strong and weak, that arise in such places, and these networks are only partially dependent upon the spatial structure. Therefore, we don't believe neighborhoods should or can be designed." Mehaffy et al., "Urban Nuclei and the Geometry of Streets."

7. "Another by-law which is not uncommon is that against roads having no through way, known as cul-de-sac roads. This action has, no doubt, been taken to avoid unwholesome yards; but for residential purposes, particularly since the development of the motor-car, the cul-de-sac roads, far from being undesirable, are especially to be desired for those who like quiet for their dwellings." Raymond Unwin quoted in Michael Southworth and Eran Ben-Joseph, *Streets and the Shaping of Towns and Cities* (Washington, D.C.: Island Press, 2003).

8. C. Alexander, S. Ishikawa, and M. Silverstein, with M. Jacobson, I. Fiksdahl-King, and S. Angel, *A Pattern Language* (New York: Oxford University Press, 1977), pattern 14 (Identifiable Neighborhood) and pattern 15 (Neighbourhood Boundary).

9. Ibid., patterns 60 (Accessible Green) and 61 (Small Public Squares).

10. Gordon Lovegrove and T. Sayed, "Macro-Level Collision Prediction Models for Evaluating Neighbourhood Traffic Safety," *Canadian Journal of Civil Engineering* 33 (2006): 609–21.

11. "In the first case [of slowing down], geometrical constraints create a lowest level like the capillaries in the human circulation system, where the flow occurs at its slowest and most diffuse, though still fed by the circulation network. Capillarity is the opposite of rapid flow. At the highest level of the network, the strongest channels are wide and smooth to optimize rapid flow. A healthy network requires all levels from the very fast to the very slow." Nikos A. Salingaros, "Connecting the Fractal City," keynote speech, 5th Biennial of Towns and Town Planners in Europe, Barcelona, Spain, 2003.

12. As we saw in Chapter 4, the frequency of access from a main artery correlates with an increase in crashes. See "Built Environment and Traffic Safety," presentation by Reid Ewing, Department of City and Metropolitan Planning, University of Utah, based on a paper of the same title, published in the *Journal of Planning Literature* (May 29, 2009).

13. "We define organic order as the kind of order that is achieved when there is a perfect balance between the needs of the parts, and the needs of the whole." Christopher Alexander, quoted at http://www.brainy quote.com/quotes/quotes/c/christophe417063.html.

Chapter 6

1. Canadian Medical Association, "No Breathing Room: National Illness Costs of Air Pollution," Summary Report, Toronto, 2008.

2. "Air pollution is Britain's forgotten environmental and public health crisis. Each year, around 29,000 deaths are attributable to man-made fine particulate air pollution in the UK, at a cost to the economy of £15 billion a year. Other pollutants cause further damage to our health and our economy." Simon Moore, *Something in the Air: The Forgotten Crisis of Britain's Poor Air Quality*, edited by Guy Newey (London: Policy Exchange, 2012). An examination of the effects of particulate matter pollution on a sample of 66,000 women in 36 U.S. cities showed that every 10-microgram rise in particulates was matched by a 76 percent rise in the chances of dying from heart disease or stroke. K.A. Miller, D.S. Siscovick, K. Sheppard, J.H. Sullivan, G. Anderson, and J.D. Kaufman, "Long-Term Exposure to Fine Particulate Matter Air Pollution and Cardiovascular Events in Women," *New England Journal of Medicine* 356 (2007): 447–58.

3. Centre for Sustainable Transportation, "Child-Friendly Transport Planning" (February 2004), 3.

4. Centre for Sustainable Transportation, "Child-Friendly Transport Planning," quoting R. Pearson, H. Wachtel, and K. Ebi, "Distance-Weighted Traffic Density in Proximity to a Home Is a Risk Factor for Leukemia and Other Childhood Cancers," *Journal of the Air & Waste Management Association* 50 (2000): 175–80.

5. "Though emissions from individual nonpoint

sources are relatively small, collectively their emissions can be of concern—particularly where large numbers of sources are located in heavily populated areas. Non-point sources contribute to over 50 percent of all particulate matter (PM) emissions, which is higher than point or mobile sources. They also emit Volatile Organic Compounds (VOC) (also known as hydrocarbons) and nitrogen dioxide (NO_2) emissions, which contribute to the formation of ground-level ozone." South Carolina Department of Health and Environmental Control, http://www.scdhec.gov/environment/baq/AirPollutants/Sources/mobile_sources.asp.

6. "Short motor vehicle trips in urban conditions tend to have relatively high per-kilometer pollution emission rates due to cold engine starts and congestion, so reductions in such trips tend to provide relatively large emission reductions." And further on, "Emissions per vehicle mile tend to be minimized at moderate traffic speeds (30–50 kilometers-per-hour) with minimum stops." Lawrence Frank, Sarah Kavage, and Todd Litman, *Promoting Public Health Through Smart Growth* (Vancouver: Smart Growth British Columbia, 2006). In summarizing the range of strategies to improve air quality, the authors suggest, "Utilize creative roadway/pathway designs in the planning and site design processes, such as connected cul-de-sacs and fused grids."

7. IBI Group, "Assessment of the Transportation Impacts of Current and Fused Grid Layouts," Phase I research report prepared for Canada Mortgage and Housing Corporation (CMHC), Ottawa, Ontario, 2007.

8. Xiongbing Jin and Roger White, "An Agent-based Model of the Influence of Neighbourhood Design on Daily Trip Patterns," *Computers, Environment and Urban Systems* 36, issue 5 (September 2012).

9. Lawrence Frank and Chris Hawkins, *Assessing Travel and Environmental Impacts of Contrasting Levels of Vehicular and Pedestrian Connectivity: Assessing Aspects of the Fused Grid* (Ottawa: Canada Mortgage and Housing Corporation [CMHC], 2008).

10. Susan Handy, Samantha Sommer, Julie Ogilvie, Xinyu Cao, and Patricia Mokhtarian, "Cul-de-Sacs and Children's Outdoor Play: Quantitative and Qualitative Evidence," Active Living, Research Conference, San Diego, February 2007.

11. Harold Marks, "Subdividing for Traffic Safety," *Traffic Quarterly* 11, no. 3 (1957): 308–25.

12. Eran Ben-Joseph, *Livability and Safety of Suburban Street Patterns: A Comparative Study*, Working Paper 642 (Berkeley: Institute of Urban and Regional Development, University of California, 1995).

13. Gordon Lovegrove and T. Sayed, "Macro-Level Collision Prediction Models for Evaluating Neighbourhood Traffic Safety," *Canadian Journal of Civil Engineering* 33 (2006): 609–21.

14. Oscar Newman, *Creating Defensible Space*, Institute for Community Design Analysis, U.S. Department of Housing and Urban Development Office of Policy Development and Research, 1996.

15. "Between 1991 and 1994 a total of 119 traffic circles were constructed throughout the NTCP. A comparison of the number of accidents occurring in the calendar year before and after construction at these intersections reveals a considerable drop in accidents. There were 187 accidents in the year before construc-

tion, compared to 11 accidents in the year after. This is a 94 percent reduction in accidents in a single year. Figure 2 displays the long-term impact of the traffic circles, as the number of accidents has remained at very low levels in the years following construction. The reduction in injuries was even more dramatic, dropping from 153 injuries in the year before the construction to a single injury in the year following the construction (Figure 3). The reduction in injuries as well as accidents is even more impressive when examining the trend-line figures, as they show increasing numbers of both injuries and accidents in the years prior to traffic circle installation." "Neighborhood Traffic Calming: Seattle's Traffic Circle Program," *Road Management & Engineering Journal*, http://www.usroads.com/journals/rmej/9801/rm980102.htm, retrieved January 2014.

16. S.R. Zein, E. Geddes, S. Hemsing, and M. Johnson, "Safety Benefits of Traffic Calming," *Transportation Research Record: Journal of the Transportation Research Board* 1578 (1997): 3–10.

17. Eric Dumbaugh and Robert Rae, "Safe Urban Form: Revisiting the Relationship Between Community Design and Traffic Safety," *Journal of the American Planning Association* 75, no. 3 (Summer 2009).

18. James Sun and Gordon Lovegrove, "Comparing the Road Safety of Neighbourhood Development Patterns: Traditional versus Sustainable Communities," *Canadian Journal of Civil Engineering* 40, no. 1 (January 2013): 35–45.

19. Dr. William H. Stewart, former surgeon general of the United States, quoted in "Noise: A Health Problem," United States Environmental Protection Agency Office of Noise Abatement and Control, Washington, D.C. 20460, August 1978 (accessed January 2014).

20. D.S. Michaud et al., "Noise Annoyance in Canada," *Noise & Health* 7, no. 27 (April–June 2005): 39–47.

21. G. Evans, P. Lercher, M. Meis, H. Ising, and W.W. Kofler, "Community Noise Exposure and Stress in Children," *Journal of the Acoustical Society of America* 109 (2001): 1023–27. (The results of this study could be interpreted to suggest that children should not live in high-density development, but it could be equally interpreted to suggest that steps be taken to reduce traffic intensities.) Quoted in Centre for Sustainable Transportation, "Child-Friendly Transport Planning."

22. Raymond Unwin, *Nothing Gained by Overcrowding!*, first published in 1912 by P.S. King & Son (Orchard House, Westminster)

23. Richard Mitchell and Frank Popham, "Effect of Exposure to Environment on Health Inequalities: An Observational Population Study," *The Lancet* 372 (2008).

24. S. de Vries, R.A. Verheij, P.P. Groenewegen, and P. Spreeuwenberg, "Natural Environments—Healthy Environments? An Exploratory Analysis of the Relationship between Green Space and Health," *Environment and Planning A* 35 (2003): 1717–31.

25. T. Takano, K. Nakamura, and M. Watanabe, "Urban Residential Environments and Senior Citizens' Longevity in Megacity Areas: The Importance of Walkable Green Spaces," *Journal of Epidemiological Community Health* 56 (2003): 913–18.

26. Mathew P. White, Ian Alcock, Benedict W. Wheeler, and Michael H. Depledge, "Would You Be

Happier Living in a Greener Urban Area? A Fixed-Effects Analysis of Panel Data," *Psychological Science* 24, no. 6 (June 2013): 920–28.

27. Health Council of the Netherlands and Dutch Advisory Council for Research on Spatial Planning, Nature and the Environment, "Nature and Health: The Influence of Nature on Social, Psychological and Physical Well-being," The Hague: Health Council of the Netherlands and RMNO, 2004 (publication no. 2004/09E).

28. Rachel Kaplan, "Nature at the Doorstep: Residential Satisfaction and the Nearby Environment," *Journal of Architectural and Planning Research* 2 (1985): 115–27.

29. *Traffic's Human Toll: A Study of the Impacts of Vehicular Traffic on New York City Residents* (New York: Transportation Alternatives, 2006).

30. Joshua Hart, "Driven to Excess: A Study of Motor Vehicle Impacts on Three Streets in Bristol," University of the West of England, 2008.

31. Oscar Newman, *Creating Defensible Space*, Institute for Community Design Analysis, U.S. Department of Housing and Urban Development Office of Policy Development and Research, 1996.

32. Bill Hillier and Ozlem Sahbaz, "An Evidence Based Approach to Crime and Urban Design: Or, Can We Have Vitality, Sustainability and Security All at Once?" Bartlett School of Graduate Studies, University College London, March 2008.

33. IBI Group, "Assessment of the Transportation Impacts of Current and Fused Grid Layouts."

34. IBI Group, "Comparing Current and Fused Grid Neighbourhood Layouts: Mobility, Infrastructure and Emission Costs," Phase II research report prepared for Canada Mortgage and Housing Corporation (CMHC), Ottawa, Ontario, 2008.

35. Michael T. Bond, Vicky L. Seiler, and Michael J. Seiler, "Residential Real Estate Prices: A Room with a View," *Journal of Real Estate Research* 23 (2002); Earl D. Benson, Julia L. Hansen, and Arthur L. Schwartz Jr., "Water Views and Residential Property Values," *Appraisal Journal* 68 (2000).

36. Bonnie Colby and Steven Wishart, "Property Value Premium for Proximity to Riparian Corridor," Department of Agricultural and Resource Economics, University of Arizona, 2002.

37. Gary Grudnitski and Quang Do, "Adjusting the Value of Houses Located on a Golf Course," *Appraisal Journal* 65 (1997).

38. Andrew Miller, "Valuing Open Space, Land Economics and Neighborhood Parks," Master's thesis, MIT Center for Real Estate, 2007.

39. Mathis Wackernagel and William E. Rees, *Our Ecological Footprint: Reducing Human Impact on the Earth* (Philadelphia: New Society Publishers, 1996).

40. Research Highlight, "A Plan for Rainy Days: Water Runoff and Site Planning," Canada Mortgage and Housing Corporation (CMHC), 2007.

41. Lawrence Frank and Chris Hawkins, *Assessing Travel and Environmental Impacts of Contrasting Levels of Vehicular and Pedestrian Connectivity: Assessing Aspects of the Fused Grid* (Ottawa: Canada Mortgage and Housing Corporation [CMHC], 2008).

42. Xiongbing Jin, "Modeling the Influence of Neighbourhood Design on Daily Trip Patterns in Urban Neighbourhoods," PhD thesis, Memorial University of Newfoundland, 2010.

43. IBI Group, "Assessment of the Transportation Impacts of Current and Fused Grid Layouts."

Chapter 7

1. IBI Group, "Assessment of the Transportation Impacts of Current and Fused Grid Layouts," Phase I research report prepared for Canada Mortgage and Housing Corporation (CMHC), Ottawa, Ontario, 2007.

2. Susan Handy, Robert G. Paterson, and Kent Butler, *Planning for Street Connectivity: Getting from Here to There* (Chicago: American Planning Association, Planning Advisory Service, 2003); J. Dill, *Measuring Network Connectivity for Bicycling and Walking*, TRB 2004, Annual Meeting CD-ROM; Paul Stangl and Jeffery M. Guinn, "Neighborhood Design, Connectivity Assessment and Obstruction," *Urban Design International* 16, no. 4 (2011): 285–96.

3. Calgary Transportation Plan, *Connectivity Handbook* (Draft Document), City of Calgary, 2010, http://www.calgary.ca/Transportation/TP/Documents/CTP2009/ctp_connectivity_handbook.pdf.

4. Eric Dumbaugh and Robert Rae, "Safe Urban Form: Revisiting the Relationship Between Community Design and Traffic Safety," *Journal of the American Planning Association* 75, no. 3 (Summer 2009); Gordon Lovegrove and T. Sayed, "Macro-Level Collision Prediction Models for Evaluating Neighbourhood Traffic Safety," *Canadian Journal of Civil Engineering* 33 (2006): 609–21.

5. Rachel Kaplan, "Nature at the Doorstep: Residential Satisfaction and the Nearby Environment," *Journal of Architectural and Planning Research* 2 (1985): 115–27; Joshua Hart, "Driven to Excess: A Study of Motor Vehicle Impacts on Three Streets in Bristol," University of the West of England, 2008.

6. "Stuyvesant Town, for example, designed in 1943 by a team led by Richmond Shreve consolidated 18 city blocks into one large parcel, housing 24,000 people in thirty five more or less identical apartment blocks. The spaces between the buildings included parks and playgrounds as well as parking lots." Witold Rybczynski, *Makeshift Metropolis: Ideas About Cities* (New York: Scribner, 2010).

7. "The Commission's report of 1811, with L'Enfant's recent plan of Washington in mind, dismisses 'those supposed improvements ... circles, ovals and stars' and stress flatly 'that a city is composed of the habitations of men, and the straight sided, and right angled houses are the most cheap to build, and the most convenient to live in.'" Spiro Kostof, *The City Shaped: Urban Patterns and Meanings Through History* (Boston: Little, Brown, 1991), 121. Further on the same page, Kostof states, "This is how the New York's Commissioners justified their decision not to provide public space in their 1811 plan. [quote follows] In plain words, when there is a chance of making money from urban land, the claims of the public good will be set aside."

8. Lawrence Frank, Jacqueline Kerr, Jim Chapman, and James Sallis, "Urban Form Relationships with Walk

Trip Frequency and Distance among Youth," *American Journal of Health Promotion* 21, no. 4 (March/April 2007).

9. Rachel Kaplan, "Nature at the Doorstep: Residential Satisfaction and the Nearby Environment," *Journal of Architectural and Planning Research* 2 (1985): 115–27.

10. "Daylight and views of nature are associated with reduced pain and depression, and high-quality air-ventilation systems are associated with lower incidence of respiratory disease and increased worker productivity." Thomas W. Eitler, Edward T. McMahon, and Theodore C. Thoerig, *Ten Principles for Building Healthy Places* (Washington, D.C.: Urban Land Institute, 2013).

11. E. Gregory McPherson, "Trees with Benefits," *American Nurseryman* 201, no. 7 (April 2003).

12. Ibid.: "Trees absorb gaseous pollutants, retain particles on their surfaces, and release oxygen and volatile organic compounds."

13. "However, in some situations they [surfaces] can substantially increase noise exposures. For example: The common situation where rows of tall buildings line both sides of downtown streets and confine traffic noise within 'urban canyons' as illustrated in Figure 7, page 20 City of Vancouver." *Noise Control Manual*, undated (c. 2002).

14. A secondary plan differs from a development plan in that it is a policy document with guidelines and objectives. Though it has the appearance of a site plan, it is actually something different altogether. Developers would be free to modify the scheme presented in the official document while still respecting its principles.

15. Michael Southworth and Eran Ben-Joseph, *Streets and the Shaping of Towns and Cities* (Washington, D.C.: Island Press, 2003), 115.

16. The complete consultant's report can be found on the City of Stratford website. A summary of it was published by CMHC, downloadable at http://www.cmhc-schl.gc.ca/odpub/pdf/63760.pdf?fr=1273232296265.

17. IBI Group, "Assessment of the Transportation Impacts of Current and Fused Grid Layouts," Phase I research report prepared for Canada Mortgage and Housing Corporation (CMHC), Ottawa, Ontario (Exhibit 3.5, page 39).

18. Calgary Transportation Plan, *Connectivity Handbook*.

19. Harold Marks, "Subdividing for Traffic Safety," *Traffic Quarterly* 11, no. 3 (1957): 308–25.

20. James Sun and Gordon Lovegrove, "Comparing the Road Safety of Neighbourhood Development Patterns: Traditional versus Sustainable Communities," *Canadian Journal of Civil Engineering* 40, no. 1 (January 2013): 35–45.

21. IBI Group, "Comparing Current and Fused Grid Neighbourhood Layouts: Mobility, Infrastructure and Emission Costs," Phase II research report prepared for Canada Mortgage and Housing Corporation (CMHC), Ottawa, Ontario, 2008 (page 13).

Appendix

1. Dan Stanislawski, "The Origin and Spread of the Grid-Pattern," *Town Geographical Review* 36, no. 1 (January 1946): 105–20.

2. Jill Grant, "The Dark Side of the Grid: Power and Urban Design," *Planning Perspectives* 16 (2001): 219–41.

3. "The British architect Sir William Chambers has said much the same thing two centuries earlier: 'on a plain where no [im]pediment obliges…. It cannot be supposed that men would go by a crooked line, where they could arrive by a straight one.'" Quoted in Spiro Kostof, *The City Shaped: Urban Patterns and Meanings Through History* (Boston: Little, Brown, 1991).

4. The sixteen determinants listed by Morris are as follows: topography; climate; construction materials and technology; economic; political; religious; the pre-urban cadaster; defense; aggrandizement; the grid-iron; urban mobility; aesthetic; legislation; urban infrastructure; social, religious and ethnic grouping; and leisure. A.E.J. Morris, *History of Urban Form: Before the Industrial Revolutions* (New York: John Wiley, 1994).

5. Spiro Kostof, *The City Shaped*, and *The City Assembled: The Elements of Urban Form Through History* (Boston: Little, Brown, 1992).

6. "Who invented the grid? Given the chapter's preamble, this is perhaps an unnecessary question; it is rather like asking who invented the right angle, that is geometry, and in fact that word carries in it the seeds of the grid's popularity, indeed inevitability" (Kostof, *The City Shaped*, 103).

7. Ibid.: "It is universal both geographically and chronologically (though its use was not continuous through history). No better urban solution recommends itself as a standard scheme for disparate sites, or as means for the equal distribution of land or the easy parceling and selling of real estate."

8. Ibid.: "Generally speaking gridded towns serve most of the purposes of towns *per se*: defense, agricultural development, trade. There is little premeditation in the choice of this street layout beyond the fact that it is, for certain periods in history, the most practical way to plan new cities" (99).

9. Ibid.: "And in terms of city-making one of the simplest ways of making order is to have horizontal and vertical coordinates in orthogonal relationship to one another…. So the grid applies to country and town, to fields and streets, and at its most basic it divides an undifferentiated stretch of land into regular, measured plots" (103).

10. Ibid.: "Here in the colonies, there was no prior Greek village structure that had to be respected, no ancient Greek sanctities. So there was no justification for the making of 'organic' cities through synoecism or other processes of assimilation, as had been the case in the homeland" (104).

11. Ibid.: "These new lands were very different from mainland Greece and the Aegean islands. There were smooth, long beaches, ample plains" (105).

12. Ibid.: "The fact is that egalitarianism is no more natural to gridded patterns than to any other urban form" (100). Further on the same page, "In the early Greek colonies for example, the grid, far from being a democratic device employed to assure and equitable allotment of property to all citizens, was the means of perpetuating the privileges of the property owning class descendent from the original settlers and bolstering a territorial aristocracy."

13. Ibid.: "And a rectilinear street pattern has also been resorted to in order to keep under watch a restless population. Refugee and prisoner camps are obvious settings ... but the siting of this planned *barrio* on a spit of harbor land outside the citadel's bastions, and the direction of the fifteen straight streets of long narrow blocks, was an intentional strategy that permitted surveillance of 'these people at sea' whose old houses had been demolished to make room for the citadel" (95).

14. Ibid., 103 (quoting J.E. Vance Jr., *This Scene of Man*).

15. Ibid.: "This Greek grid with its rational subdivisions was alien to the old cultures overwhelmed by Alexander. The people reverted to their pre–Greek habits as soon as the Hellenistic episode was over, and the grids were suitably remade. The tidy subdivision of blocks came undone, the open space of agoras was taken over by stalls and small shops. The transformation of Dura Europos on the Syrian frontier is an excellent instance of this process" (105).

16. Ibid.: "There is precise information, however, about the theoretical design of Hindu cities on a modular grid in texts like the *Manasara*, a section of the *Silpa Shastra*, probably of the first century BC but reliant on much earlier sources; and as far back as 1000 BC *Vastuvidya*, the occult doctrines of city-making and architecture, provided for geometric urban *mandalas* that included rectilinear formulas" (104).

17. Ibid.: "Mohenjo Daro ... had a citadel on the western edge of the town and blocks of roughly equal size. A distinction was made between principal streets (as much as 20 to 30 feet—6 to 9 m—wide) and the alleys on to which the houses looked. A carry-over of this planning tradition into the later phase of Indian History cannot be demonstrated" (104).

18. Ibid.: "At the end of the Classical world we lose track of the grid for several centuries. The old gridded Greco-Roman cities lose their physical integrity or disappear altogether" (108).

19. Ibid., 99.

20. In the Sumerian Farmer's Almanac, the first on record (c. 1700–1500), the farmer was instructed to make sure that he had an extra ox for the plow. The written almanac, as with all other early written documents, can be assumed to be a transcription of age-old traditions that were transmitted orally for many generations since the ox and plow became the prevalent method of cultivation. Emphasizing the primordial origin of the practice, "The writer of the Sumerian Farmer's Almanac said that the agricultural instructions were not his, however those of the god Ninurta, the son and 'true farmer' of the leading Sumerian deity, Enlil." Wikipedia, "Sumerian Farmer's Almanac," http://en.wikipedia.org/wiki/Sumerian_Farmer's_Almanac. Similarly, Hesiod's *Works and Days* gives instructions to the farmer that continue the ancient tradition: "Get two ploughs ready work on them at home, one all of a piece, and the other jointed.... *Get two oxen*, bulls of nine years; for their strength is unspent and they are in the prime of their age: they are best for work. They will not fight in the furrow and break the plough and then leave the work undone." *Works and Days*, translated by Hugh G. Evelyn-White, first published in 1914. In the same source, Hesiod also warns about the plowing season: "Mark, when you hear the voice of the crane (17) who

cries year by year from the clouds above, for she gives the signal for plowing and shows the season of rainy winter; *but she vexes the heart of the man who has no oxen* [plural]. Then is the time to feed up your horned oxen in the byre" (22).

21. Hesiod, *Works and Days*: "Let a brisk fellow of forty years follow them, with a loaf of four quarters and eight slices for his dinner, one who will attend to his work *and drive a straight furrow* and is past the age for gaping after his fellows, but will keep his mind on his work."

22. The Egyptian land surveyors are depicted bearing ropes and they are referred to as "rope stretchers," while their trade is "rope stretching."

23. One section of the Code of Hammurabi gives the precise penalty per unit of land damaged: "If a man opens [an irrigation gate and releases] waters and thereby he allows the water to carry away whatever work has been done in his neighbor's field, he shall measure and deliver 3,000 silas of grain per 18 ikus [of field]." Quoted in Robert C. Ellickson and Charles DiA. Thorland, "Ancient Land Law: Mesopotamia, Egypt, Israel," *Faculty Scholarship Series*, paper 410 (1995).

24. Marcel Mazoyer and Laurence Roudart, *A History of World Agriculture from the Neolithic Age to the Current Crisis* (New York: Monthly Review Press, 2006), Figure 10.1, "Stages in the Development of Equipment and Motomechanization in Grain Cultivation," page 384.

25. Ibid., Figure 1.5, "The Growth of Human Population in Connection with the Development of Agrarian Systems throughout the World," page 63. Further on in their book, Mazoyer and Roudart state, "It remains the case, however, that beginning in the Iron Age the new systems based on fallowing were predominant in this immense area, and for more than a millennium they supplied the basic essentials of subsistence for circum–Mediterranean and European societies" (229).

26. Herodotus (484–425 BCE) believed the Greeks imported geometry from Egypt, where it was used to calculate lands that were to the annual flooding of the Nile [Herodotus 1998 II, 109, 136]. Rachel Fletcher, "Introduction to the Geometer's Angle," *Nexus Network Journal* 6, no. 2 (Autumn 2004), pp. 93–94. http://www.nexusjournal.com/GA-intro.html.

27. Quoting Proclus, James Gow writes, "Geometry is said by many to have been invented among the Egyptians, its origin being due to the measurement of plots of land. This was necessary there because of the rising of the Nile, which obliterated the boundaries appertaining to separate owners." He continues: "Nor is it marvelous that the discovery of this and the other sciences should have arisen from such an occasion, since everything which moves in development will advance from the imperfect to the perfect. *From mere sense-perception to calculation, and from this to reasoning, is a natural transition*. Just as among the Phoenicians, through commerce and exchange, an accurate knowledge of numbers was originated, so also among the Egyptians geometry was invented for the reason above stated." James Gow, *A Short History of Greek Mathematics* (Cambridge: Cambridge University Press, 1884), 134 (inspected on Google e-books archives, January 2014).

28. Interestingly, one surviving unit of land meas-

urement relates directly to plowing—the furlong: "**fur-long**, old English unit of *length*, based on the length of an average plowed furrow (hence 'furrow-long,' or furlong) in the English open- or common-field system. Each furrow ran the length of a 40 _ 4-rod acre.... The standardization of such linear units as the yard, foot, and inch—begun by government enactment sometime between 1266 and 1303—recognized the traditional sizes of rods, furlongs, and acres as fixed and therefore simply redefined them in terms of the newly standardized units.... Today, the furlong is used almost exclusively in horse racing." *Encyclopedia Britannica*, retrieved January 2014. A Wikipedia article likewise indicates that, due to an acre being formed by one furlong length and one chain width, "the furlong was once also called an **acre's length**." According to this source, a furlong was considered a practical length of a straight plowing effort before turning the ox team and plow, and the resulting acre was the area that a person with a plow and one ox could do in one day. Wikipedia, "Furlong," http://en.wikipedia.org/wiki/Furlong.

29. "Whoever said that farming is the foundation of all the arts, is quite correct. When all is well on the farms, all is well elsewhere." Xenophon in *Oeconomicus* (c. 370 BCE), quoted in Stewart Ross's *Daily Life* (Lincolnwood, IL: P. Bedrick Books, 1999).

30. The very earliest plough was the simple scratch-plough, or ard, which is dragged through the topsoil (still used in many parts of the world). It breaks up a strip of land directly along the plowed path, which can then be planted. "Because the ard leaves a strip of undisturbed earth between the furrows, fields are often cross-ploughed lengthwise and across, and this tends to lead to squarish fields" (Wikipedia, "Plough," http://en.wikipedia.org/wiki/Plough).

31. Mazoyer and Roudart, *A History of World Agriculture*: "The fields that make up the *ager* are permanent, quadrangular, and contiguous, as opposed to the generally dispersed, multiform, and temporarily occupied parcels characteristic of slash-and-burn cultivation. On light, easy-to-work lands, two animals harnessed in front suffice to pull the ard. The harnessing is short enough to allow an easy turn at the end of the field. As a result, it is not necessary to stretch out the length of the fields in order to avoid difficult maneuvers. But since a second pass of the ard, at a right angle to the first one, is often practiced, the fields must not be too narrow. This is why cultivation with the ard accommodates fields that are rather small, not very long, or even quasi-square on soils that are easy to work. On the other hand, on heavy soil that requires a team of two pairs of oxen or more, which makes turning difficult, the fields must be larger."

32. "The Emperor Frederick II made specific mention of this revival [of classical Rome] in his inauguration in 1247 of Vittoria, near Parma in Italy, and he traced the perimeter of the town with a plough in imitation of the *sulcus primigenius* of the Etruscan/Roman town-founding ritual" (Kostof, *The City Shaped*).

33. The Romans founded their cities according to a ritual borrowed from the Etruscans: "No one in antiq-uity denies them this merit, and the finest praise one could give to a city was that it had been founded *Etrusco ritu*, according to the Etruscan rite. It was known that they possessed 'ritual books' in which was prescribed 'by what rite towns are founded, altars and temples are consecrated; what made walls inviolable and gates permissible.'" And, describing the ritual, "The founder, his head covered with a part of his toga, would cut the primal furrow with a bronze plowshare harnessed to a bull and a heifer; He was careful to cast the soil of this boundary furrow (*sulcus primigenius*) inwards, and when he arrived at where that gates (*porta*) would stand, he would lift and carry (*portare*) his plough." Jacques Heurgon, *Daily Life of the Etruscans* (London: Weidenfeld and Nicolson, 1964).

34. Nicholas Wade reporting in *New York Times* on the work of Torroni and Alessandro Achilli, published in the April 2007 issue of the *American Journal of Human Genetics*: "Origins of the Etruscans: Was Herodotus Right?" *New York Times*, April 3, 2007.

35. Morris, *History of Urban Form*.

36. Ibid., 22, 23.

37. "The city stands on a broad plain, *and is an exact square*, a hundred and twenty furlongs in length each way, so that the entire circuit is four hundred and eighty furlongs. While such is its size, in magnificence there is no other city that approaches to it. It is surrounded, in the first place, by a broad and deep moat, full of water, behind which rises a wall fifty royal cubits in width, and two hundred in height.... On the top, along the edges of the wall, they constructed buildings of a single chamber facing one another, leaving between them room for *a four-horse chariot to turn*.... The houses are mostly three and four stories high; the streets *all run in straight lines*, not only those parallel to the river, but also the cross streets which lead down to the water-side.... The city, as I said, was divided by the river into two distinct portions. Under the former kings, if a man wanted to pass from one of these divisions to the other, he had to cross in a boat; which must, it seems to me, have been very troublesome ... after which, with the materials which had been prepared, she [the Queen] built, as near the middle of the town as possible, a stone bridge, the blocks whereof were bound together with iron and lead." Herodotus, *The History of the Persian Wars*, c. 430 BCE, in *Ancient History Sourcebook: Greek Reports of Babylonia, Chaldea, and Assyria*, http://www.fordham.edu/halsall/ancient/greek-babylon.asp.

38. "Secondly, there were from the start plenty of towns that did not in the least look natural or organic. Some like El Lahun, were dormitory communities for workers, not full-fledged towns in reality. But they showed ... the knowledge to design totally ordered environments, with streets, seriated housing units, and a residential hierarchy that is anything but random" (Kostof, *The City Shaped*, 34).

39. "Given the need to build a settlement paid for from a single source in one stage, it is hard to see what alternative to a gridiron could have existed." Morris, *History of Urban Form*, quoting Kemp, "Temple and town in Ancient Egypt" (29).

Bibliography

Alberti, Leon Battista. *Ten Books on Architecture* (1485). Edited by James Rykwert. New York: Transatlantic Arts, 1966.

Alexander, C., S. Ishikawa, and M. Silverstein, with M. Jacobson, I. Fiksdahl-King, and S. Angel. *A Pattern Language*. New York: Oxford University Press, 1977.

Al Sayyad, Nezar. *Cities and Caliphs: On the Genesis of Arab Muslim Urbanism*. New York: Greenwood Press, 1991.

Andersen, Paul, and David L. Salomon. *The Architecture of Patterns*. New York: W.W. Norton, 2010.

Appleyard, Donald, M.S. Gerson, and M. Lintell. *Livable Streets*. Berkeley: University of California Press, 1981.

Aristotle. *The Politics*. Translated by T.A. Sinclair. New York: Penguin, 1962.

Ausubel, Jesse H., Cesare Marchetti, and Perrin Meyer. "Toward Green Mobility: The Evolution of Transport." *European Review* 6, no. 2 (1998): 137–56.

Banerjee, T., and M. Southworth. *City Sense and City Design Writings and Projects of Kevin Lynch*. Cambridge, MA: MIT Press, 1990.

Batty, M., and P. Longley. *Fractal Cities: A Geometry of Form and Function*. London and San Diego: Academic Press, 1994.

Ben-Joseph, Eran. *Livability and Safety of Suburban Street Patterns: A Comparative Study*. Working Paper 642. Berkeley: Institute of Urban and Regional Development, University of California, 1995.

Benson, Earl D., Julia L. Hansen, and Arthur L. Schwartz Jr. "Water Views and Residential Property Values." *Appraisal Journal* 68 (2000).

Bond, Michael T., Vicky L. Seiler, and Michael J. Seiler. "Residential Real Estate Prices: A Room with a View." *Journal of Real Estate Research* 23 (2002).

Bucholz, Robert O., and Joseph P. Ward. *London: A Social and Cultural History, 1550–1750*. Cambridge: Cambridge University Press, 2012.

Byles, Jeff. *Rubble: Unearthing the History of Demolition*. New York: Three Rivers Press, 2005.

Calthorpe, Peter. *The Urban Network: A New Framework for Growth*. 2002. http://www.calthorpe.com/publications/urban-network-new-framework-growth.

Calthorpe, Peter, and Douglas Kelbaugh. *The Pedes-*

trian Pocket Book: A New Suburban Design Strategy. New York: Princeton Architectural Press, 1989.

Canadian Medical Association. "No Breathing Room: National Illness Costs of Air Pollution." Summary Report. Toronto, 2008.

Carcopino, Jerome. *Daily Life in Ancient Rome*. New Haven, CT: Yale University Press, 1941.

Centre for Sustainable Transportation. "Child-Friendly Transport Planning." February 2004.

Childs, M.C. *Squares: A Public Space Design Guide for Urbanists*. Albuquerque: University of New Mexico Press, 2002.

Colby, Bonnie, and Steven Wishart. "Property Value Premium for Proximity to Riparian Corridor." Department of Agricultural and Resource Economics, University of Arizona, 2002.

Le Corbusier. *La Ville Radieuse (The Radiant City)*. Boulogne-sur-Seine: Editions de l'Architecture d'aujourd'hui, 1935.

Cullen, Gordon. *Concise Townscape*. London: Architectural Press, 1971.

De Long, J. Bradford, and Andrei Shleifer. *Princes and Merchants: European City Growth Before the Industrial Revolution*. Cambridge, MA: National Bureau of Economic Research, 1993.

Delucchi, Mark, and Kenneth S. Kurani. "Can We Have Sustainable Transportation Without Making People Drive Less or Give Up Suburban Living?" *Journal of Urban Planning and Development* (June 2013).

de Vries, S., R.A. Verheij, P.P. Groenewegen, and P. Spreeuwenberg. "Natural Environments—Healthy Environments? An Exploratory Analysis of the Relationship Between Green Space and Health." *Environment and Planning A* 35 (2003): 1717–31.

Dill, J. *Measuring Network Connectivity for Bicycling and Walking*. TRB 2004. Annual Meeting CD-ROM.

DK Eyewitness Books. London: DK Publishing, 2011.

Doxiadis, Constantinos. *Anthropopolis: City for Human Development*. W.W. Norton, 1975.

Duany, Andres, and E. Plater-Zyberk. "The Second Coming of the American Small Town." *Wilson Quarterly* 16, no. 1 (1992): 19–49.

Dumbaugh, Eric. "Safe Streets, Livable Streets." *Journal of the American Planning Association* 71, no. 3 (2005): 283–98.

Dumbaugh, Eric, and Robert Rae. "Safe Urban Form:

Revisiting the Relationship Between Community Design and Traffic Safety." *Journal of the American Planning Association* 75, no. 3 (Summer 2009).

Duranton, Gilles. "Distance, Land, and Proximity: Economic Analysis and the Evolution of Cities." *Research Papers in Environmental and Spatial Analysis*, no. 53. Department of Geography & Environment, London School of Economics, January 1999.

Eitler, Thomas W., Edward T. McMahon, and Theodore C. Thoerig. *Ten Principles for Building Healthy Places.* Washington, D.C.: Urban Land Institute, 2013.

Ellickson, Robert C., and Charles DiA. Thorland. "Ancient Land Law: Mesopotamia, Egypt, Israel." *Faculty Scholarship Series*, Paper 410. 1995.

Evans, G., P. Lercher, M. Meis, H. Ising, and W.W. Kofler. "Community Noise Exposure and Stress in Children." *Journal of the Acoustical Society of America* 109 (2001): 1023–27.

Ewing, Reid. *Traffic Calming: State of the Practice.* Washington, D.C.: Institute of Transportation Engineers, 1999.

FHA. *Planning Neighbourhoods for Small Houses.* Technical Bulletin No. 5. Washington, D.C., 1936.

Filion, Pierre, Trudi Bunting, Kathleen McSpurren, and Alan Tse. "Canada-U.S. Metropolitan Density Patterns: Zonal Convergence and Divergence." *Urban Geography* 25, issue 1 (2004): 42–65.

Frank, Lawrence, and Chris Hawkins. *Assessing Travel and Environmental Impacts of Contrasting Levels of Vehicular and Pedestrian Connectivity: Assessing Aspects of the Fused Grid.* Ottawa: Canada Mortgage and Housing Corporation (CMHC), 2008.

Frank, Lawrence, Sarah Kavage, and Todd Litman. *Promoting Public Health Through Smart Growth.* Vancouver: Smart Growth British Columbia, 2006.

Frank, Lawrence, Jacqueline Kerr, Jim Chapman, and James Sallis. "Urban Form Relationships with Walk Trip Frequency and Distance Among Youth." *American Journal of Health Promotion* 21, no. 4 (March/April 2007).

Gallion, Arthur, and Simon Eisner. *The Urban Pattern: City Planning and Design.* New York: Van Nostrand Reinhold, 1986.

Girouard, Mark. *Cities & People: A Social and Architectural History.* New Haven, CT, and London: Yale University Press, 1985.

Gow, James. *A Short History of Greek Mathematics.* Cambridge: Cambridge University Press, 1884.

Grammenos, Fanis, Sevag Pogharian, and Julie Tasker-Brown. *Residential Street Pattern Design: A Proposal.* Ottawa: Canadian Mortgage and Housing Corporation (CMHC), 2005.

Grant, Jill. "The Dark Side of the Grid: Power and Urban Design." *Planning Perspectives* 16 (2001): 219–41.

Grudnitski, Gary, and Quang Do. "Adjusting the Value of Houses Located on a Golf Course." *Appraisal Journal* 65 (1997).

Hakim, Besim. *Arabic-Islamic Cities: Building and Planning Principles.* London: Kegan Paul International, 1986.

_____. "Generative Processes for Revitalizing Historic Towns or Heritage Districts." *Urban Design International* 12 (2007): 87–99.

_____. "Julian of Ascalon's Treatise of Construction and Design Rules from Sixth-Century Palestine." *Journal of the Society of Architectural Historians* 60, no. 1 (March 2001): 4–25.

Handy, Susan, Robert G. Paterson, and Kent Butler. *Planning for Street Connectivity: Getting from Here to There.* Chicago: American Planning Association, Planning Advisory Service, 2003.

Handy, Susan, Samantha Sommer, Julie Ogilvie, Xinyu Cao, and Patricia Mokhtarian. "Cul-de-Sacs and Children's Outdoor Play: Quantitative and Qualitative Evidence." Active Living, Research Conference, San Diego, February 2007.

Hart, Joshua. "Driven to Excess: A Study of Motor Vehicle Impacts on Three Streets in Bristol." University of the West of England, 2008.

Heurgon, Jacques. *Daily Life of the Etruscans.* London: Weidenfield and Nicolson, 1964.

Hillier, Bill, and Ozlem Sahbaz. "An Evidence Based Approach to Crime and Urban Design: Or, Can We Have Vitality, Sustainability and Security All at Once?" Bartlett School of Graduate Studies, University College London, March 2008.

IBI Group. "Assessment of the Transportation Impacts of Current and Fused Grid Layouts." Phase I research report prepared for Canada Mortgage and Housing Corporation (CMHC), Ottawa, Ontario, 2007.

_____. "Comparing Current and Fused Grid Neighbourhood Layouts: Mobility, Infrastructure and Emission Costs." Phase II research report prepared for Canada Mortgage and Housing Corporation (CMHC), Ottawa, Ontario, 2008.

ITE Transportation Planning. *Traditional Neighborhood Development: Street Design Guidelines.* Institute of Transportation Engineers, 1999.

Jacobs, Allan B. *Great Streets.* Cambridge, MA: MIT Press, 1993.

Jacobs, Jane. *The Death and Life of Great American Cities.* New York: Random House, 1961.

Kaplan, Rachel. "Nature at the Doorstep: Residential Satisfaction and the Nearby Environment." *Journal of Architectural and Planning Research* 2 (1985): 115–27.

Kirkland, Stephane. *Paris Reborn: Napoléon III, Baron Haussmann, and the Quest to Build a Modern City.* New York: St. Martin's Press, 2013.

Kostof, Spiro. *The City Assembled: The Elements of Urban Form Through History.* Boston: Little, Brown, 1992.

_____. *The City Shaped: Urban Patterns and Meanings Through History*. Boston: Little, Brown, 1991.

Kotkin, Joel. *The City: A Global History*. New York: Random House, 2007.

Kulash, Walter, Joe Anglin, and David Marks. "Traditional Neighborhood Development: Will the Traffic Work?" *Development* 21 (July/August 1990): 21–24.

Kutzbach, Mark. "Megacities and Megatraffic." *ACCESS*, no. 37 (Fall 2010).

Lay, M.G. *Ways of the World: A History of the World's Roads and of the Vehicles That Used Them*. New Brunswick, NJ: Rutgers University Press, 1992.

Lee, C-M., and K-H. Ahn. "Is Kentlands Better than Radburn? The American Garden City and New Urbanist Paradigms." *Journal of the American Planning Association* 69, no. 1 (2003): 50–71.

Lovegrove, Gordon, and T. Sayed. "Macro-level Collision Models for Evaluating Neighbourhood Traffic Safety." *Canadian Journal of Civil Engineering* 33 (2006): 609–21.

Lynch, Kevin. *The Image of the City*. Cambridge, MA: MIT Press, 1960.

Lynch, Kevin, and Michael Southworth. "Designing and Managing the Strip." In *City Sense and City Design: Writings and Projects by Kevin Lynch*, edited by T. Banerjee and M. Southworth. Cambridge, MA: MIT Press, 1974.

Marks, Harold. "Subdividing for Traffic Safety." *Traffic Quarterly* 11, no. 3 (1957): 308–25.

Marshall, Alex. *How Cities Work: Suburbs, Sprawl, and the Roads Not Taken*. Austin: University of Texas Press, 2000.

_____. *The Surprising Design of Market Economies*. Austin: University of Texas Press, 2012.

Marshall, Stephen. *Streets & Patterns: The Structure of Urban Geometry*. London and New York: Spoon Press, 2005.

Mazoyer, Marcel, and Laurence Roudart. *A History of World Agriculture from the Neolithic Age to the Current Crisis*. New York: Monthly Review Press, 2006.

Mehaffy, Michael, Sergio Porta, Yodan Rofe, and Nikos Salingaros. "Urban Nuclei and the Geometry of Streets: The 'Emergent Neighborhoods' Model." *Urban Design International* 15, no. 1 (2010): 22–46.

Michaud, D.S., et al. "Noise Annoyance in Canada." *Noise & Health* 7, no. 27 (April–June 2005): 39–47.

Miller, Andrew. "Valuing Open Space, Land Economics and Neighborhood Parks." Master's thesis, MIT Center for Real Estate, 2007.

Miller, K.A., D.S. Siscovick, K. Sheppard, J.H. Sullivan, G. Anderson, and J.D. Kaufman. "Long-Term Exposure to Fine Particulate Matter Air Pollution and Cardiovascular Events in Women." *New England Journal of Medicine* 356 (2007): 447–58.

Mitchell, Richard, and Frank Popham. "Effect of Exposure to Environment on Health Inequalities: An Observational Population Study." *The Lancet* 372 (2008).

Moore, Simon. *Something in the Air: The Forgotten Crisis of Britain's Poor Air Quality*. Edited by Guy Newey. London: Policy Exchange, 2012.

Morris, A.E.J. *History of Urban Form: Before the Industrial Revolutions*. New York: John Wiley, 1994.

Morris, Eric. "From Horse Power to Horsepower." *ACCESS*, no. 30 (Spring 2007): 2–8.

Newman, Oscar. *Creating Defensible Space*. Institute for Community Design Analysis, U.S. Department of Housing and Urban Development Office of Policy Development and Research, 1996.

Palen, J. *The Suburbs*. New York: McGraw-Hill, 1995.

Perry, Clarence. *Housing for the Machine Age*. New York: Russell Sage Foundation, 1939.

Ross, Stewart. *Daily Life*. Lincolnwood, IL: P. Bedrick Books, 1999.

Rybczynski, Witold. *Makeshift Metropolis: Ideas About Cities*. New York: Scribner, 2010.

Salat, Serge, Françoise Labbé, Caroline Nowacki, and Gila Walker. *Cities and Forms: On Sustainable Urbanism*. Paris: Hermann Editeurs des Sciences et des Arts, 2011.

Salingaros, Nikos A. "Connecting the Fractal City." Keynote speech, 5th Biennial of Towns and Town Planners in Europe, Barcelona, Spain, 2003.

Salingaros, Nikos A., and Bruce J. West. "A Universal Rule for the Distribution of Sizes." *Environment and Planning B: Planning and Design* 26, no. 6 (1999): 909–23.

Sijpkes, Pieter, and David Brown. "Montreal's Indoor City: 35 Years of Development." Paper presented at the 7th International Conference of Underground Space, Montreal, 1997.

Southworth, Michael, with Tridib Banerjee. *City Sense and City Design: Writings and Projects of Kevin Lynch*. Cambridge, MA: MIT Press, 1990; paperback edition 1995.

Southworth, Michael, and Eran Ben-Joseph. *Streets and the Shaping of Towns and Cities*. Washington, D.C.: Island Press, 2003.

Southworth, Michael, and Peter Owens. "The Evolving Metropolis: Studies of Community, Neighbourhood, and Street Form at the Urban Edge." *Journal of the American Planning Association* 59, no. 3 (1993): 271–87.

Stangl, Paul. "The Pedestrian Route Directness Test: A New Level-of-Service Model." *Urban Design International* 17, no. 3 (2012): 228–38.

Stangl, Paul, and Jeffery M. Guinn. "Neighborhood Design, Connectivity Assessment and Obstruction." *Urban Design International* 16, no. 4 (2011): 285–96.

Stanislawski, Dan. "The Origin and Spread of the

Grid-Pattern." *Town Geographical Review* 36, no. 1 (January 1946): 105–20.

Stein, Clarence. *Towards New Towns for America.* Cambridge, MA: MIT Press, 1957.

Sun, James, and Gordon Lovegrove. "Comparing the Road Safety of Neighbourhood Development Patterns: Traditional versus Sustainable Communities." *Canadian Journal of Civil Engineering* 40, no. 1 (January 2013): 35–45.

_____, and _____. "Research Study on Evaluating the Level of Safety of the Fused Grid Road Pattern." External Research Project for Canada Mortgage and Housing Corporation (CMHC), Ottawa, Ontario, 2009.

SWOV Road Safety Research Institute (2013). SWOV Fact Sheet: Road Fatalities in the Netherlands, Leidschendam, the Netherlands. July 2013.

Takano, T., K. Nakamura, and M. Watanabe. "Urban Residential Environments and Senior Citizens' Longevity in Megacity Areas: The Importance of Walkable Green Spaces." *Journal of Epidemiological Community Health* 56 (2003): 913–18.

Traffic's Human Toll: A Study of the Impacts of Vehicular Traffic on New York City Residents. New York: Transportation Alternatives, 2006.

USDOT (2011), "Fatality Analysis Reporting System (FARS) General Estimates System: 2011 Data Summary," National Highway Traffic Safety Administration, National Center for Statistics and Analysis (NCSA), Report NVS-424, Washington, D.C.

Wackernagel, Mathis, and William E. Rees. *Our Ecological Footprint: Reducing Human Impact on the Earth.* Philadelphia: New Society Publishers, 1996.

White, Mathew P., Ian Alcock, Benedict W. Wheeler, and Michael H. Depledge. "Would You Be Happier Living in a Greener Urban Area? A Fixed-Effects Analysis of Panel Data." *Psychological Science* 24, no. 6 (June 2013): 920–28.

Wolf, P.M. *Eugene Henard and the Beginning of Urbanism in Paris, 1900–1914.* The Hague: International Federation for Housing and Planning, 1968.

World Health Organization. *Global Status Report on Road Safety 2013: Supporting a Decade of Action.* Geneva, Switzerland: WHO Press.

Xiongbing Jin. "Modeling the Influence of Neighbourhood Design on Daily Trip Patterns in Urban Neighbourhoods." PhD thesis, Memorial University of Newfoundland, 2010.

Xiongbing Jin and Roger White. "An Agent-based Model of the Influence of Neighbourhood Design on Daily Trip Patterns." *Computers, Environment and Urban Systems* 36, issue 5 (September 2012).

Zein, S.R., E. Geddes, S. Hemsing, and M. Johnson. "Safety Benefits of Traffic Calming." *Transportation Research Record: Journal of the Transportation Research Board* 1578 (1997): 3–10.

Resources

The fused grid network model first appeared in the public domain in 2003. Since then, the authors have continued refining and expanding the model, adding new descriptive drawings, pictures and articles—too many to include in this book. A good number of these resources have been uploaded on the web and can be found on the following sites:

www.fusedgrid.ca (the authors' website, which includes articles, images, papers and presentations)

http://www.flickr.com/photos/22392855@N08/sets/72157612393017935/ (a set of drawings on a personal Flickr photo stream)

http://www.flickr.com/photos/22392855@N08/sets/72157626176042534/ (drawings, images, and videos on Flickr photo stream)

http://www.flickr.com/photos/22392855@N08/sets/72157626048951233/ (images of international cases of city retrofits of existing networks into fused grids)

http://en.wikipedia.org/wiki/Fused_Grid (English Wikipedia article)

http://zh.wikipedia.org/wiki/%E8%9E%8D%E5%90%88%E5%9E%8B%E8%B7%AF%E7%BD%91 (Chinese Wikipedia article)

Index

Numbers in *bold italics* indicate pages with photographs.